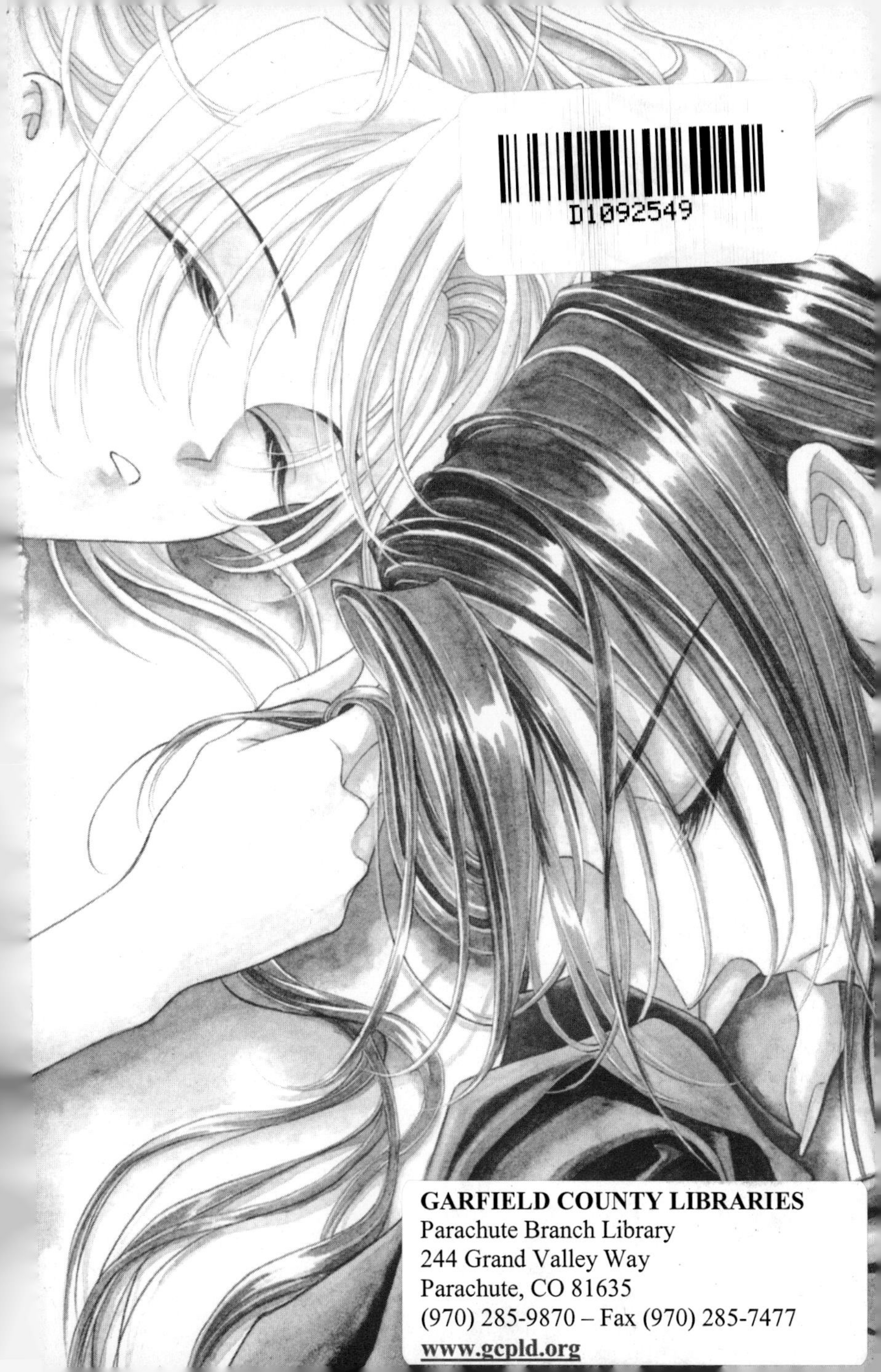

ART BY KARA
STORY BY LEE YUN HEE

DEMON DIARY

Translator - Lauren Na
English Adaptation - Kelly Sue DeConnick
Retouch and Lettering - Christina R. Siri
Cover Layout - Aaron Suhr
Graphic Designer - Deron Bennett

Editor - Rob Tokar
Digital Imaging Manager - Chris Buford
Pre-Press Manager - Antonio DePietro
Production Managers - Jennifer Miller, Mutsumi Miyazaki
Art Director - Matt Alford
Managing Editor - Jill Freshney
VP of Production - Ron Klamert
President & C.O.O. - John Parker
Publisher & C.E.O. - Stuart Levy

Email: info@TOKYOPOP.com
Come visit us online at www.TOKYOPOP.com

A  **TOKYOPOP** Manga

TOKYOPOP Inc.
5900 Wilshire Blvd. Suite 2000
Los Angeles, CA 90036

Demon Diary Vol. 7

MAWAN-IGLI 1 ©2000 by KARA. All rights reserved.
First published in KOREA in 2000 by SIGONGSA Co., Ltd.
English translation rights arranged by SIGONGSA Co., Ltd.

English text copyright ©2004 TOKYOPOP Inc.

All rights reserved. No portion of this book may be reproduced or transmitted
in any form or by any means without written permission from the copyright
holders. This manga is a work of fiction. Any resemblance to actual events
or locales or persons, living or dead, is entirely coincidental.

ISBN: 1-59182-432-X

First TOKYOPOP printing: May 2004

10 9 8 7 6 5 4 3 2 1
Printed in the USA

DEMON DIARY

ART BY KARA
STORY BY LEE YUN HEE

VOLUME 7

TOKYOPOP®

LOS ANGELES • TOKYO • LONDON

WHO'S WHO IN DEMON DIARY

RAENEF

AN ORPHAN, RAENEF HAD TO JOIN THIEVES AT AN EARLY AGE IN ORDER TO SURVIVE. AMONG THE THIEVES, RAENEF'S KIND, GENTLE, AND SOMEWHAT DITZY NATURE MADE HIM STAND OUT. APPROACHED BY ECLIPSE, RAENEF WAS EAGER FOR A CHANGE FROM HIS LIFE OF STEALING JUST TO EAT. UNFORTUNATELY, RAENEF'S CHEERFUL AND KIND-HEARTED QUALITIES ARE EVEN LESS DESIRABLE IN A DEMON LORD THAN THEY ARE IN A THIEF. THOUGH A POOR STUDENT AND A REGULAR SOURCE OF EMBARRASSMENT FOR ECLIPSE, RAENEF DESPERATELY WANTS TO BECOME THE GREATEST DEMON LORD EVER.
RECENTLY, IT WAS REVEALED THAT RAENEF IS ACTUALLY THE TIME-DISPLACED SON OF RAENEF IV FROM THE DISTANT FUTURE, AND THAT RAENEF V'S PERSONALITY WAS FRACTURED BY HIS TRAUMATIC JOURNEY THROUGH TIME. "GOOD" RAENEF HAD TO COMBAT HIS "EVIL" HALF AND, WITH THE HELP OF HIS FRIENDS AND RAENEF IV, THE TWO ASPECTS OF RAENEF V WERE HARMONIZED AS ONE.

UNFORTUNATELY, THE BATTLE WAS FAR FROM OVER, AS RAENEF IV ANNOUNCED HIS PLAN TO USURP RAENEF V'S EXISTENCE AND TAKE OVER AS THE REIGNING DEMON LORD RAENEF. EVEN WITH HIS NEWFOUND UNITY OF MIND, RAENEF V WAS HARD-PRESSED TO DEFEAT HIS PREDECESSOR...AND ONLY SUCCEEDED WITH THE HELP OF ECLIPSE, ERUTIS, AND CHRIS.

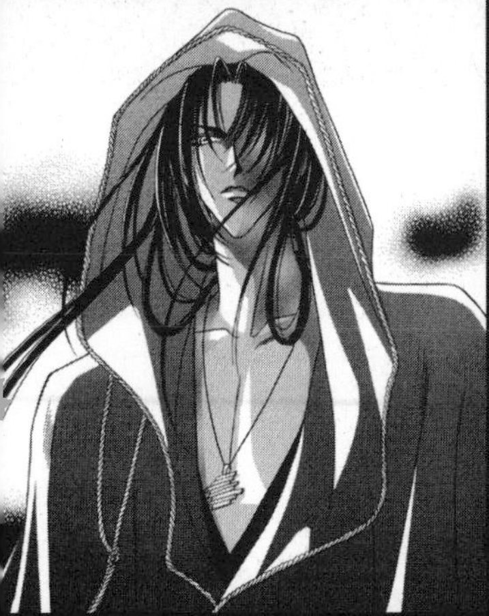

Eclipse

...ysterious, Eclipse is a wise and noble demon ...gods to mentor Raenef. His new pupil's ineptitude ...ipse's prestige, especially since Raenef's first ...rrassing visit to the Demon Courts. Despite their ...ipse finds himself strangely drawn to Raenef.

...s only rely on themselves, even as vassals. A ... do what he himself wants to do--he cannot be ...uaded. However, when the Demon Lord Krayon ...Raenef to recruit Eclipse's services, Eclipse stood ...ster's side. When Lord Krayon abducted Raenef V ...g demon lord's worthiness of Eclipse's servitude, ...d aid his master.

...Meruhesae told Eclipse that the greatest gift a ...s master is his trust. Despite Raenef's many ...nflinchingly refused to leave Raenef for Krayon ... life in danger to protect the demon lord-in-train-...n's attacks.

...ntly, Eclipse risked his life on his master's behalf ... (Eclipse's former master) tried to usurp Raenef ...mon Lord Raenef. Though Eclipse swore loyalty ...st, he chose to uphold his current oath of loyal-

SENSING POWERFUL MAGIC COMING FROM RAENEF'S CASTLE, THE HUMAN KNIGHT ERUTIS INTENDED TO BUILD HER REPUTATION BY SLAYING THE DEMON LORD WITHIN. AT FIRST, SHE FOUND IT HARD TO TAKE RAENEF SERIOUSLY BUT, AFTER BREAKING HER SWORD ON THE DEMON-LORD-IN-TRAINING'S HEAD, ERUTIS SOON FOUND HERSELF OUTMATCHED. TO SAVE HER LIFE, SHE CONVINCED RAENEF TO TAKE HER ON AS HIS HENCHMAN RATHER THAN KILLING HER. SINCE THEN, SHE HAS BECOME RAENEF'S CLOSE FRIEND...AND CHRIS'S DAILY TORMENTOR.

ERUTIS

FIVE YEARS AGO, A FORCE OF DEMONS DESCENDED ON A TOWN AND UTTERLY DESTROYED IT. DURING THE ATTACK, ONLY CHRIS' HEART CALLED OUT FOR THE GOD RASED AND, THUS, RASED SPARED CHRIS'S YOUNG LIFE. THE SOLE SURVIVOR OF THE ATTACK, CHRIS WAS RESCUED BY HEJEM, HIGH CLERIC OF THE NEARBY TEMPLE OF RASED. SENSING THAT CHRIS WAS BRIMMING WITH THE POWER OF THE GREAT GOD RASED, HEJEM TOOK THE YOUNGSTER AS HIS DISCIPLE AND DESIGNATED CHRIS TO BE THE TEMPLE'S NEXT HIGH CLERIC. AS AN ACT OF MERCY, RASED SUPPRESSED CHRIS'S TRAUMATIC MEMORIES, TELLING HEJEM THAT THEY WOULD ONE DAY RESURFACE. RASED ALSO INDICATED THAT THE WORLD OF THE DEMON LORDS IS SOON TO CHANGE AND, AT THAT TIME, CHRIS WILL LEAD RASED'S PEOPLE. UNAWARE OF RASED'S PROPHESIES, CHRIS HAS GROWN INTO A HEADSTRONG, EGOTISTICAL, DEMON-HATING, BRATTY YOUNG MAN. AGAINST HEJEM'S WISHES, CHRIS CREATED A DEMON SUMMONING SIGN AND CAPTURED RAENEF. THE SCUFFLE BETWEEN THE DEMON LORD-IN-TRAINING AND THE FUTURE HIGH CLERIC WAS BRIEF AND, AS AN APOLOGY (AND TO TEACH CHRIS HUMILITY), HEJEM SENT CHRIS TO LIVE WITH RAENEF FOR A SHORT TIME. DESPITE HIMSELF, CHRIS HAS DEVELOPED A FRIENDSHIP WITH RAENEF.

CHRIS

A BEAUTIFUL FEMALE DEMON SEER WITH AN UNREQUITED CRUSH ON ECLIPSE. WHEN ECLIPSE WAS ASSIGNED TO LOCATE RAENEF THE FIFTH, IT WAS MERUHESAE WHO POINTED THE DEMON IN THE RIGHT DIRECTION. WHEN RAENEF THE FOURTH RETURNED FROM THE DEAD, HE WARNED MERUHESAE--AND THE REST OF DEMONKIND--NOT TO INTERFERE WITH EVENTS AT CASTLE RAENEF

RAENEF IV

THE DEMON LORD RAENEF THE FOURTH WAS A POWERFUL AND RESPECTED DEMON LORD WHO, THROUGH THE MASTERY OF INCANTATIONS, BECAME THE MOST POWERFUL OF HIS KIND. 150 YEARS AGO, DURING THE HANGMA WAR, RAENEF WAS EXTERMINATING THE CREATURES OF HEAVEN WITH IMPUNITY. REALIZING THAT RAENEF COULD NOT BE STOPPED BY ANY CONVENTIONAL MEANS, MANY OF THE CREATURES OF HEAVEN SACRIFICED THEIR LIVES TO CURSE RAENEF WITH THE ANNIHILATION OF THE NAME, A CURSE DESIGNED TO SHORTEN A DEMON LORD'S LIFE...AND TO DESTROY HIS HEIRS. RAENEF WITHDREW IN AN ATTEMPT TO STUDY AND COUNTER THE CURSE AND, TWO DAYS AFTER HE CLAIMED TO HAVE SUCCEEDED, THE DEMON LORD RAENEF THE FOURTH DIED. RECENTLY, RAENEF IV MADE A SURPRISE RETURN TO THE WORLD OF THE LIVING...THOUGH IT WAS AS SHORT-LIVED AS HIS FAILED ATTEMPT TO USURP RAENEF V'S PLACE AS THE CURRENT DEMON LORD RAENEF.

THE DEMON LORD OF EGAE, KRAYON IS ONE OF THE FIVE OLDEST DEMONS IN EXISTENCE (THOUGH HE CERTAINLY DOESN'T LOOK IT.) DURING KRAYON'S FAILED ATTEMPT TO LURE ECLIPSE AWAY FROM SERVING RAENEF, KRAYON MET--AND, APPARENTLY, FELL FOR--THE KNIGHT KNOWN AS ERUTIS. KRAYON EVEN WENT SO FAR AS TO SPECIFICALLY REQUEST THAT RAENEF IV NOT HARM ERUTIS IN HIS BID TO RETURN TO POWER

KRAYON

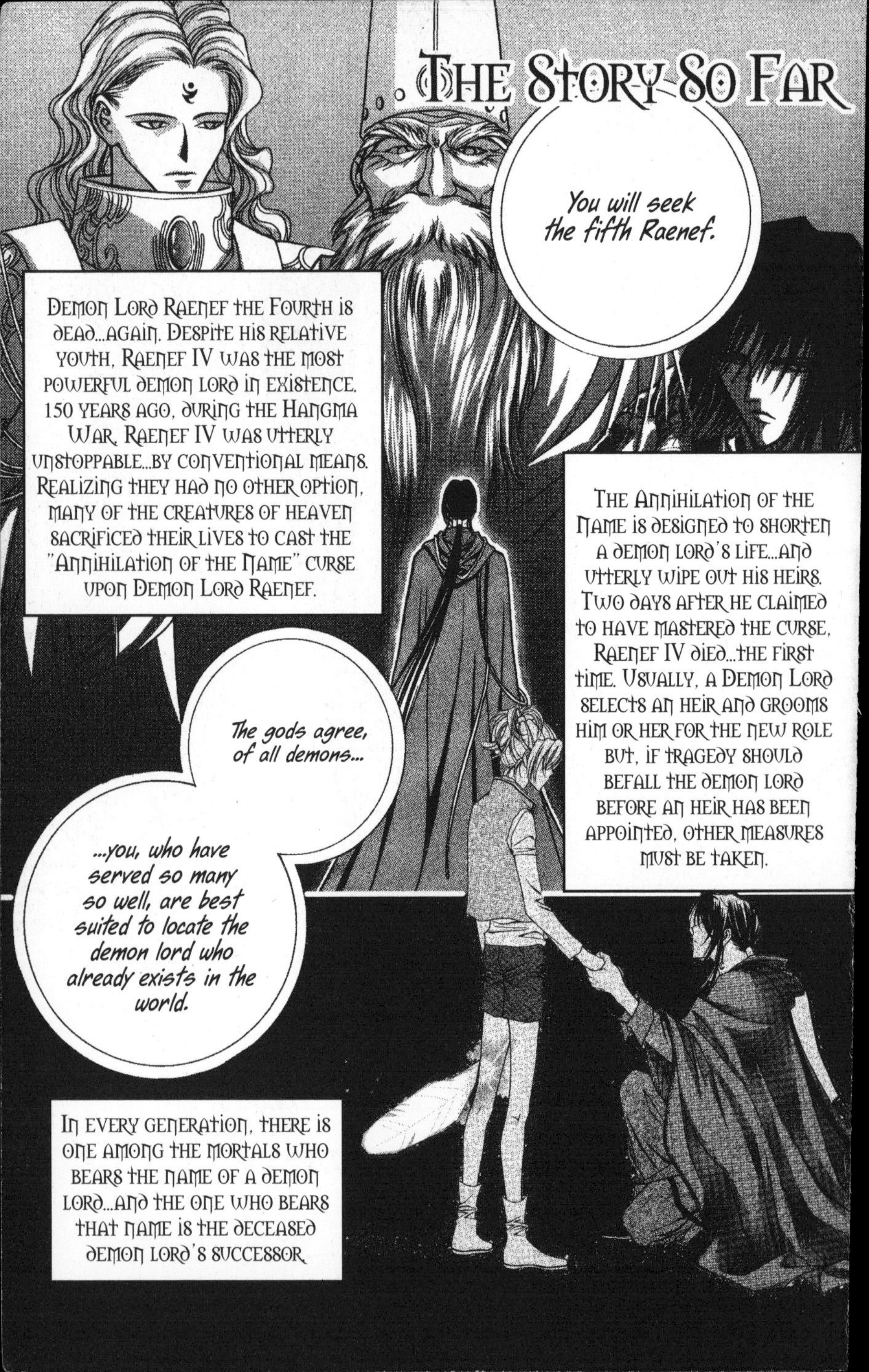
THE STORY SO FAR
You will seek the fifth Raenef.
DEMON LORD RAENEF THE FOURTH IS DEAD...AGAIN. DESPITE HIS RELATIVE YOUTH, RAENEF IV WAS THE MOST POWERFUL DEMON LORD IN EXISTENCE. 150 YEARS AGO, DURING THE HANGMA WAR, RAENEF IV WAS UTTERLY UNSTOPPABLE...BY CONVENTIONAL MEANS. REALIZING THEY HAD NO OTHER OPTION, MANY OF THE CREATURES OF HEAVEN SACRIFICED THEIR LIVES TO CAST THE "ANNIHILATION OF THE NAME" CURSE UPON DEMON LORD RAENEF.
THE ANNIHILATION OF THE NAME IS DESIGNED TO SHORTEN A DEMON LORD'S LIFE...AND UTTERLY WIPE OUT HIS HEIRS. TWO DAYS AFTER HE CLAIMED TO HAVE MASTERED THE CURSE, RAENEF IV DIED...THE FIRST TIME. USUALLY, A DEMON LORD SELECTS AN HEIR AND GROOMS HIM OR HER FOR THE NEW ROLE BUT, IF TRAGEDY SHOULD BEFALL THE DEMON LORD BEFORE AN HEIR HAS BEEN APPOINTED, OTHER MEASURES MUST BE TAKEN.
The gods agree, of all demons...
...you, who have served so many so well, are best suited to locate the demon lord who already exists in the world.
IN EVERY GENERATION, THERE IS ONE AMONG THE MORTALS WHO BEARS THE NAME OF A DEMON LORD...AND THE ONE WHO BEARS THAT NAME IS THE DECEASED DEMON LORD'S SUCCESSOR.

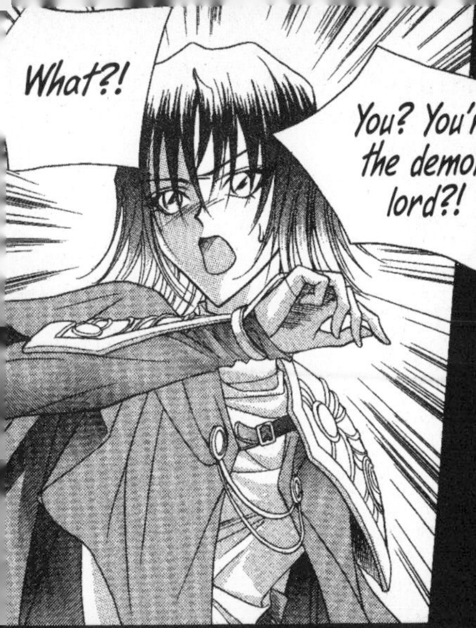
What?!
You? You're the demon lord?!

Enter Raenef, an orphaned street urchin and, unbeknownst to him, the heir to demon royalty. Unfortunately, with a personality that is incredibly sweet, nice and friendly, Raenef the Fifth couldn't be further from demon lord material. Assigned by the gods to be Raenef's tutor, Eclipse is a wise and noble demon faced with the seemingly impossible task of molding Raenef into a proper demon lord.

A demon lord's life is not without peril, and Raenef has already faced several attacks by those bent on destroying his kind. However, thanks to Raenef's lovable nature, two of his attackers (a human knight known as Erutis and the future High Cleric to the Temple of Rased named Chris) now live in Raenef's castle as his companions.

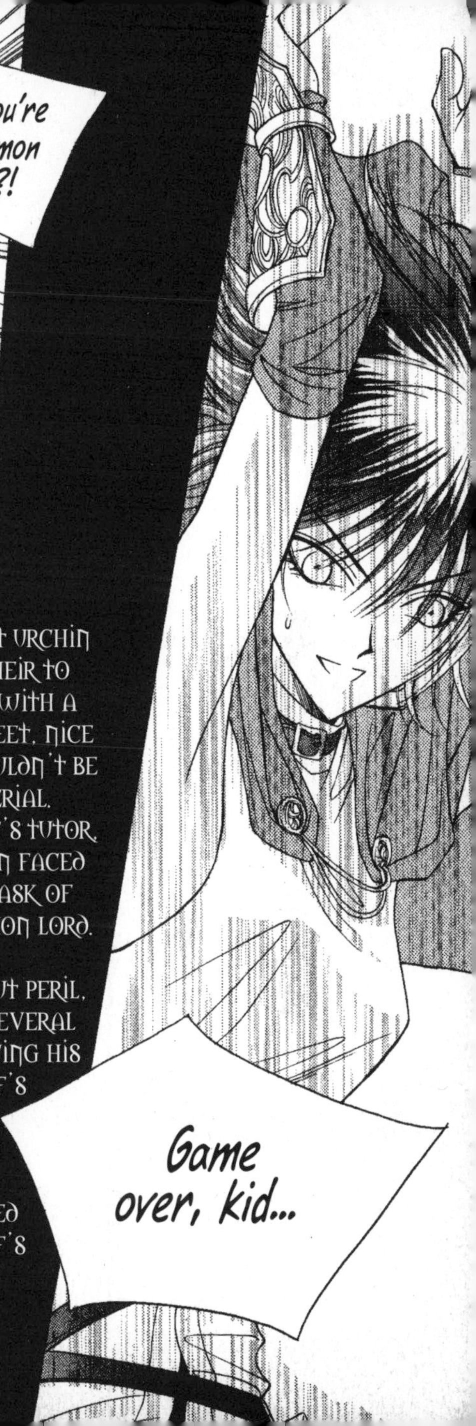
Game over, kid...

OST WHEN IT SEEMED THAT LIFE IN CASTLE
ENEF COULDN'T GET ANY CRAZIER, A FLOCK OF
AVEN'S CREATURES DESCENDED TO CARRY OUT
REST OF THE ANNIHILATION OF THE NAME. AS
CREATURES OF HEAVEN BROUGHT RAENEF V'S
EVIL" PERSONALITY TO THE FORE, ALL WERE
OCKED BY THE SUDDEN APPEARANCE OF RAENEF
V. THE FORMERLY DECEASED DEMON LORD THEN
RDERED CHRIS TO SUMMON THE POWER OF THE
GOD RASED AND USE IT TO ATTACK RAENEF V!

A FIERCE BATTLE ENSUED AND RAENEF'S DUAL
ERSONALITIES HARMONIZED INTO ONE. BEFORE
ANYONE COULD CATCH A BREATH, RAENEF IV
ANNOUNCED HIS PLAN TO USURP RAENEF V'S
EXISTENCE AND TAKE OVER AS THE REIGNING
MON LORD RAENEF. EVEN WITH HIS NEWFOUND
TY OF MIND, RAENEF V WAS HARD-PRESSED TO
EFEAT HIS PREDECESSOR...AND ONLY SUCCEEDED
ITH THE HELP OF ECLIPSE, ERUTIS, AND CHRIS.

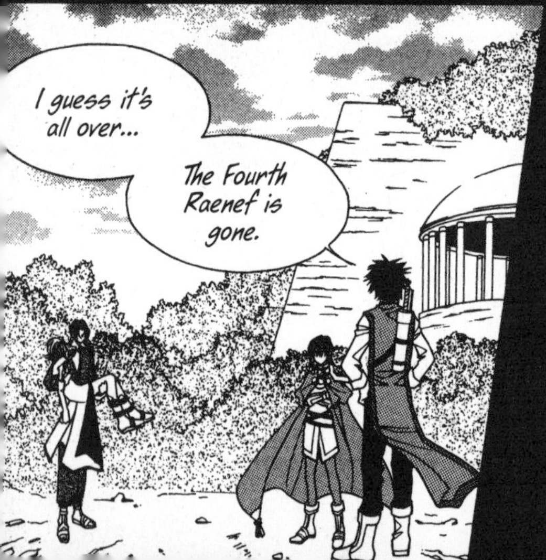
I guess it's all over...
The Fourth Raenef is gone.

In the aftermath, Eclipse observed that Raenef had finally mastered his powers and congratulated his young charge on becoming a true demon lord. Exhausted, Raenef collapsed in Eclipse's arms.

As Eclipse tucked the young demon lord into bed, Raenef's companions wondered about their friend's immediate future...

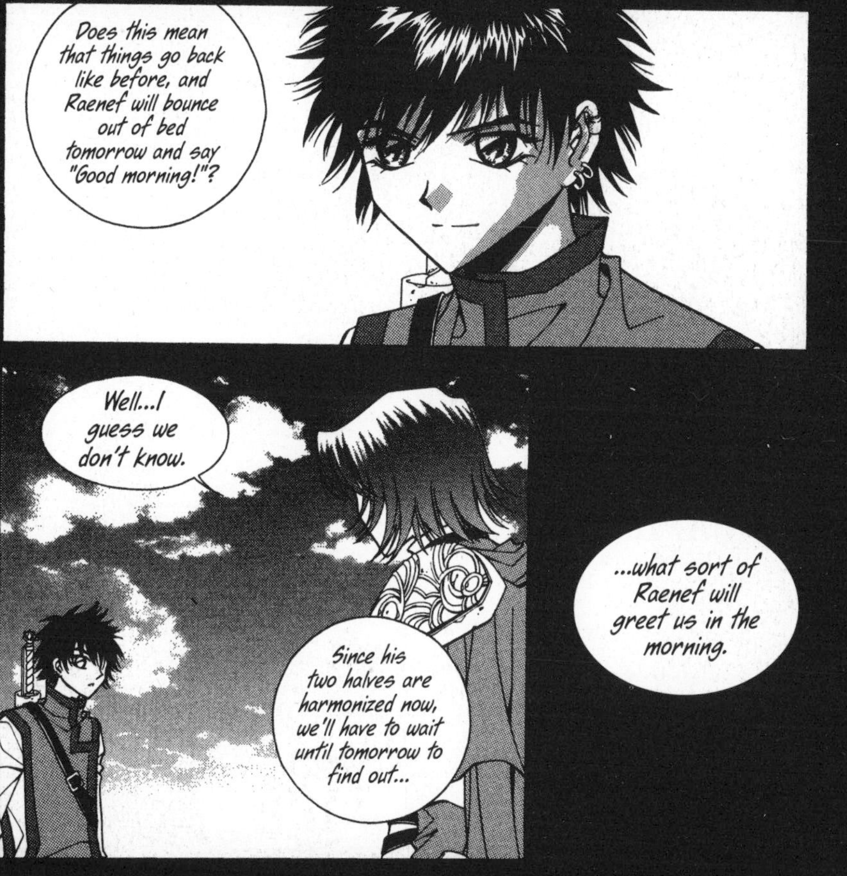
Does this mean that things go back like before, and Raenef will bounce out of bed tomorrow and say "Good morning!"?
Well...I guess we don't know.
Since his two halves are harmonized now, we'll have to wait until tomorrow to find out...
...what sort of Raenef will greet us in the morning.

Contents

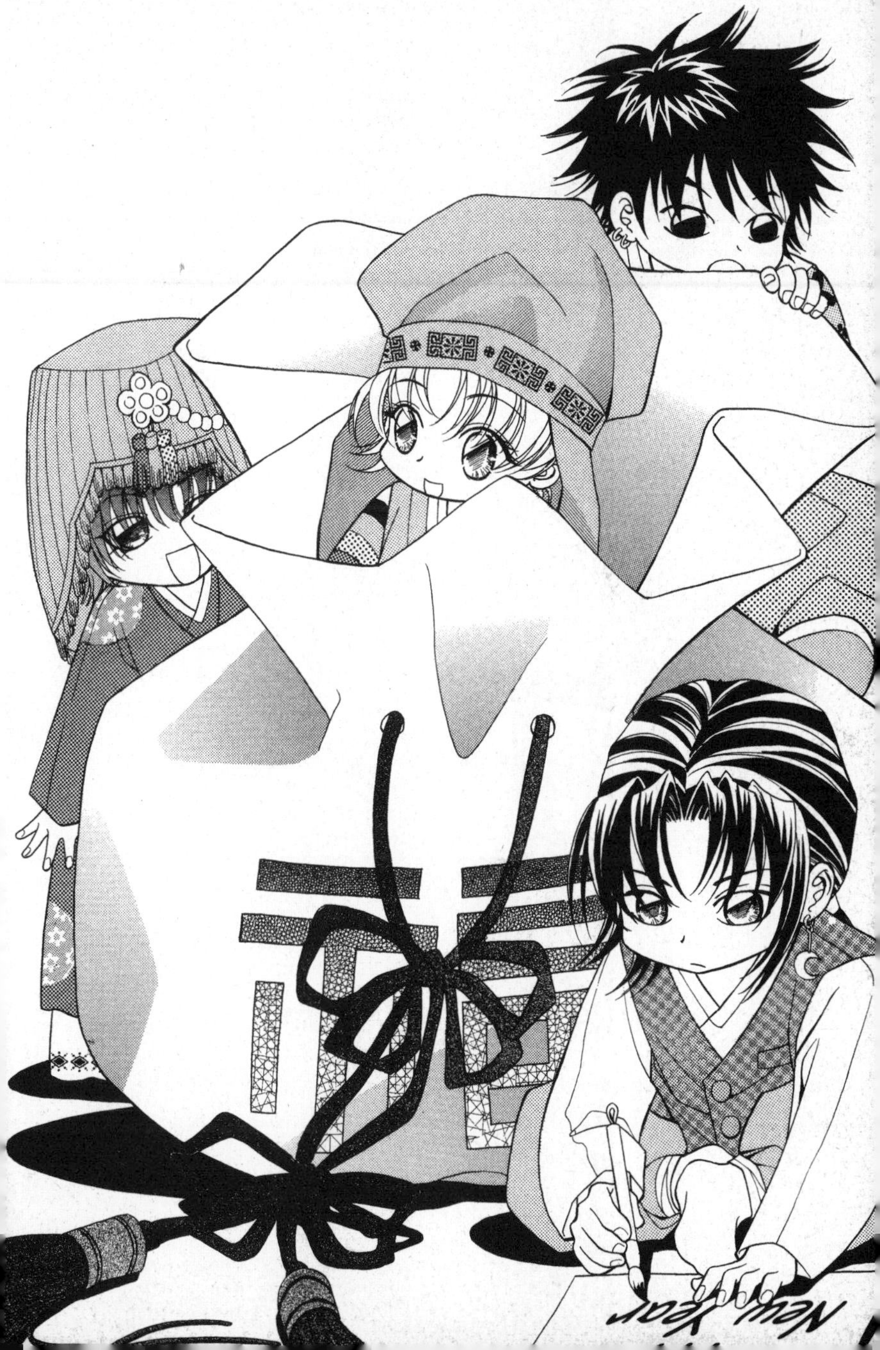
New Year

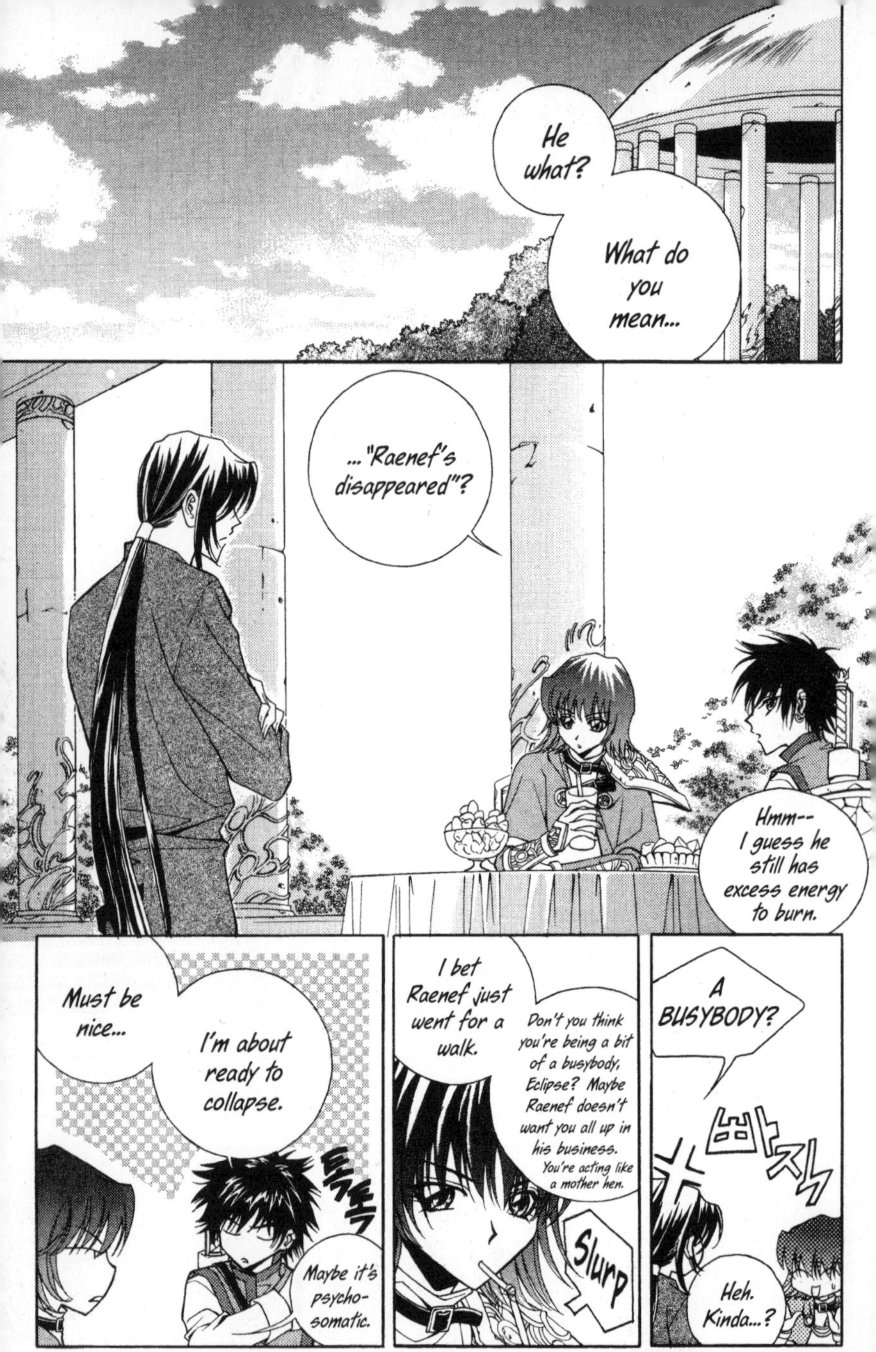
He what?
What do you mean...
..."Raenef's disappeared"?
Hmm-- I guess he still has excess energy to burn.
Must be nice...
I'm about ready to collapse.
Maybe it's psycho-somatic.
I bet Raenef just went for a walk.
Don't you think you're being a bit of a busybody, Eclipse? Maybe Raenef doesn't want you all up in his business. You're acting like a mother hen.
Slurp
A BUSYBODY?
Heh. Kinda...?

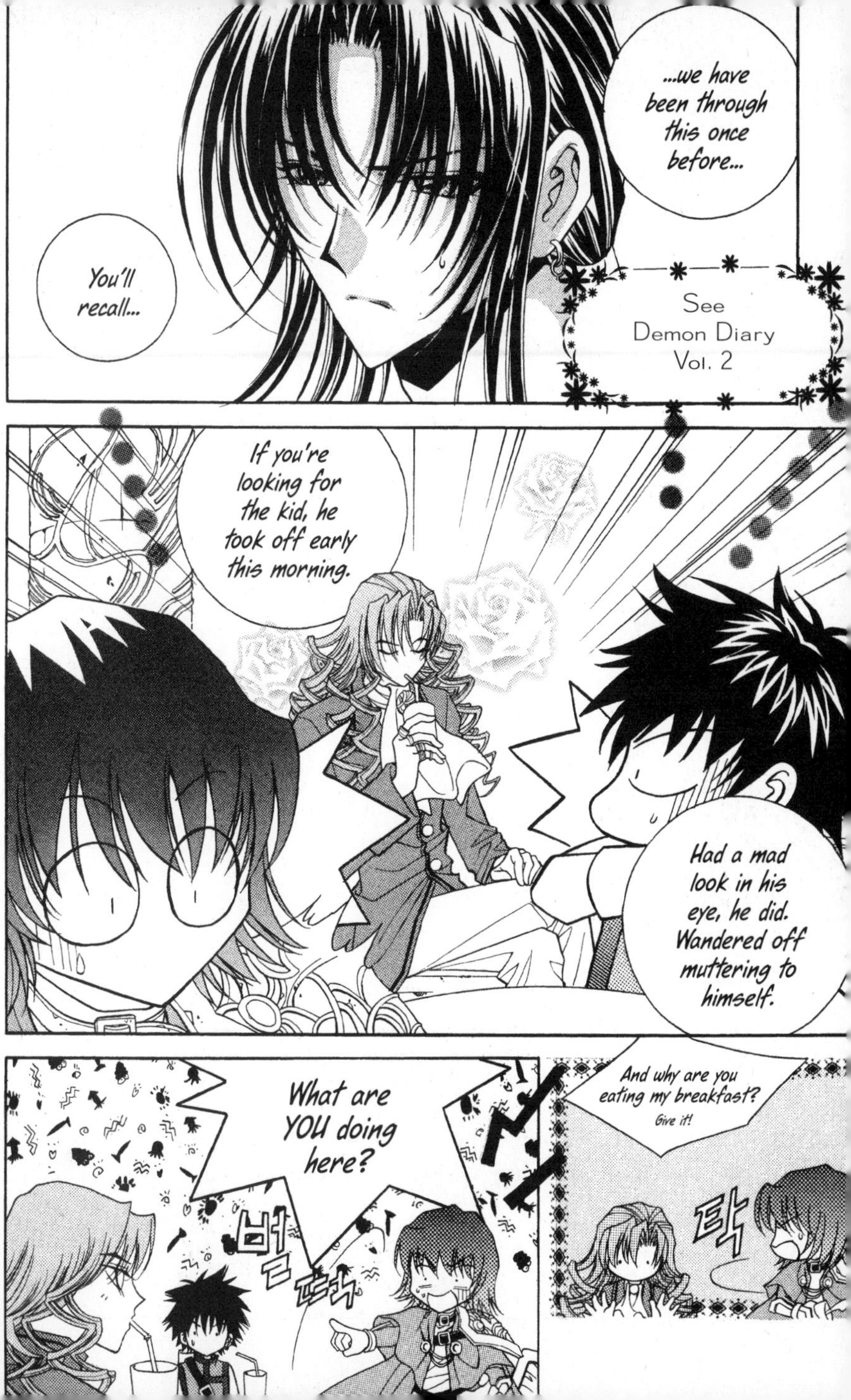

You'll recall...
...we have been through this once before...
See Demon Diary Vol. 2
If you're looking for the kid, he took off early this morning.
Had a mad look in his eye, he did. Wandered off muttering to himself.
What are YOU doing here?
벌떡
And why are you eating my breakfast?
Give it!
탁

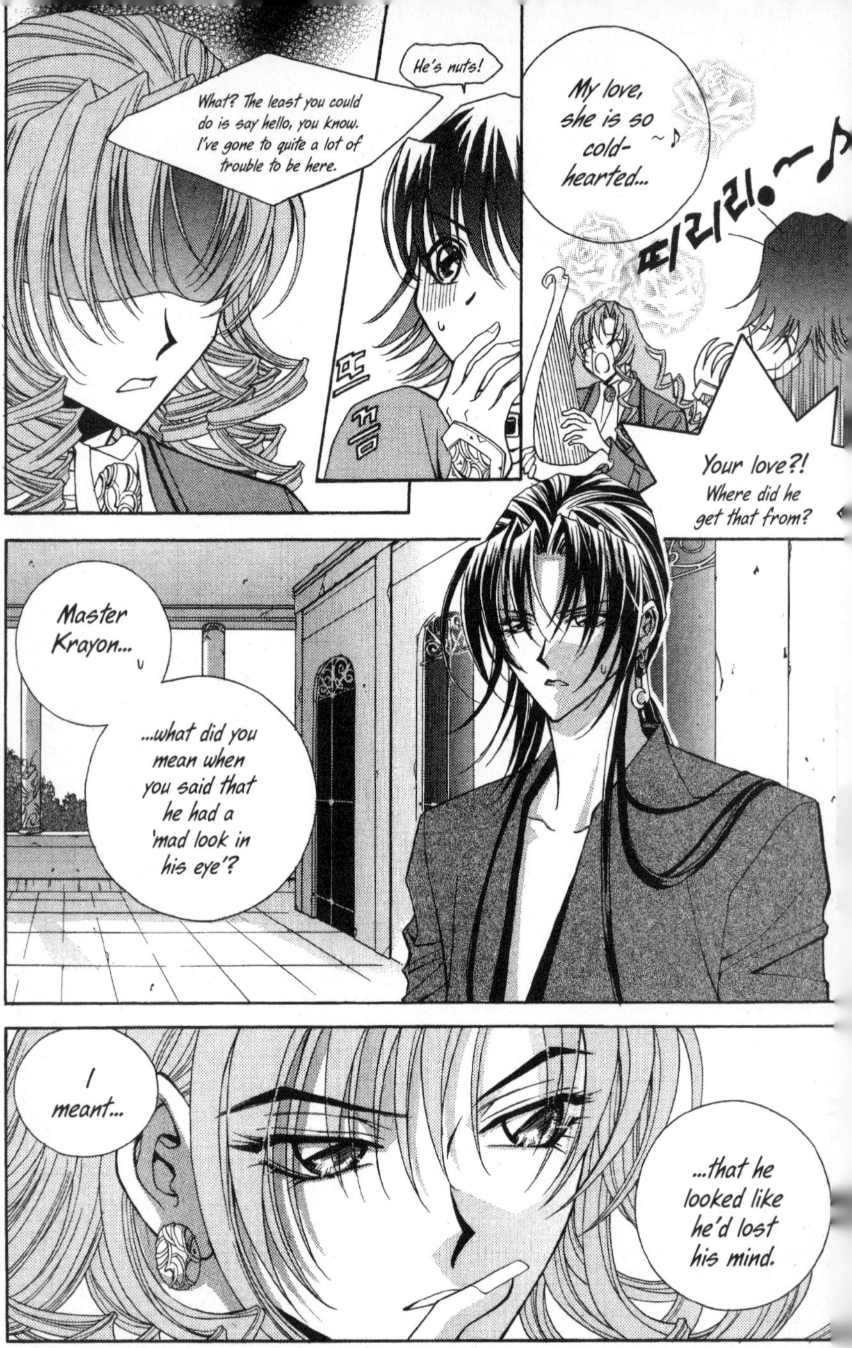
What? The least you could do is say hello, you know. I've gone to quite a lot of trouble to be here.
He's nuts!
My love, she is so cold-hearted... ~♪
Your love?! Where did he get that from?
Master Krayon...
...what did you mean when you said that he had a 'mad look in his eye'?
I meant...
...that he looked like he'd lost his mind.

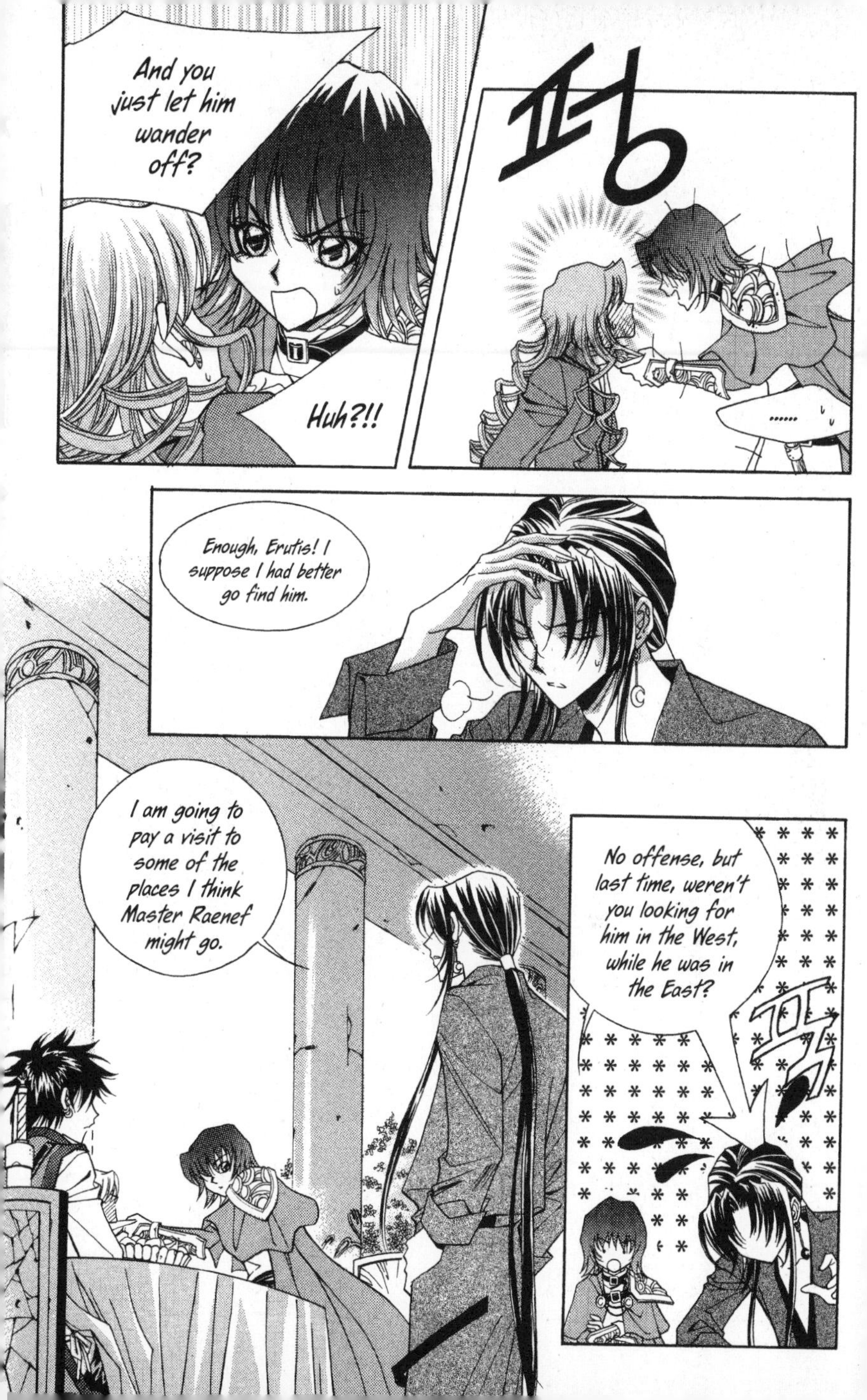
And you just let him wander off?
Huh?!!
......
Enough, Erutis! I suppose I had better go find him.
I am going to pay a visit to some of the places I think Master Raenef might go.
No offense, but last time, weren't you looking for him in the West, while he was in the East?

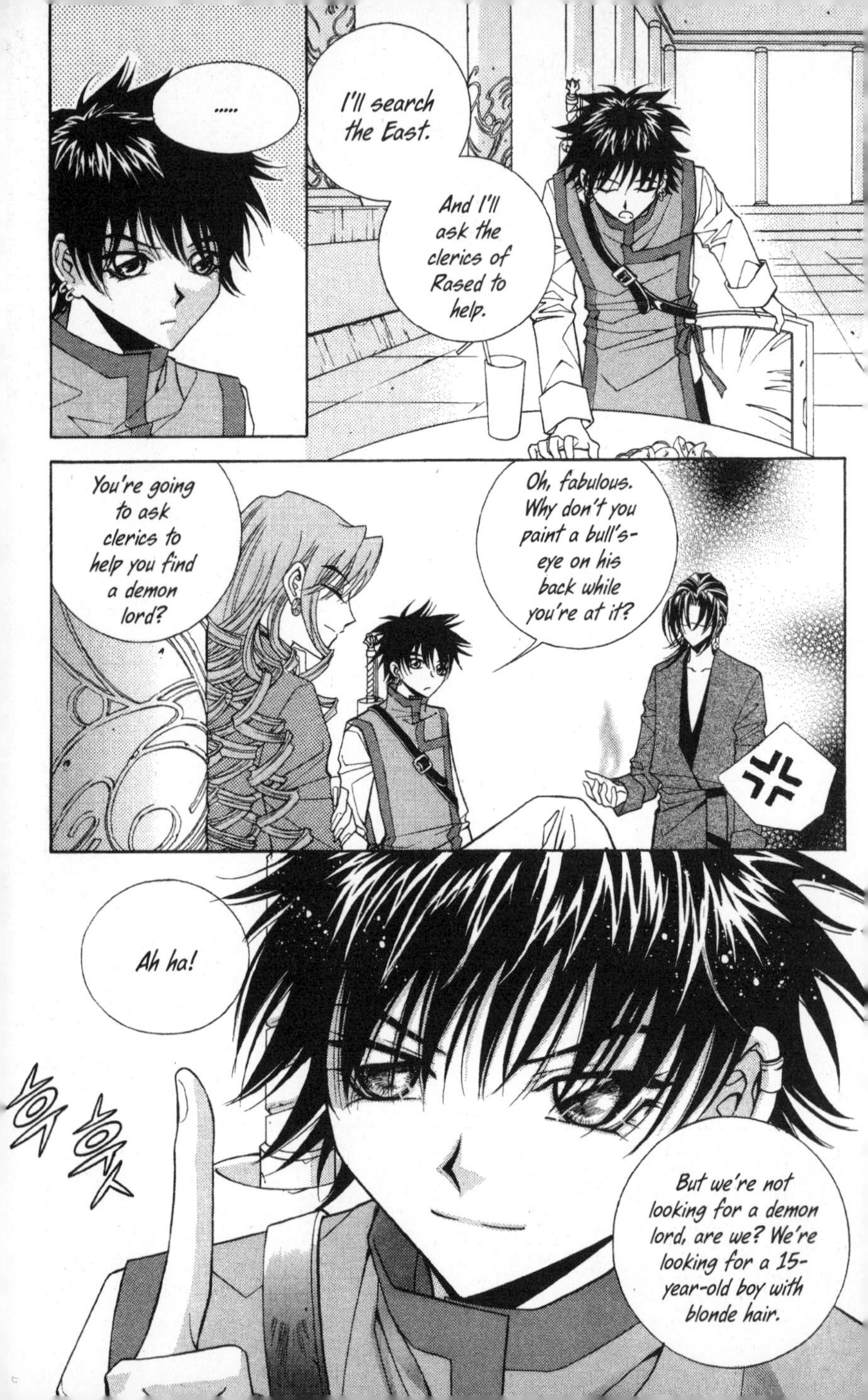
.....
I'll search the East.
And I'll ask the clerics of Rased to help.
You're going to ask clerics to help you find a demon lord?
Oh, fabulous. Why don't you paint a bull's-eye on his back while you're at it?
Ah ha!
TOK TOK
But we're not looking for a demon lord, are we? We're looking for a 15-year-old boy with blonde hair.

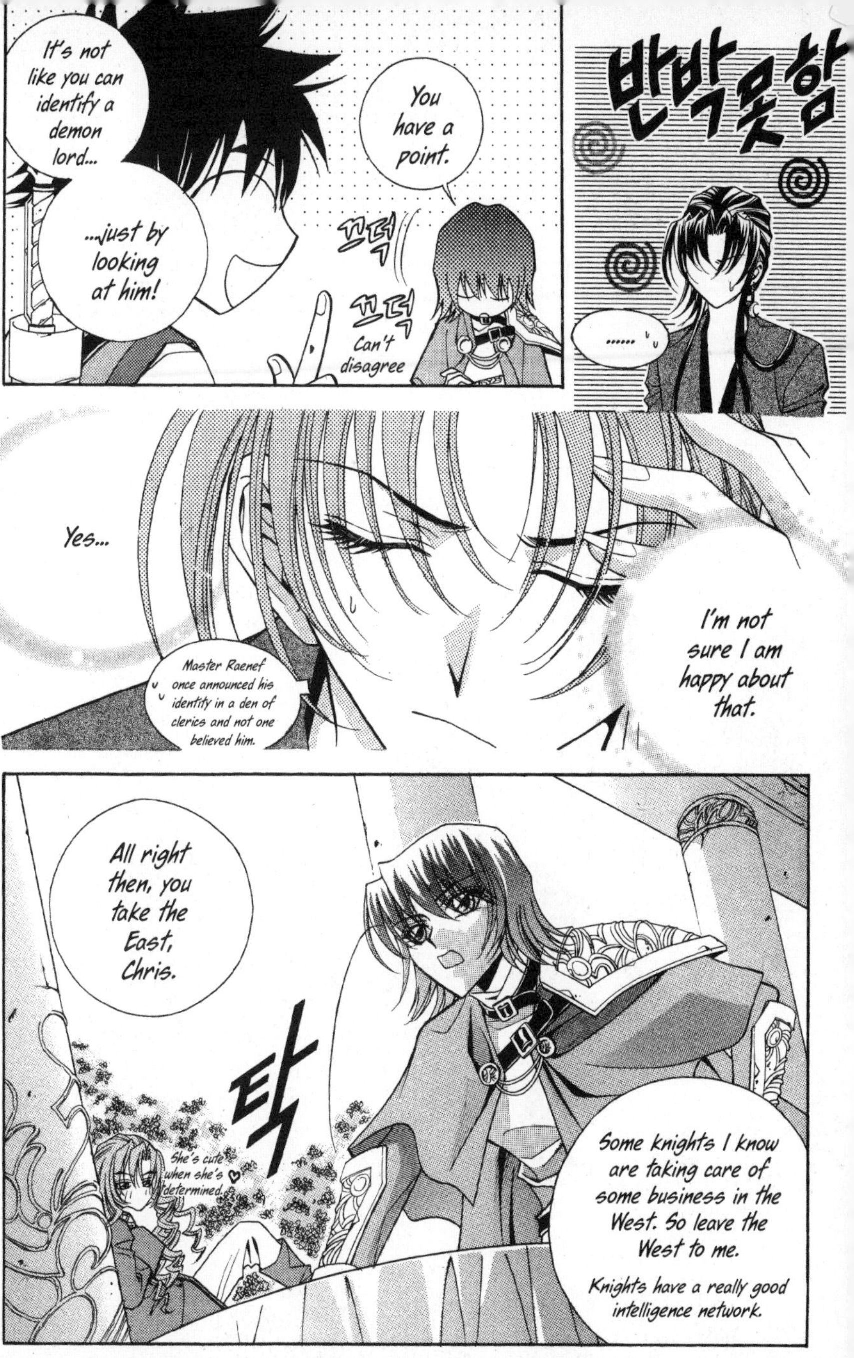
It's not like you can identify a demon lord...
...just by looking at him!
You have a point.
끄덕
끄덕
Can't disagree
반박못함
......
Yes...
Master Raenef once announced his identity in a den of clerics and not one believed him.
I'm not sure I am happy about that.
All right then, you take the East, Chris.
탁
She's cute when she's determined.
Some knights I know are taking care of some business in the West. So leave the West to me.
Knights have a really good intelligence network.

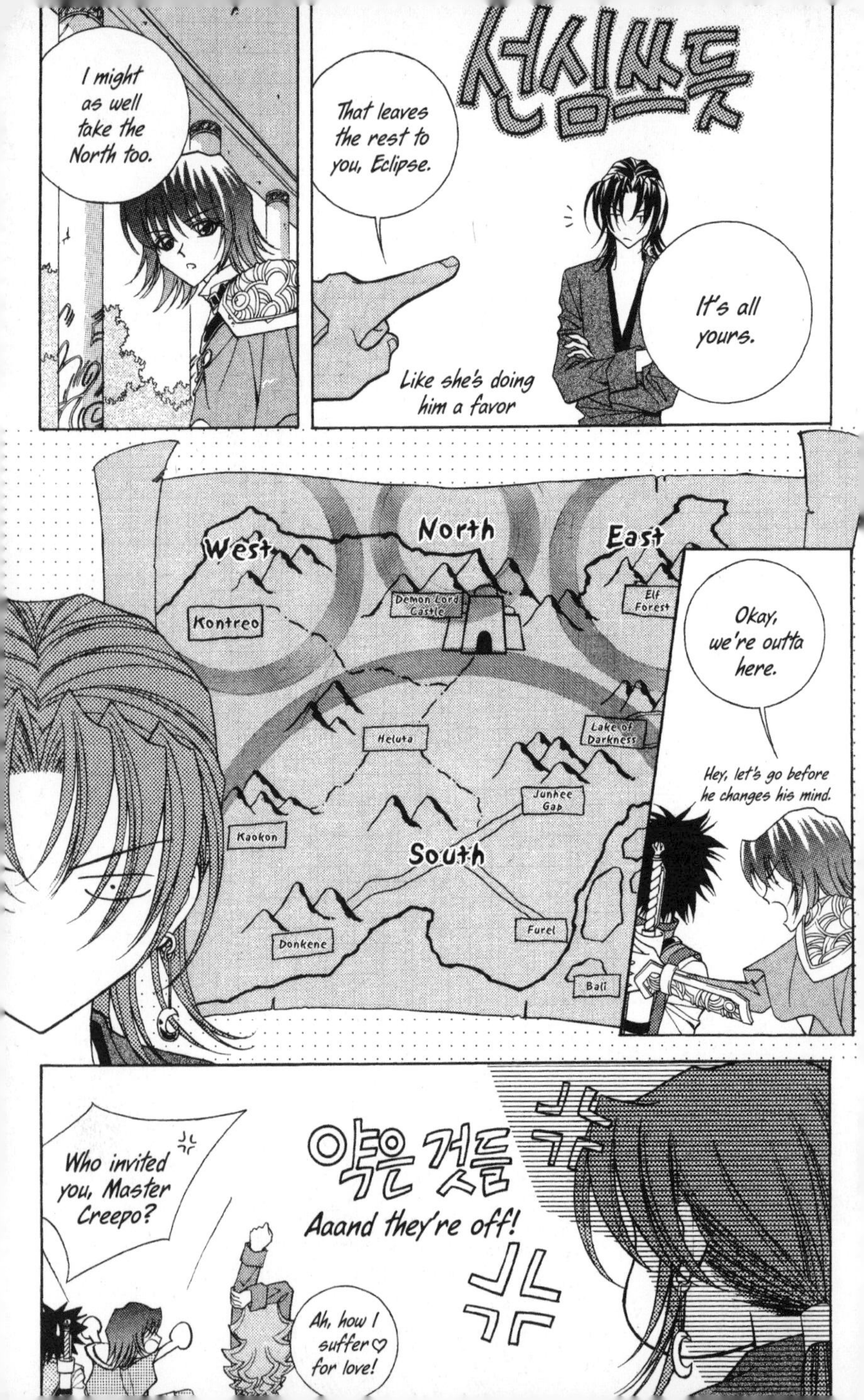
I might as well take the North too.
선심쓰듯
That leaves the rest to you, Eclipse.
It's all yours.
Like she's doing him a favor
West
North
East
Kontreo
Demon Lord Castle
Elf Forest
Heluta
Lake of Darkness
Junhee Gab
Kaokon
South
Donkene
Furel
Bali
Okay, we're outta here.
Hey, let's go before he changes his mind.
Who invited you, Master Creepo?
약은 것들
Aaand they're off!
Ah, how I suffer♡ for love!

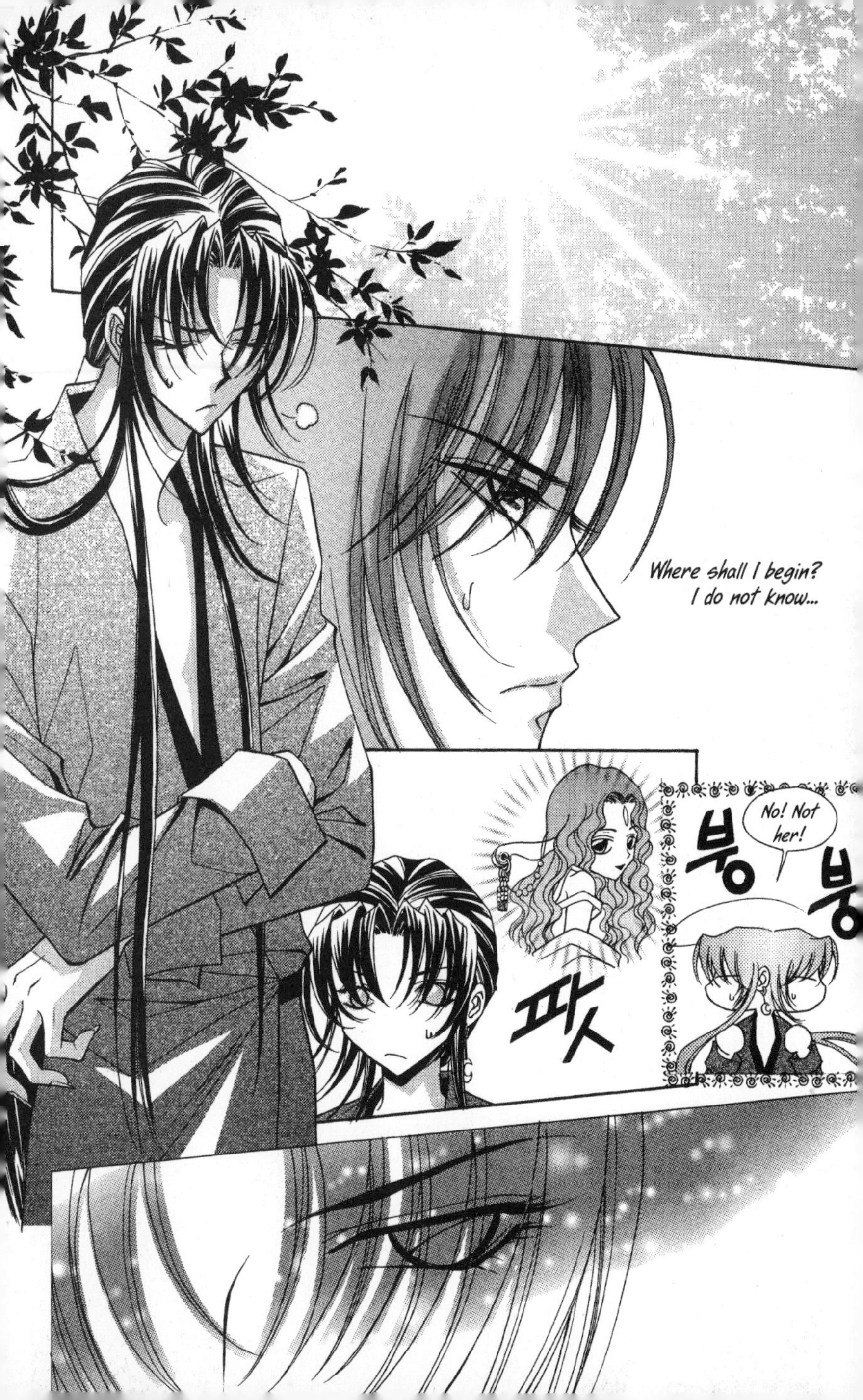
Where shall I begin?
I do not know...
파人
붕
No! Not her!
붕

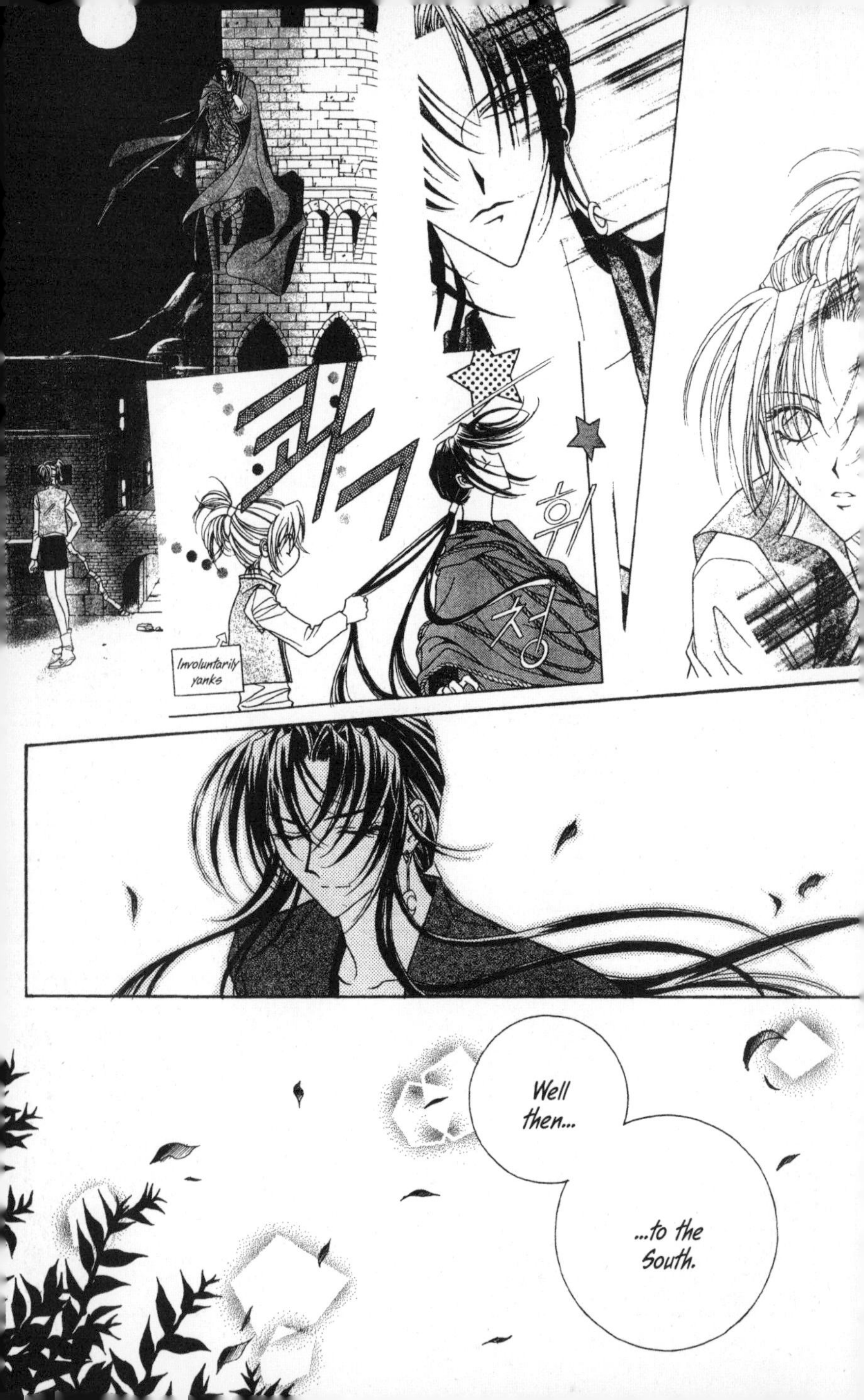
콱
휘청
Involuntarily yanks
Well then...
...to the South.

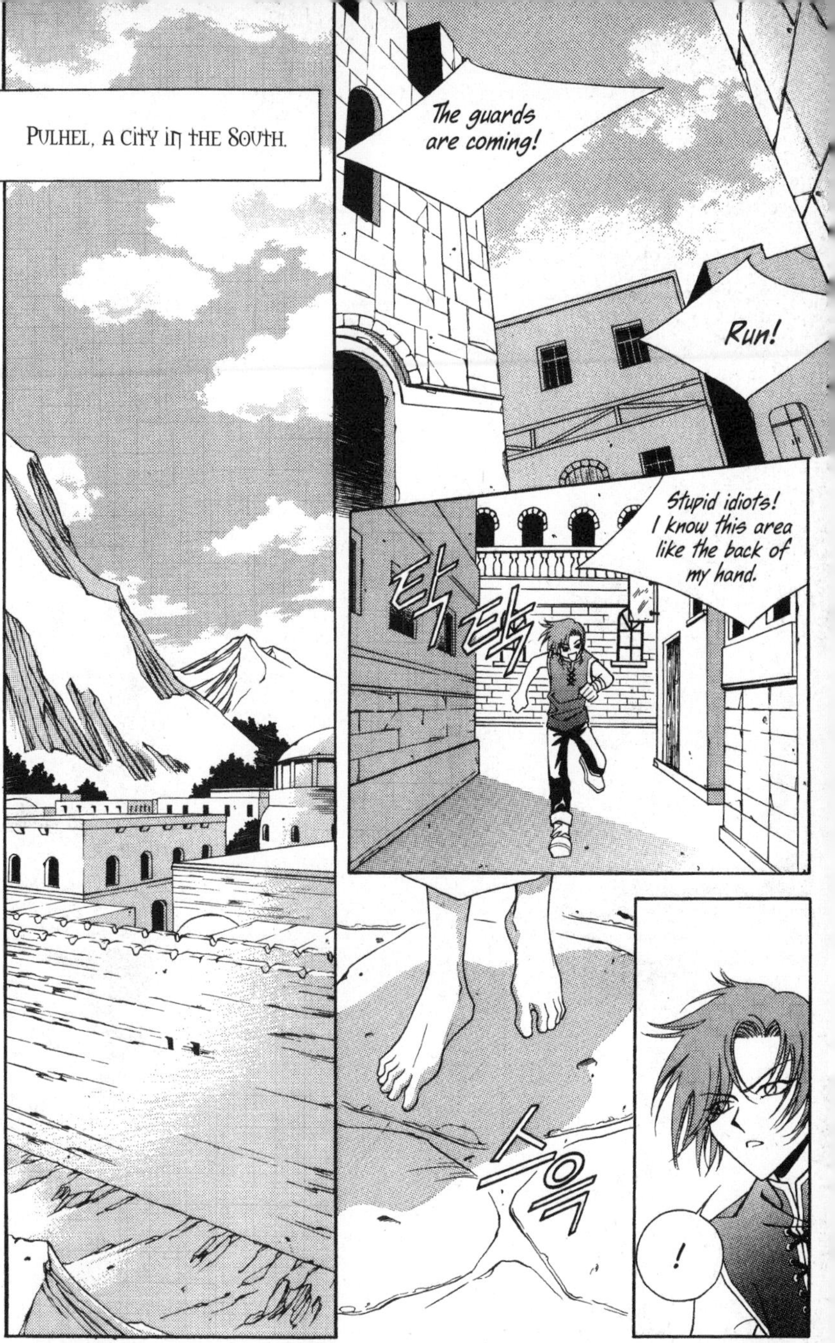

Pulhel, a city in the South.
The guards are coming!
Run!
탁
탁
Stupid idiots! I know this area like the back of my hand.
!

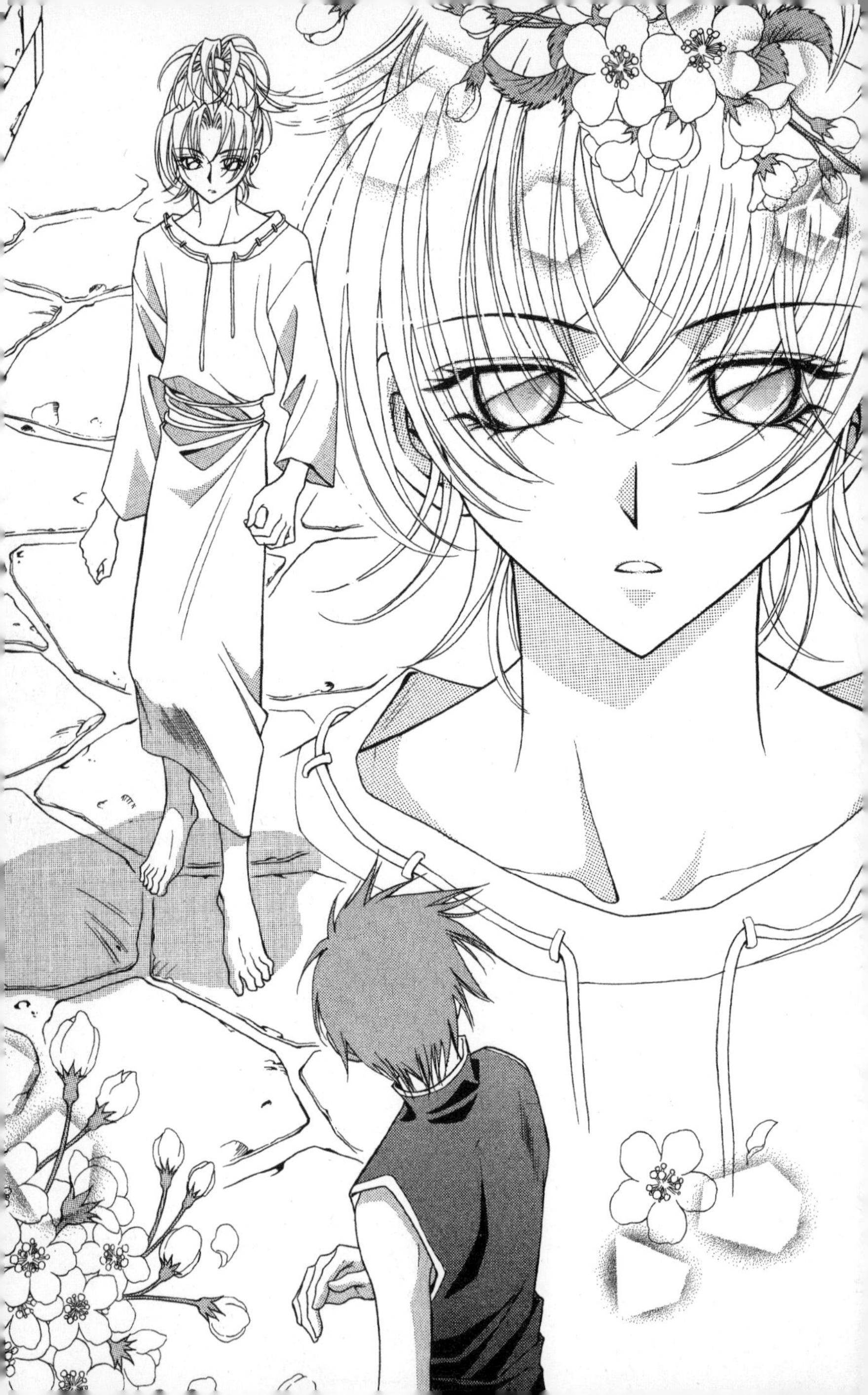

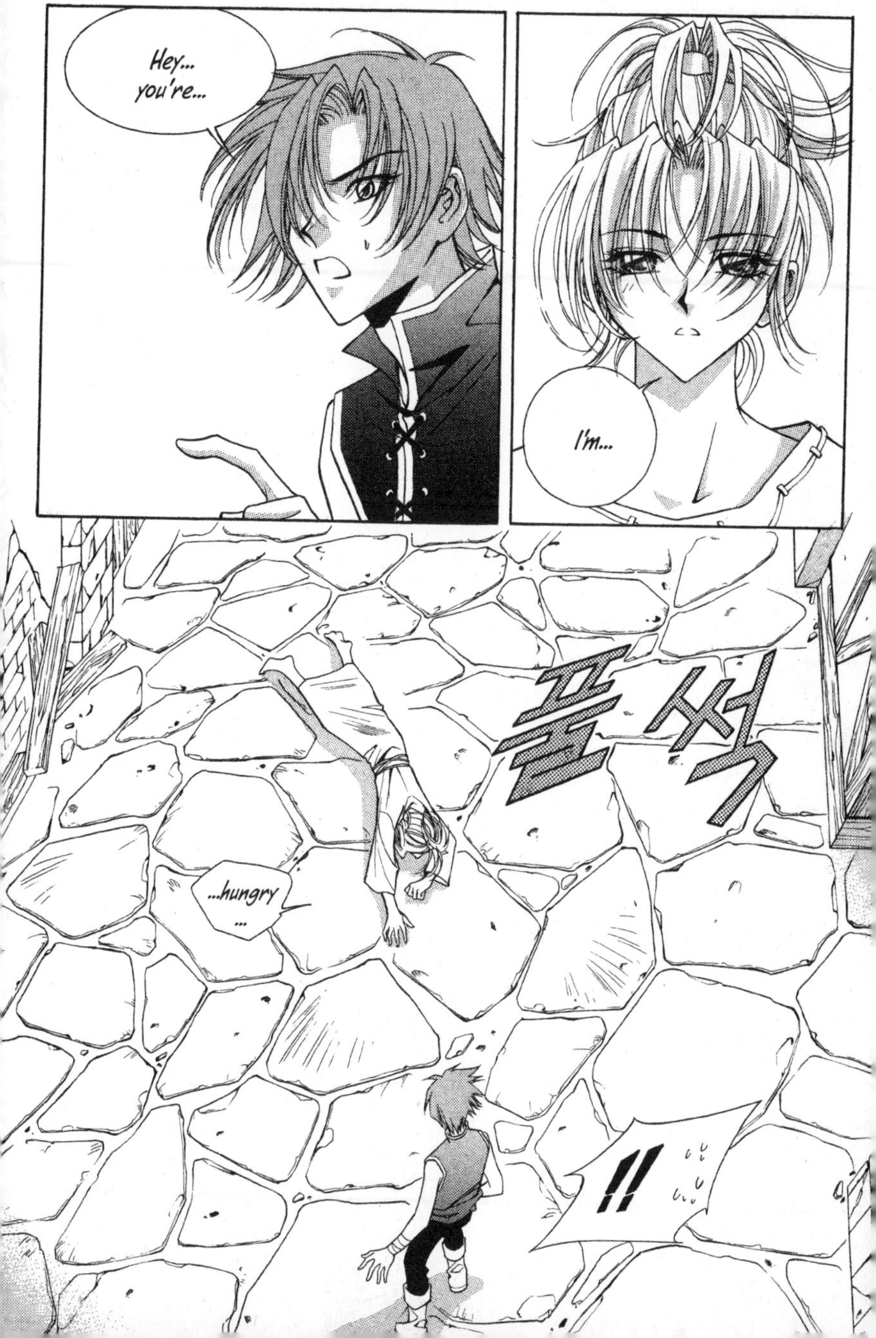
Hey... you're...
I'm...
풀썩
...hungry ...
!!

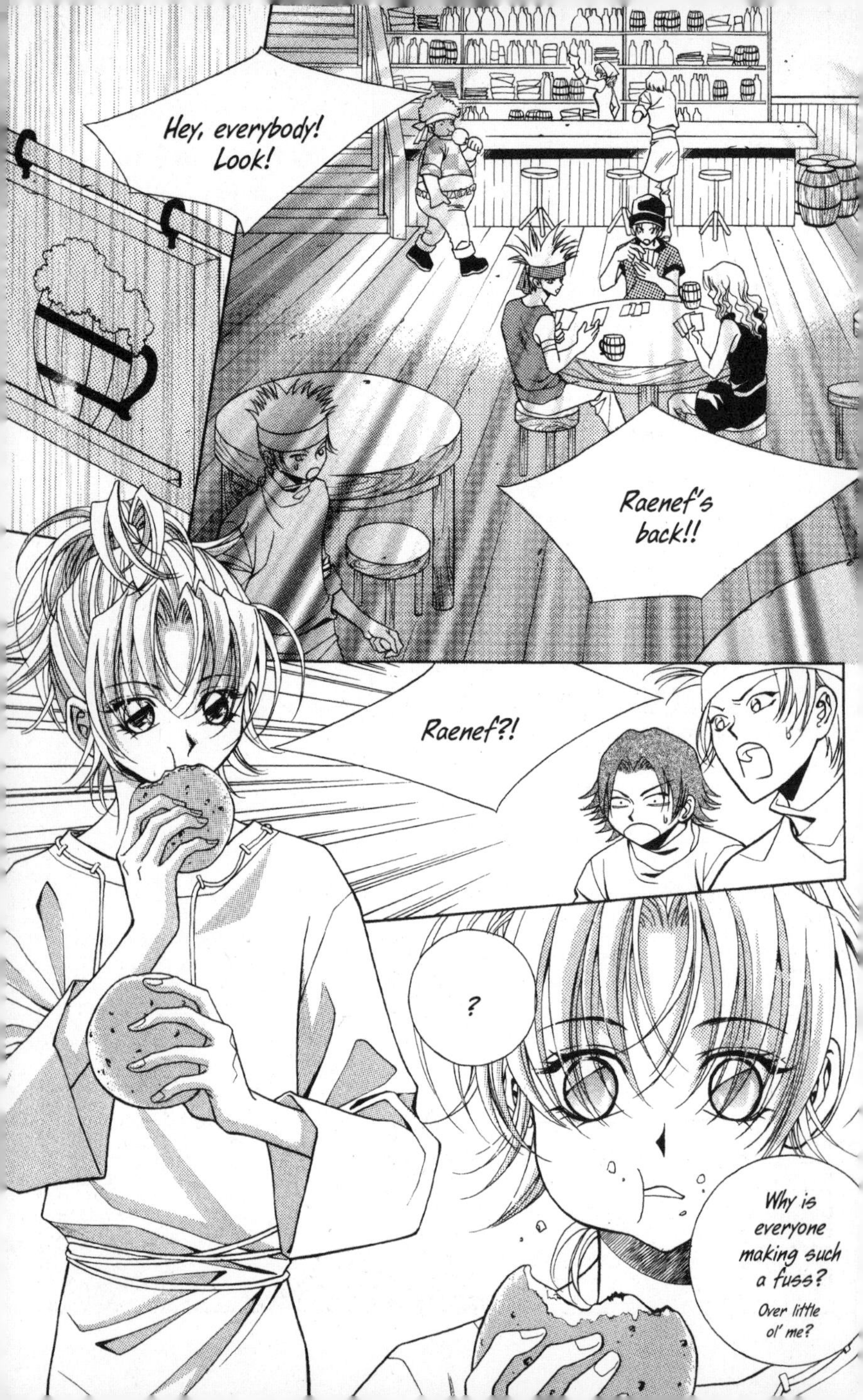
Hey, everybody! Look!
Raenef's back!!
Raenef?!
?
Why is everyone making such a fuss?
Over little ol' me?

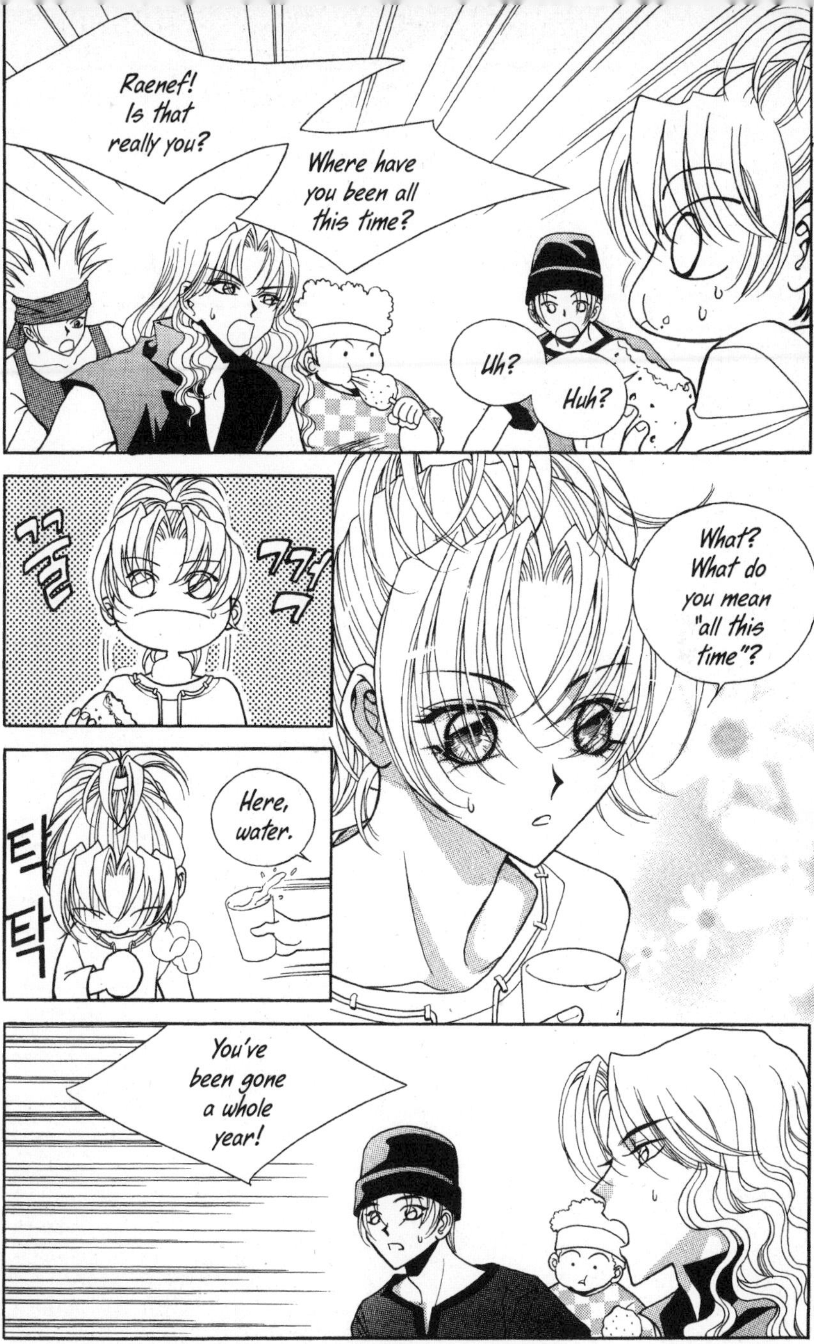
Raenef! Is that really you?
Where have you been all this time?
Uh?
Huh?
꿀꺽
Here, water.
탁탁
What? What do you mean "all this time"?
You've been gone a whole year!

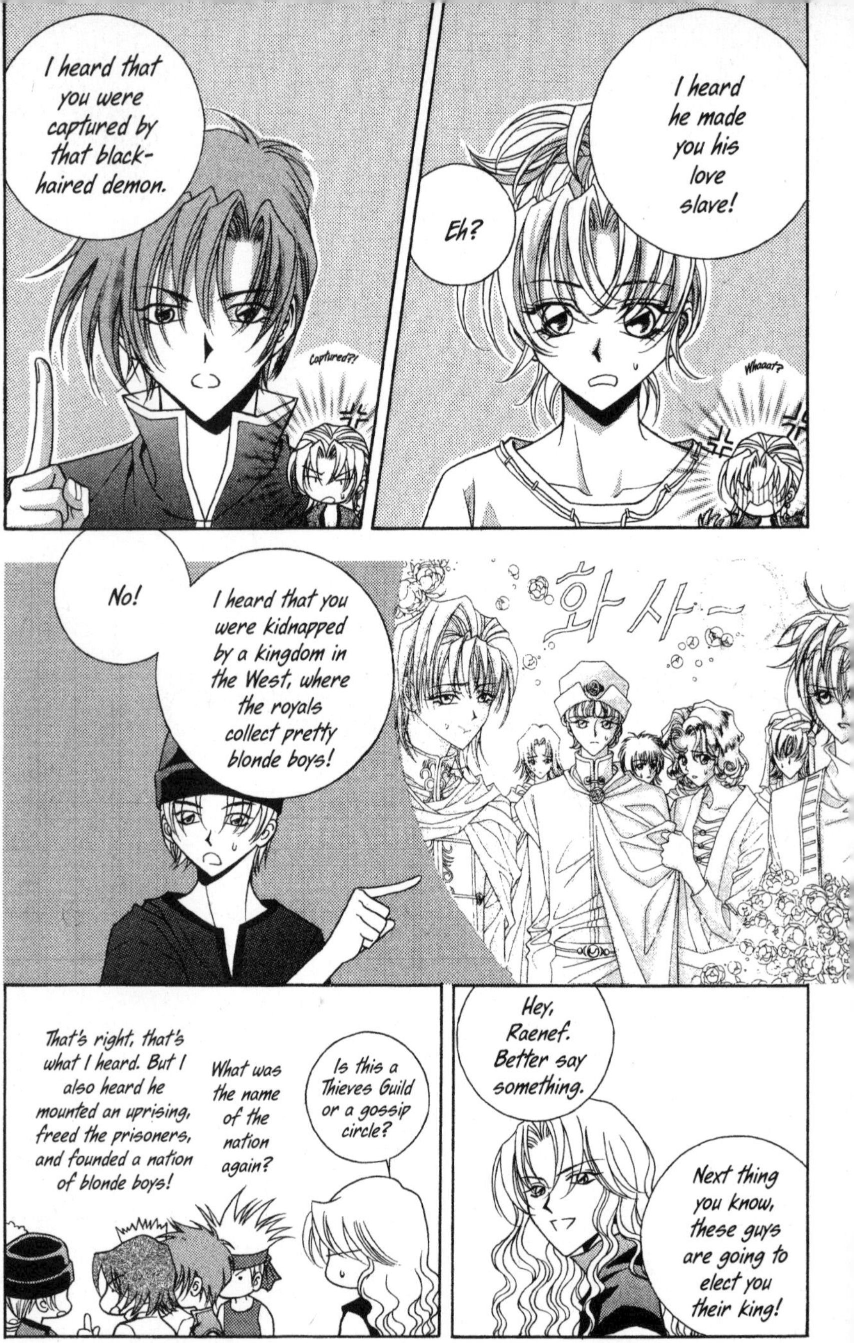
I heard that you were captured by that black-haired demon.
Captured?!
Eh?
I heard he made you his love slave!
Whaaat?
No!
I heard that you were kidnapped by a kingdom in the West, where the royals collect pretty blonde boys!
화사~
That's right, that's what I heard. But I also heard he mounted an uprising, freed the prisoners, and founded a nation of blonde boys!
What was the name of the nation again?
Is this a Thieves Guild or a gossip circle?
Hey, Raenef. Better say something.
Next thing you know, these guys are going to elect you their king!

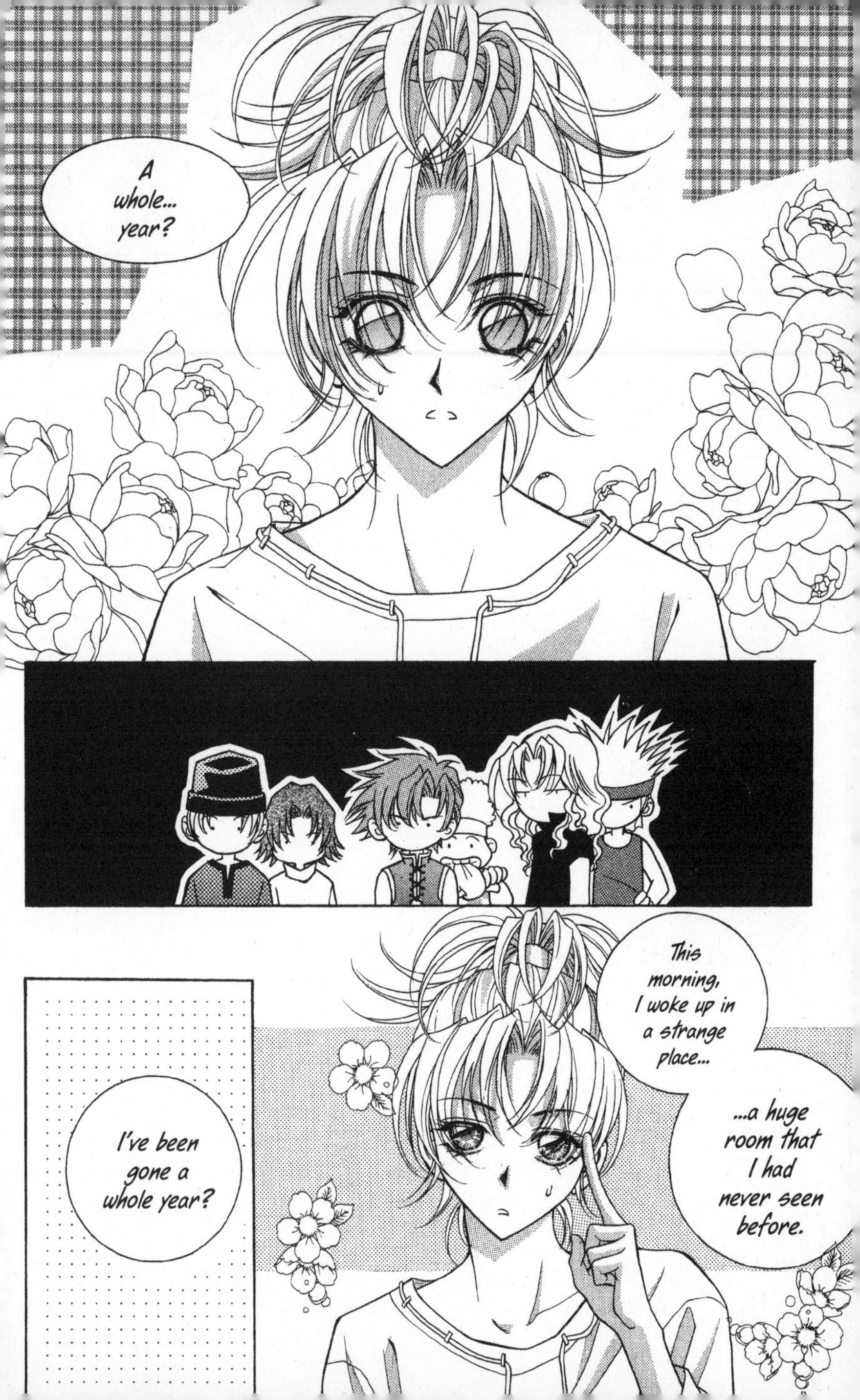
A whole... year?
I've been gone a whole year?
This morning, I woke up in a strange place...
...a huge room that I had never seen before.

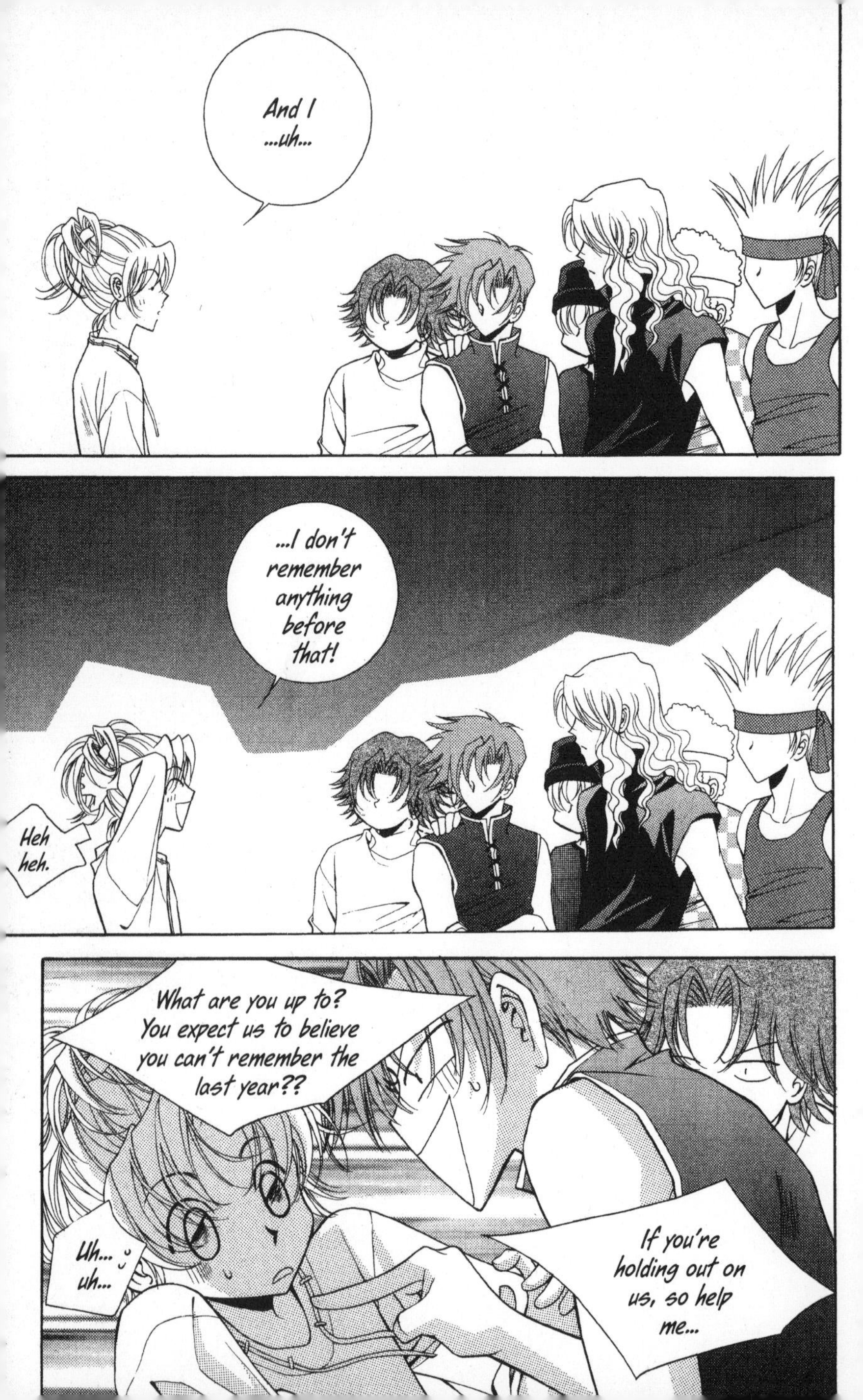
And I ...uh...
...I don't remember anything before that!
Heh heh.
What are you up to? You expect us to believe you can't remember the last year??
Uh... uh...
If you're holding out on us, so help me...

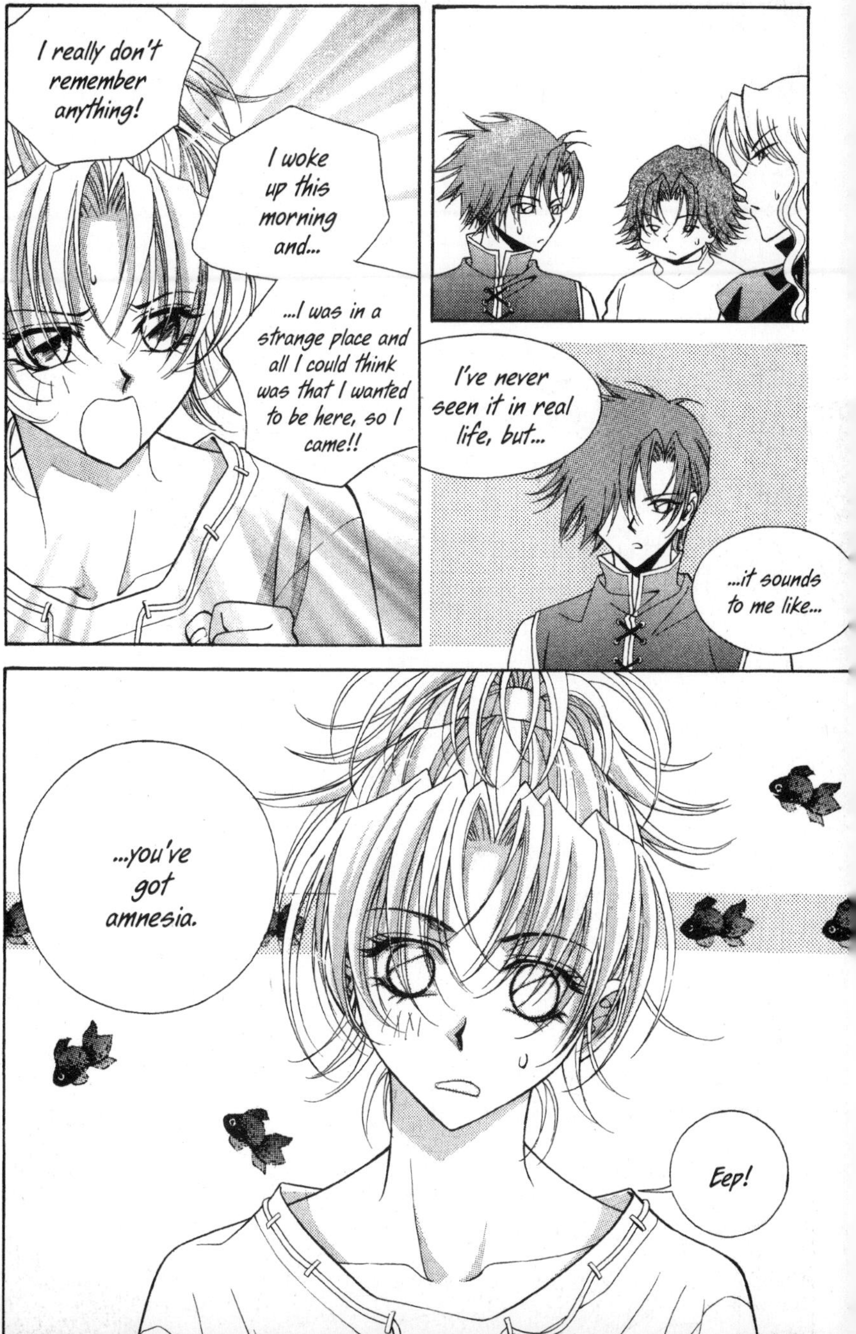
I really don't remember anything!
I woke up this morning and...
...I was in a strange place and all I could think was that I wanted to be here, so I came!!
I've never seen it in real life, but...
...it sounds to me like...
...you've got amnesia.
Eep!

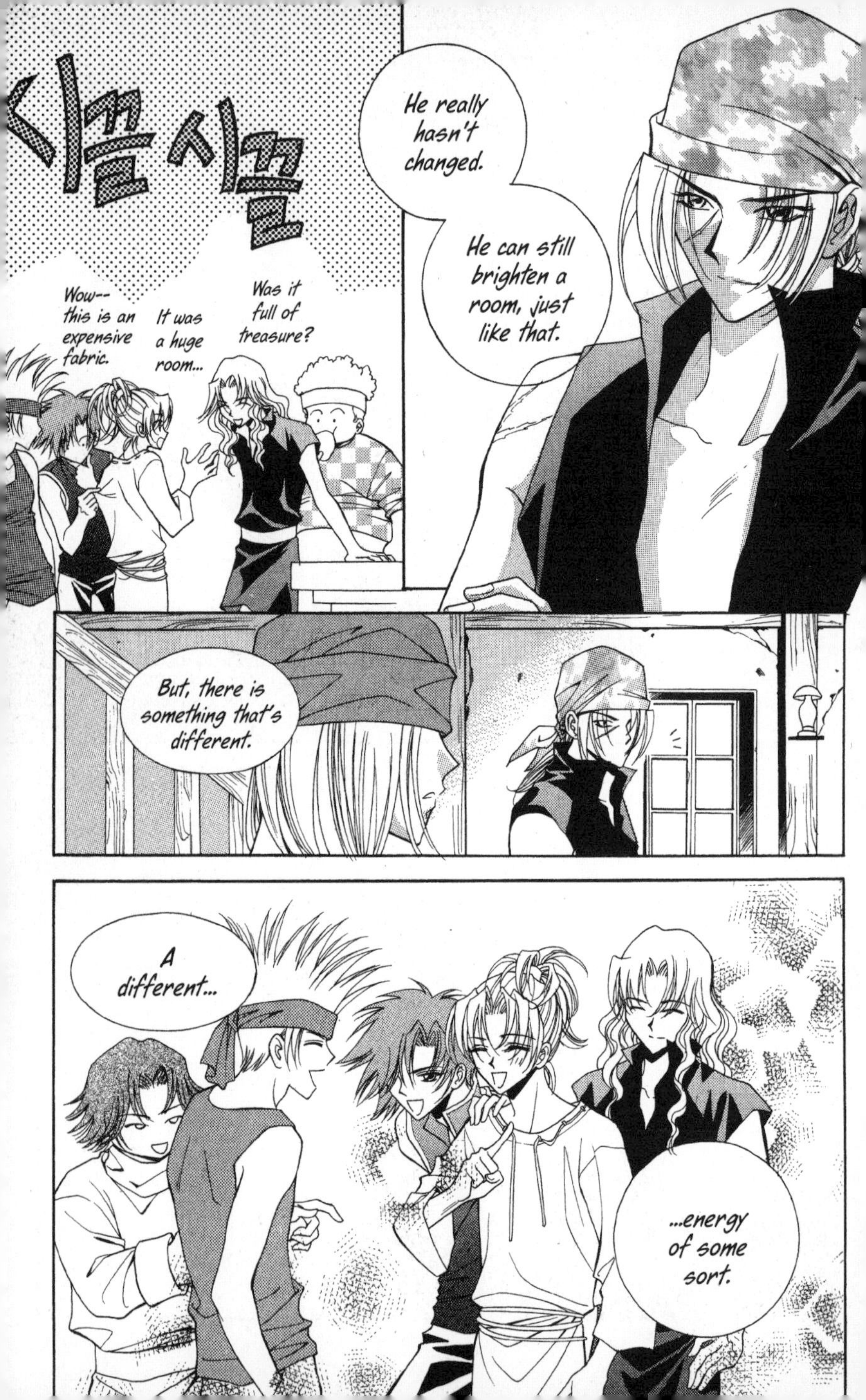
시끌시끌
Wow-- this is an expensive fabric.
It was a huge room...
Was it full of treasure?
He really hasn't changed.
He can still brighten a room, just like that.
But, there is something that's different.
A different...
...energy of some sort.

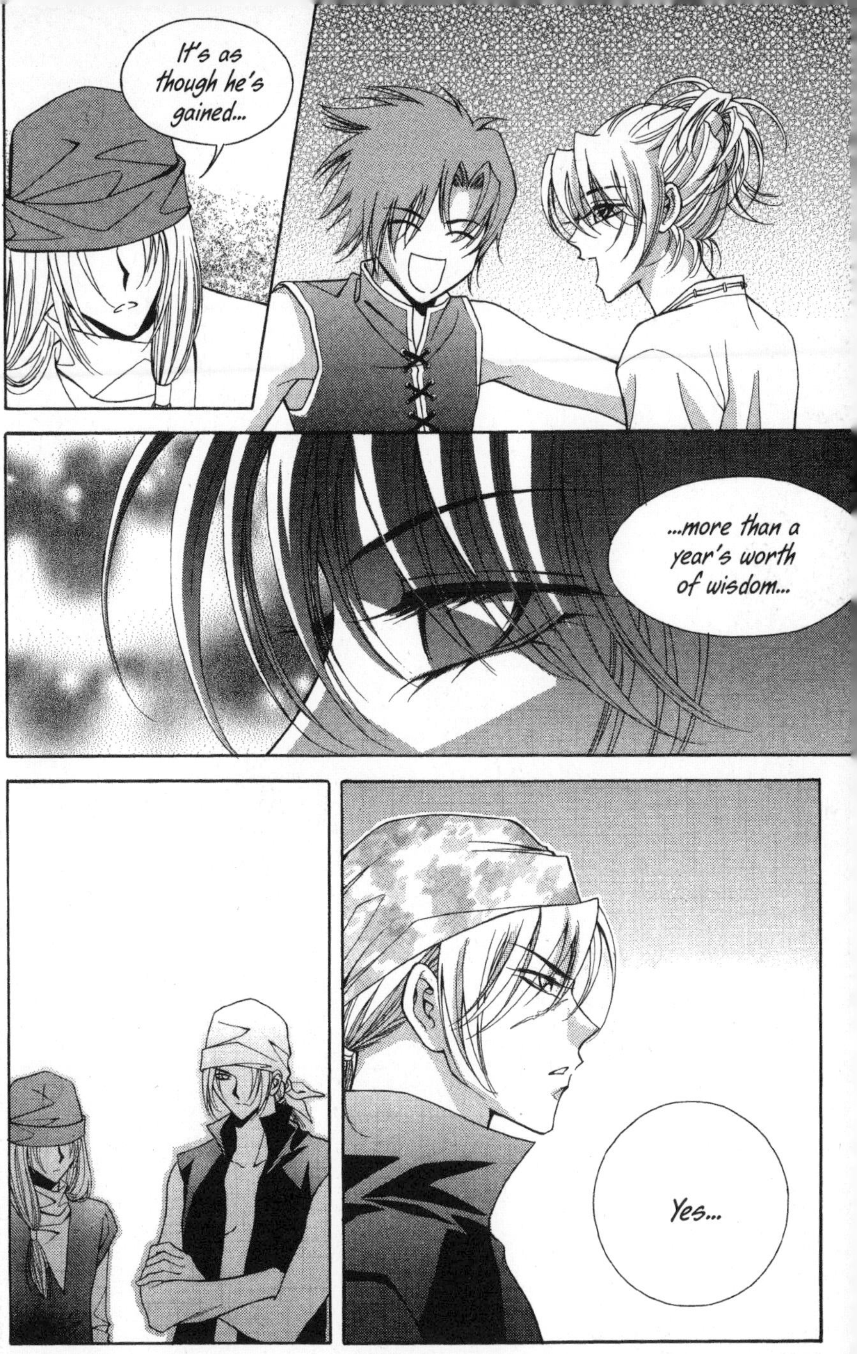
It's as though he's gained...
...more than a year's worth of wisdom...
Yes...

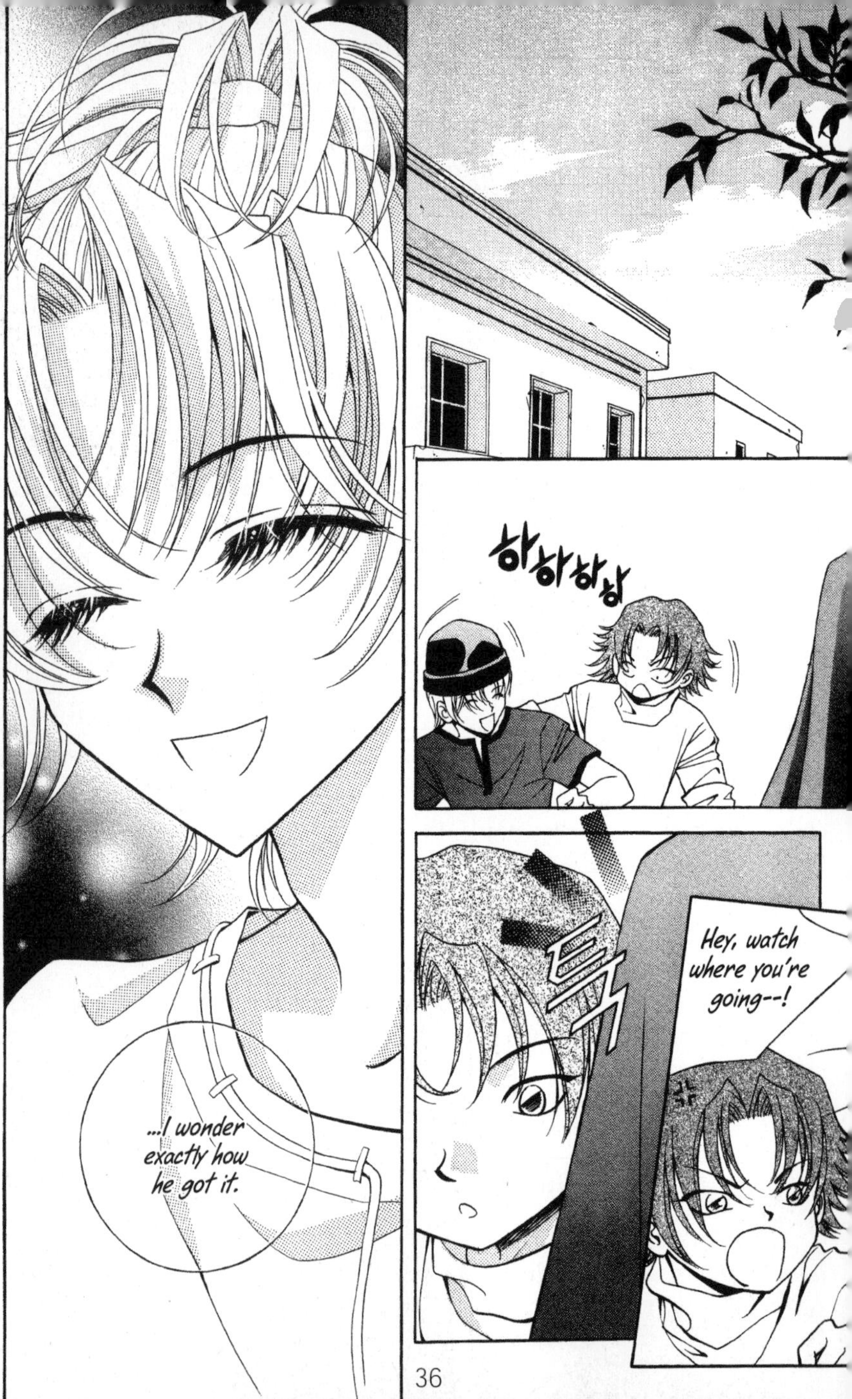
...I wonder exactly how he got it.
하하하하
툭
Hey, watch where you're going--!

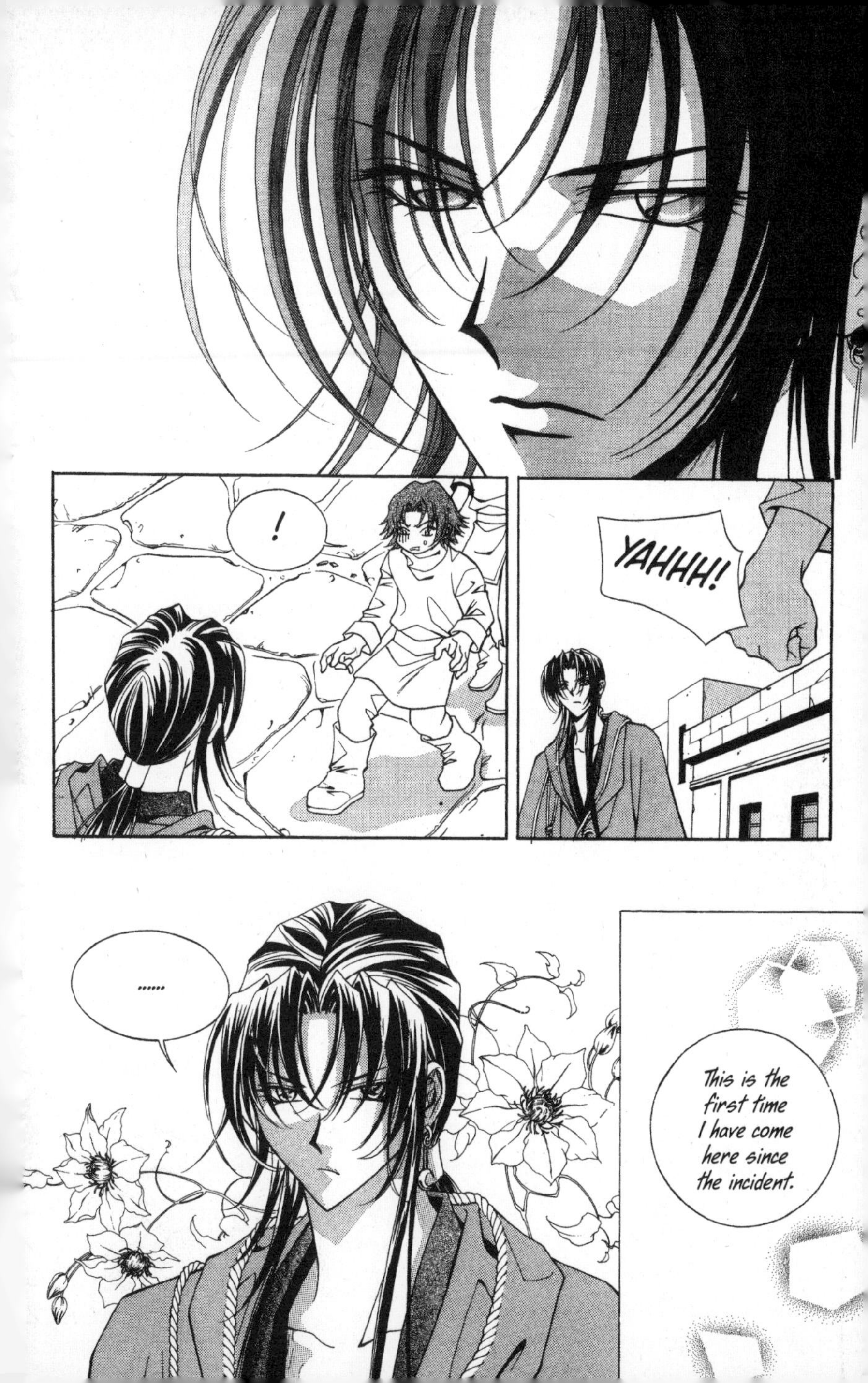
!
YAHHH!
......
This is the first time I have come here since the incident.

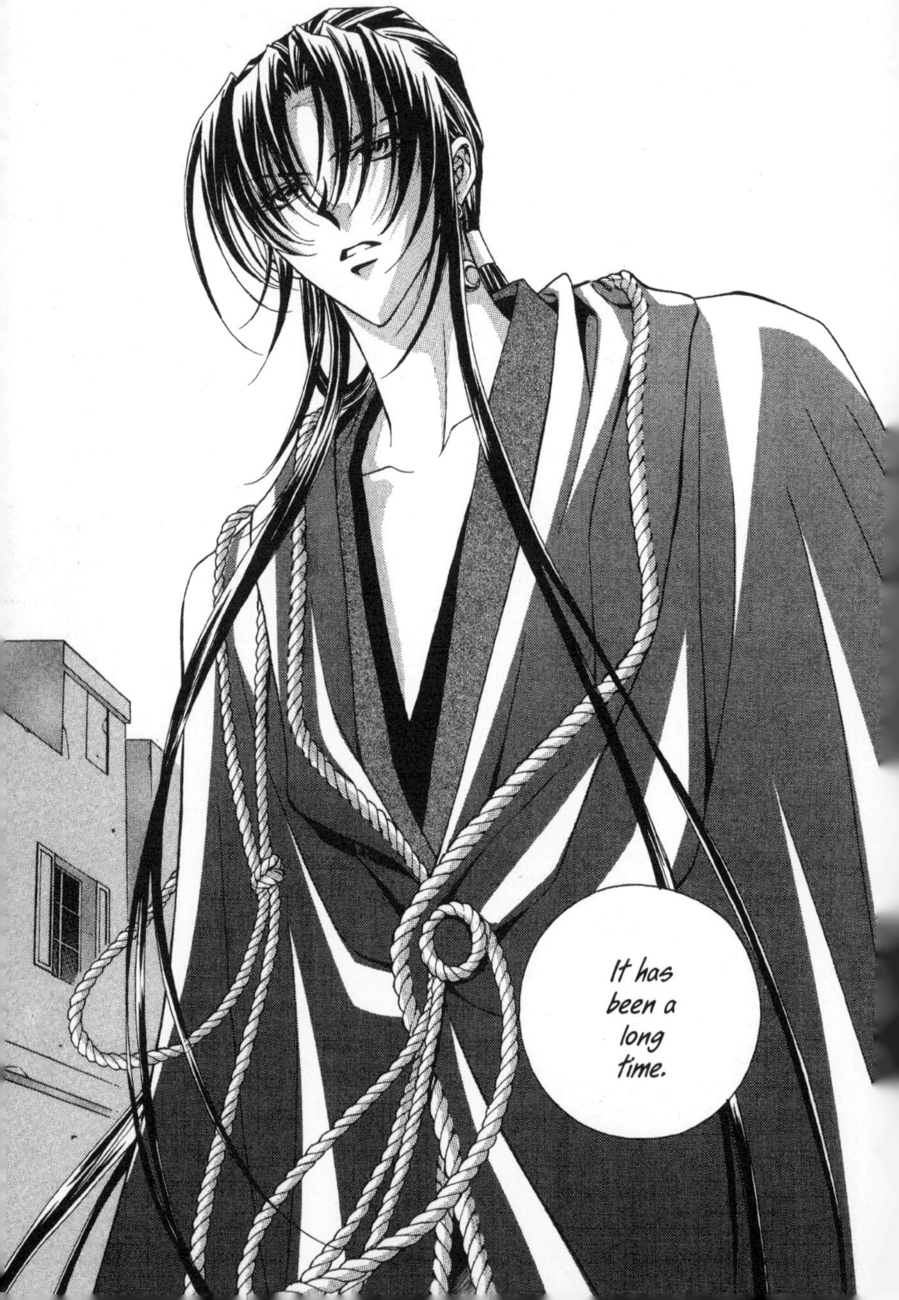
It has been a long time.

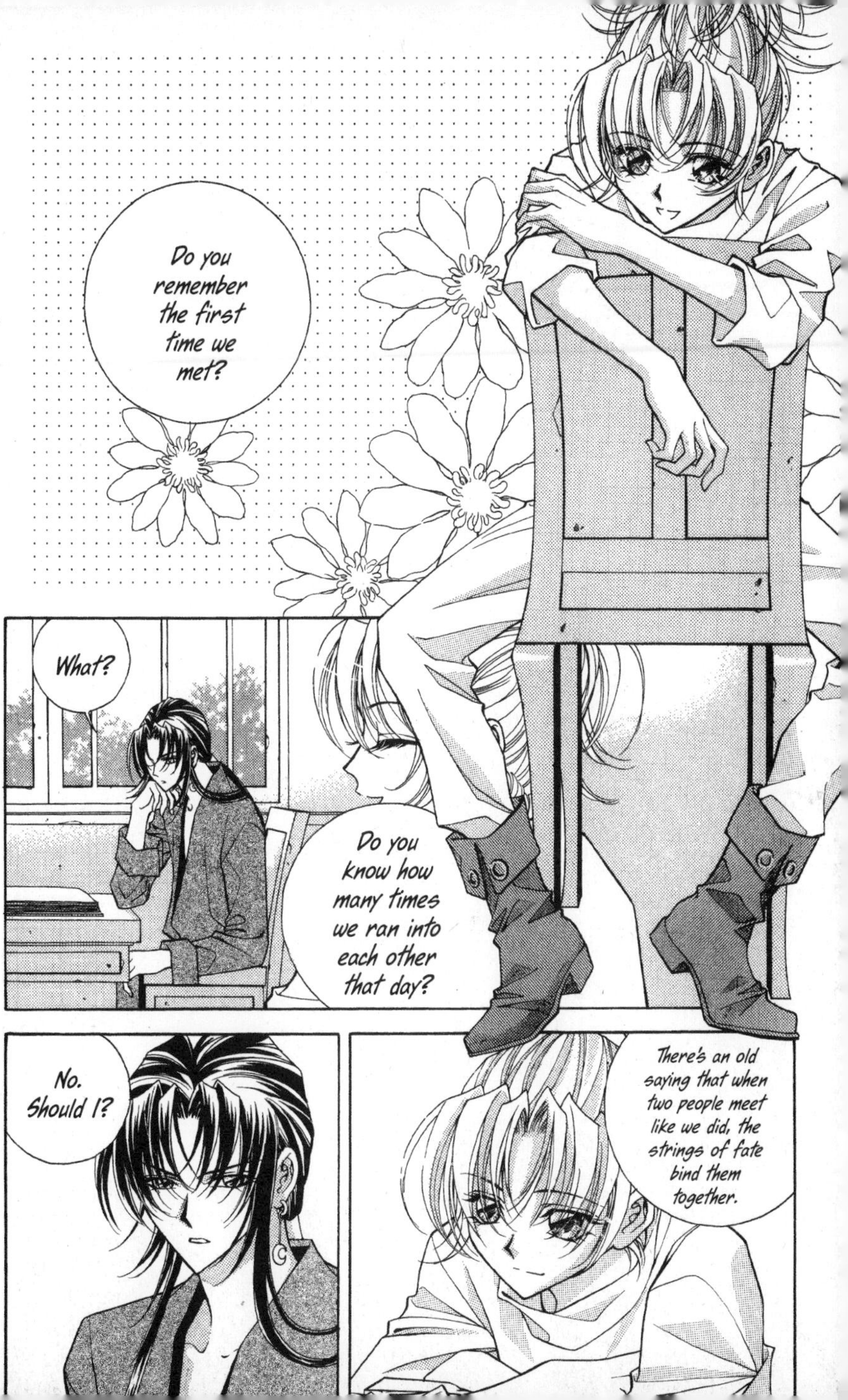
Do you remember the first time we met?
What?
Do you know how many times we ran into each other that day?
No. Should I?
There's an old saying that when two people meet like we did, the strings of fate bind them together.

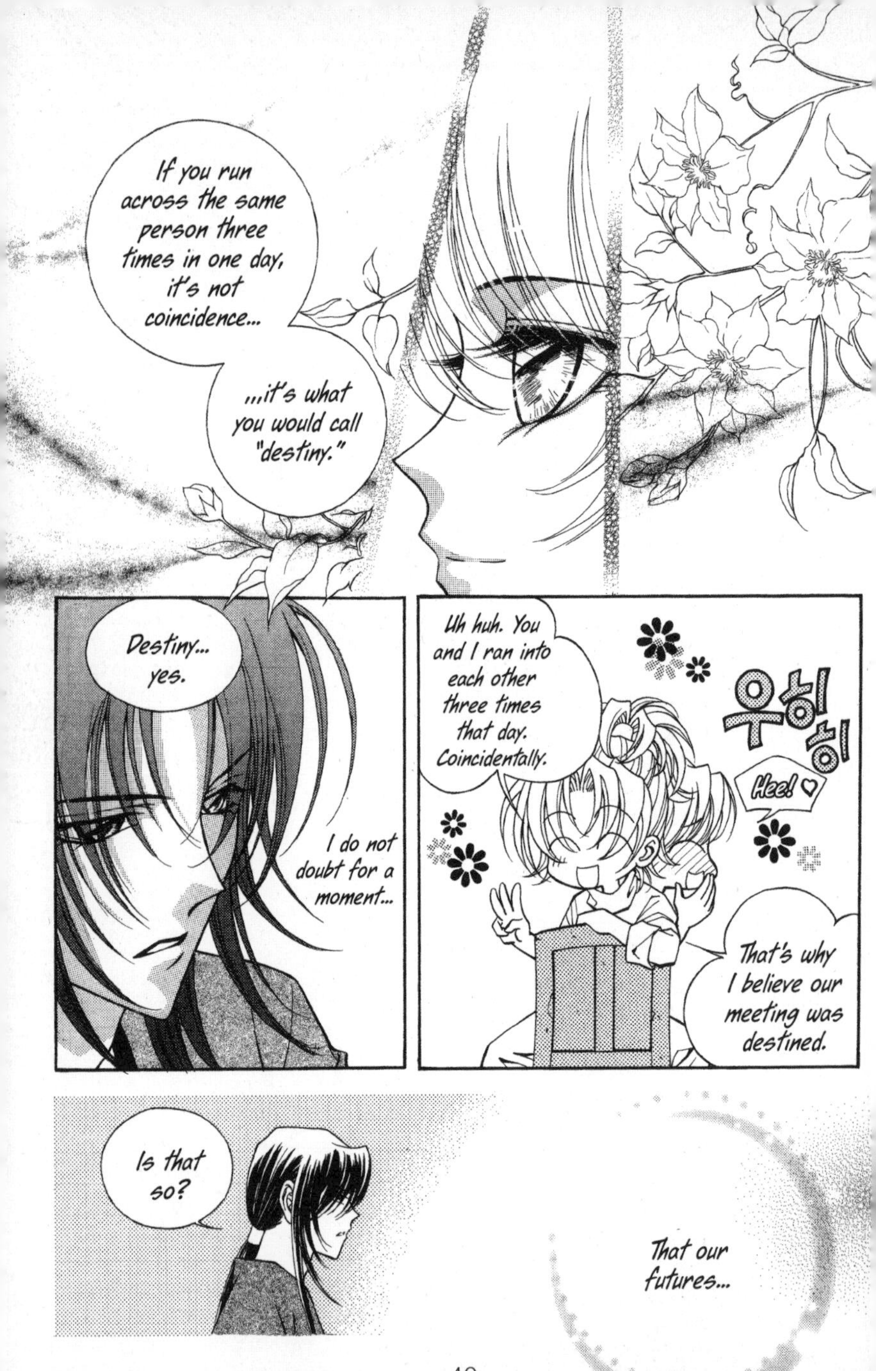
If you run across the same person three times in one day, it's not coincidence...
...it's what you would call "destiny."
Destiny... yes.
I do not doubt for a moment...
Uh huh. You and I ran into each other three times that day. Coincidentally.
우히힝
Hee! ♡
That's why I believe our meeting was destined.
Is that so?
That our futures...

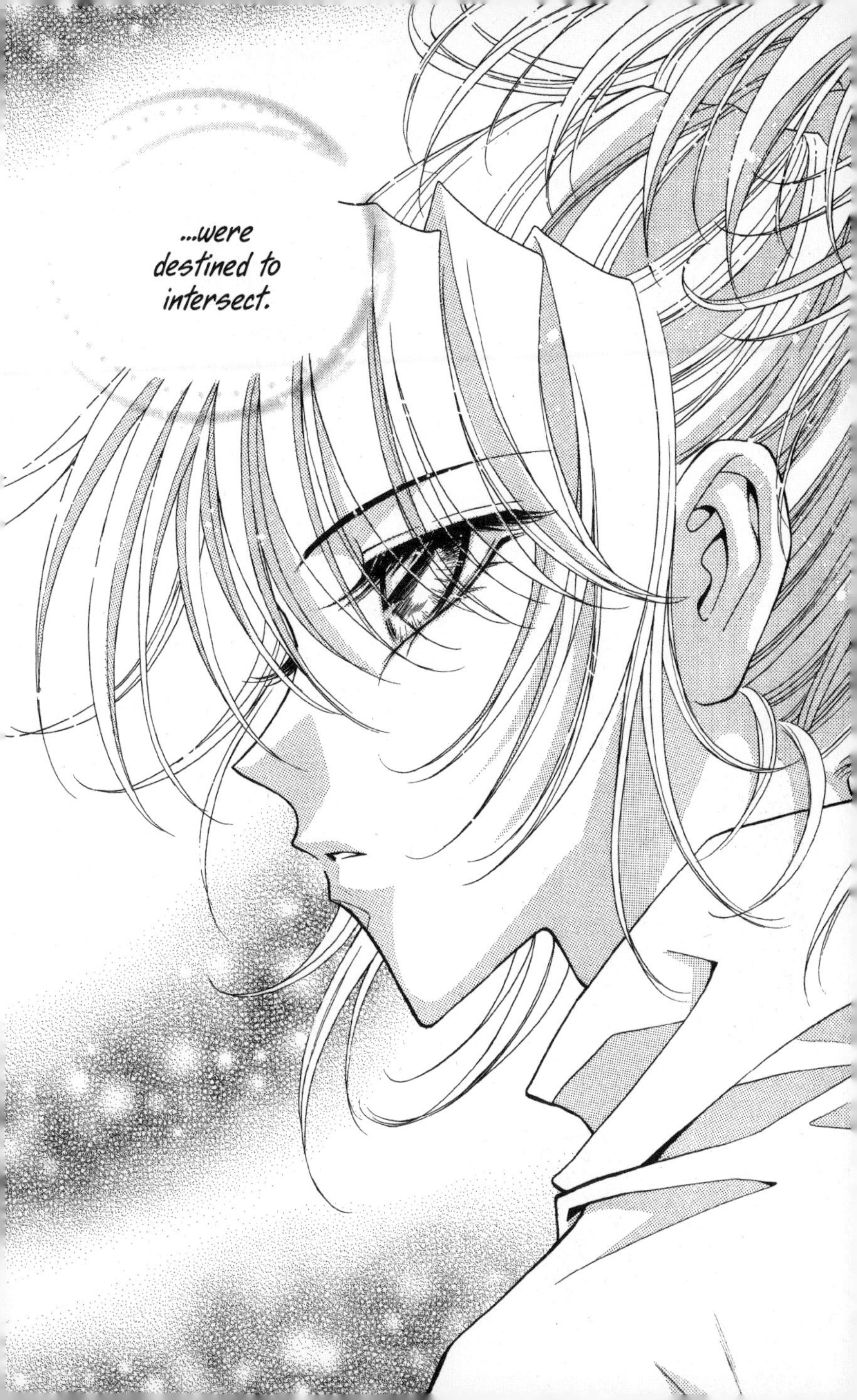
...were destined to intersect.

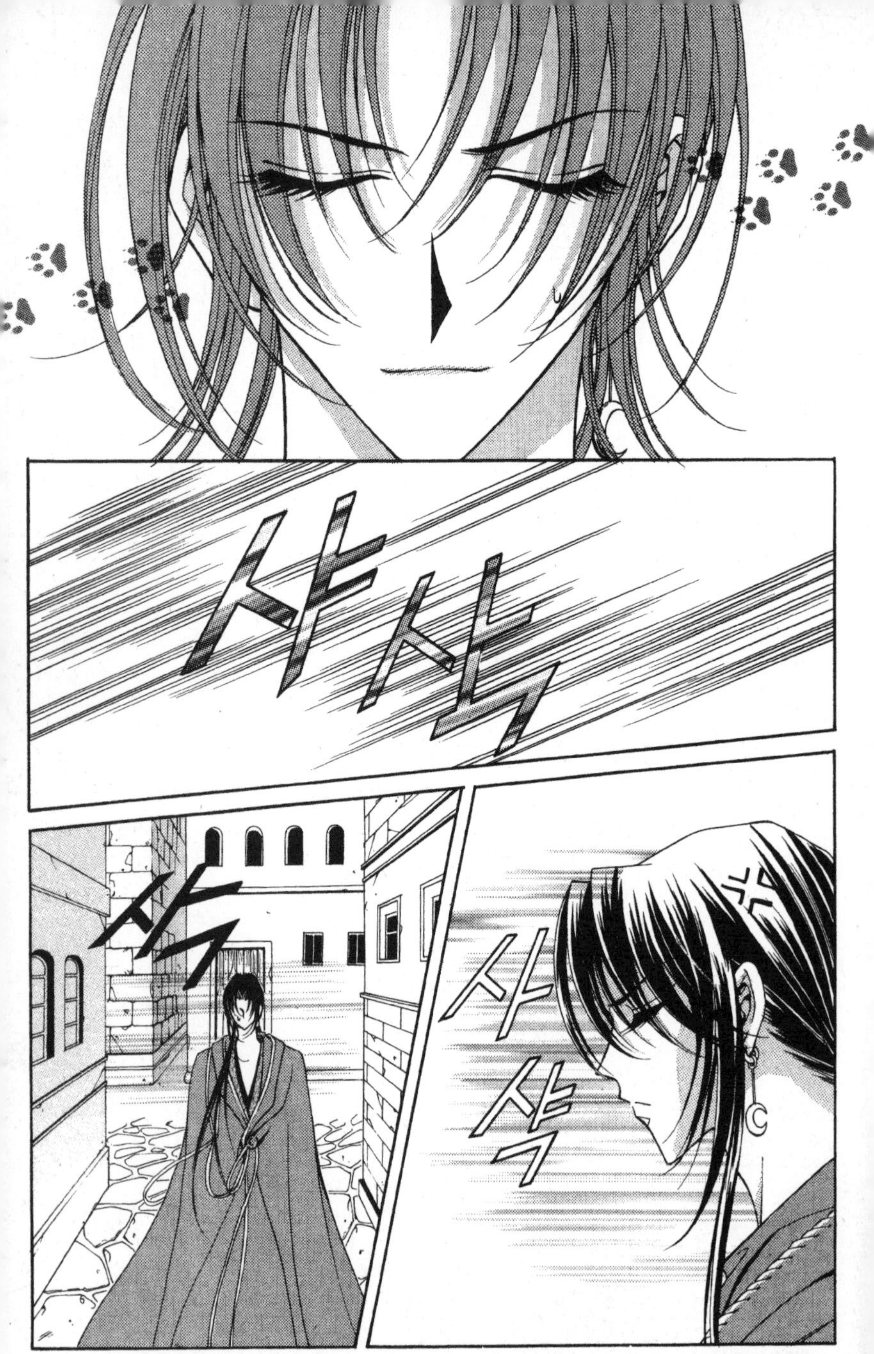

샤샥
샥
사샥

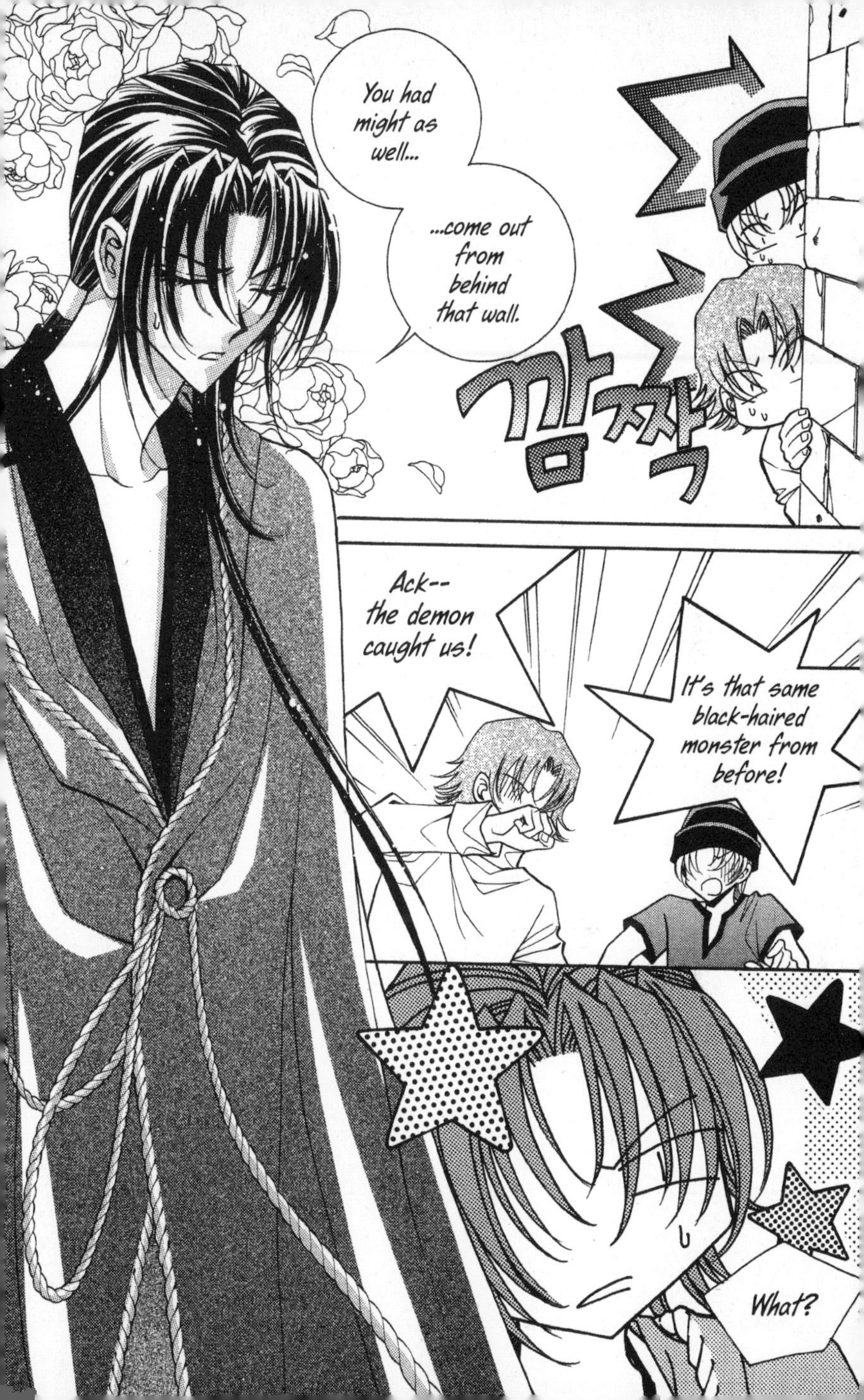
You had might as well...
...come out from behind that wall.
깜짝
Ack-- the demon caught us!
It's that same black-haired monster from before!
What?

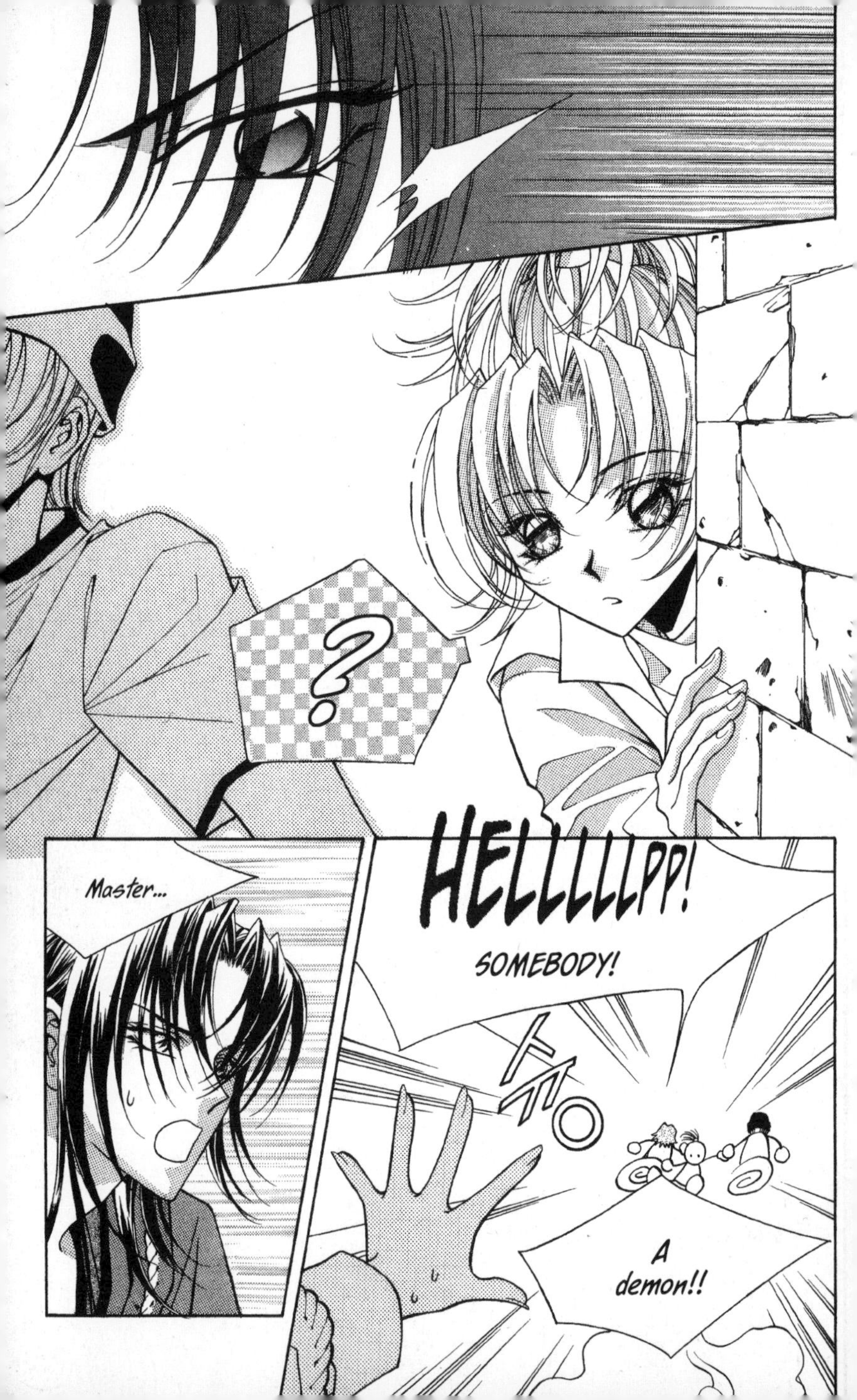
?
Master...
HELLLLLPP!
SOMEBODY!
A demon!!

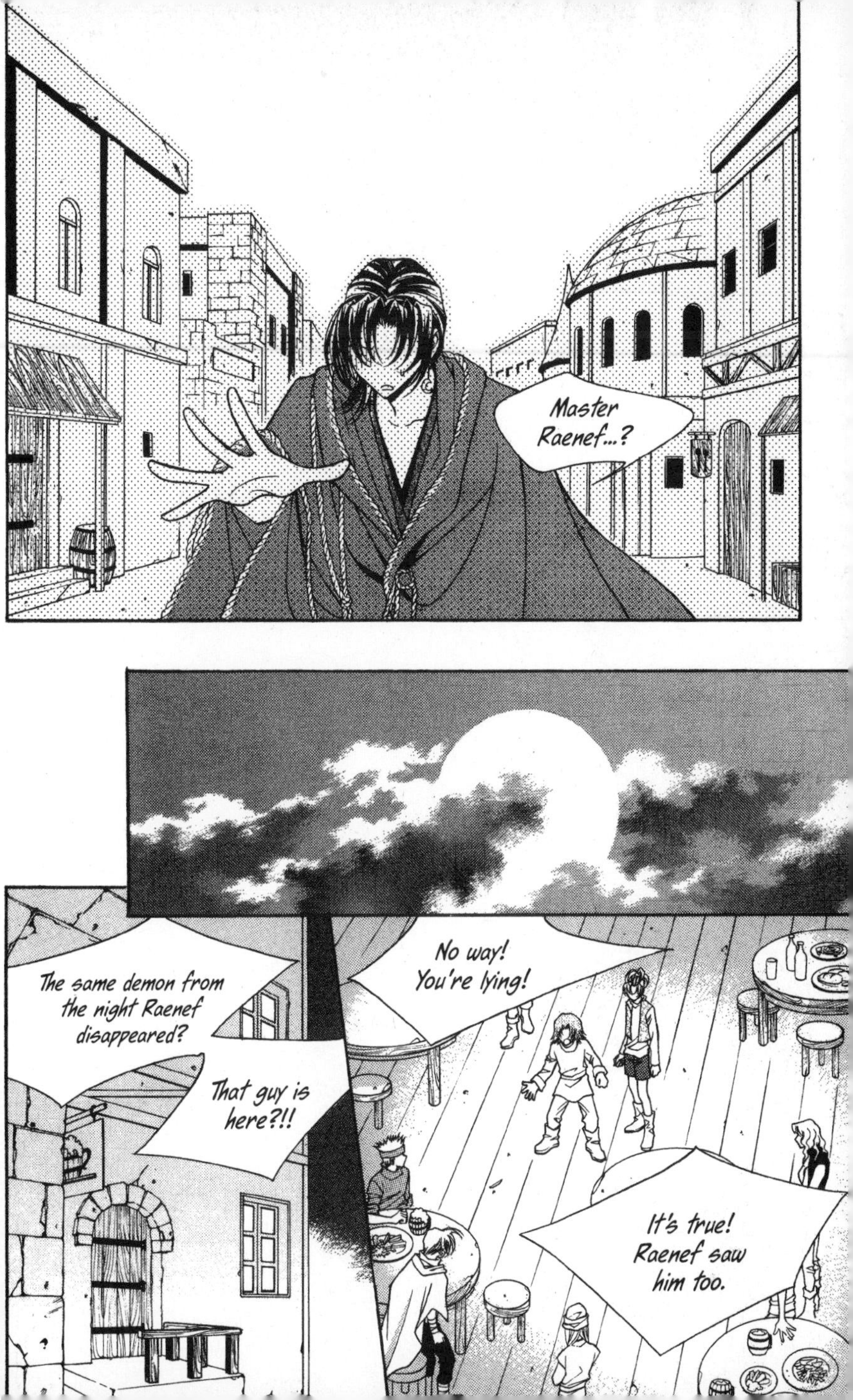
Master Raenef...?
The same demon from the night Raenef disappeared?
That guy is here?!!
No way! You're lying!
It's true! Raenef saw him too.

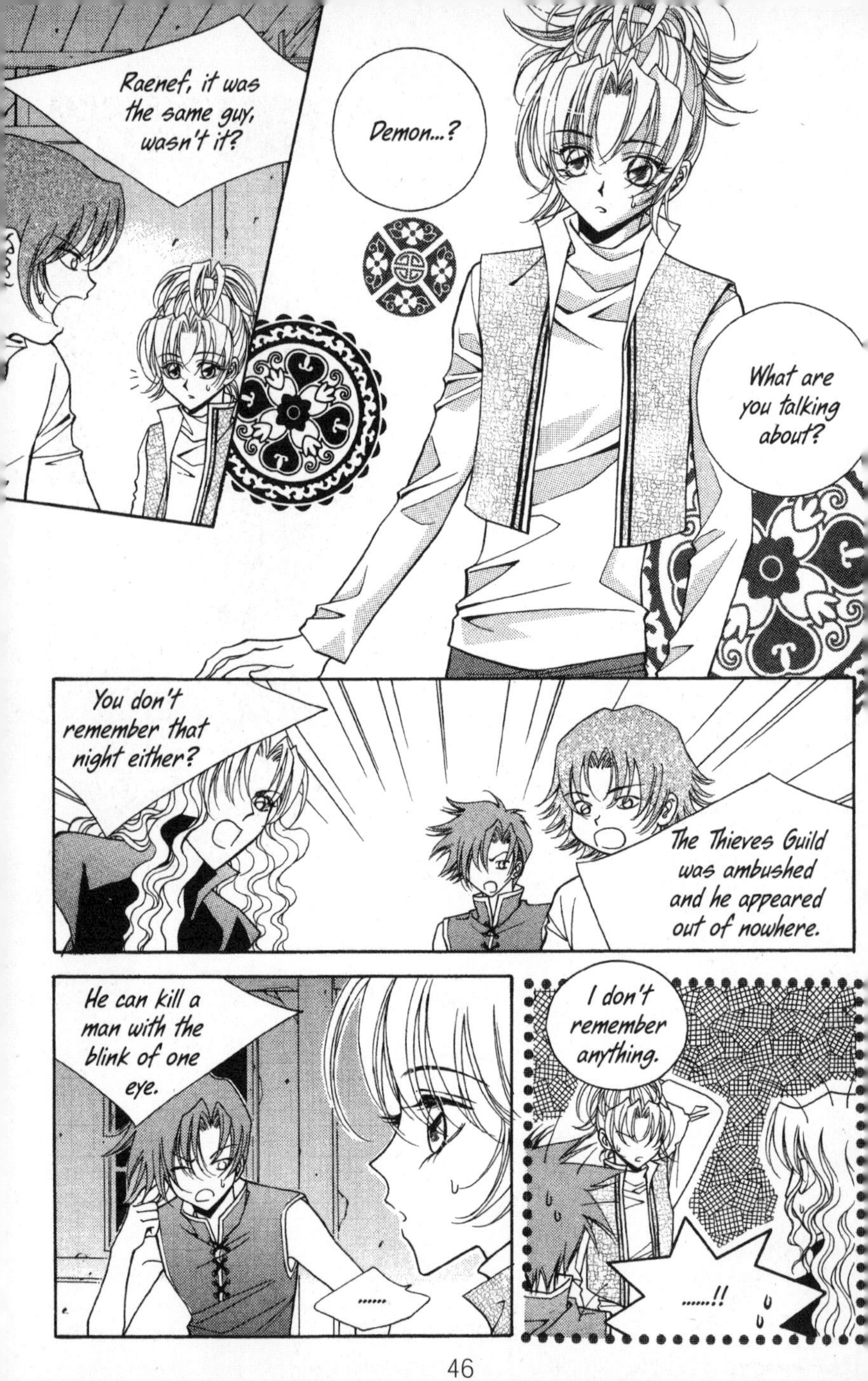

Raenef, it was the same guy, wasn't it?
Demon...?
What are you talking about?
You don't remember that night either?
The Thieves Guild was ambushed and he appeared out of nowhere.
He can kill a man with the blink of one eye.
......
I don't remember anything.
......!!

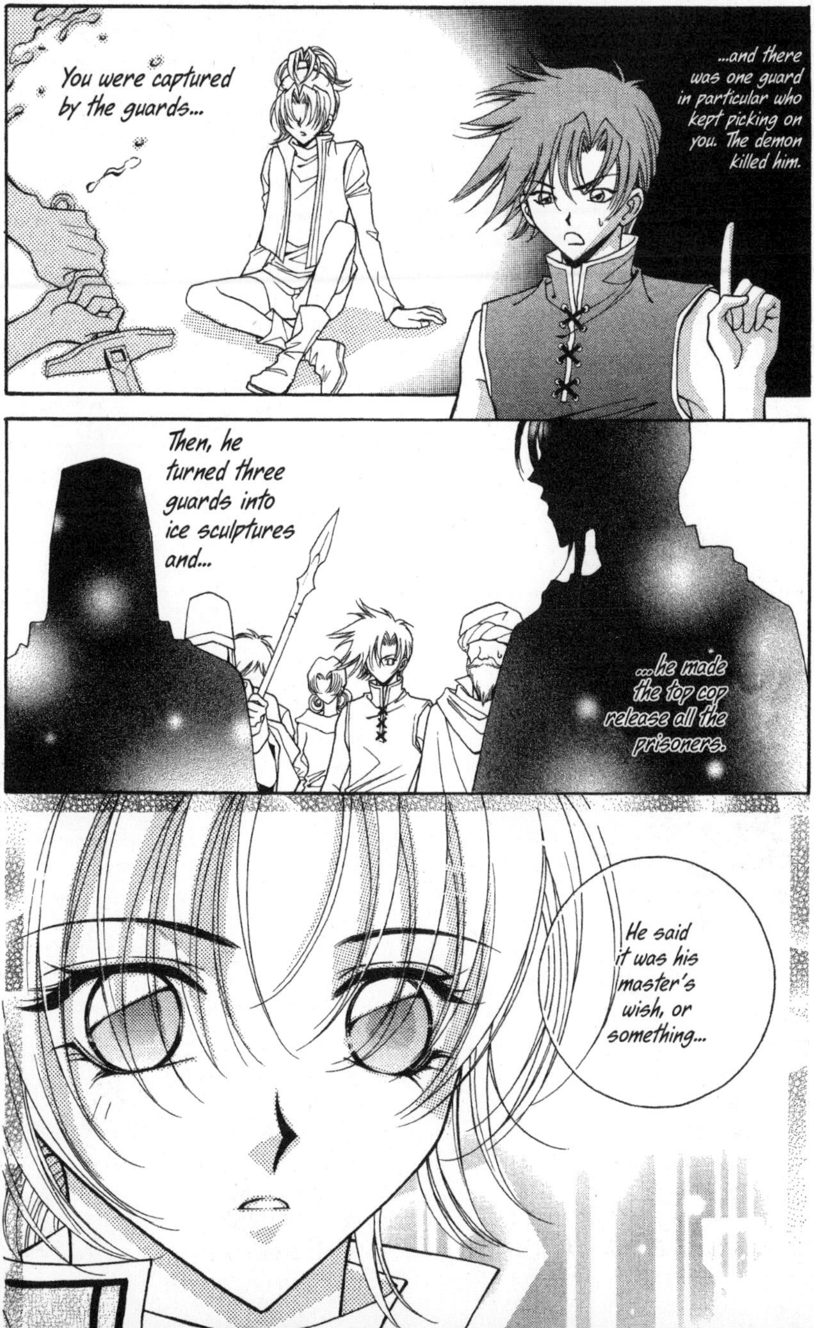
You were captured by the guards...
...and there was one guard in particular who kept picking on you. The demon killed him.
Then, he turned three guards into ice sculptures and...
...he made the top cop release all the prisoners.
He said it was his master's wish, or something...

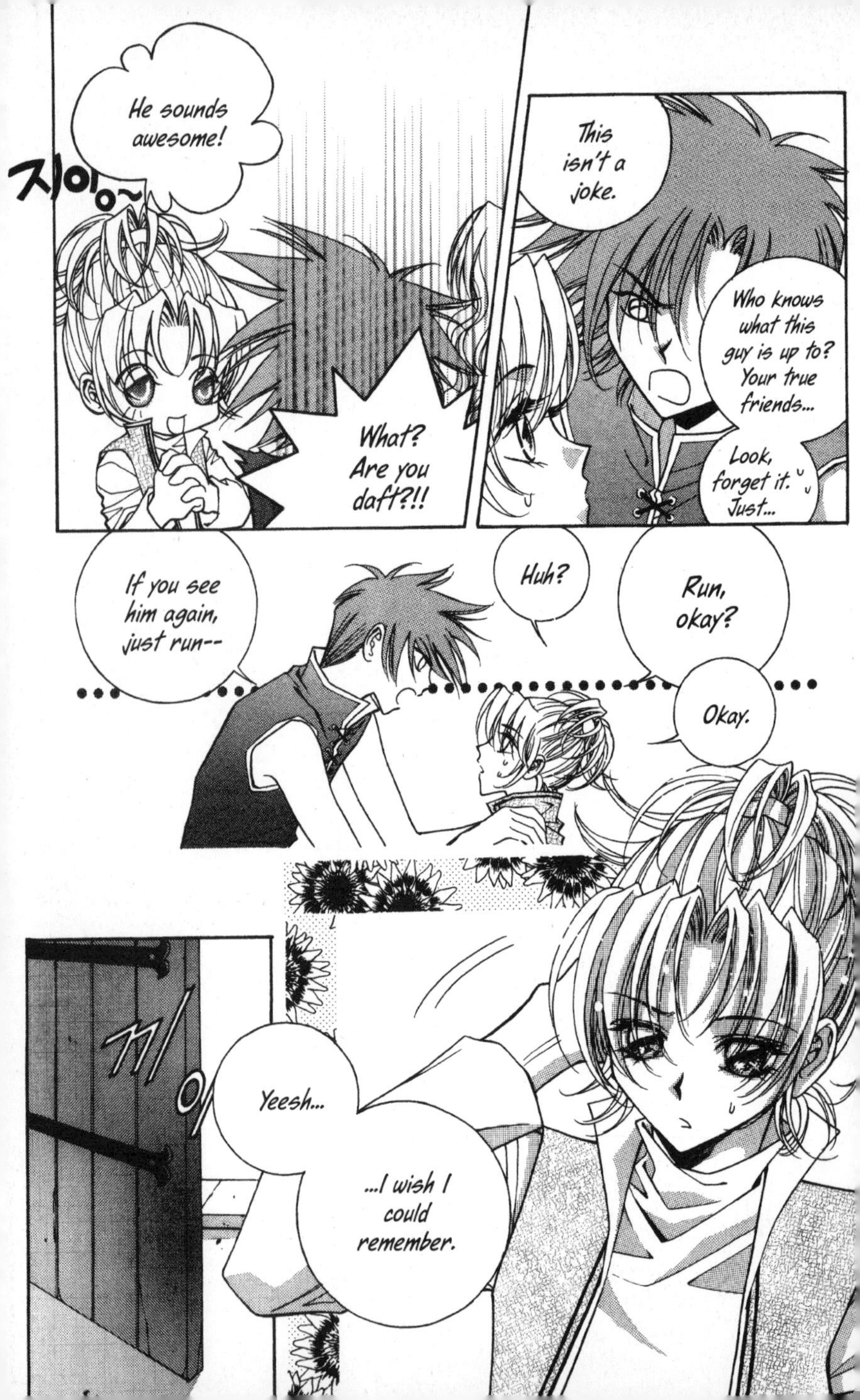
He sounds awesome!
지이잉~
What? Are you daft?!!
This isn't a joke.
Who knows what this guy is up to? Your true friends...
Look, forget it. Just...
If you see him again, just run--
Huh?
Run, okay?
Okay.
끼이
Yeesh...
...I wish I could remember.

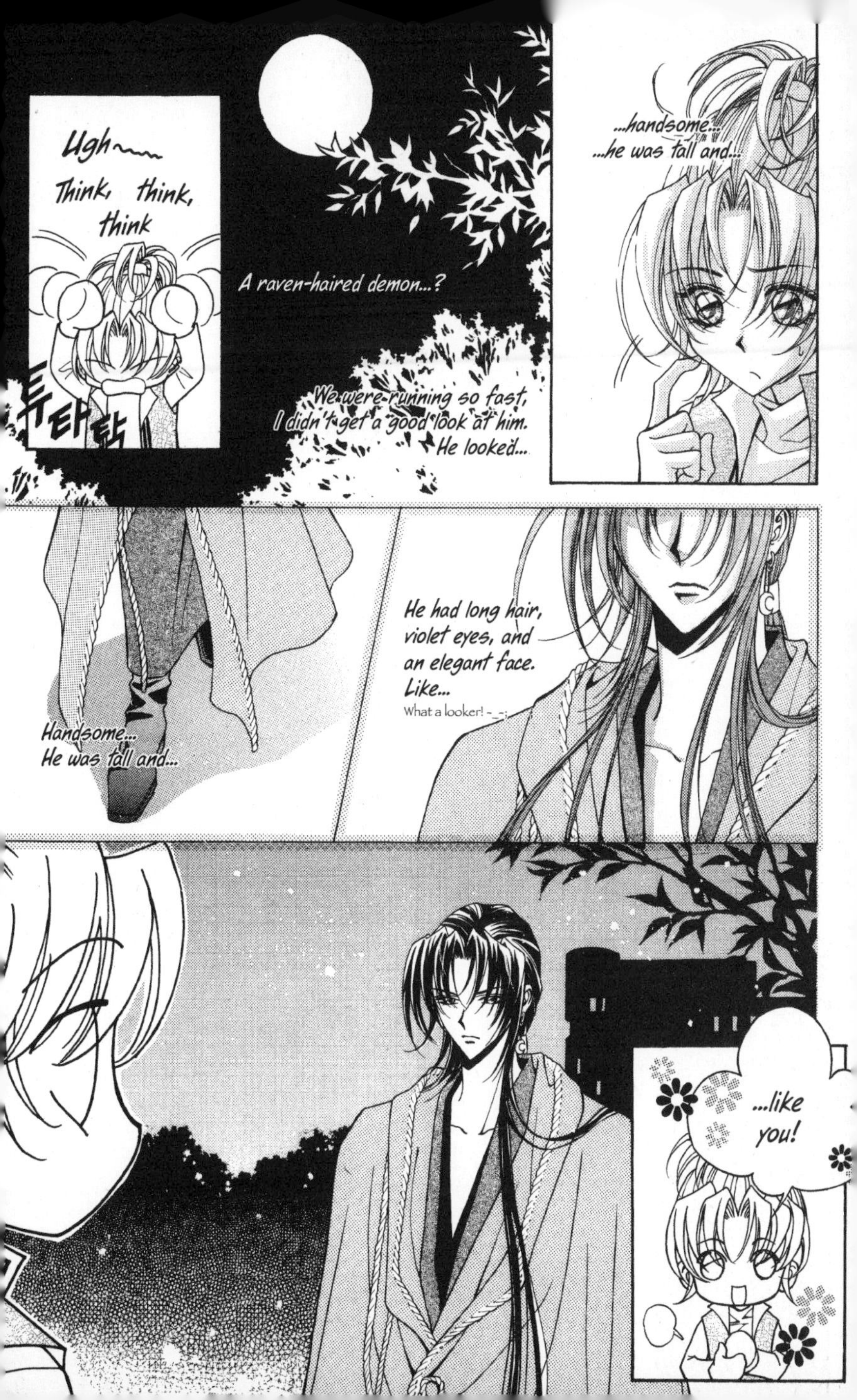
Ugh~~~
Think, think, think
A raven-haired demon...?
We were running so fast, I didn't get a good look at him. He looked...
...handsome... ...he was tall and...
Handsome... He was tall and...
He had long hair, violet eyes, and an elegant face. Like...
What a looker! -_-;
...like you!

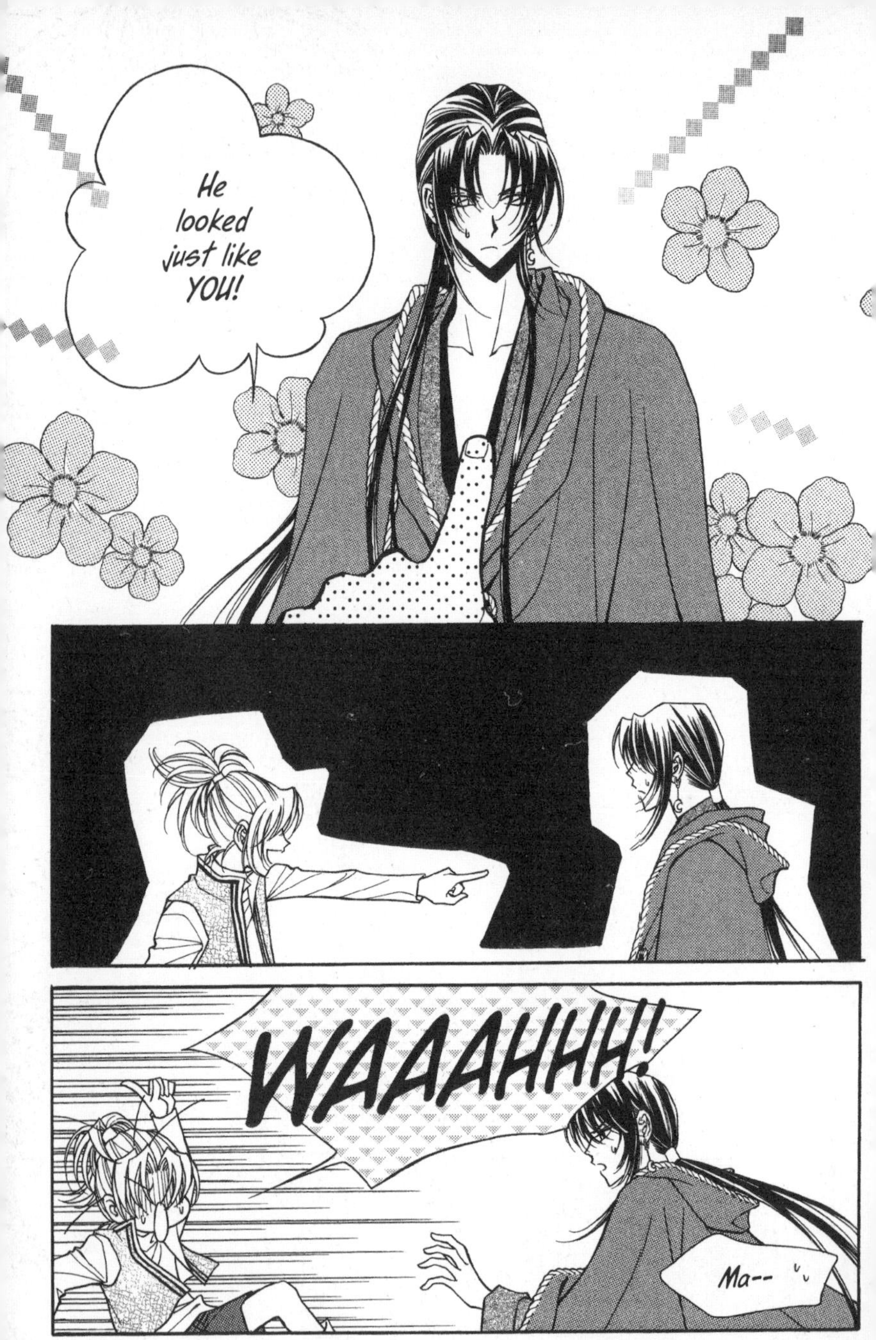
He looked just like YOU!
WAAAHHH!
Ma--

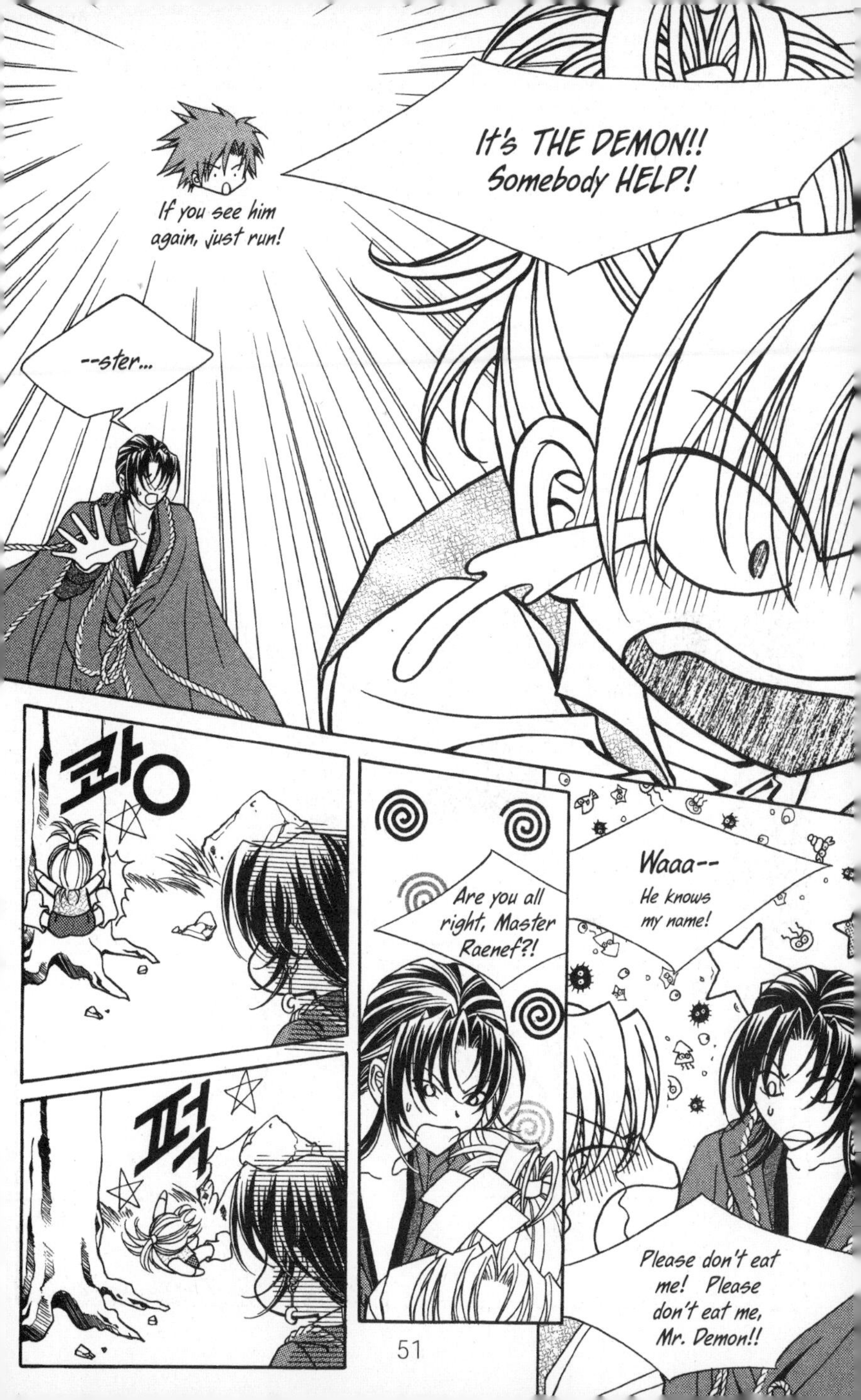
If you see him again, just run!
It's THE DEMON!! Somebody HELP!
--ster...
콰ㅇ
퍽
Are you all right, Master Raenef?!
Waaa-- He knows my name!
Please don't eat me! Please don't eat me, Mr. Demon!!

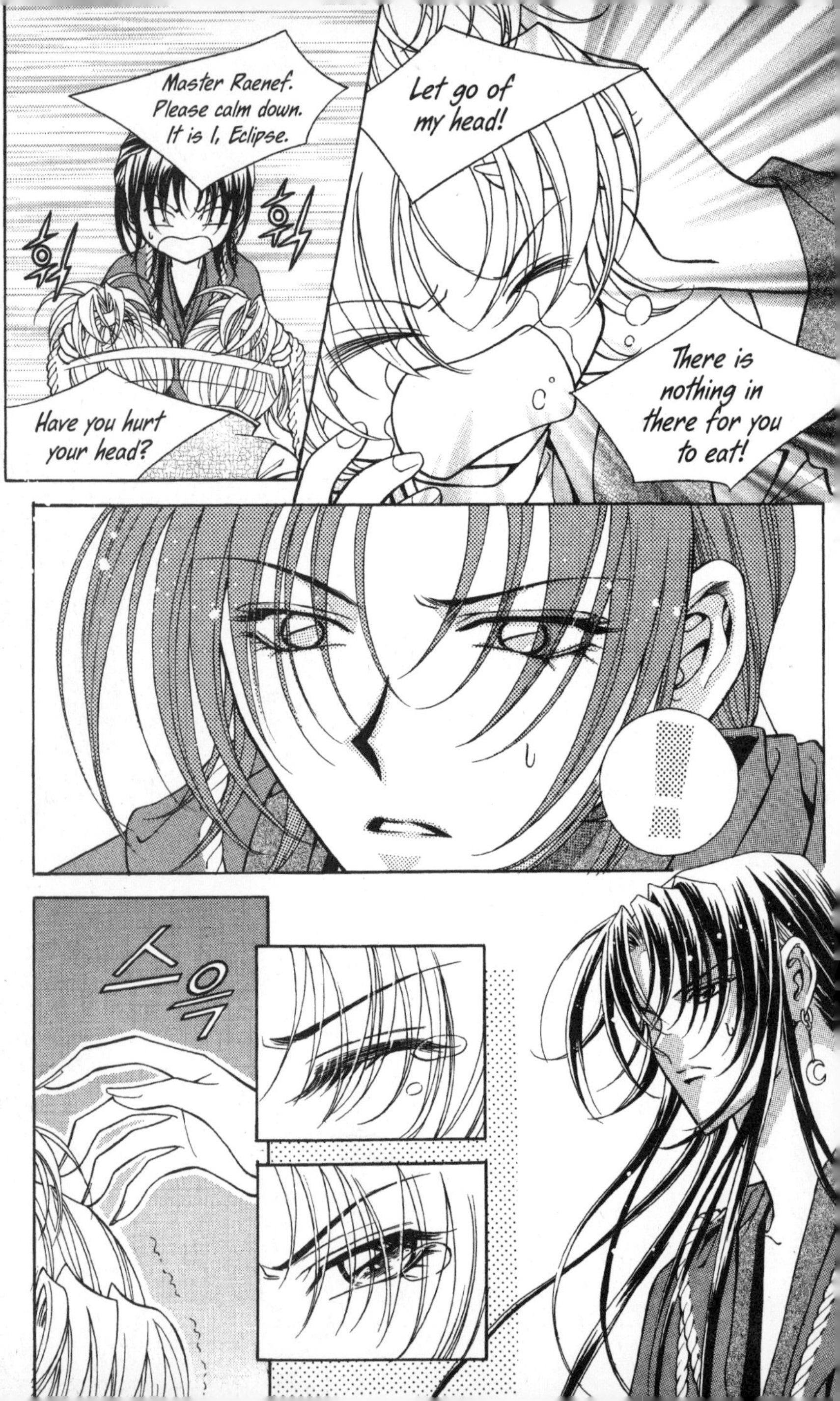
Master Raenef. Please calm down. It is I, Eclipse.
Have you hurt your head?
Let go of my head!
There is nothing in there for you to eat!
!!
스윽

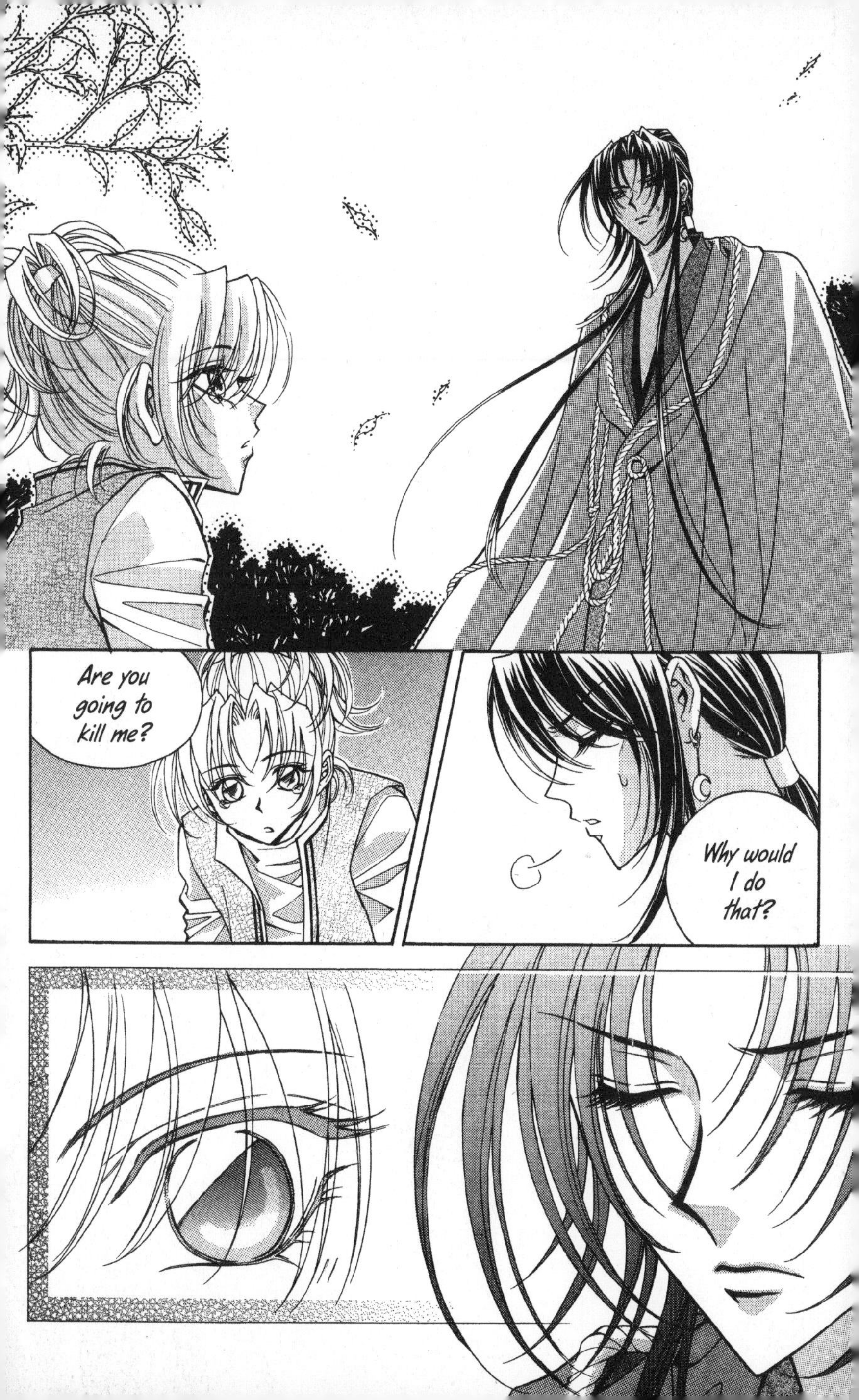
Are you going to kill me?
Why would I do that?

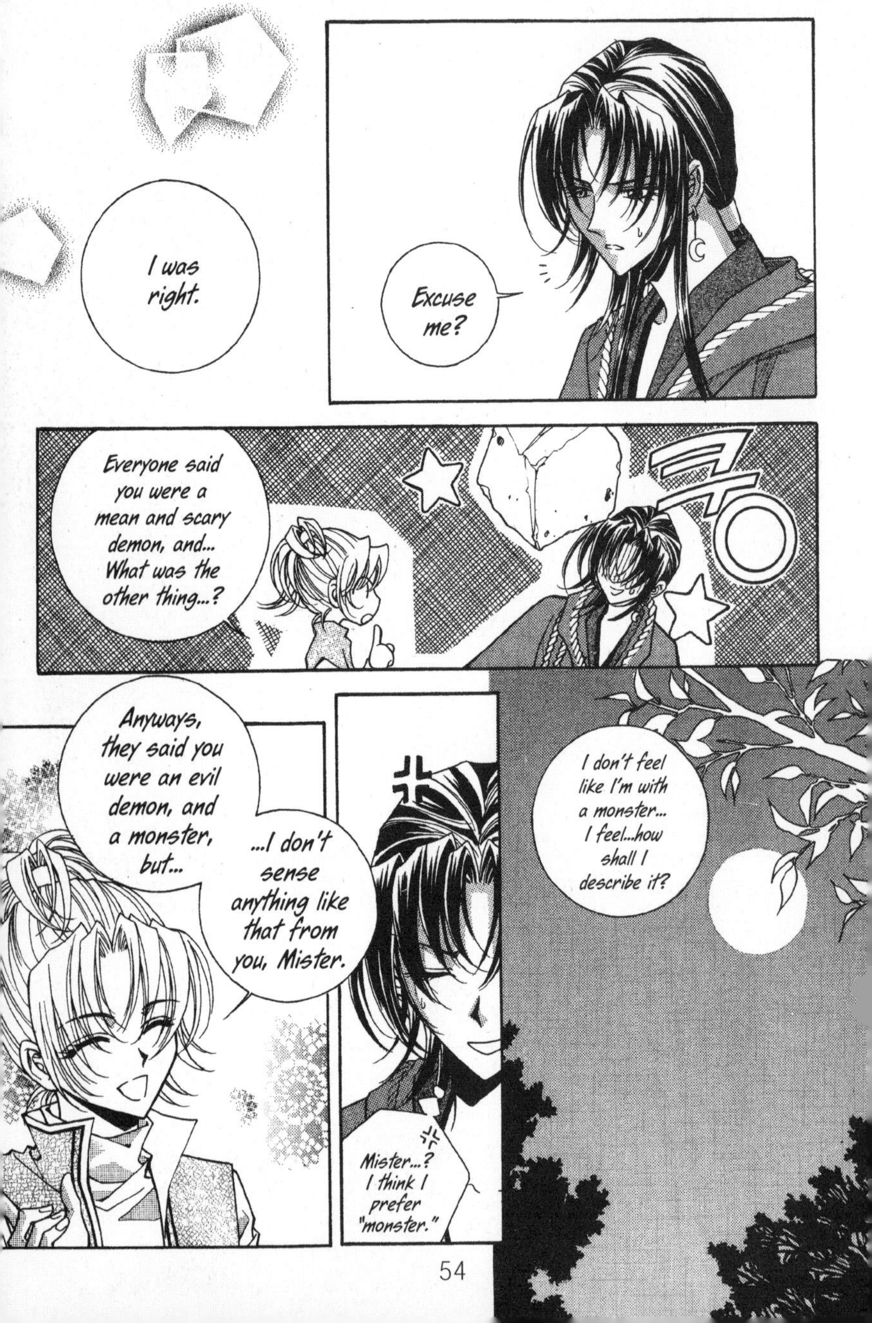

I was right.
Excuse me?
Everyone said you were a mean and scary demon, and... What was the other thing...?
Anyways, they said you were an evil demon, and a monster, but...
...I don't sense anything like that from you, Mister.
Mister...? I think I prefer "monster."
I don't feel like I'm with a monster... I feel...how shall I describe it?

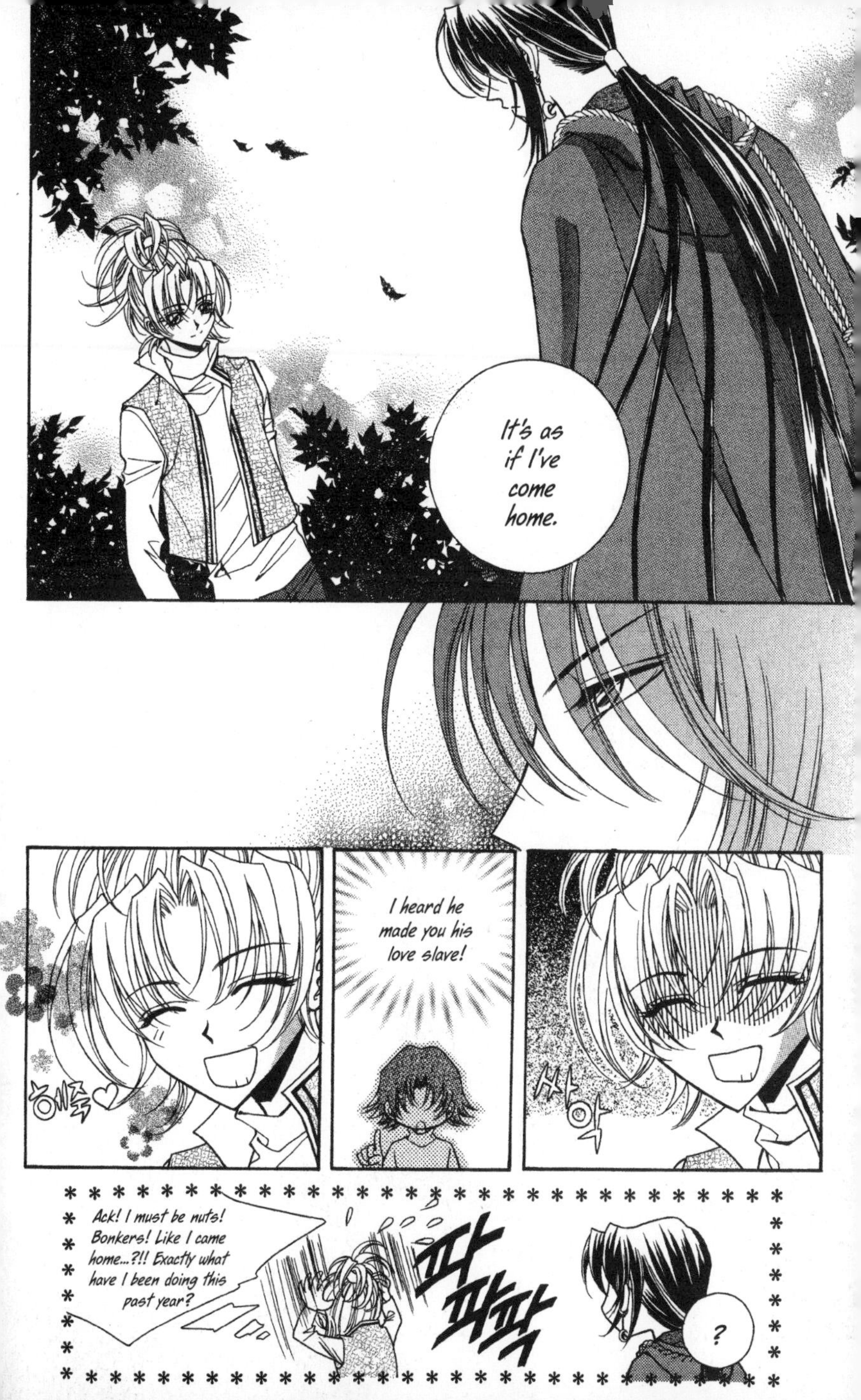
It's as if I've come home.
I heard he made you his love slave!
Ack! I must be nuts! Bonkers! Like I came home...?!! Exactly what have I been doing this past year?
파파팍
?

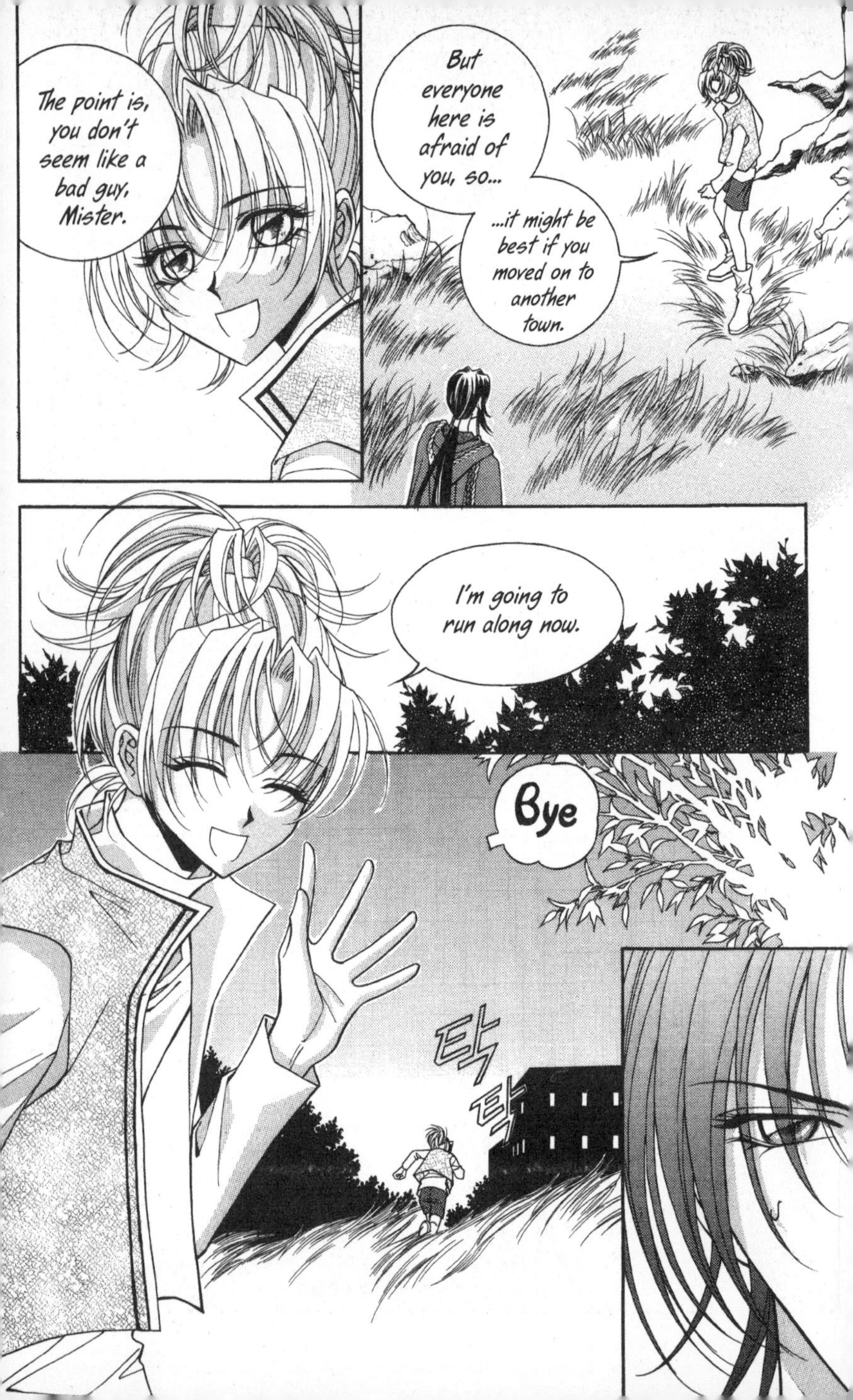
The point is, you don't seem like a bad guy, Mister.
But everyone here is afraid of you, so...
...it might be best if you moved on to another town.
I'm going to run along now.
Bye
탁
탁

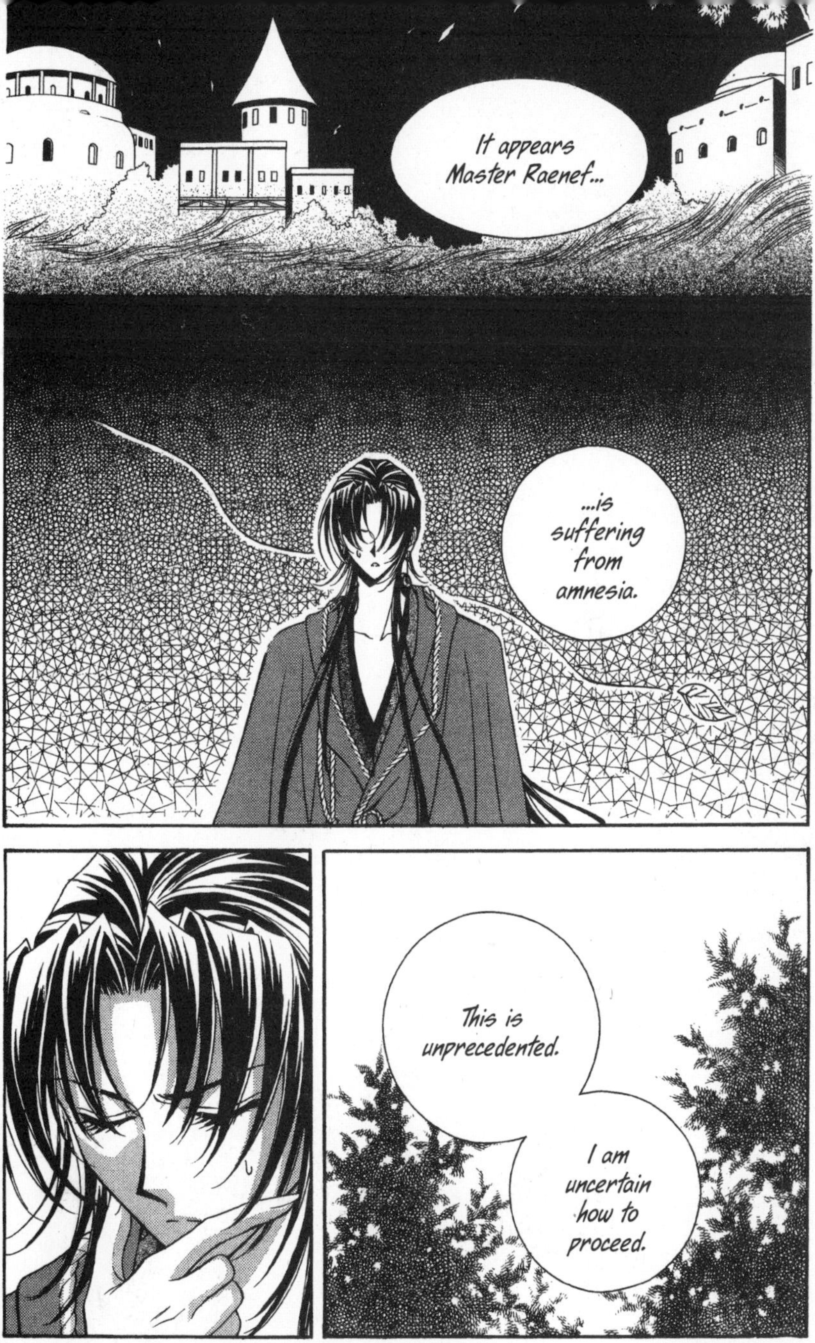
It appears Master Raenef...
...is suffering from amnesia.
This is unprecedented.
I am uncertain how to proceed.

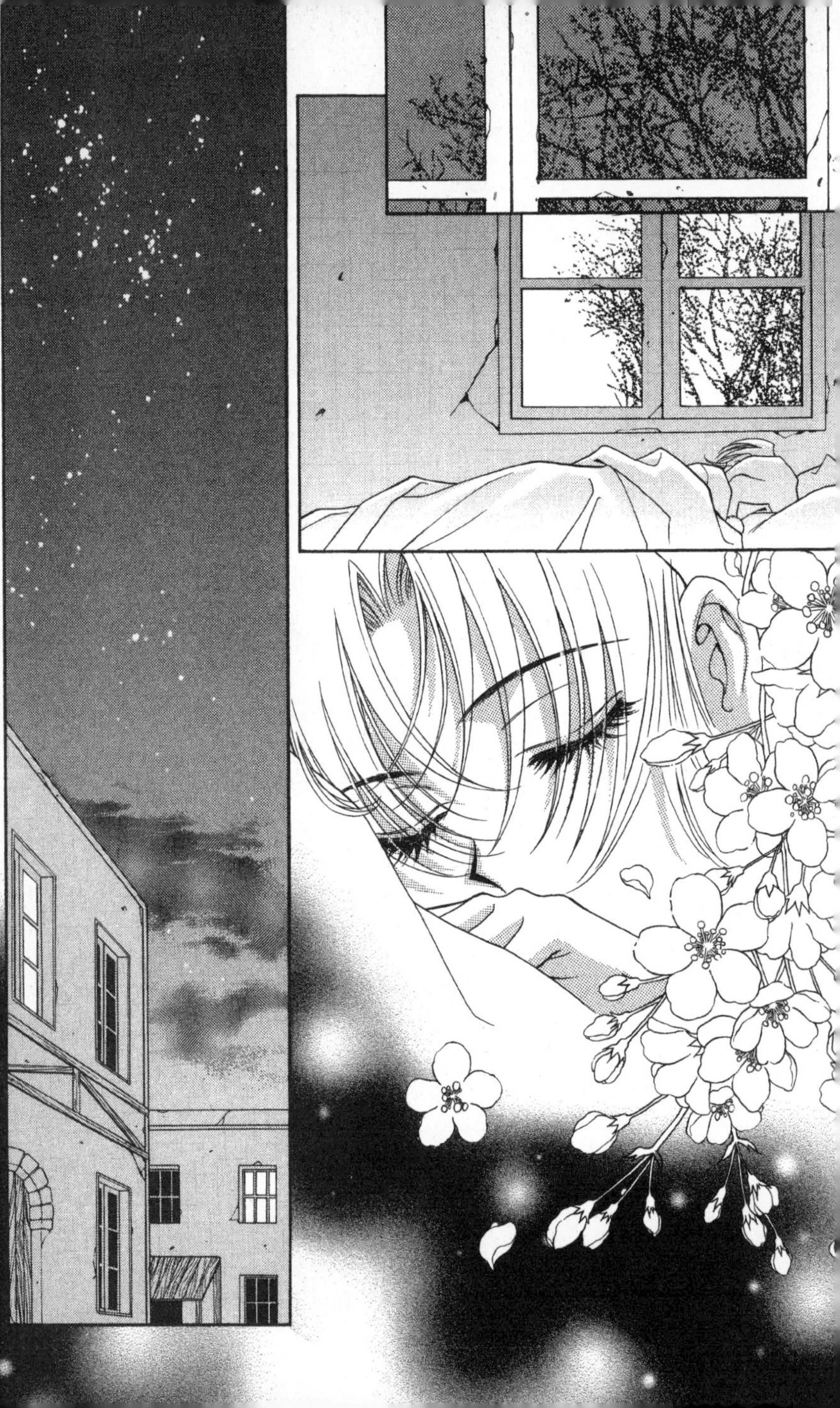

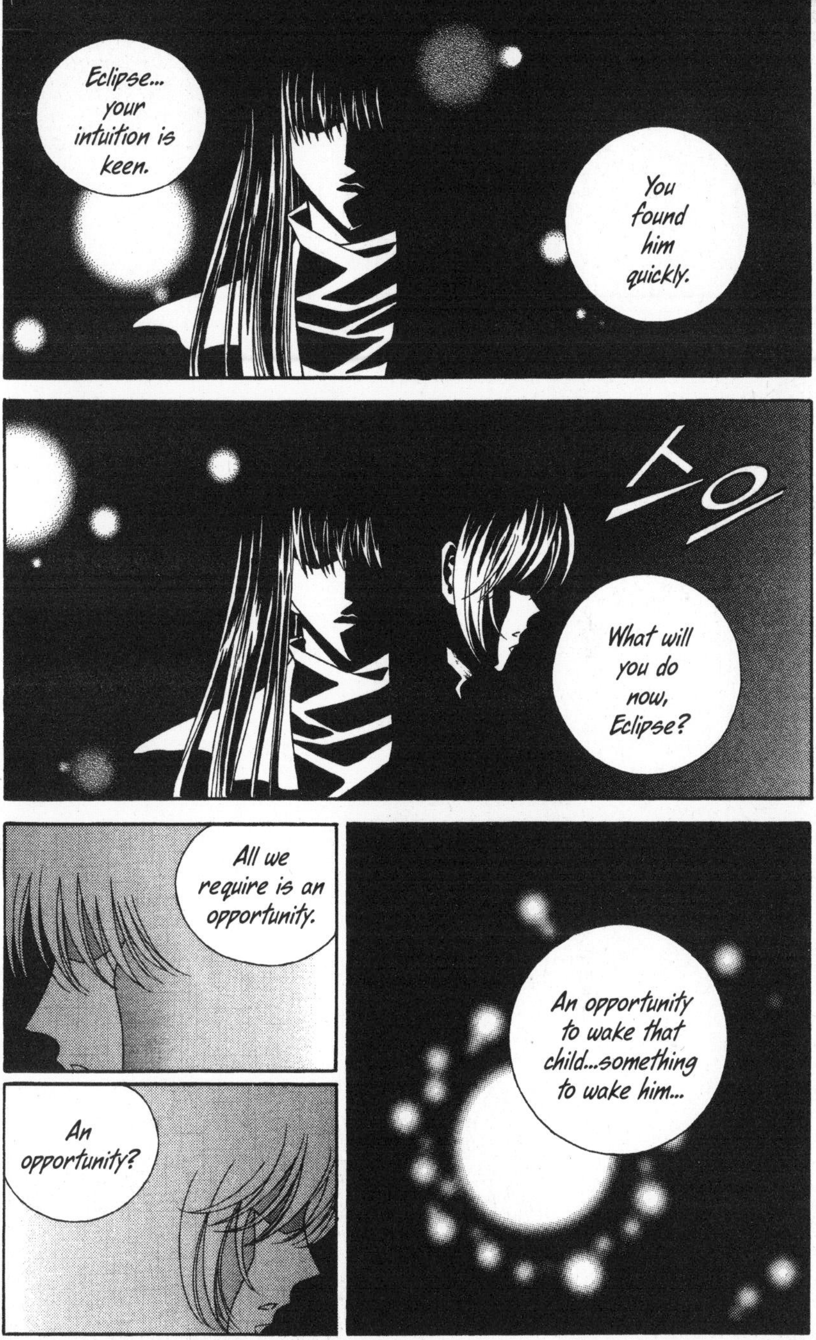
Eclipse... your intuition is keen.
You found him quickly.
스이
What will you do now, Eclipse?
All we require is an opportunity.
An opportunity?
An opportunity to wake that child...something to wake him...

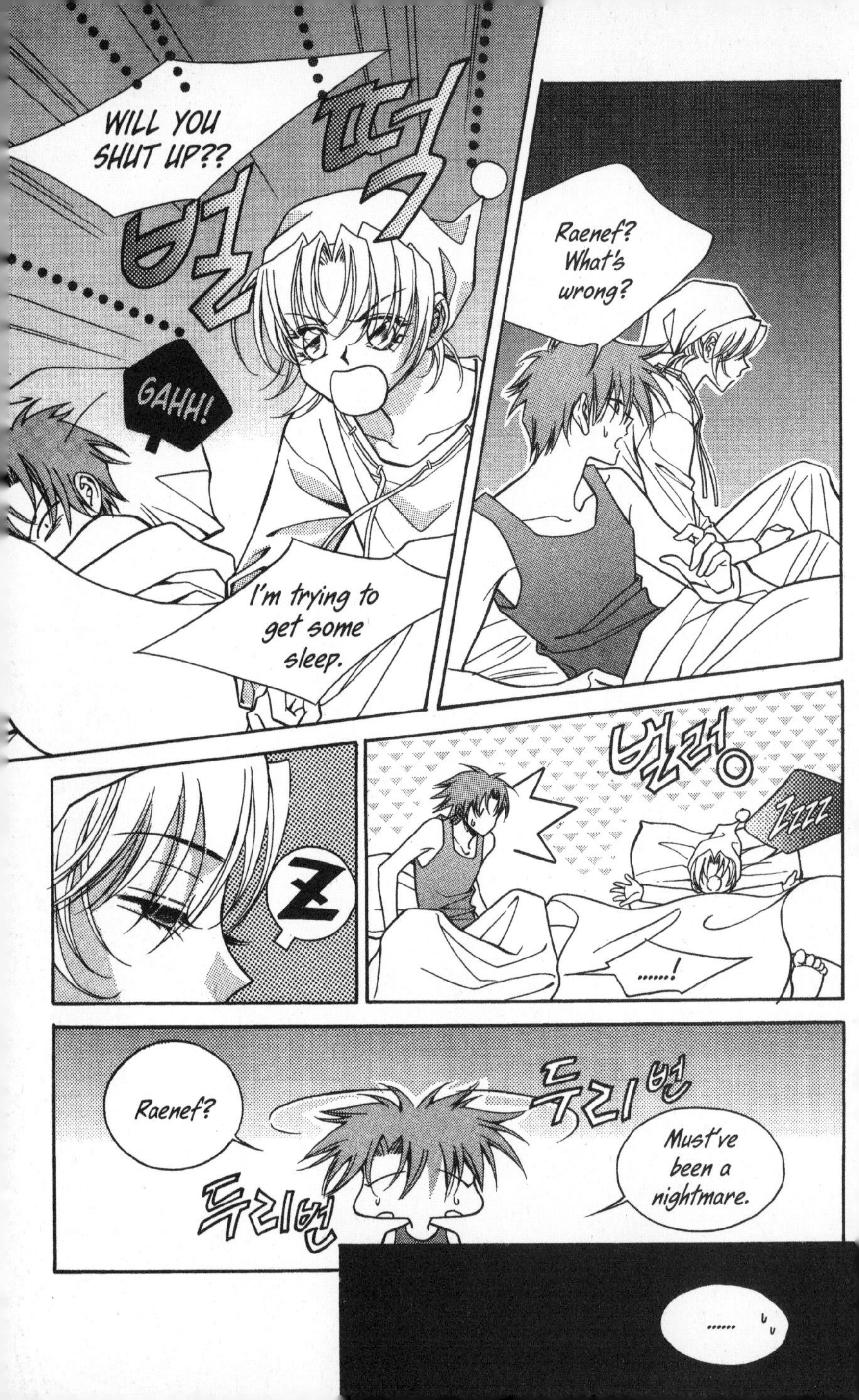
WILL YOU SHUT UP??
벌떡
GAHH!
I'm trying to get some sleep.
Raenef? What's wrong?
Z
벌러
ZZZZ
......!
Raenef?
두리번
Must've been a nightmare.
두리번
......

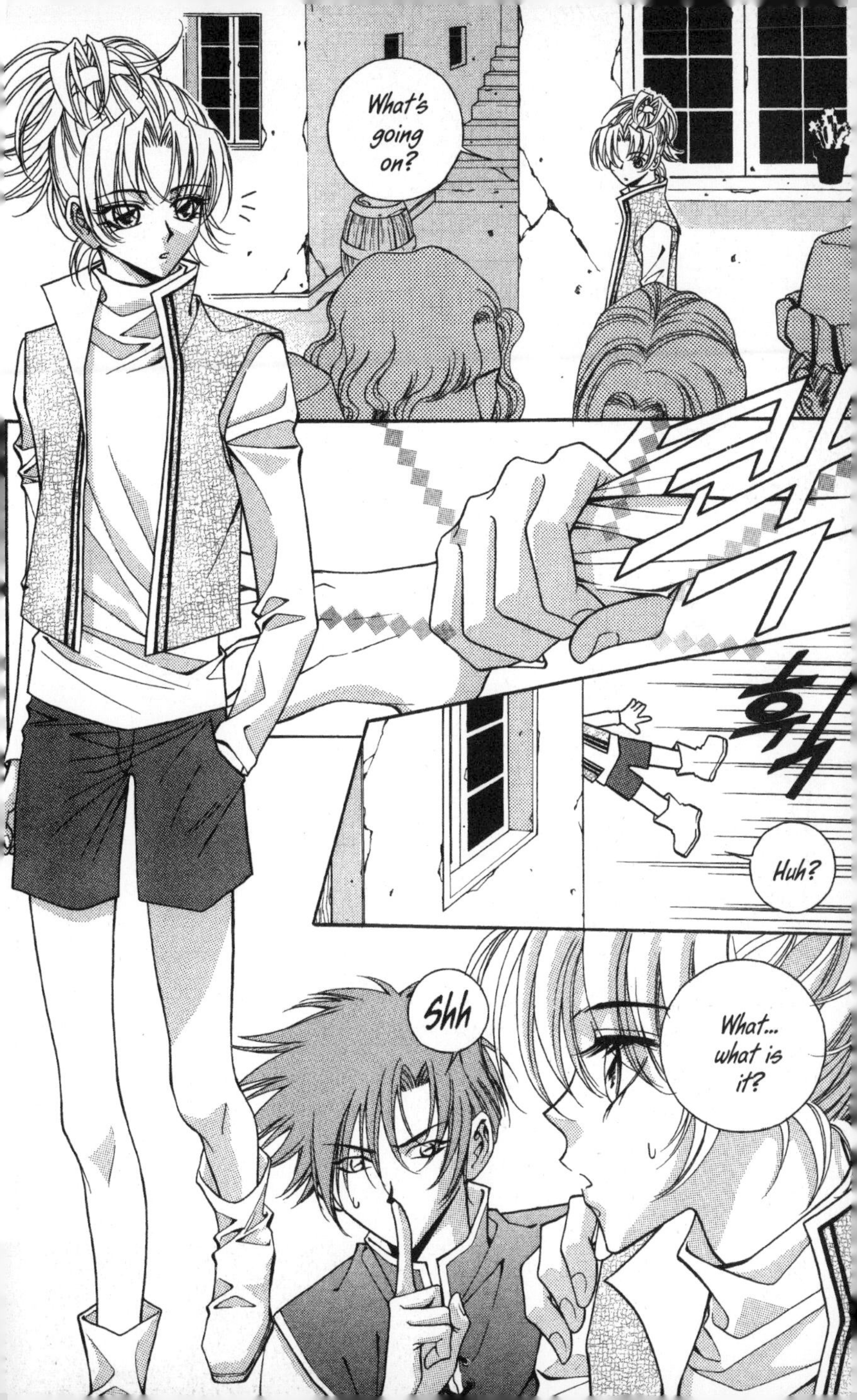
What's going on?
Huh?
Shh
What... what is it?

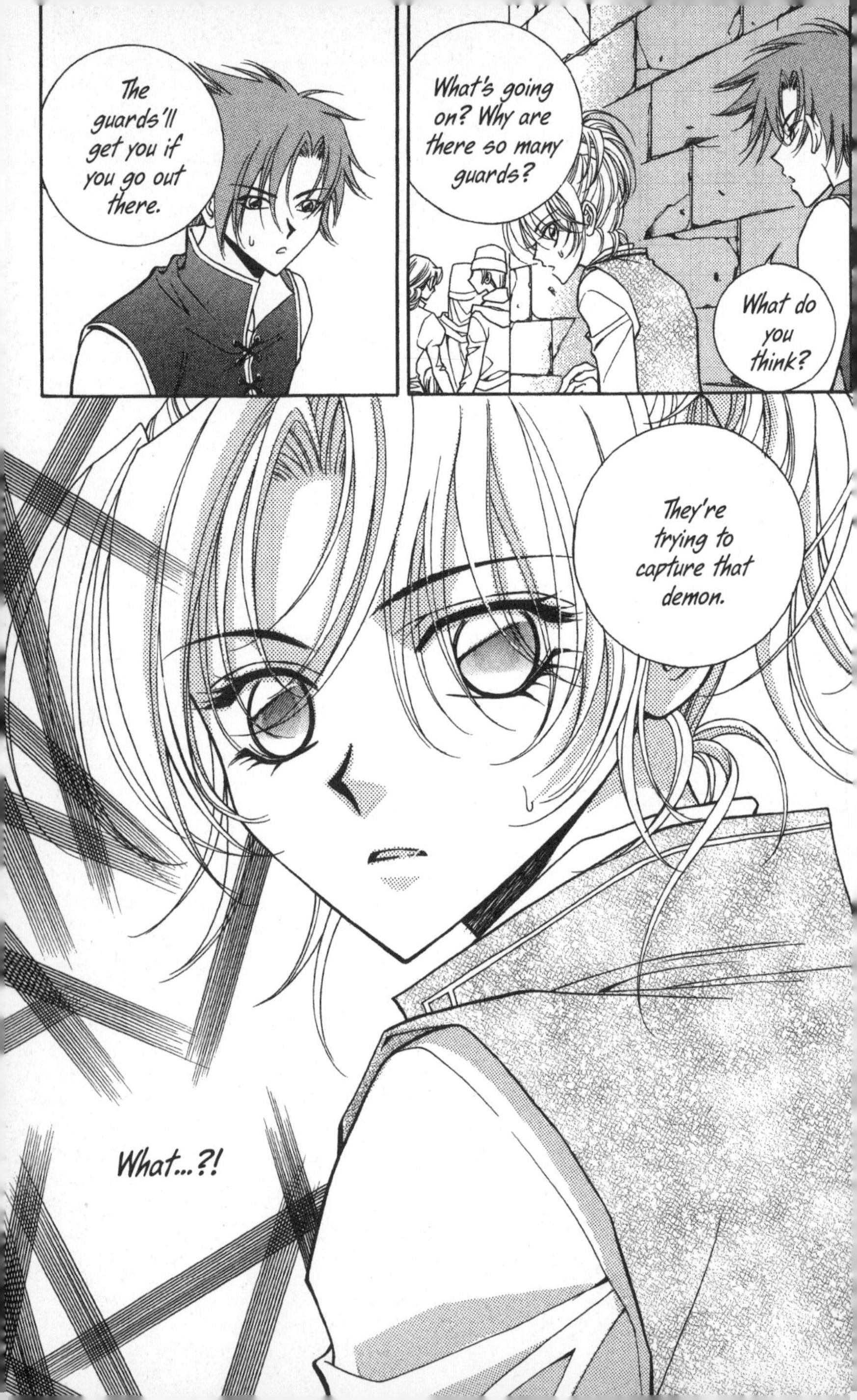
What's going on? Why are there so many guards?
What do you think?
The guards'll get you if you go out there.
They're trying to capture that demon.
What...?!

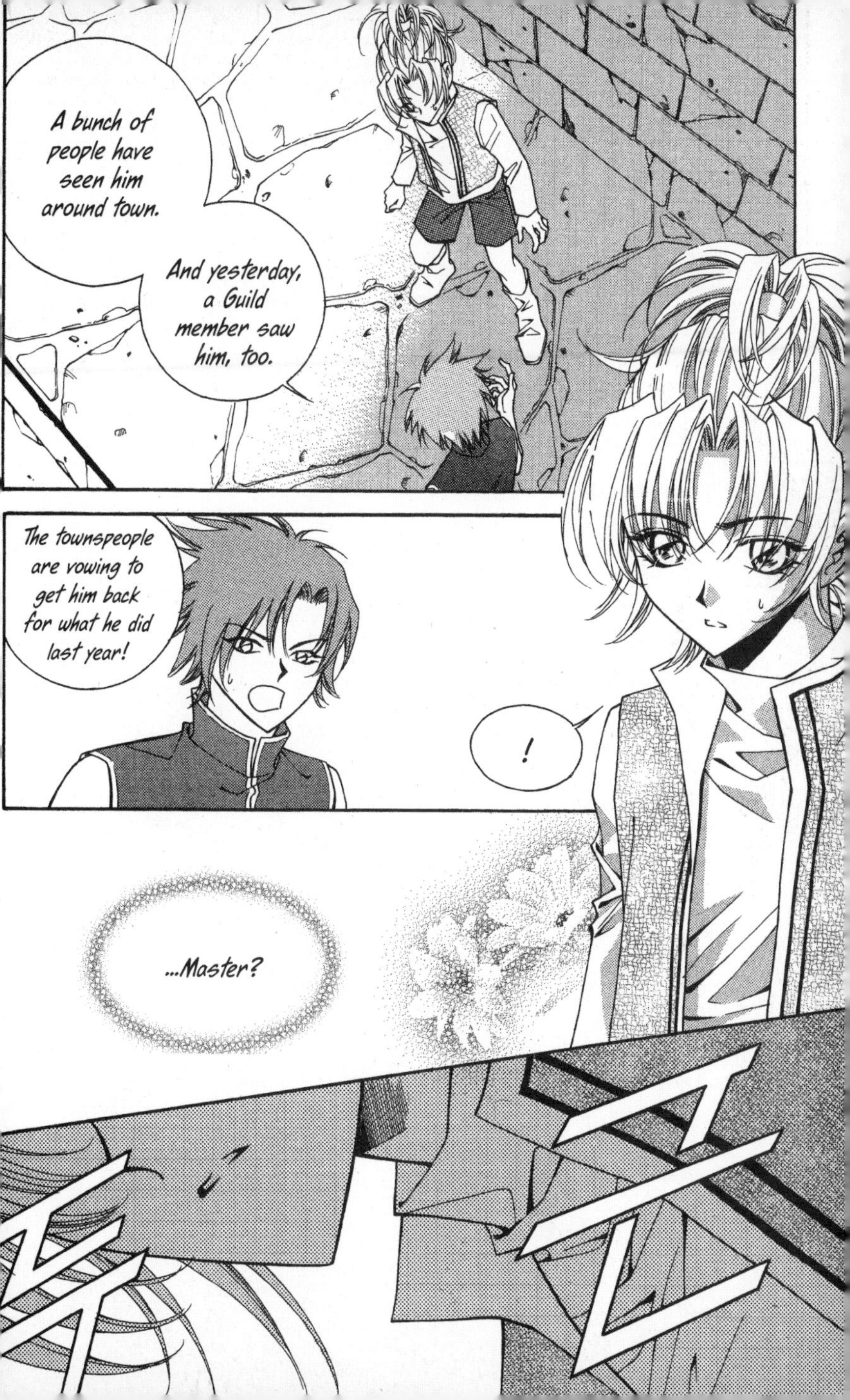
A bunch of people have seen him around town.
And yesterday, a Guild member saw him, too.
The townspeople are vowing to get him back for what he did last year!
!
...Master?

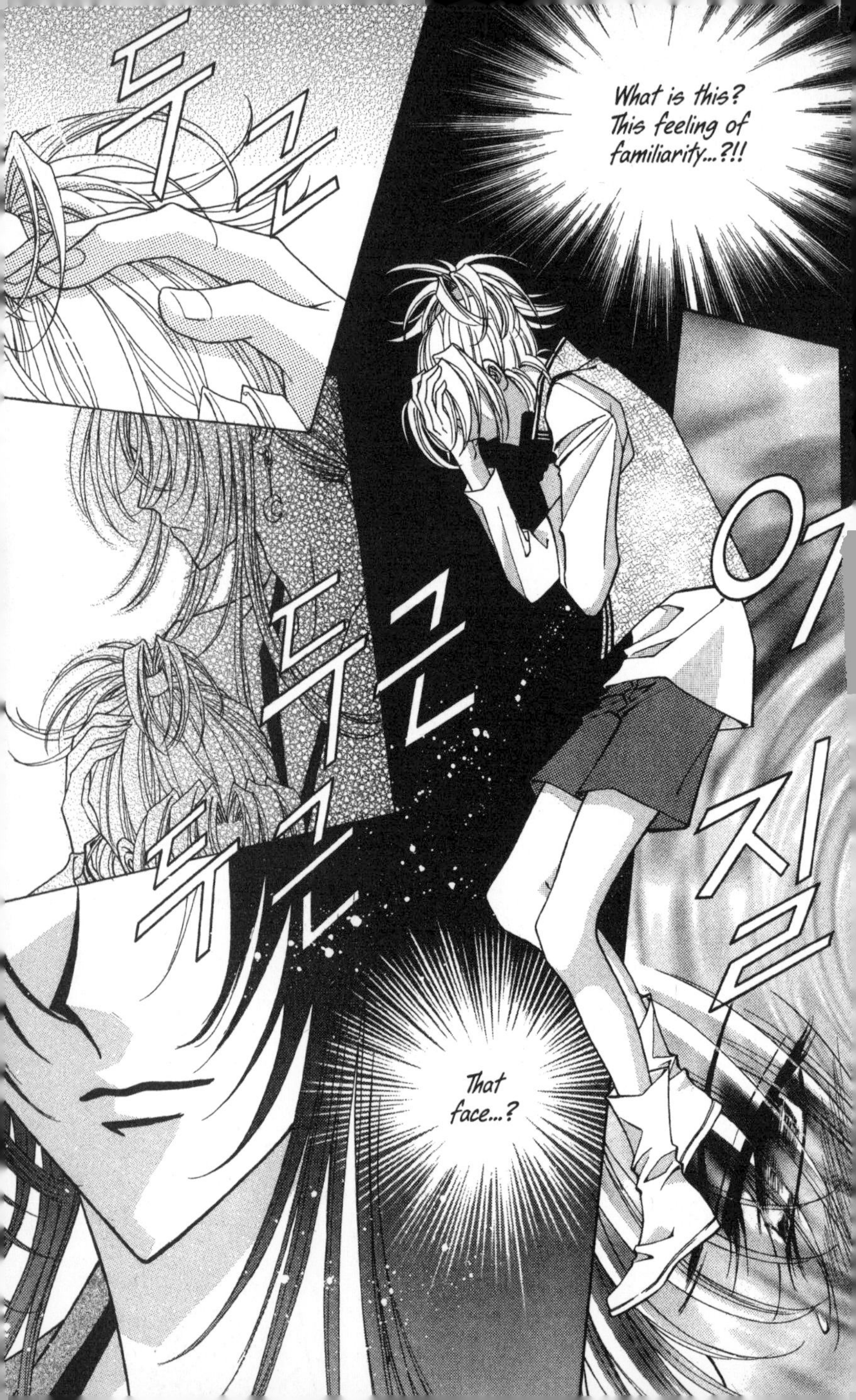

What is this? This feeling of familiarity...?!!
That face...?

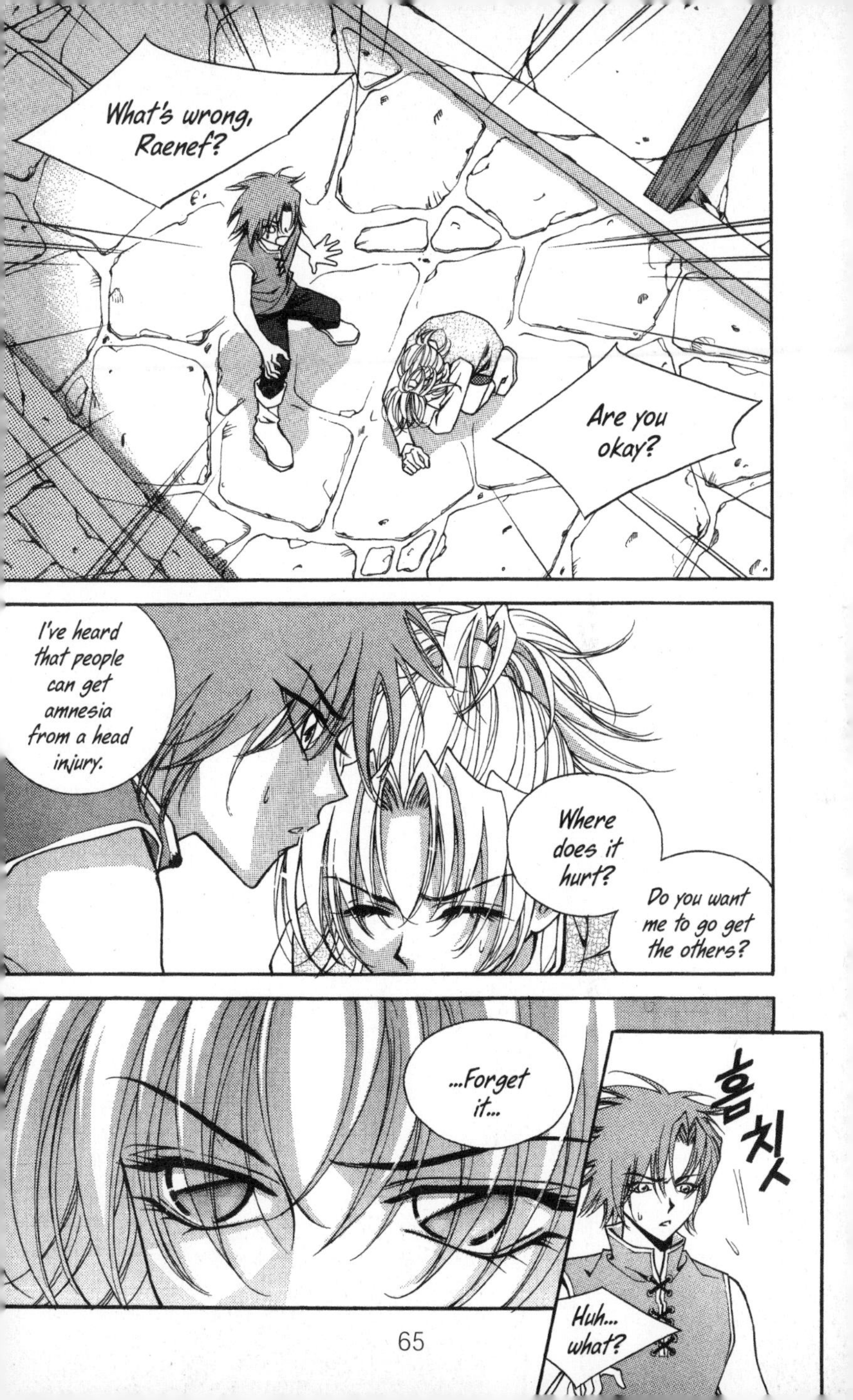
What's wrong, Raenef?
Are you okay?
I've heard that people can get amnesia from a head injury.
Where does it hurt?
Do you want me to go get the others?
...Forget it...
흠칫
Huh... what?

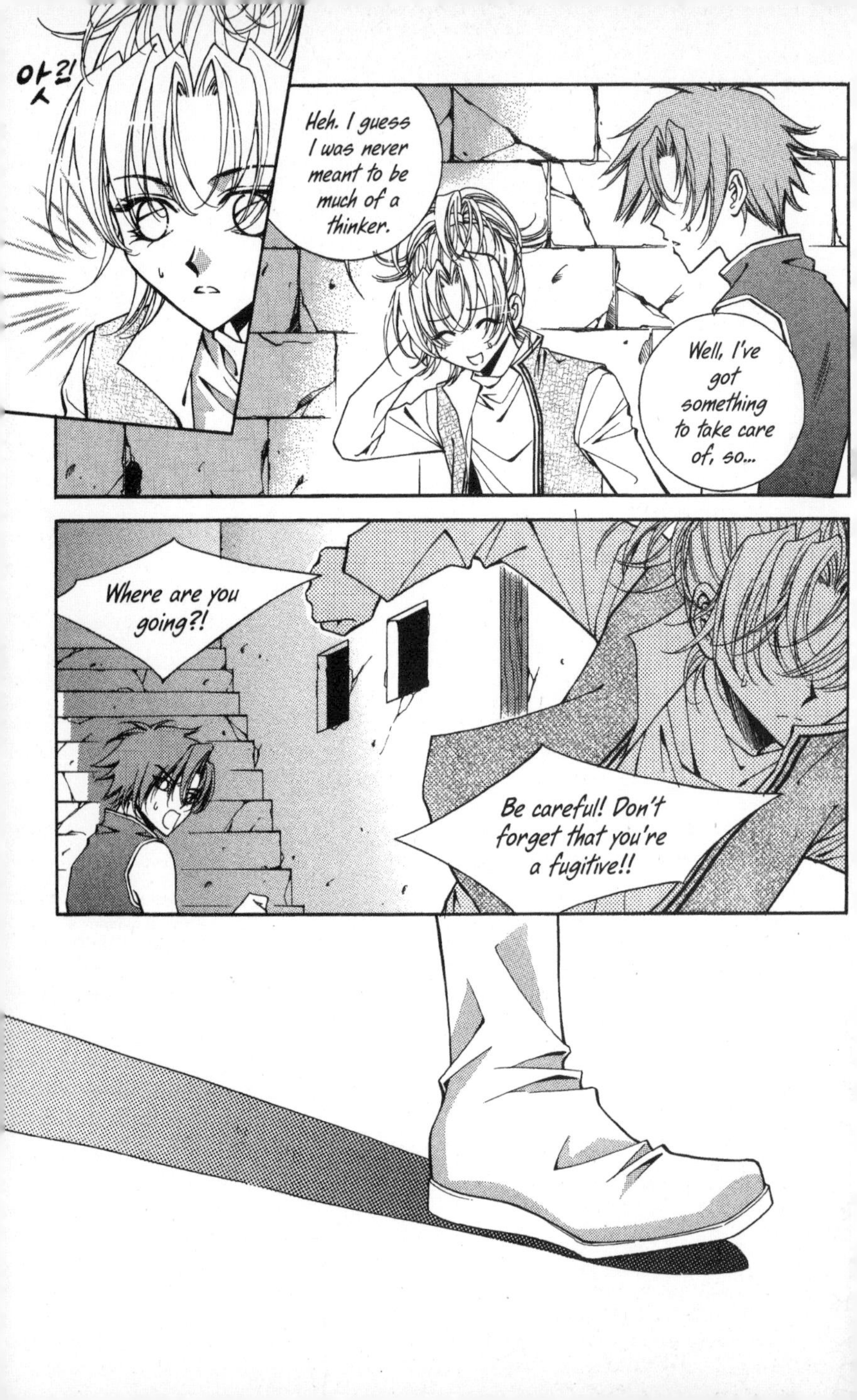
앗!
Heh. I guess I was never meant to be much of a thinker.
Well, I've got something to take care of, so...
Where are you going?!
Be careful! Don't forget that you're a fugitive!!

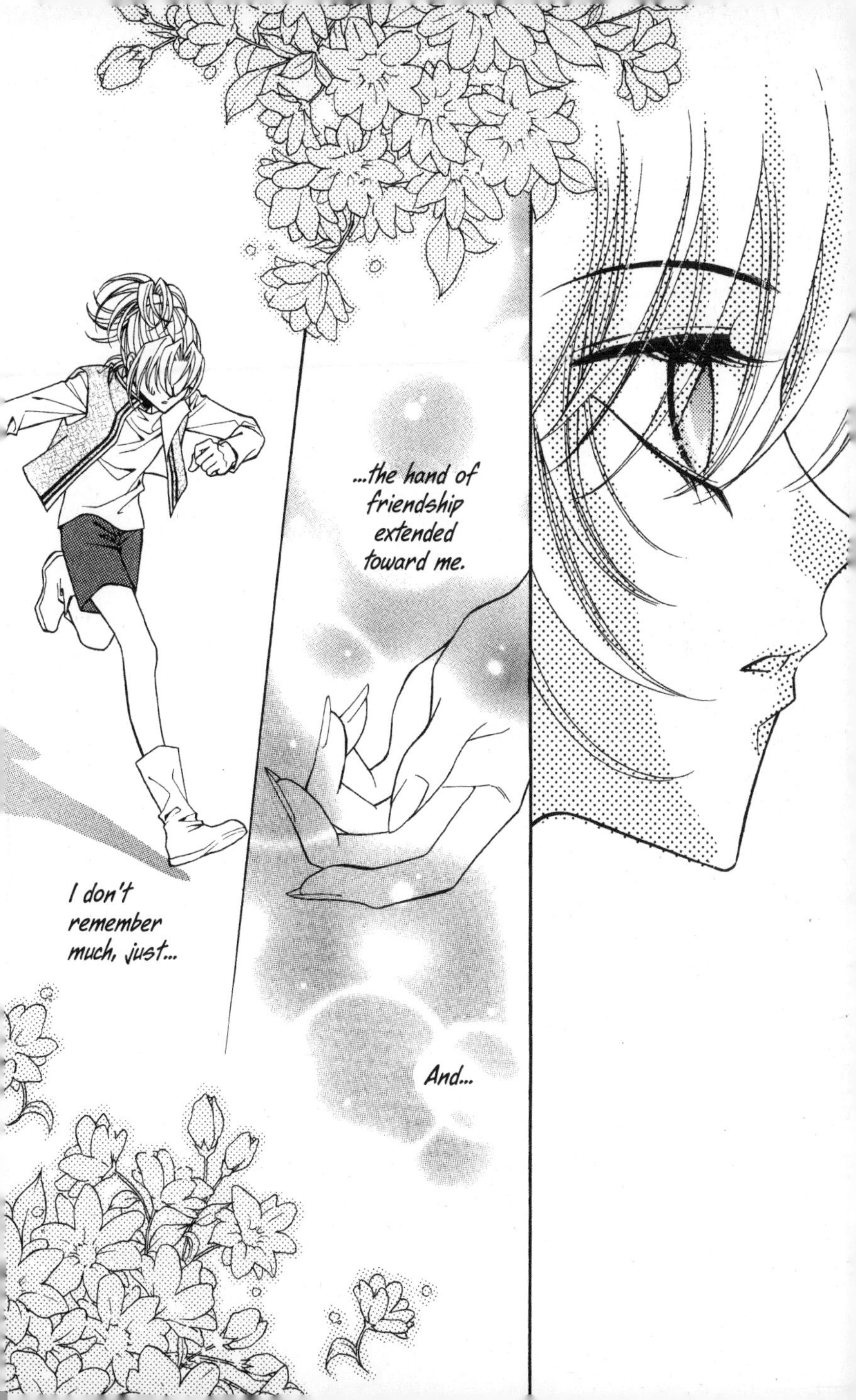
I don't remember much, just...
...the hand of friendship extended toward me.
And...

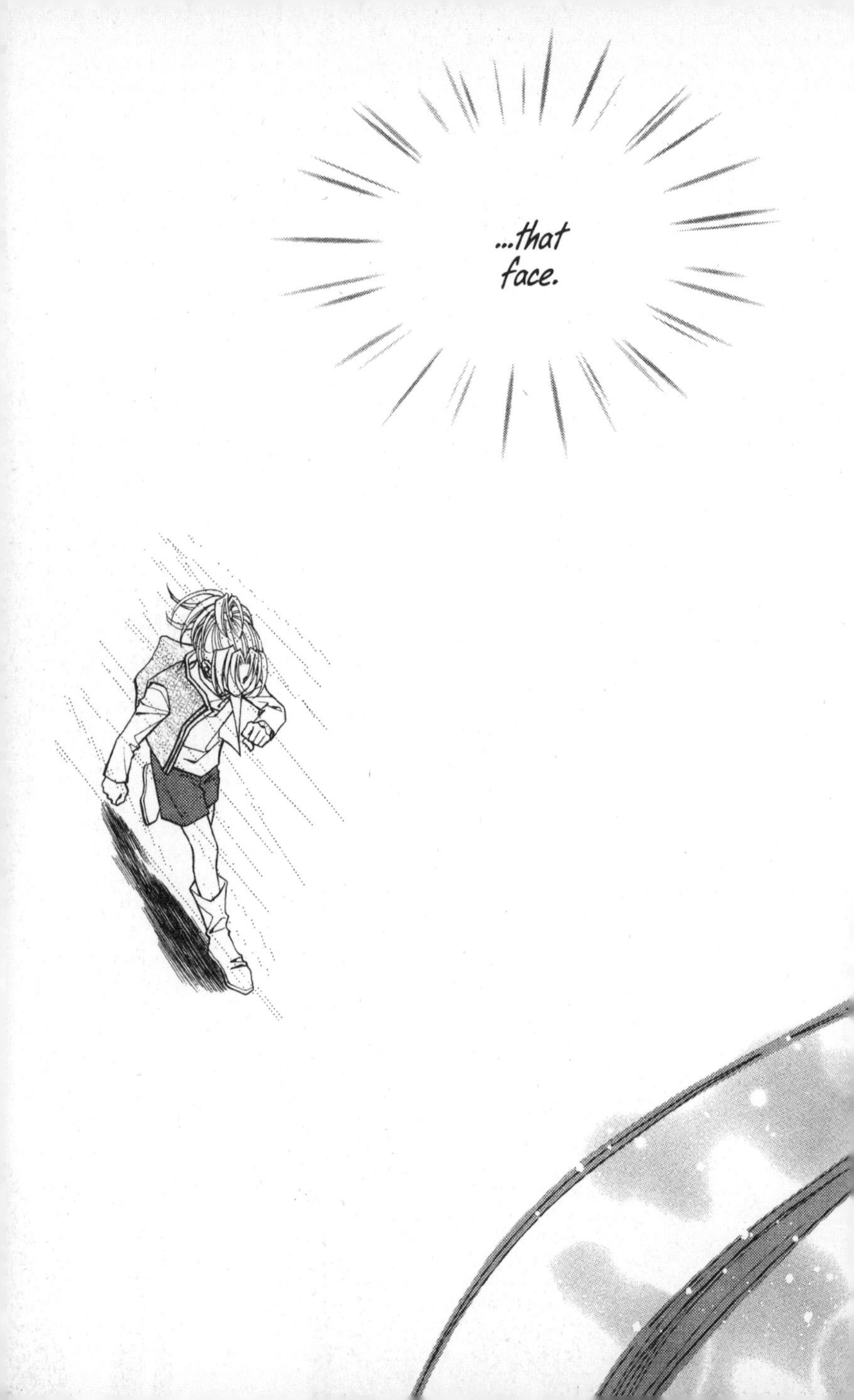
...that face.

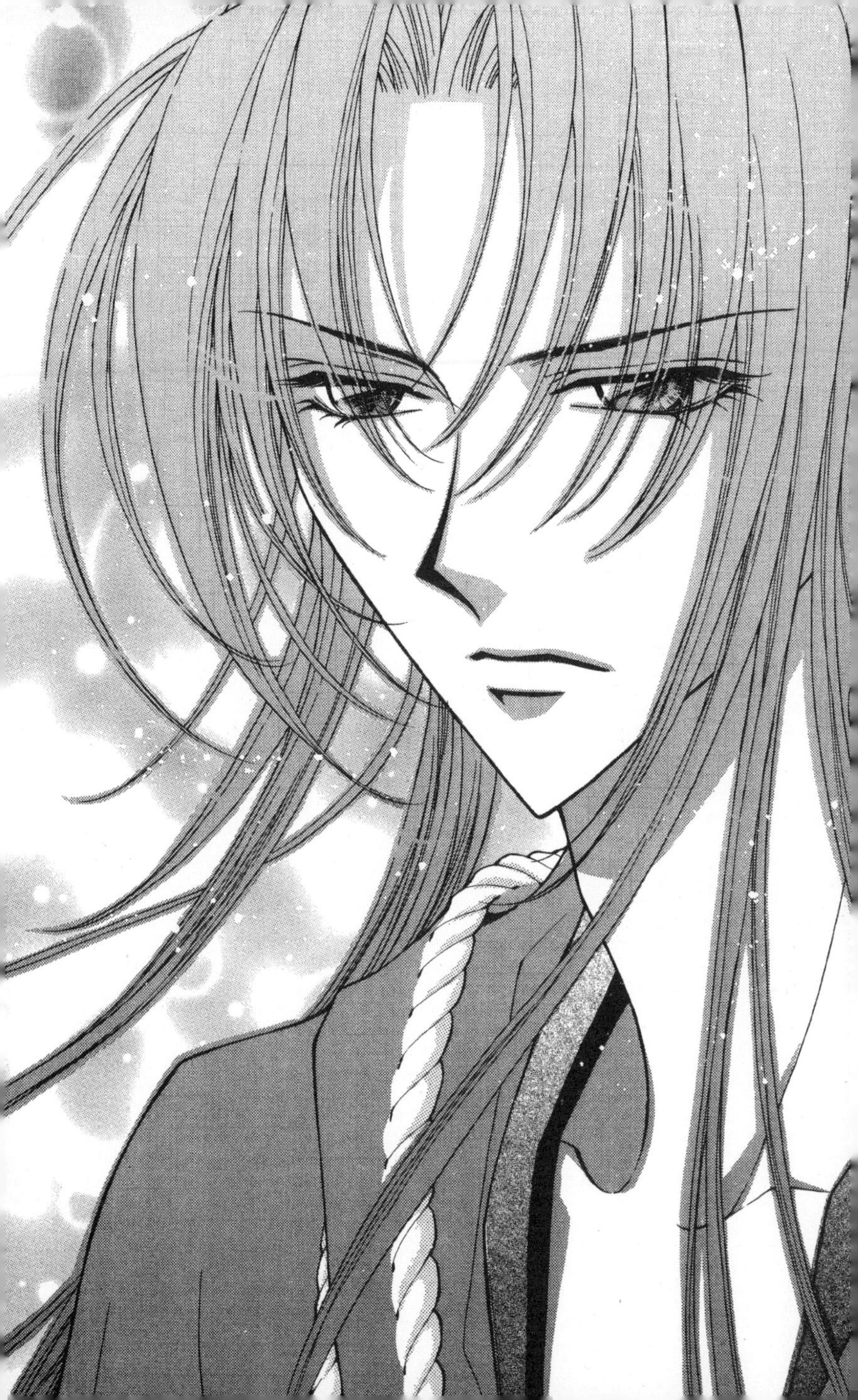

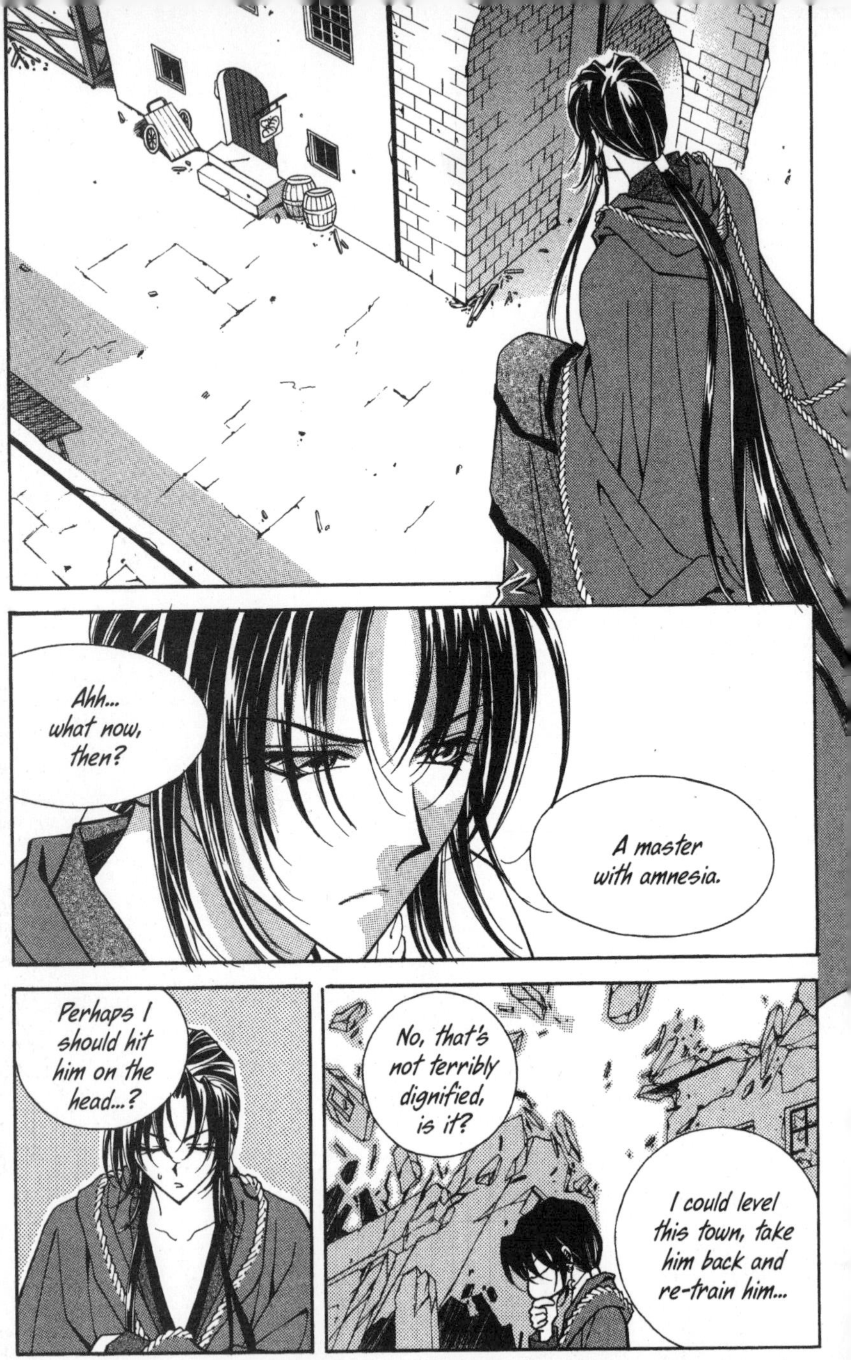
Ahh... what now, then?
A master with amnesia.
Perhaps I should hit him on the head...?
No, that's not terribly dignified, is it?
I could level this town, take him back and re-train him...

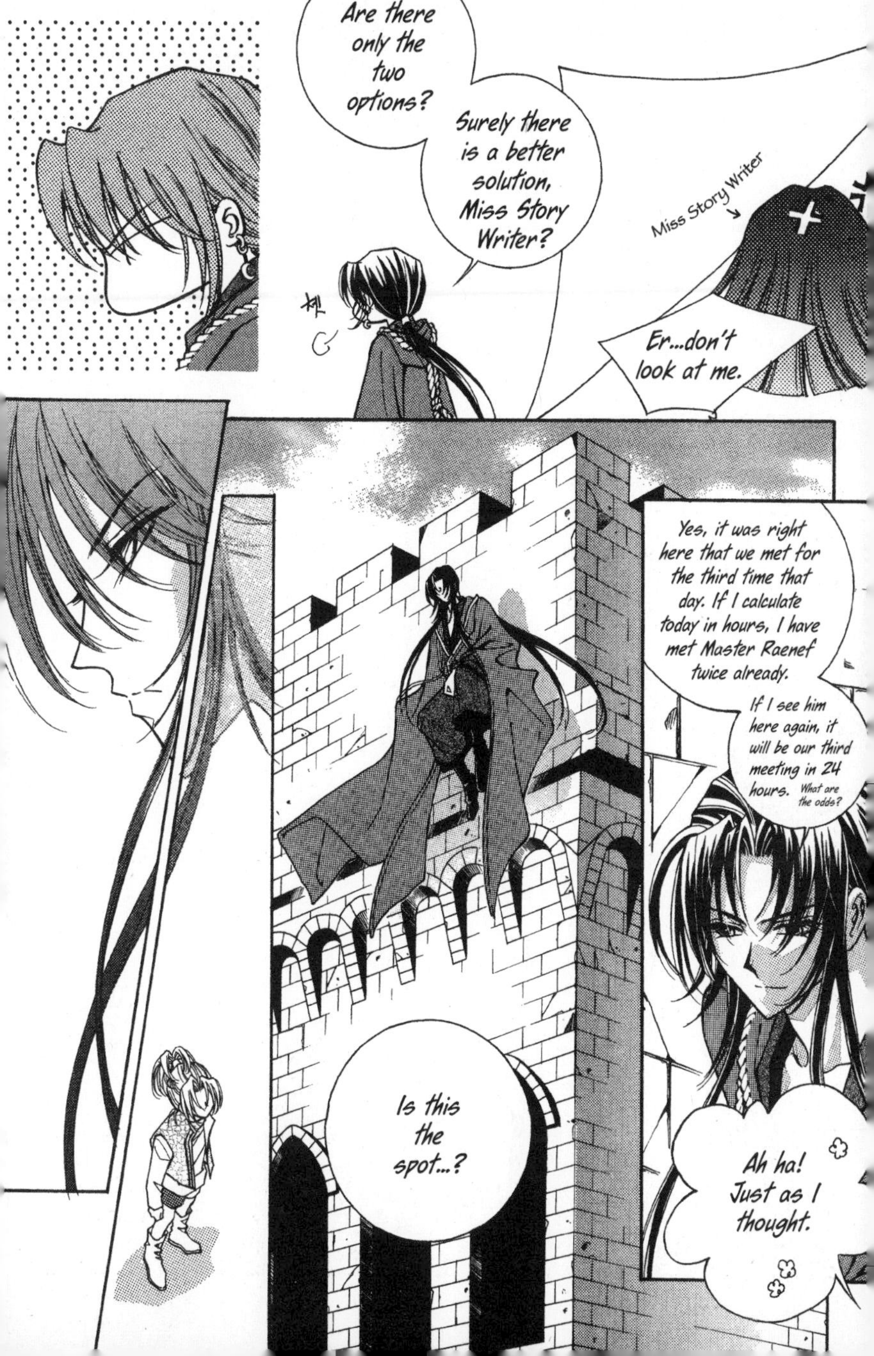

Are there only the two options?
Surely there is a better solution, Miss Story Writer?
Miss Story Writer
Er...don't look at me.
Is this the spot...?
Yes, it was right here that we met for the third time that day. If I calculate today in hours, I have met Master Raenef twice already.
If I see him here again, it will be our third meeting in 24 hours.
What are the odds?
Ah ha! Just as I thought.

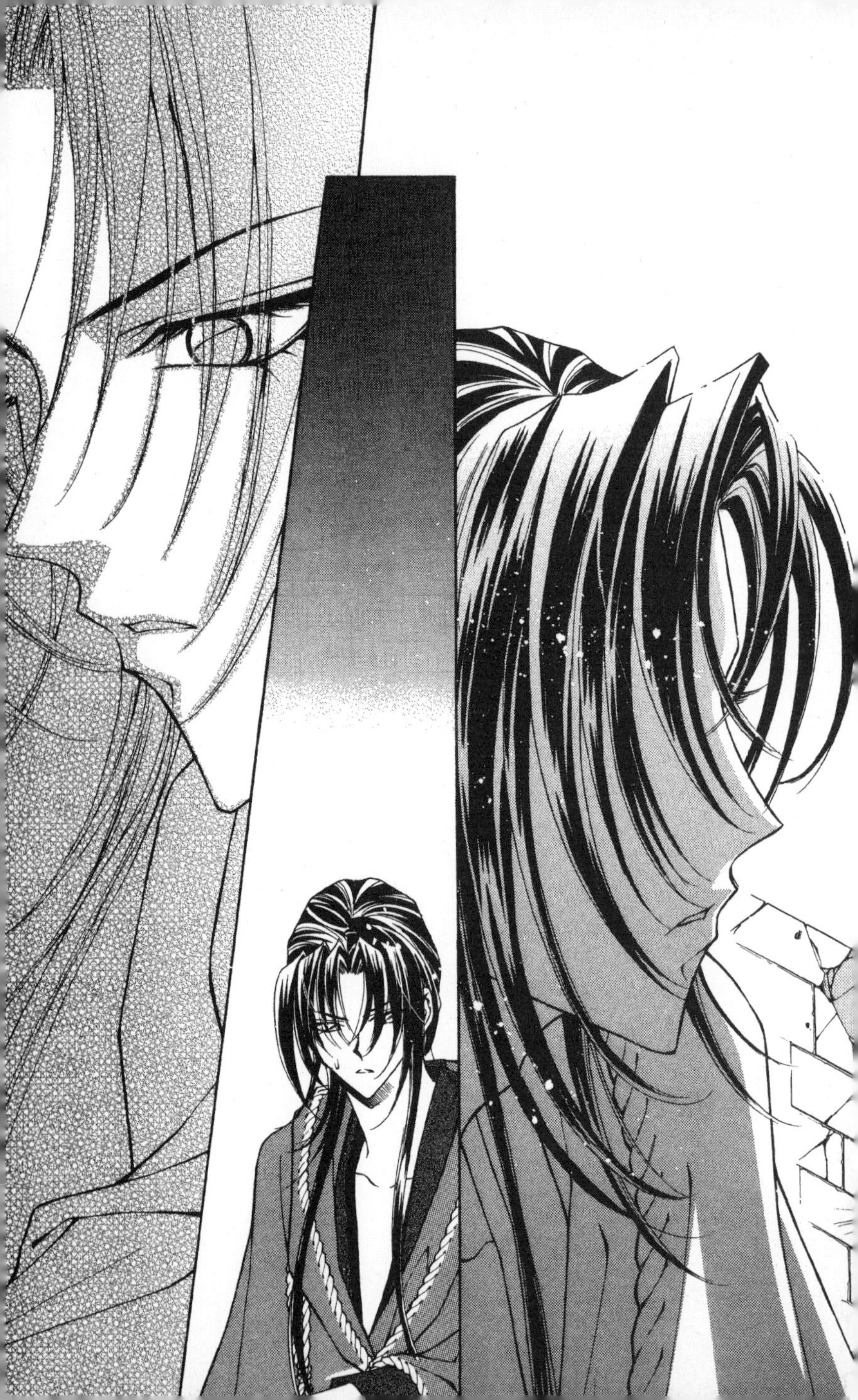

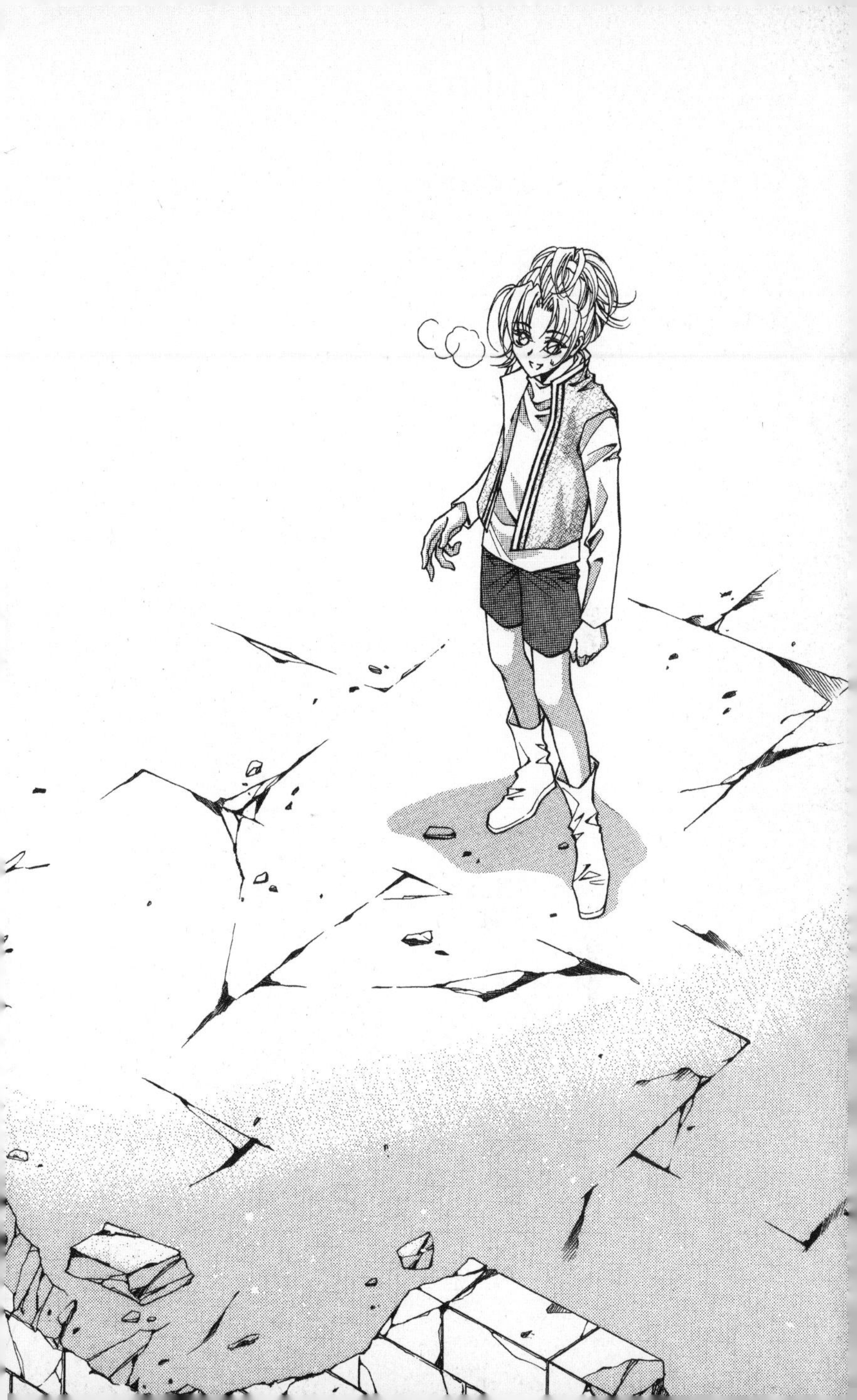

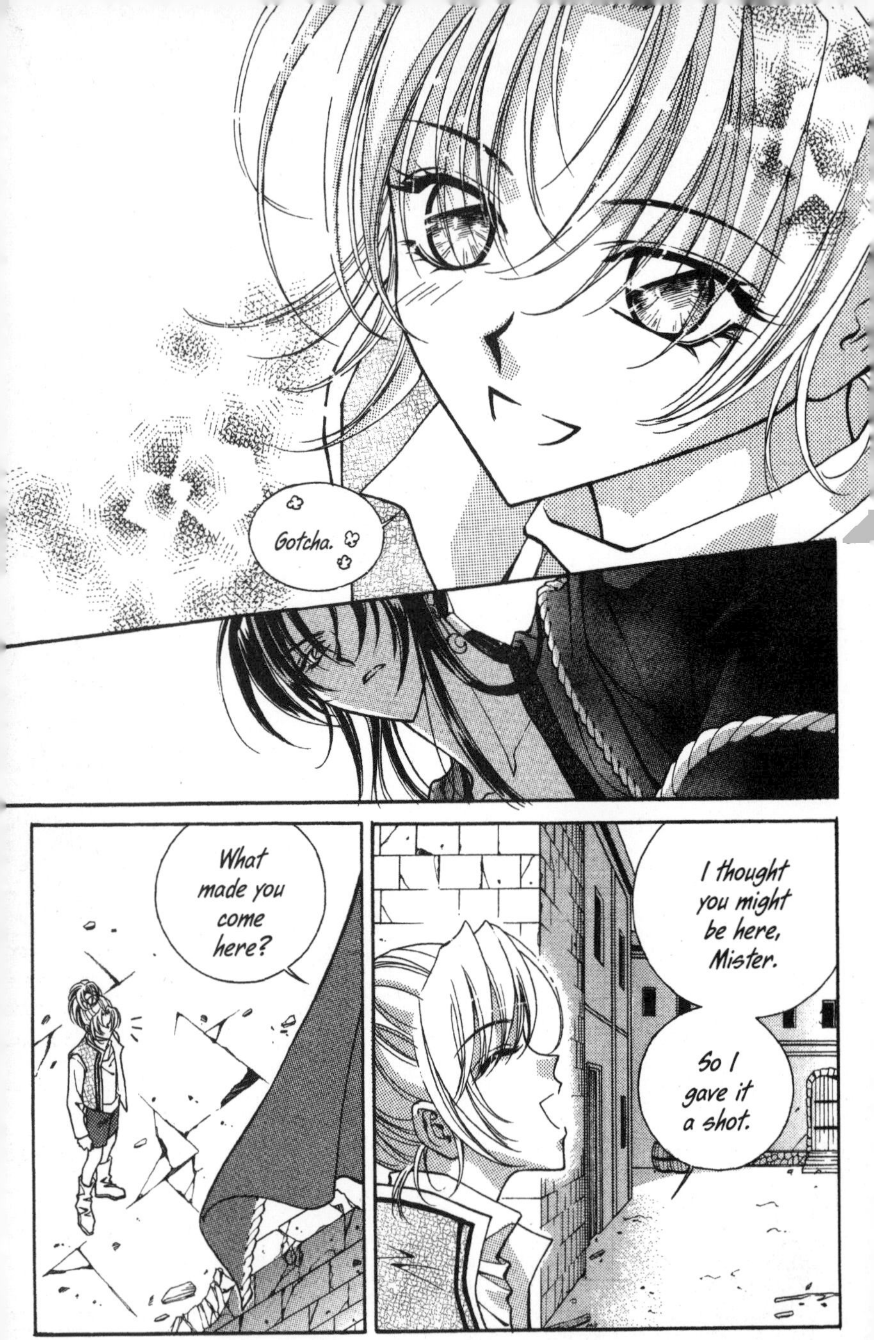
Gotcha.
What made you come here?
I thought you might be here, Mister.
So I gave it a shot.

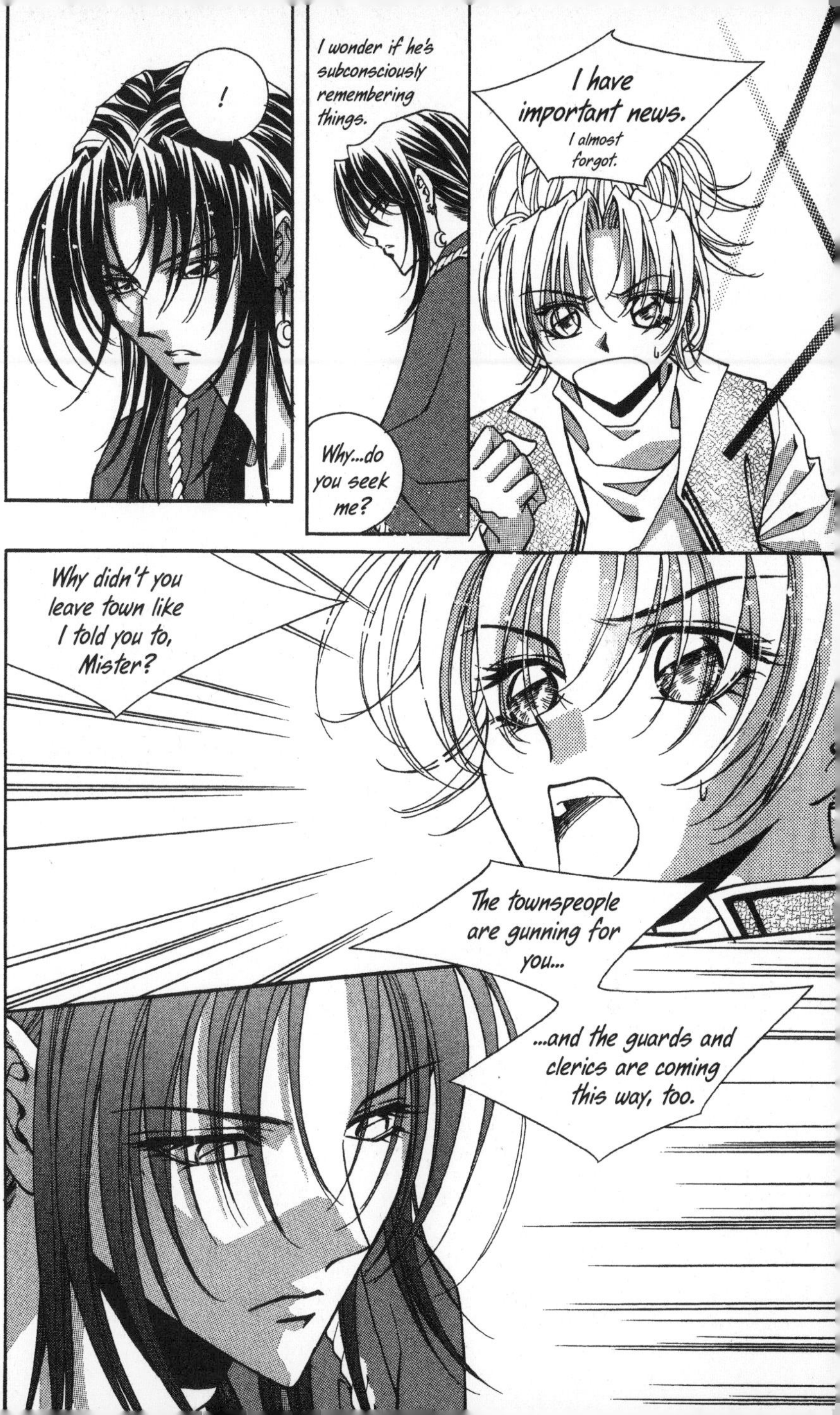
!
I wonder if he's subconsciously remembering things.
Why...do you seek me?
I have important news.
I almost forgot.
Why didn't you leave town like I told you to, Mister?
The townspeople are gunning for you...
...and the guards and clerics are coming this way, too.

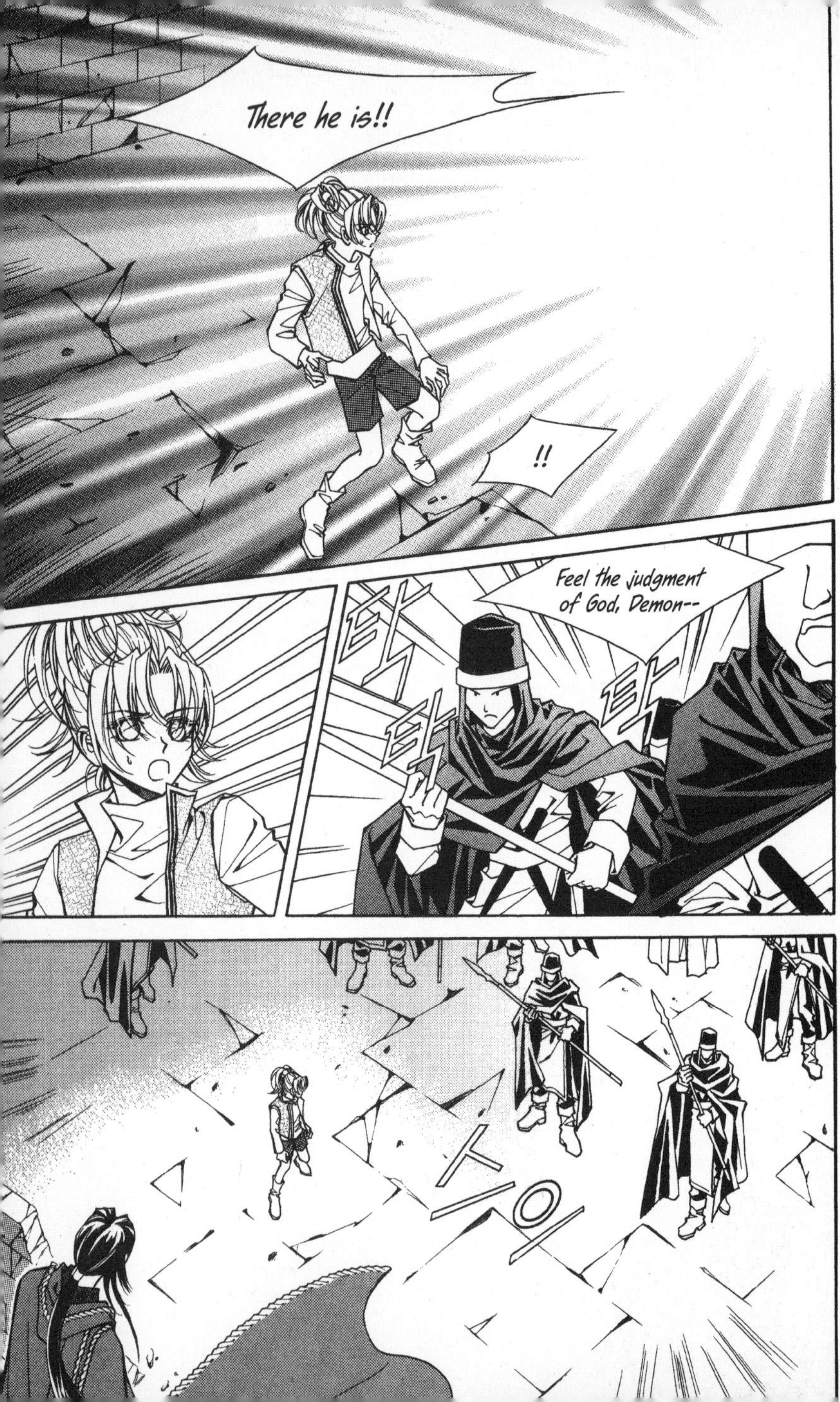
There he is!!
!!
탁
탁
Feel the judgment of God, Demon--
탁

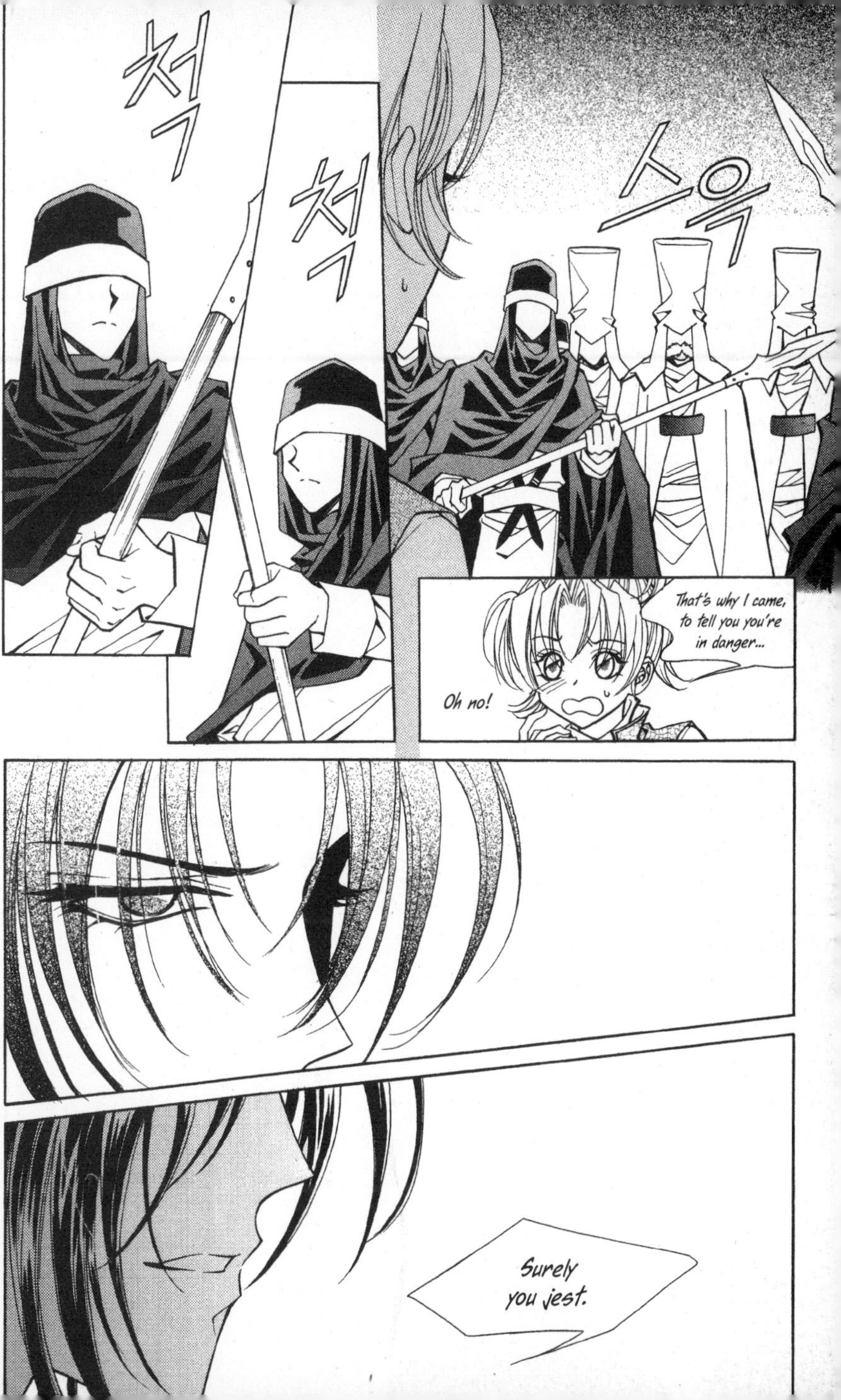
척
척
스윽
Oh no!
That's why I came, to tell you you're in danger...
Surely you jest.

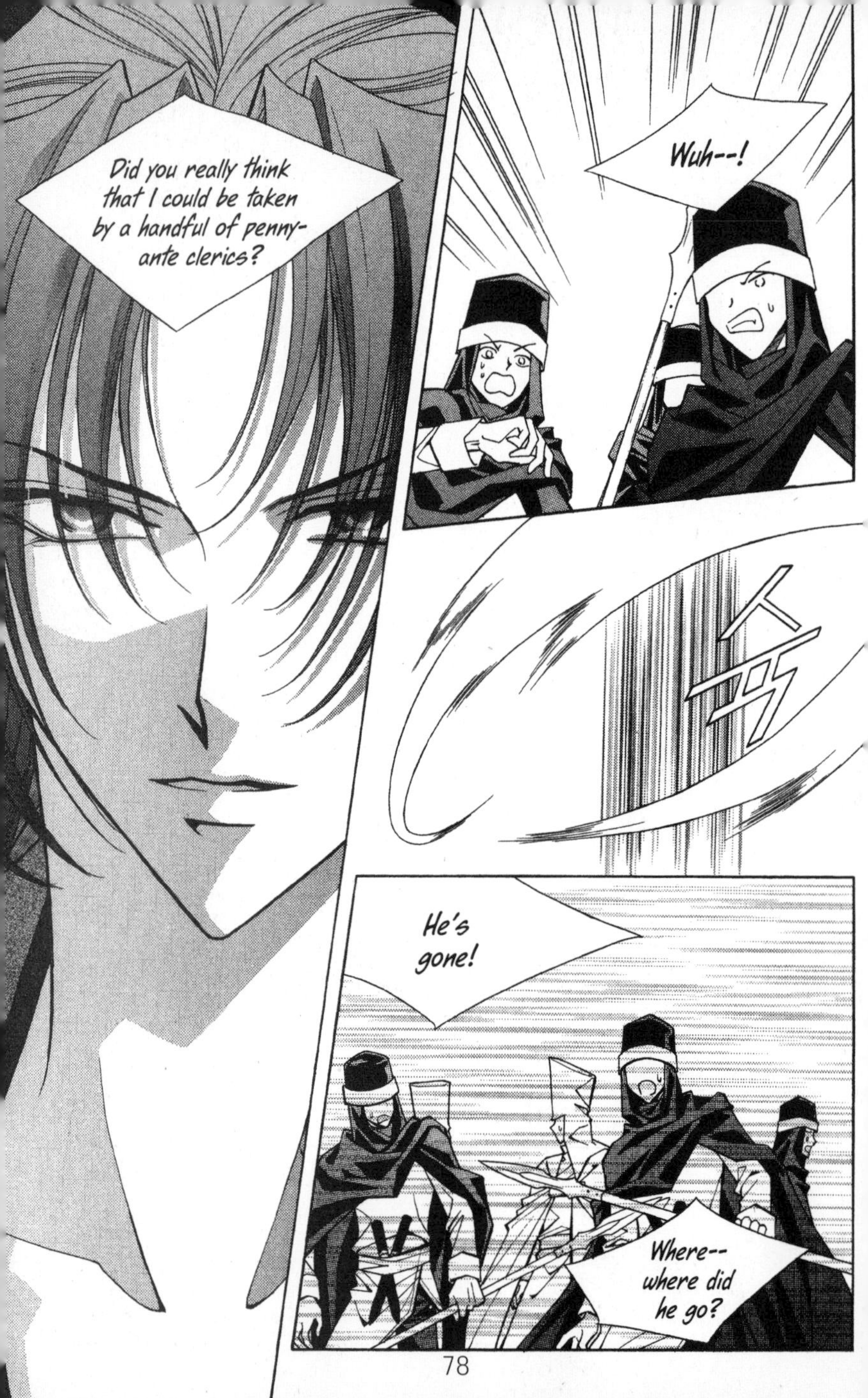
Did you really think that I could be taken by a handful of penny-ante clerics?
Wuh--!
He's gone!
Where-- where did he go?

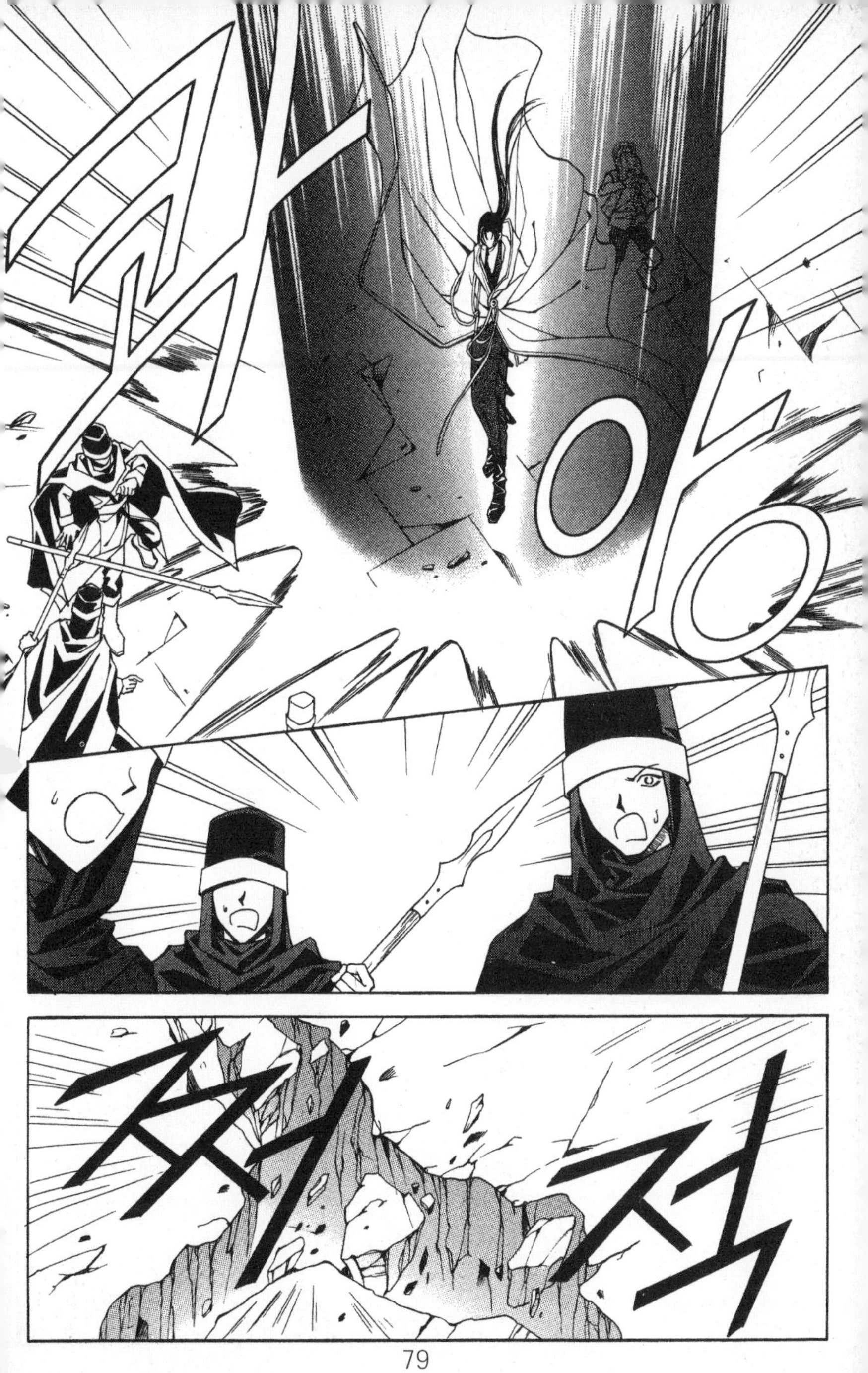

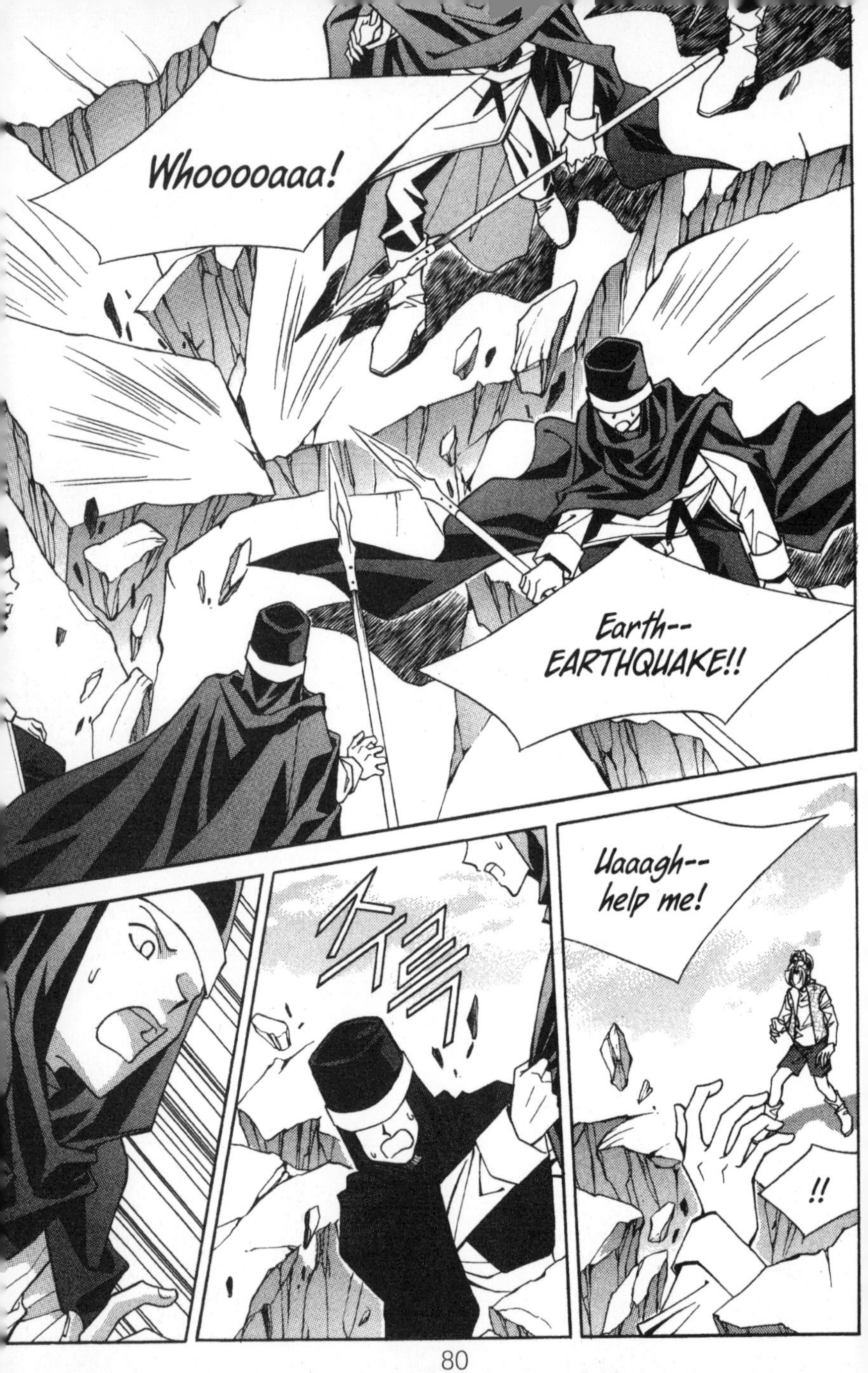
Whoooaaa!
Earth-- EARTHQUAKE!!
Uaaagh-- help me!
!!

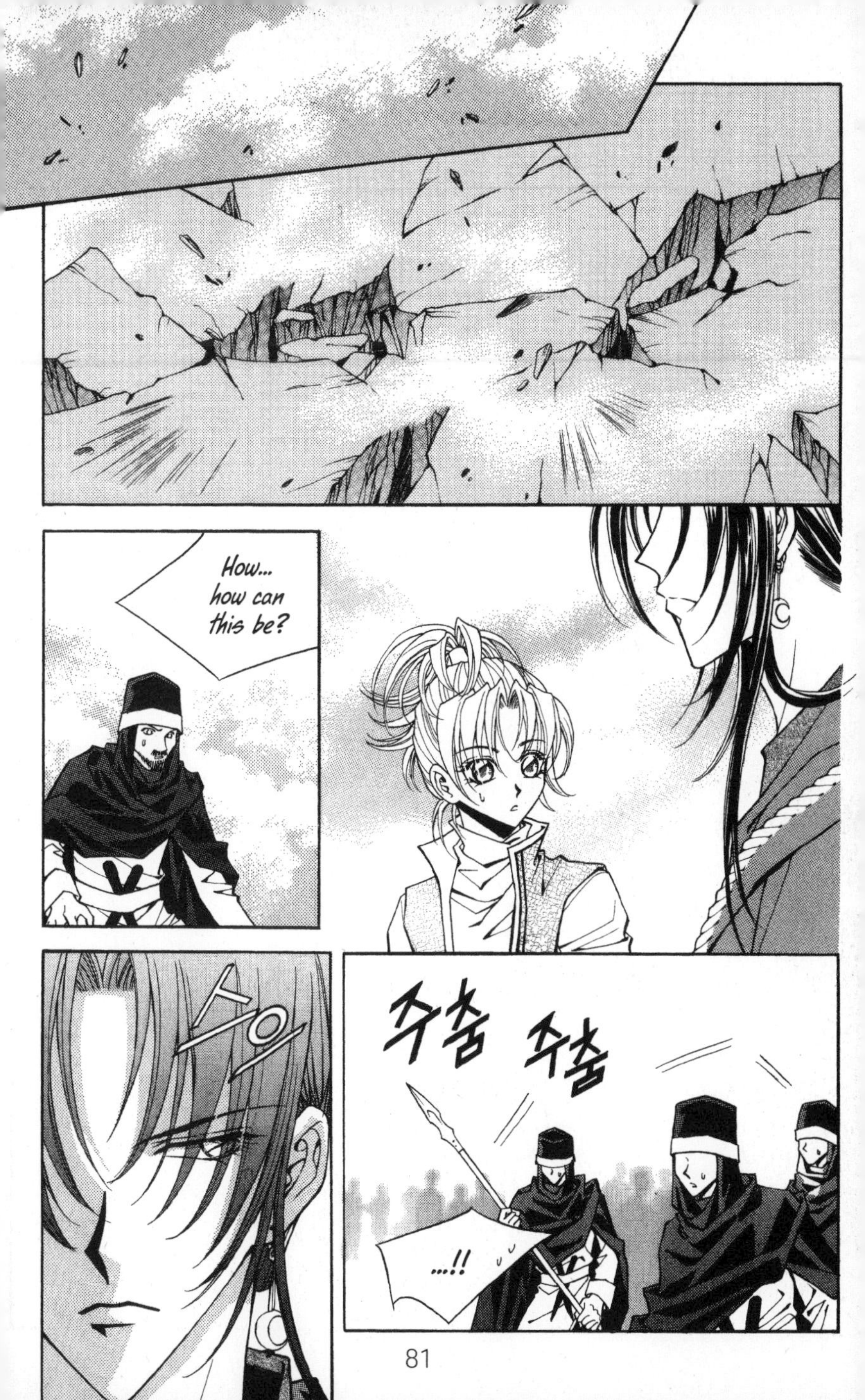
How... how can this be?
스윽
주춤 주춤
...!!

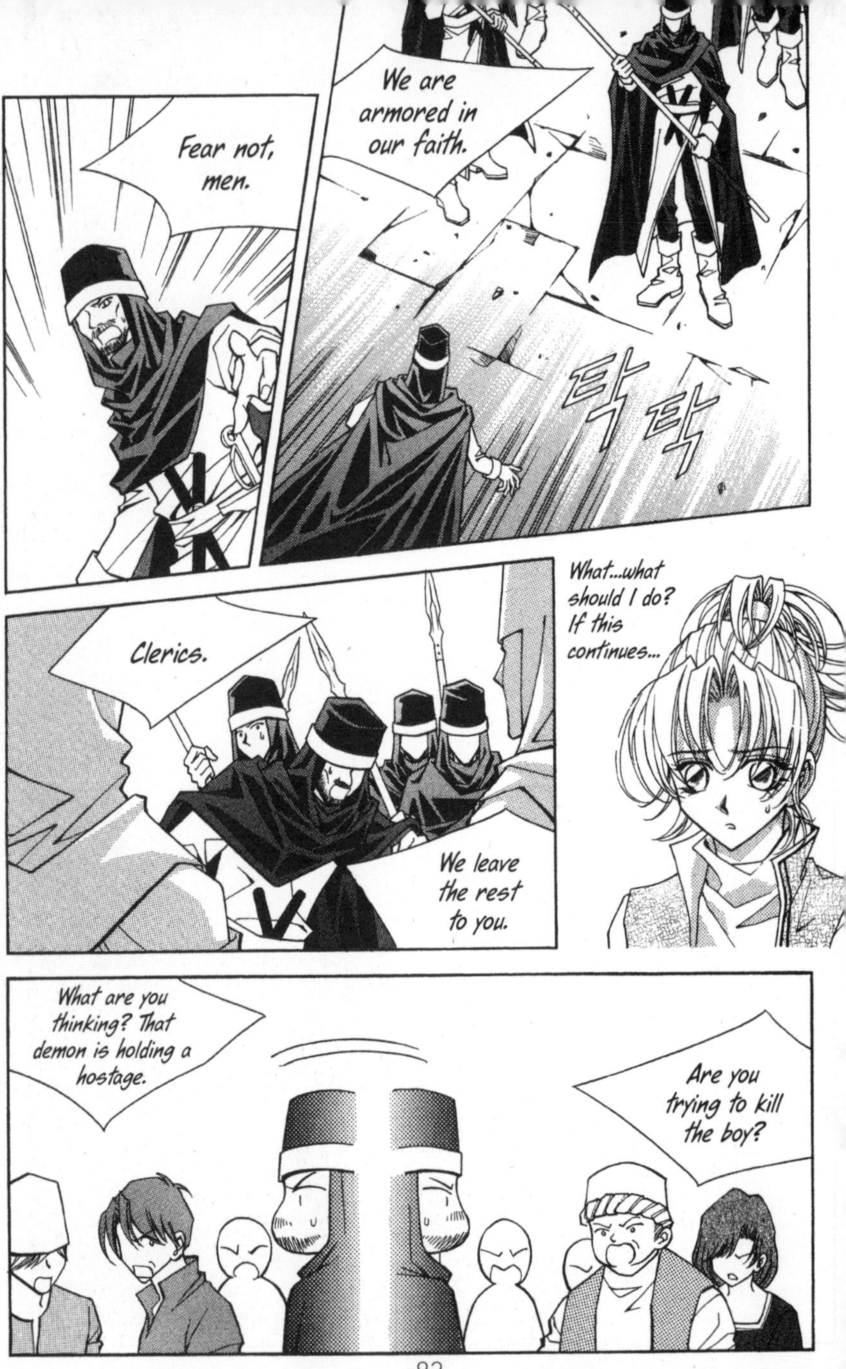

Fear not, men.
We are armored in our faith.
탁 탁
Clerics.
We leave the rest to you.
What...what should I do? If this continues...
What are you thinking? That demon is holding a hostage.
Are you trying to kill the boy?

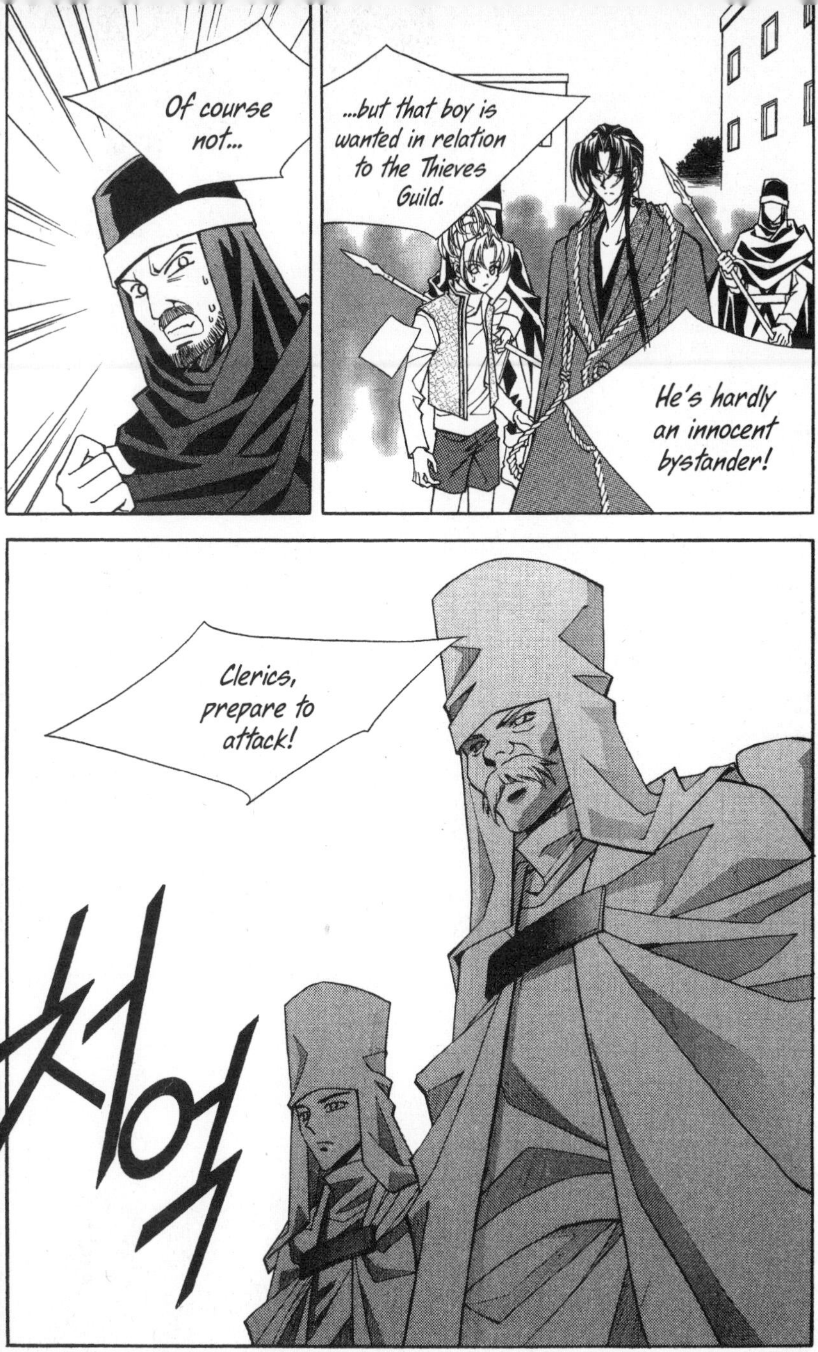
Of course not...
...but that boy is wanted in relation to the Thieves Guild.
He's hardly an innocent bystander!
Clerics, prepare to attack!

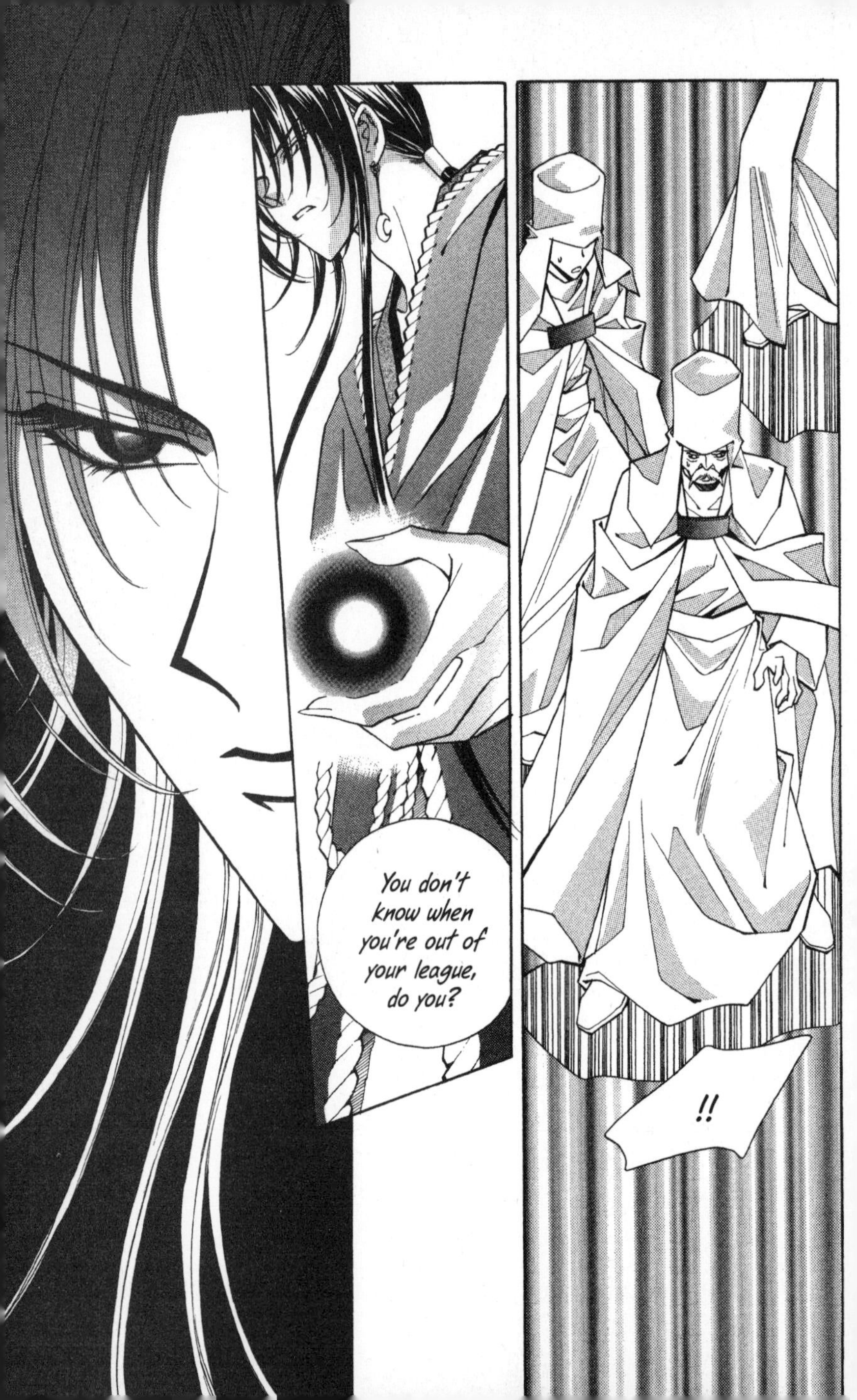
You don't know when you're out of your league, do you?
!!

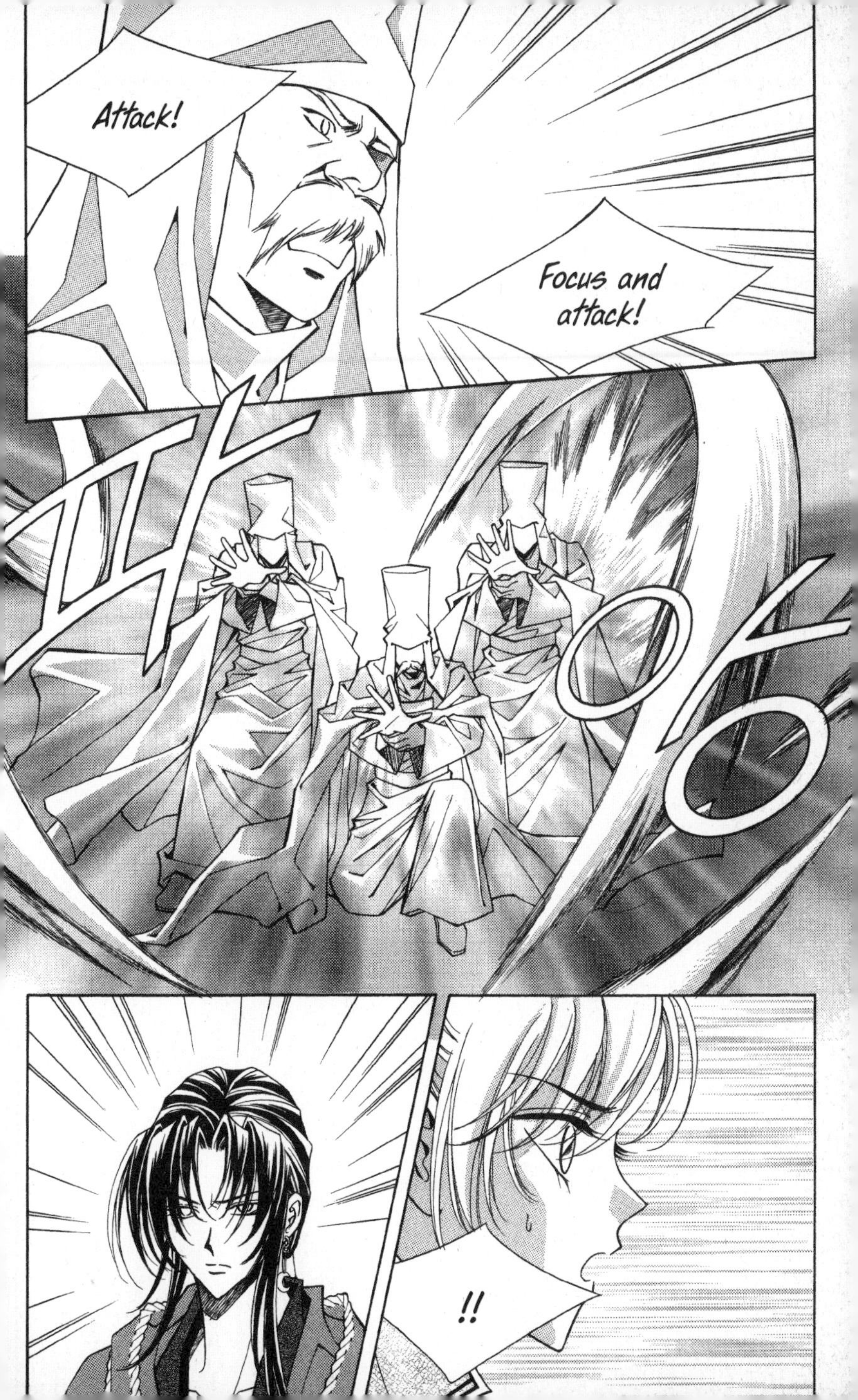
Attack!
Focus and attack!
!!

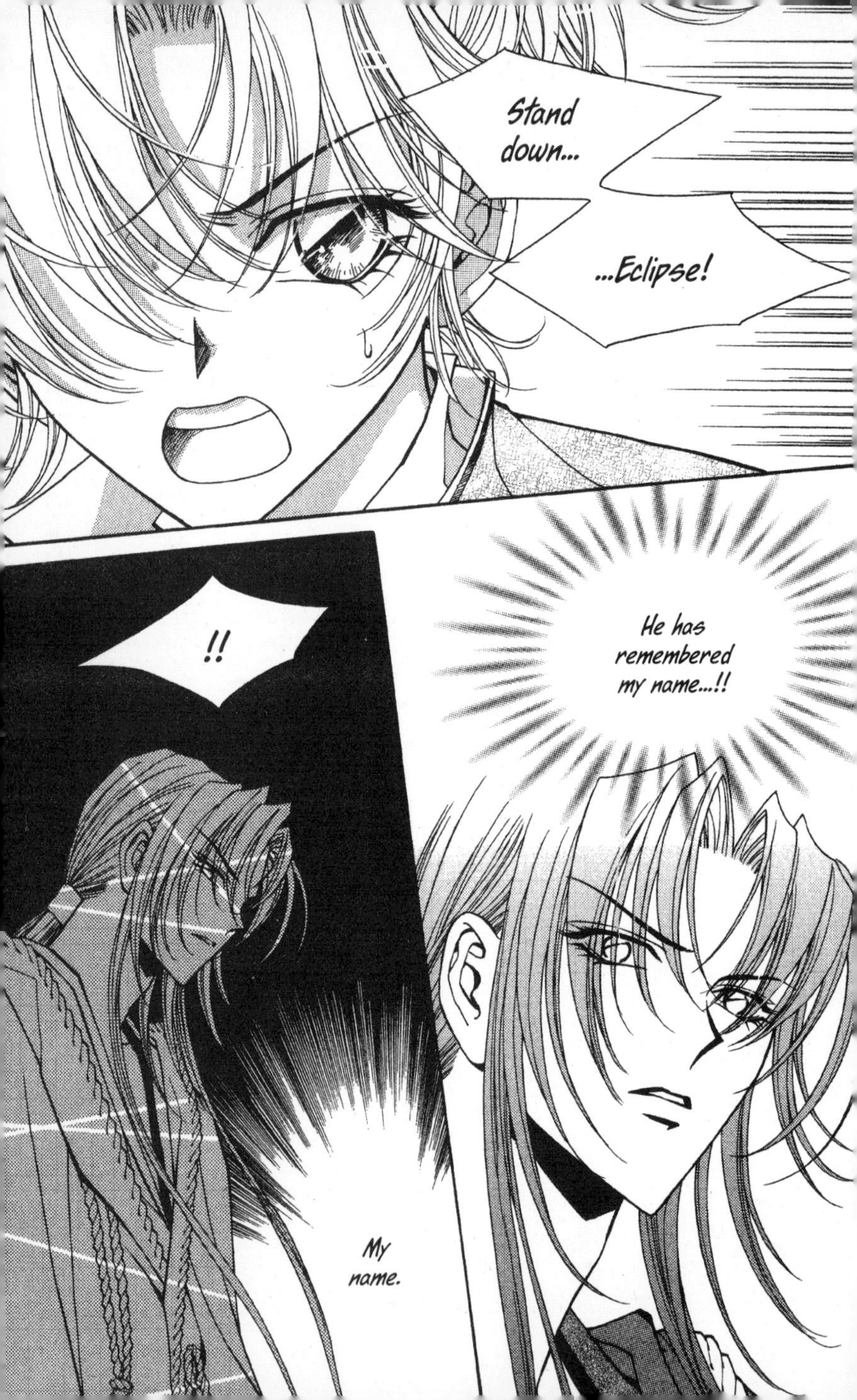
Stand down...
...Eclipse!
!!
My name.
He has remembered my name...!!

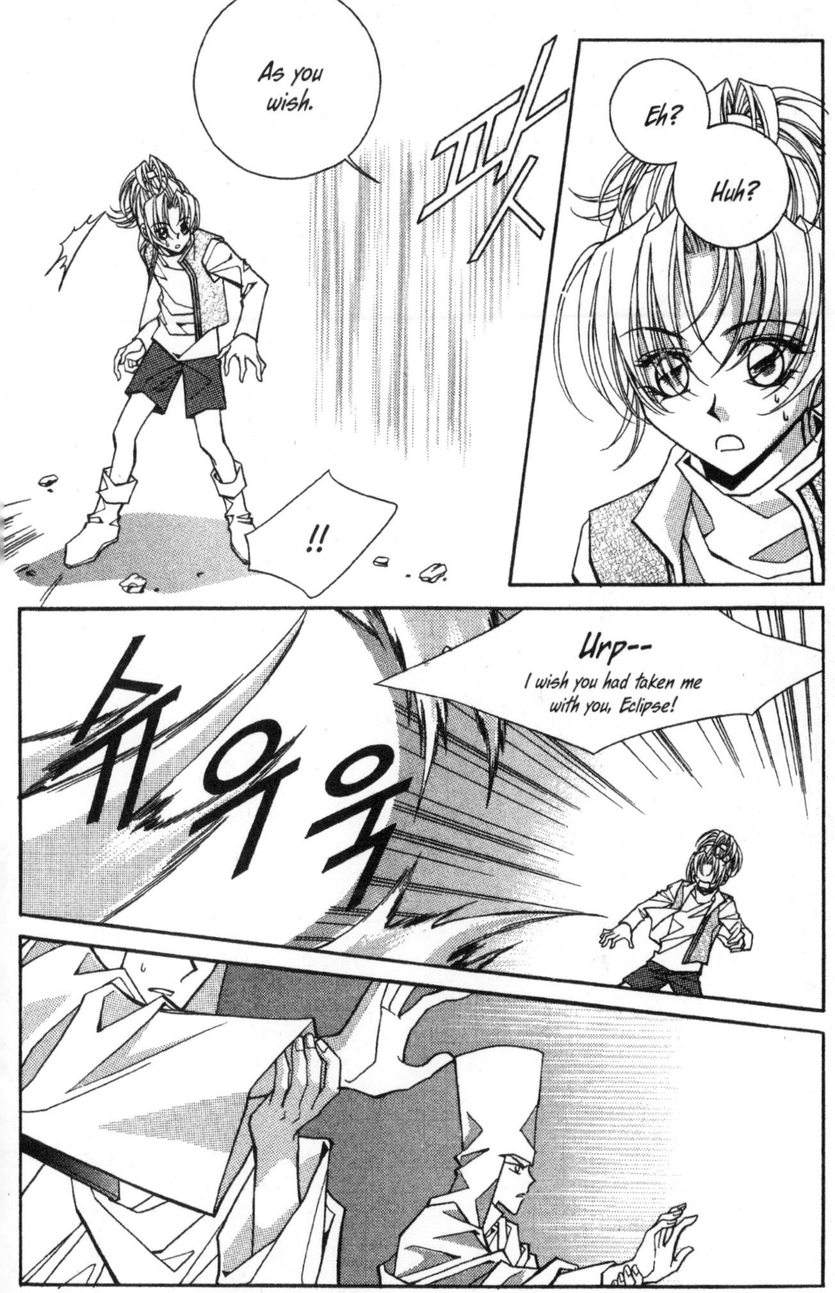
As you wish.
!!
Eh?
Huh?
Urp--
I wish you had taken me with you, Eclipse!

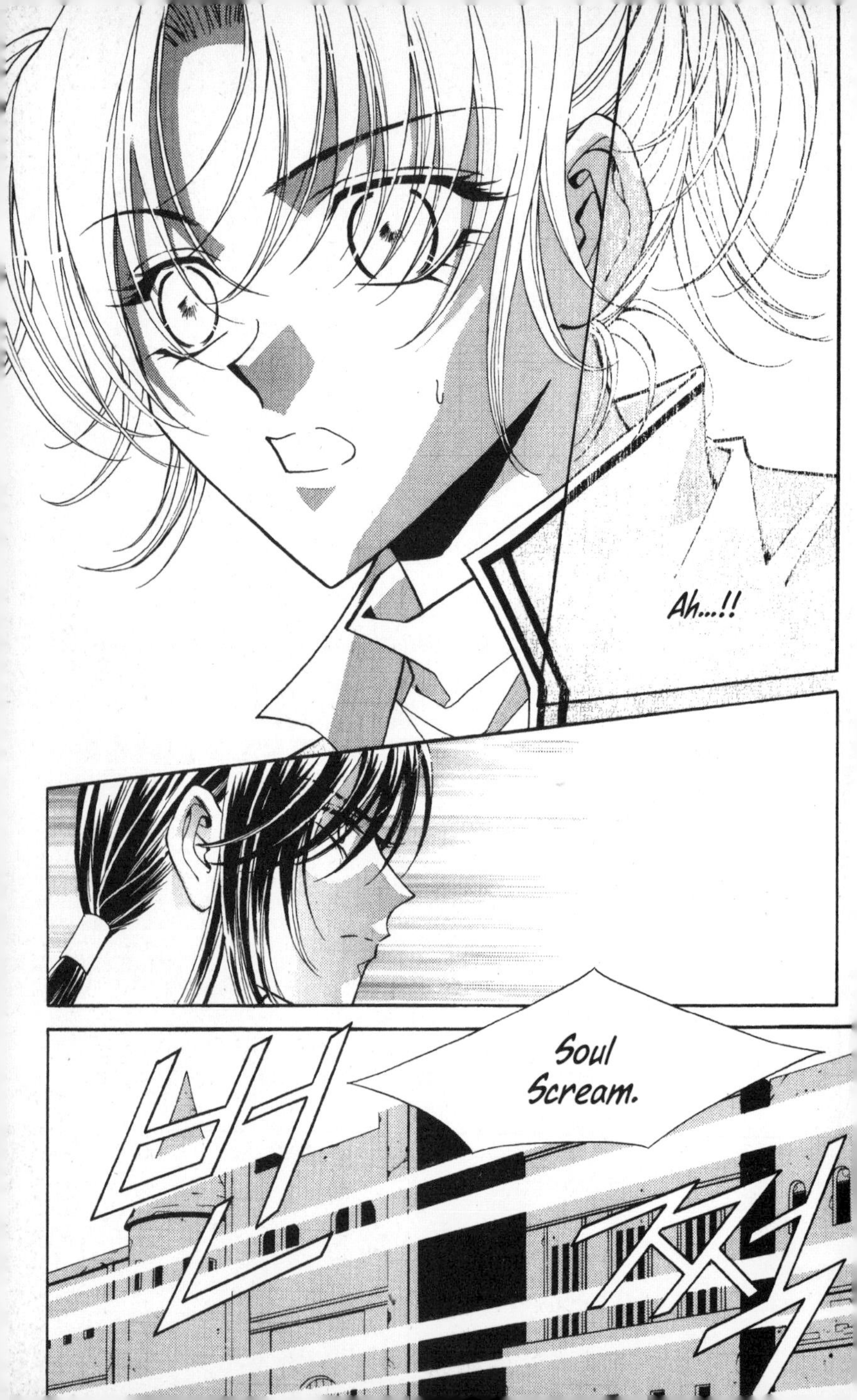
Ah...!!
Soul Scream.

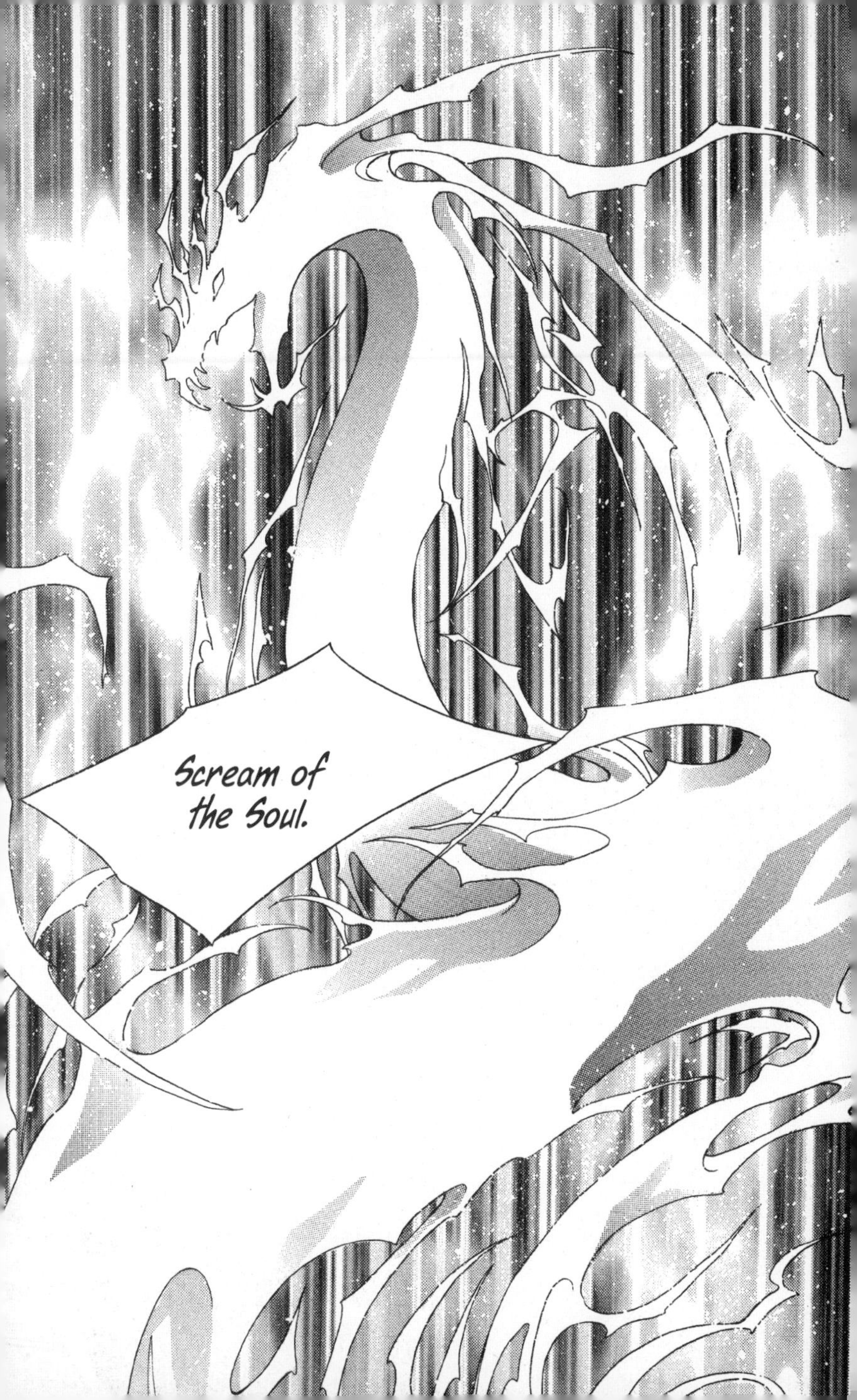
Scream of the Soul.

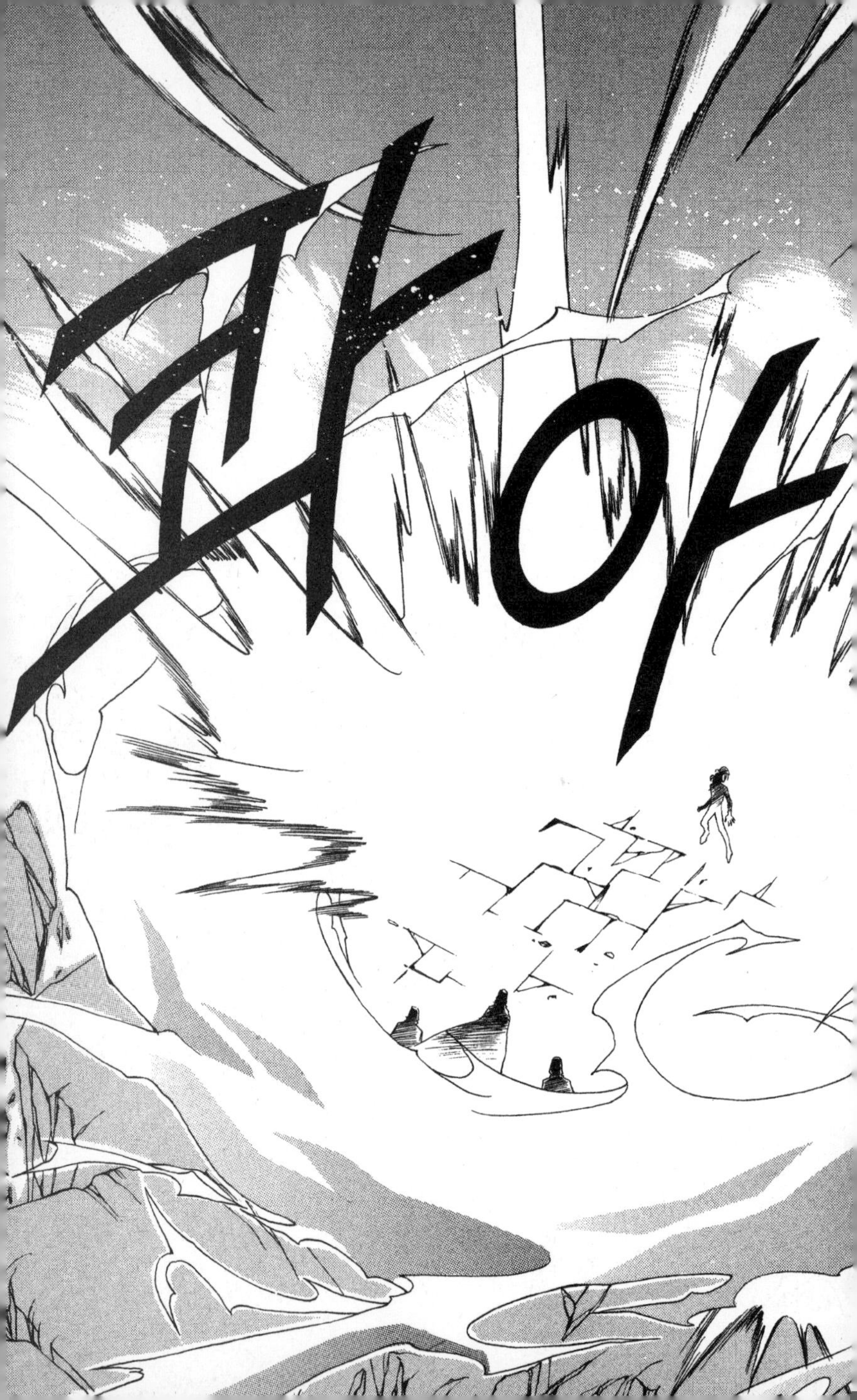
콰아

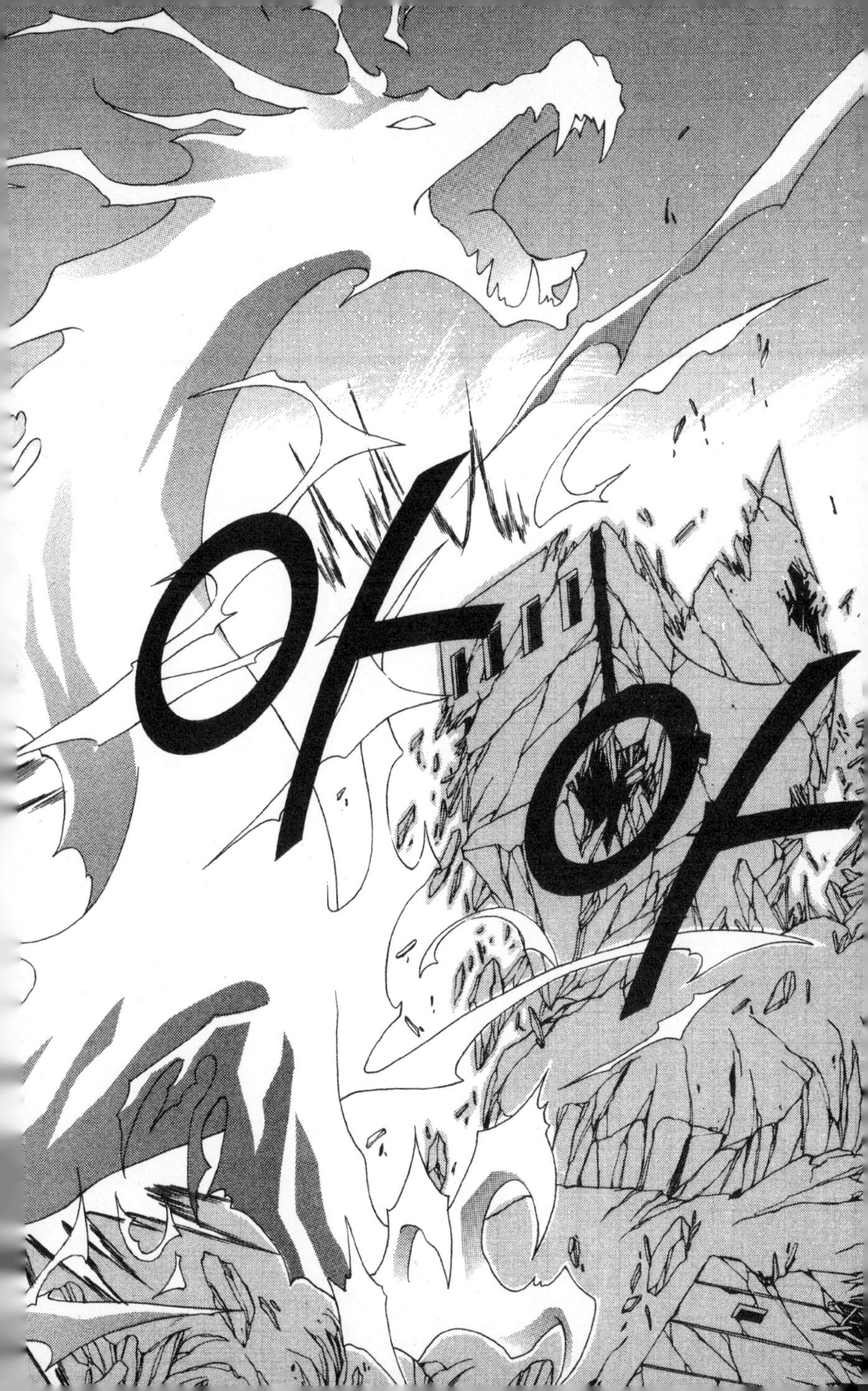

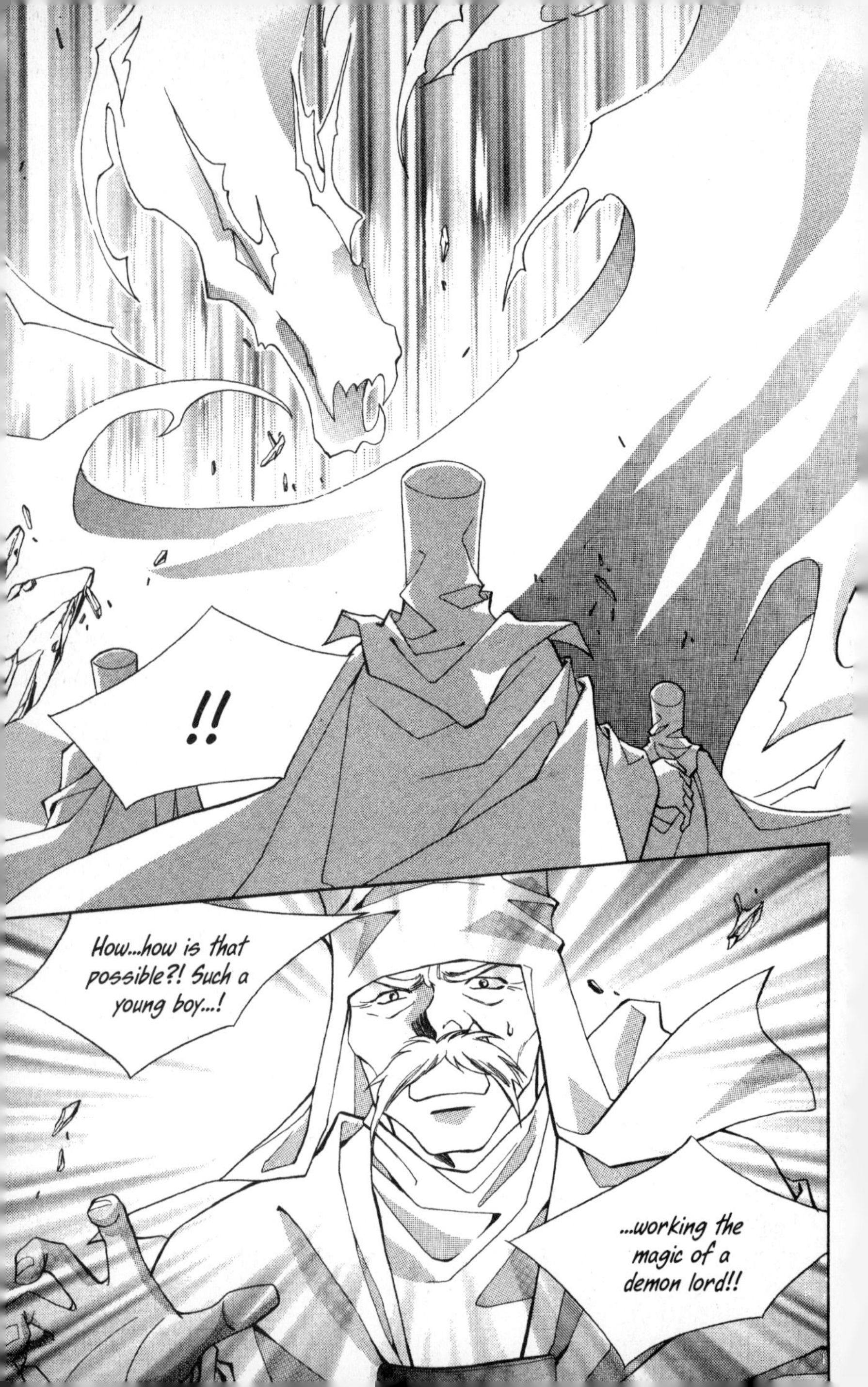
!!
How...how is that possible?! Such a young boy...!
...working the magic of a demon lord!!

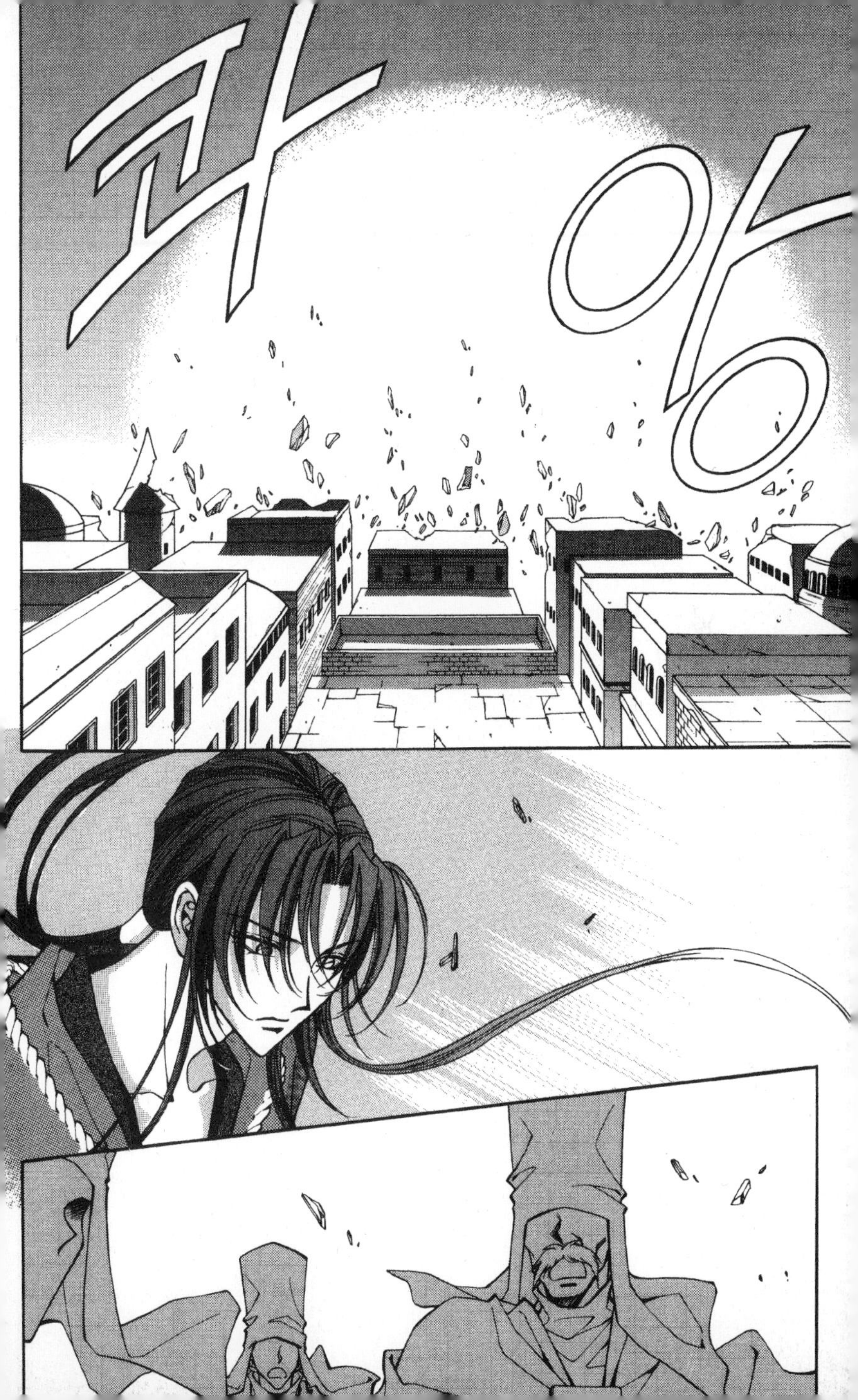
콰앙

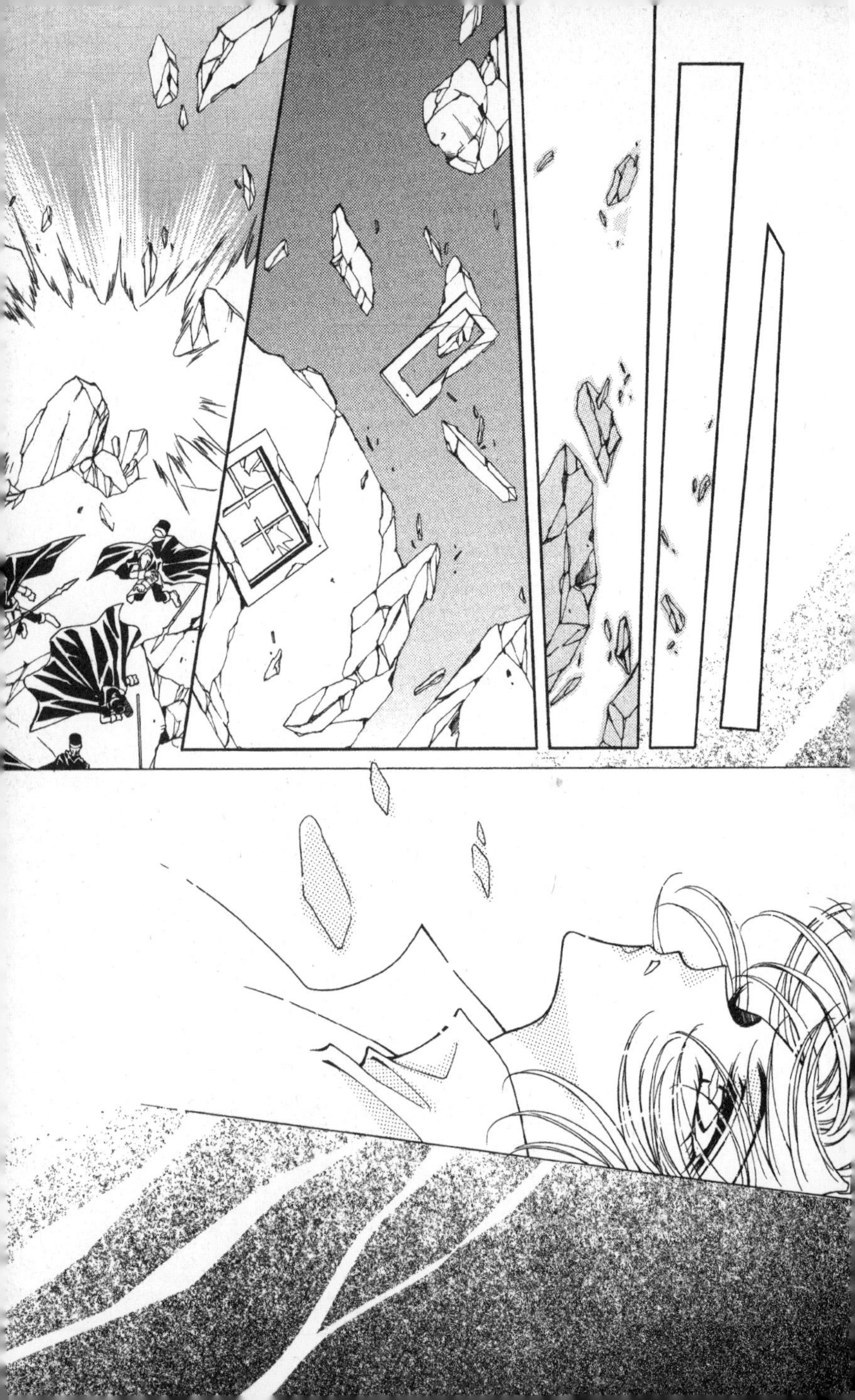

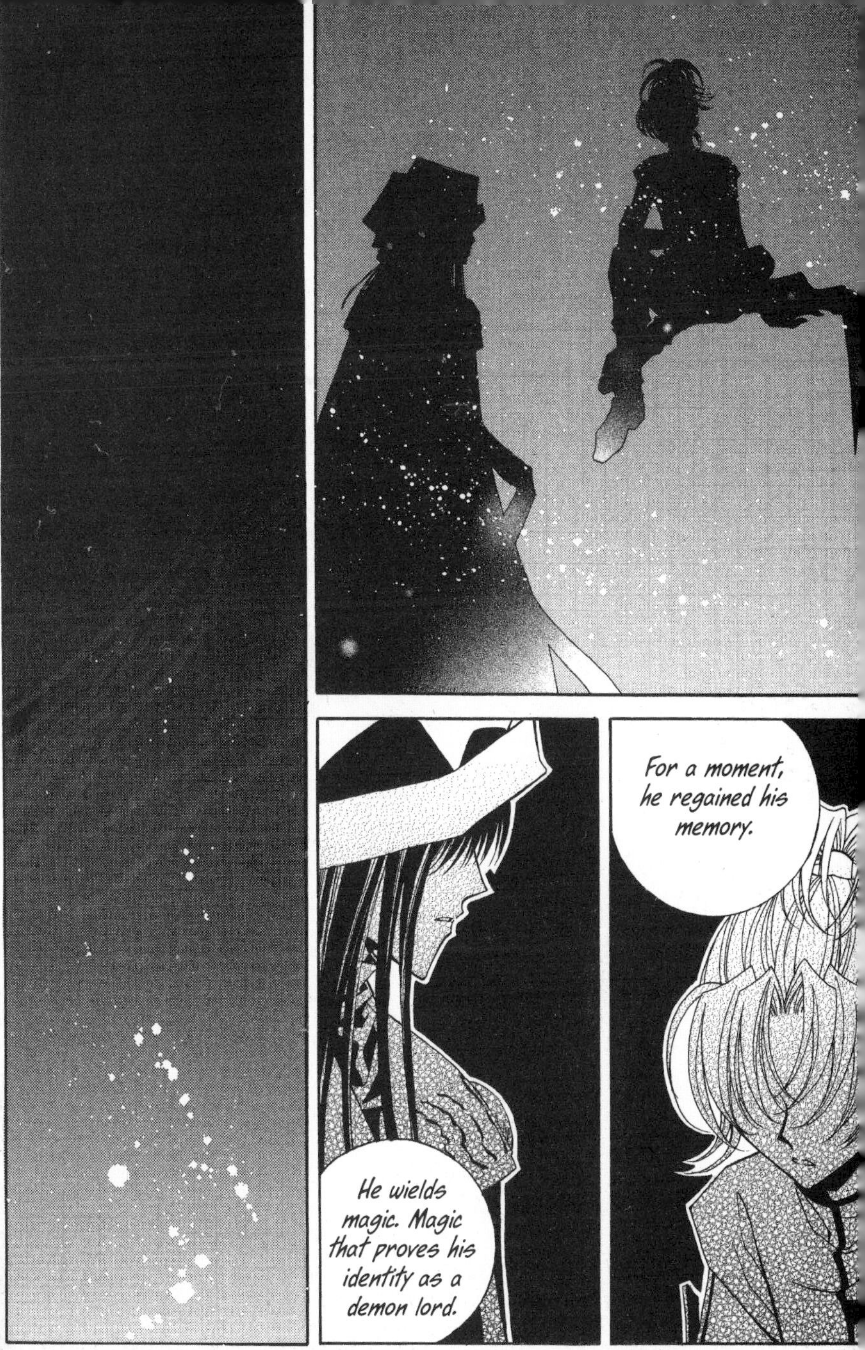
He wields magic. Magic that proves his identity as a demon lord.
For a moment, he regained his memory.

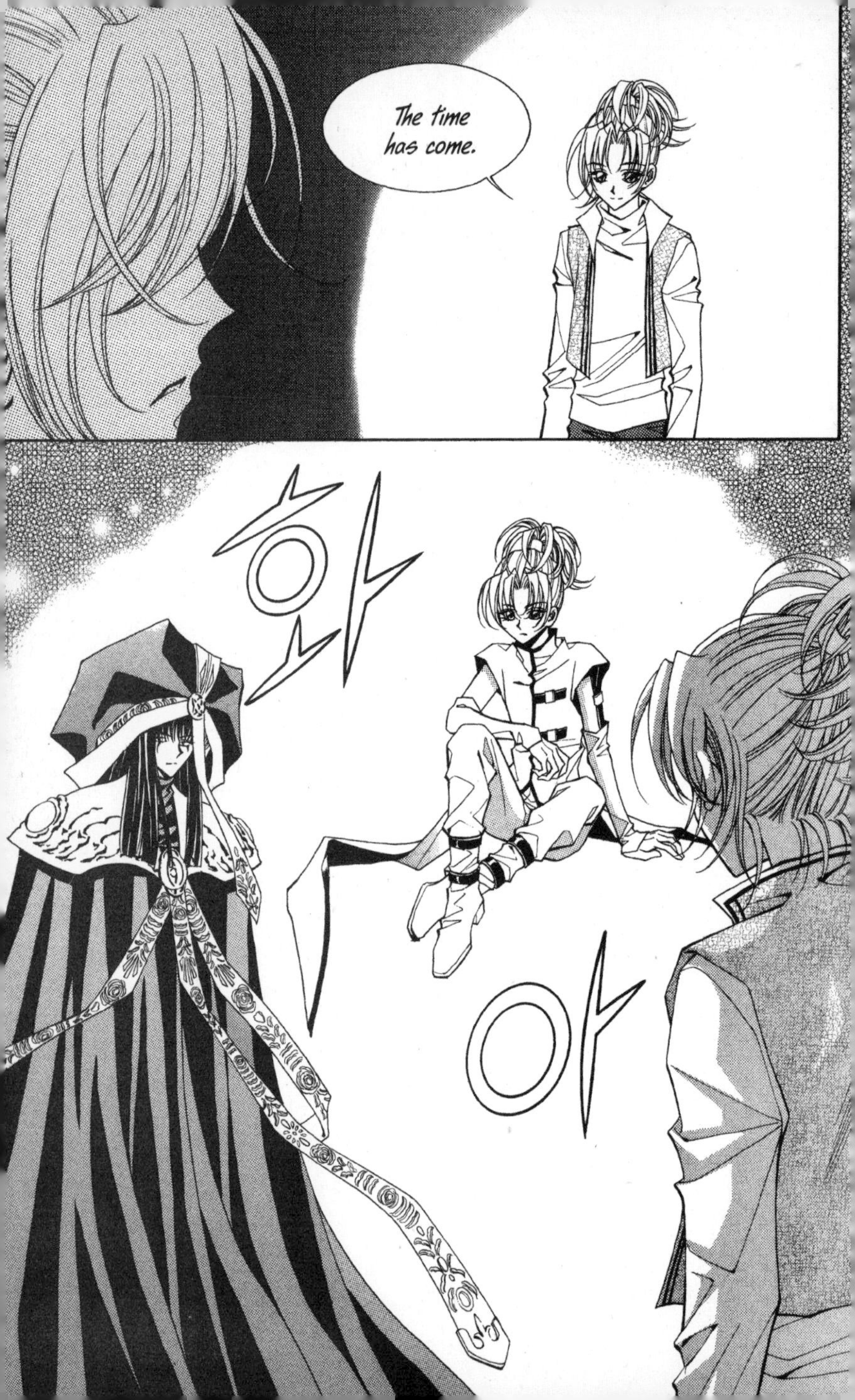
The time has come.

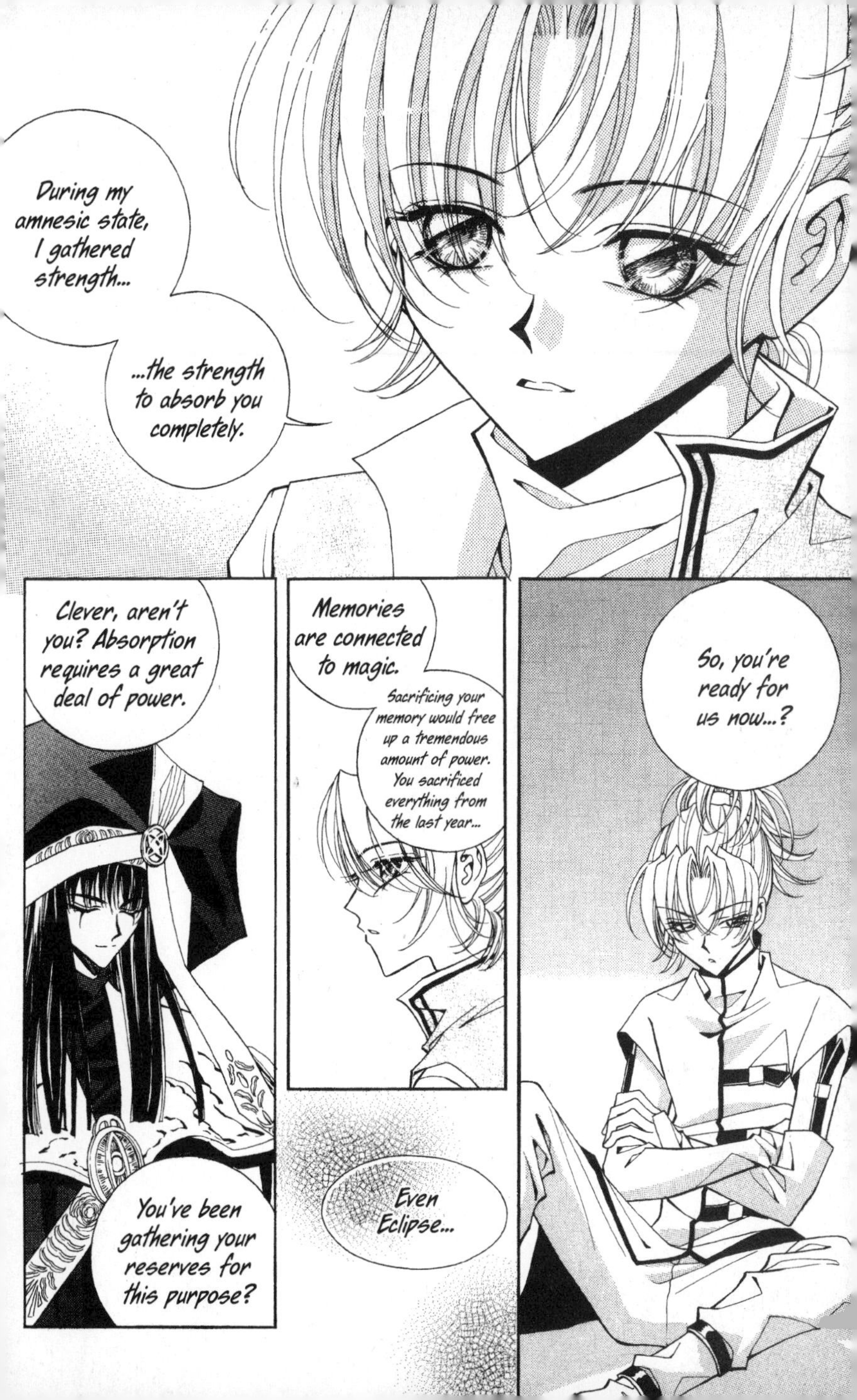
During my amnesic state, I gathered strength...
...the strength to absorb you completely.
Clever, aren't you? Absorption requires a great deal of power.
You've been gathering your reserves for this purpose?
Memories are connected to magic.
Sacrificing your memory would free up a tremendous amount of power. You sacrificed everything from the last year...
Even Eclipse...
So, you're ready for us now...?

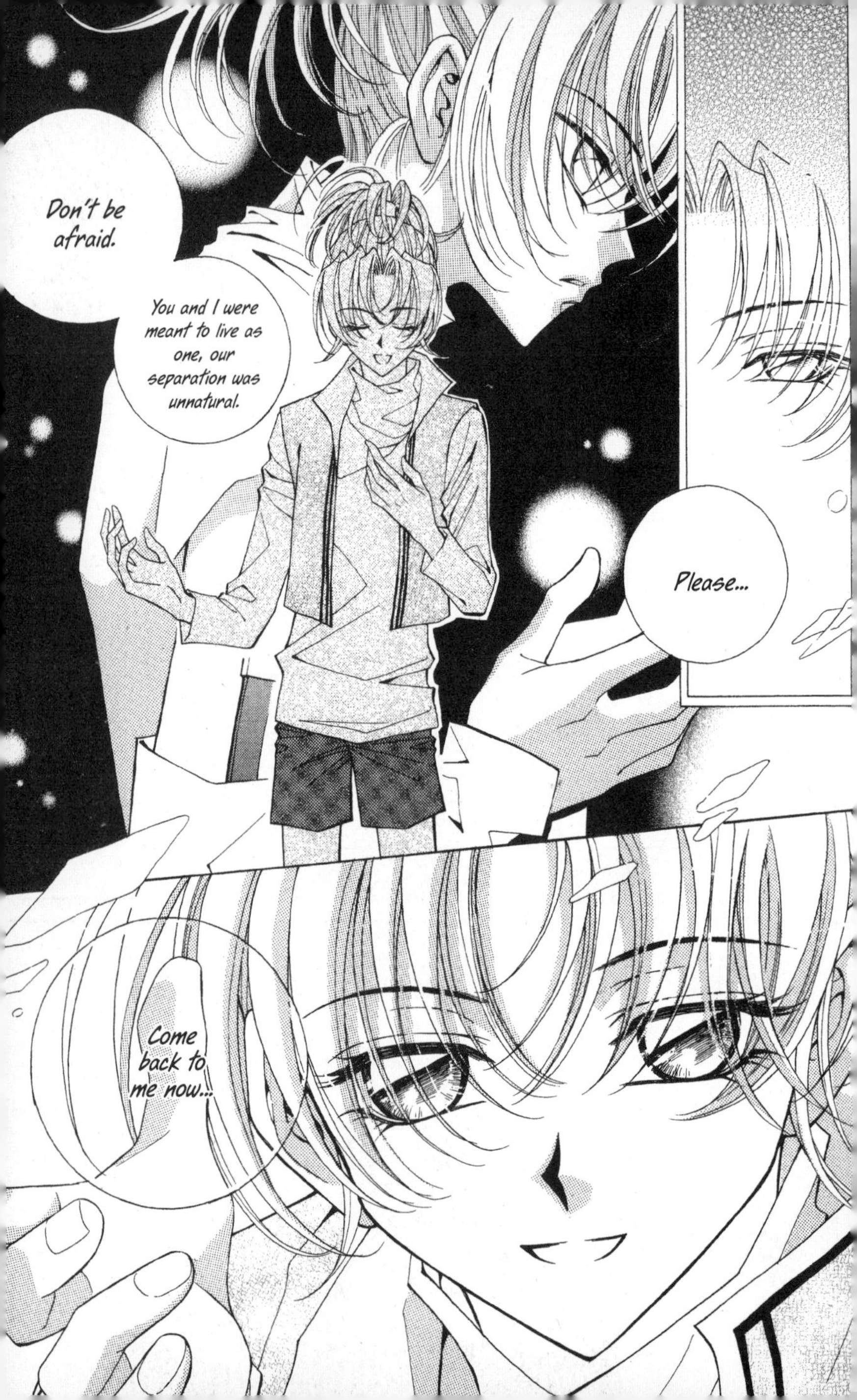
Don't be afraid.
You and I were meant to live as one, our separation was unnatural.
Please...
Come back to me now...

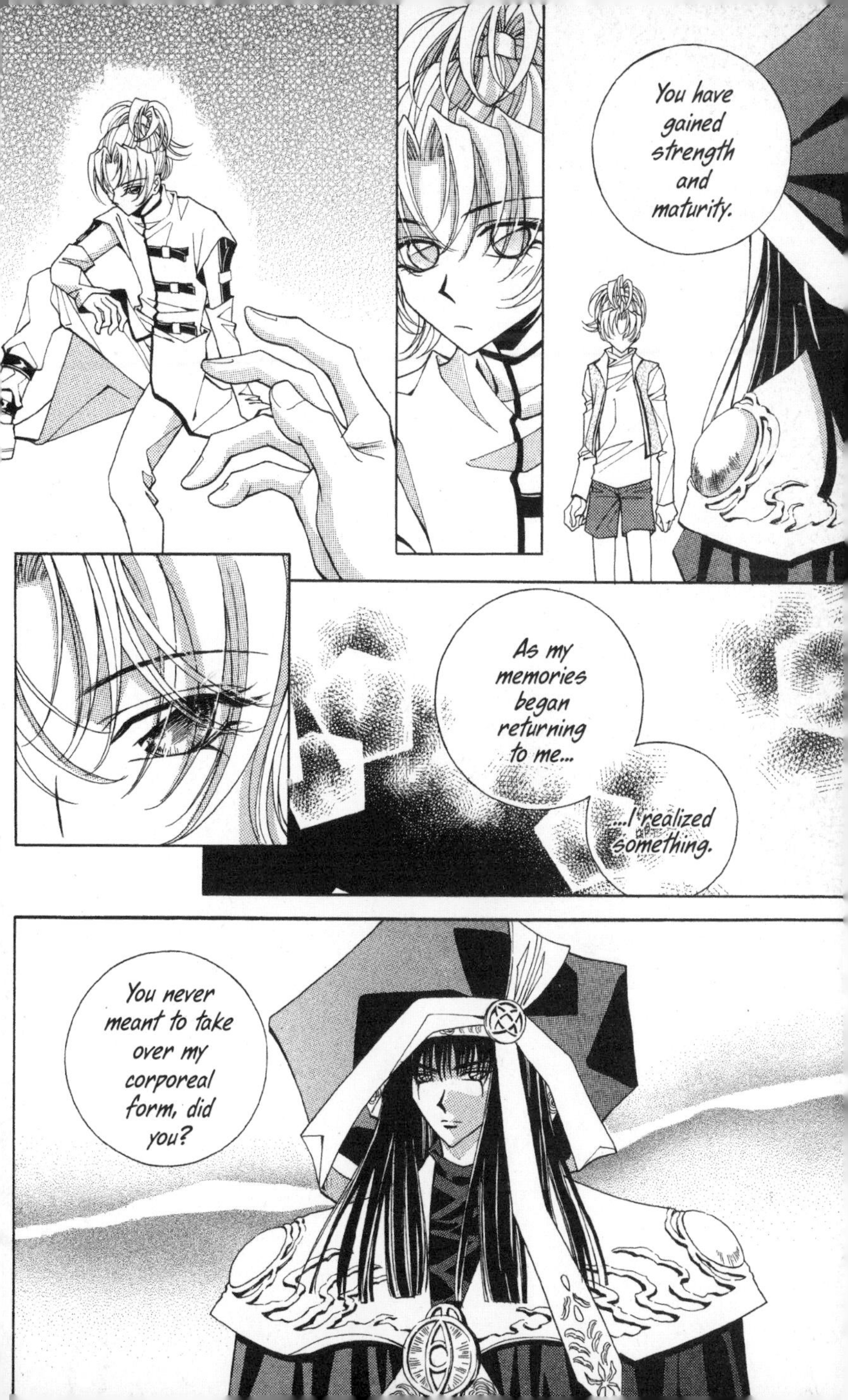
You have gained strength and maturity.
As my memories began returning to me...
...I realized something.
You never meant to take over my corporeal form, did you?

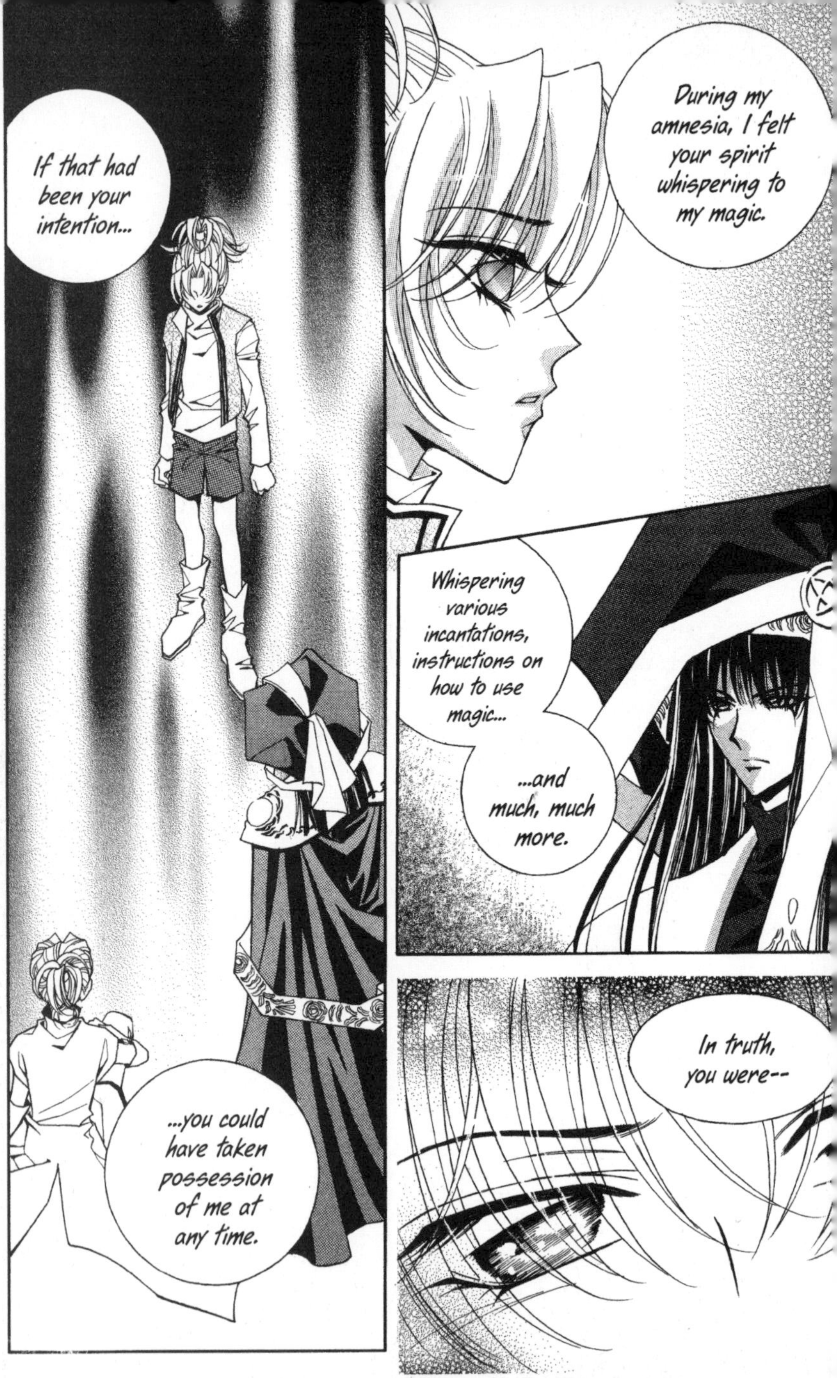
If that had been your intention...
...you could have taken possession of me at any time.
During my amnesia, I felt your spirit whispering to my magic.
Whispering various incantations, instructions on how to use magic...
...and much, much more.
In truth, you were--

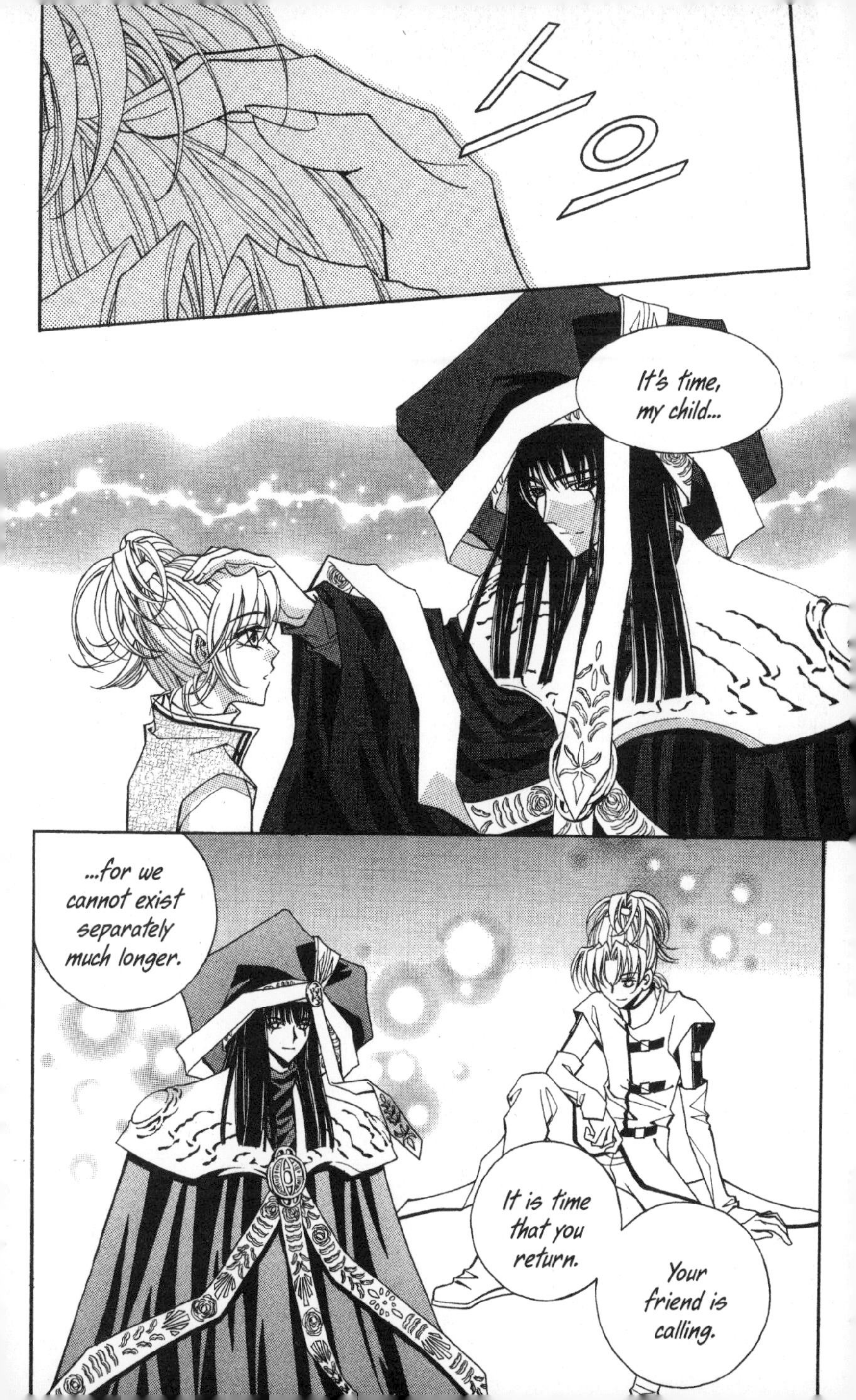
It's time, my child...
...for we cannot exist separately much longer.
It is time that you return.
Your friend is calling.

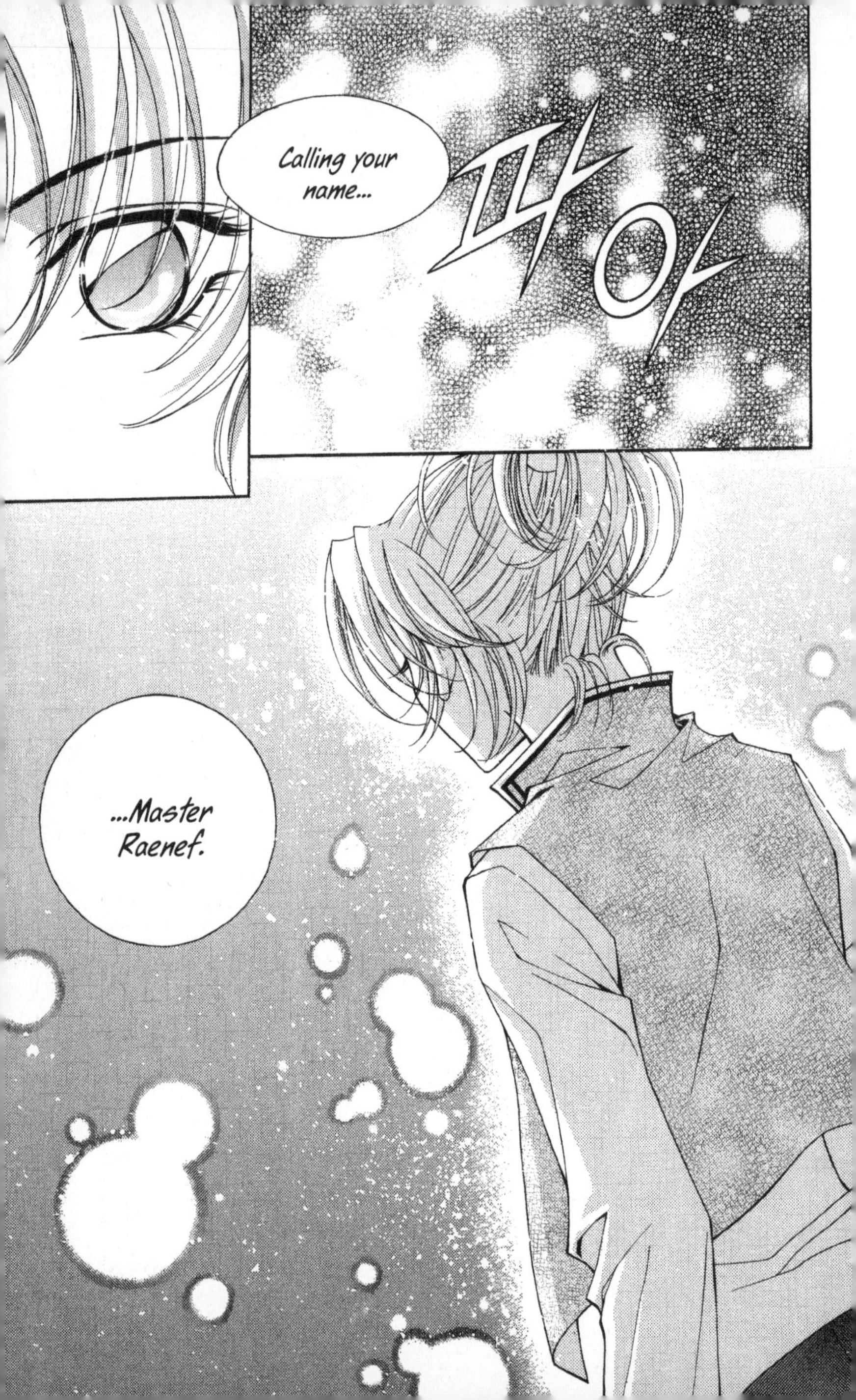
Calling your name...
...Master Raenef.

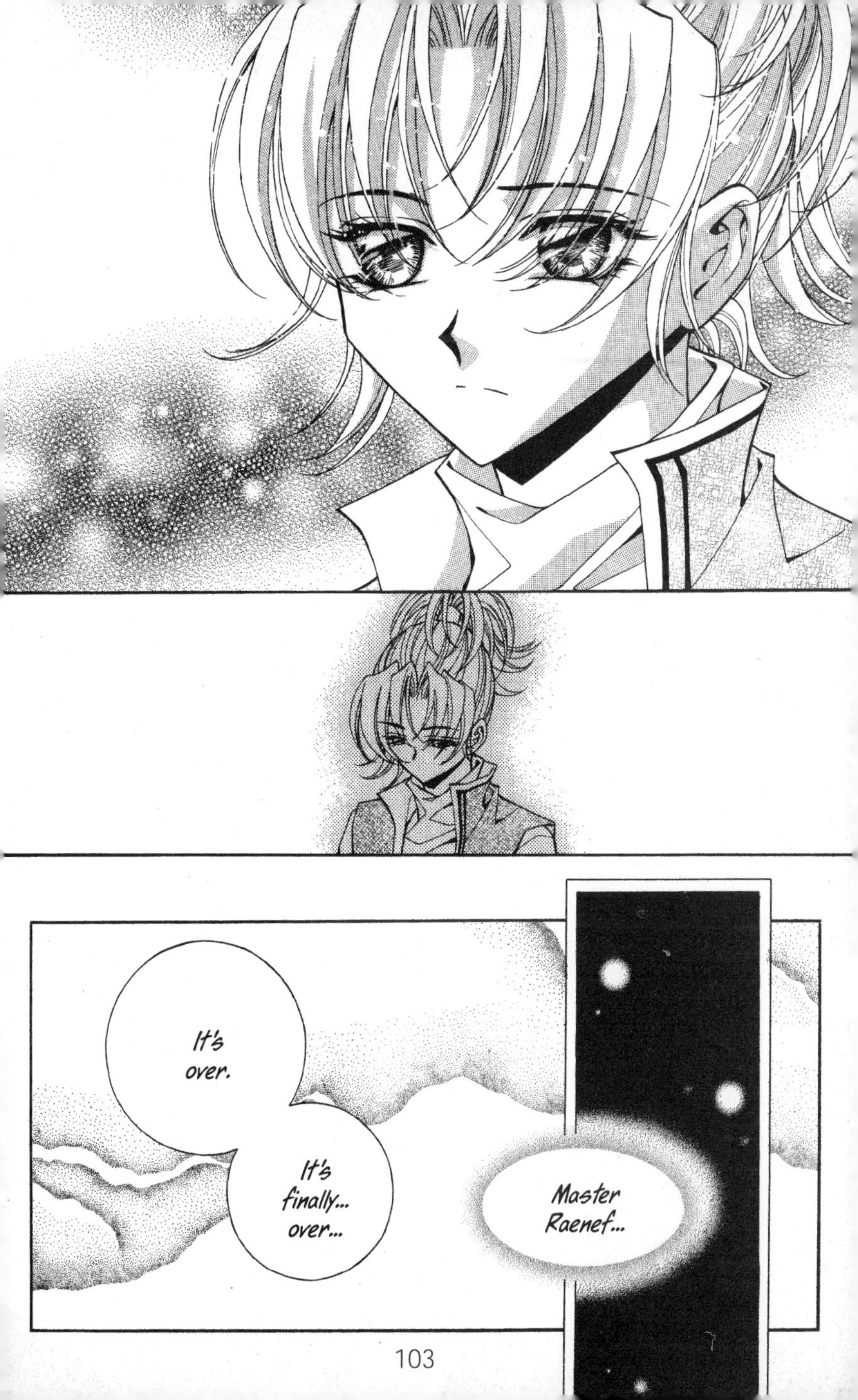
It's over.
It's finally... over...
Master Raenef...

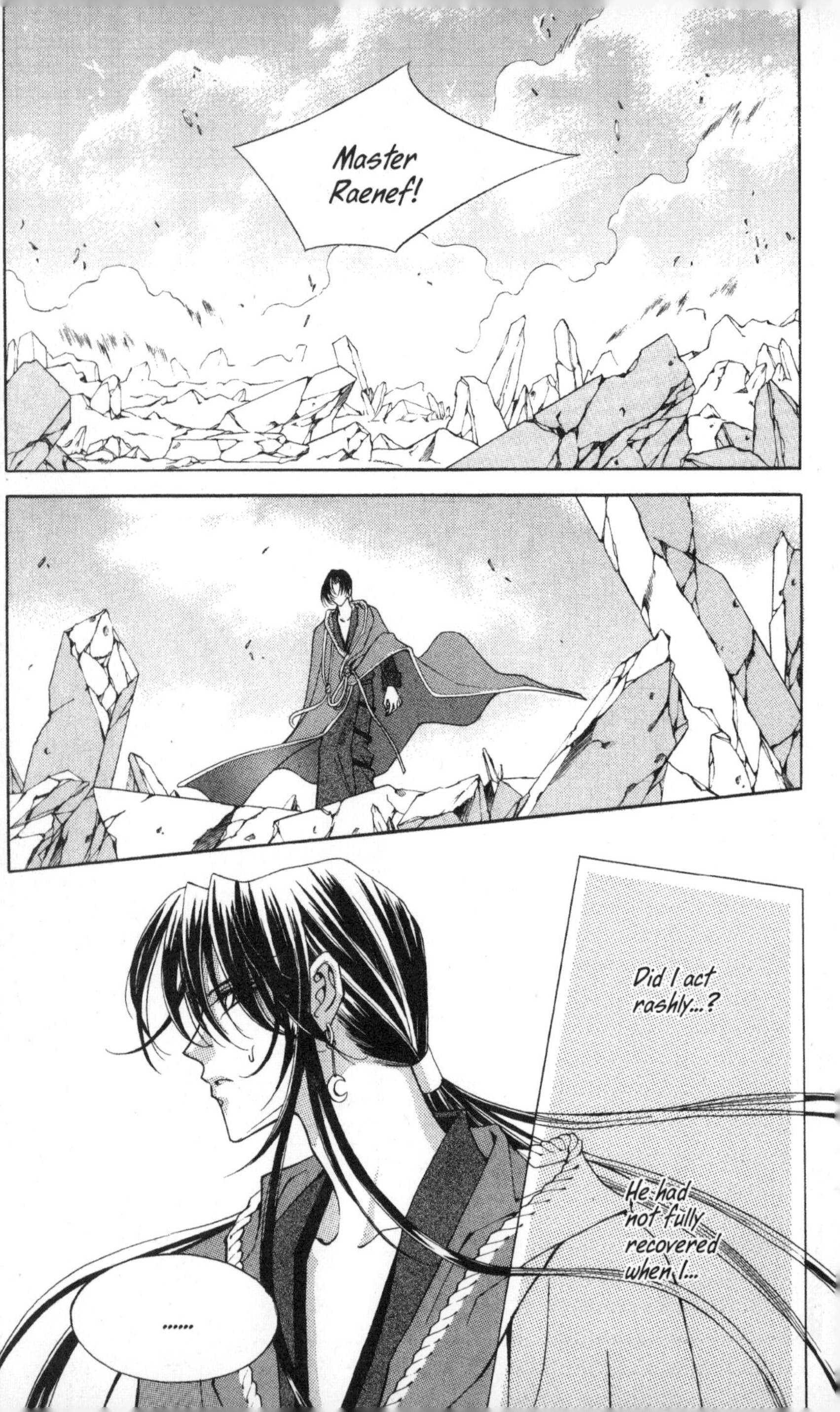
Master Raenef!
Did I act rashly...?
He had not fully recovered when I...
......

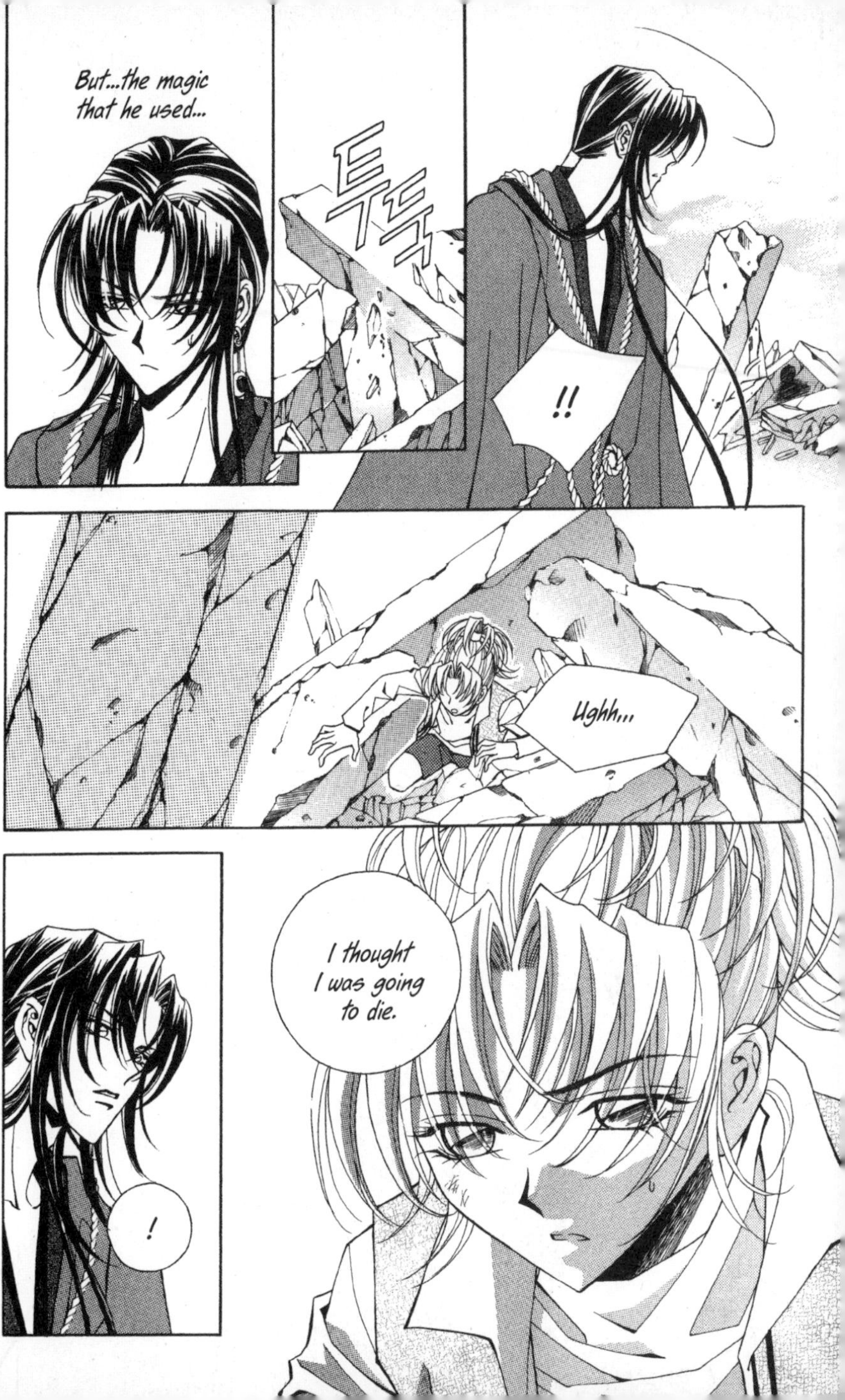
But...the magic that he used...
투득
!!
Ughh...
!
I thought I was going to die.

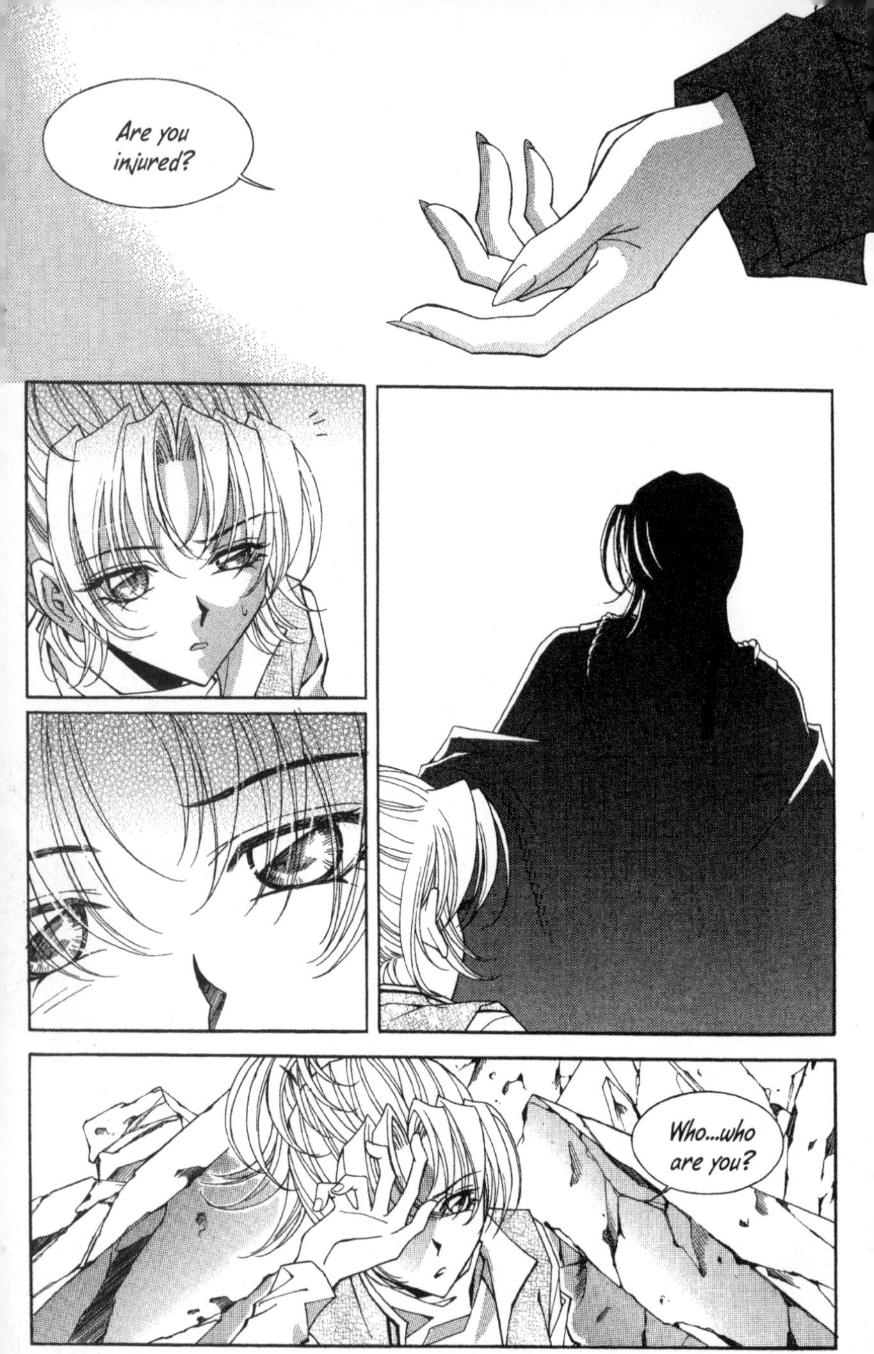
Are you injured?
Who...who are you?

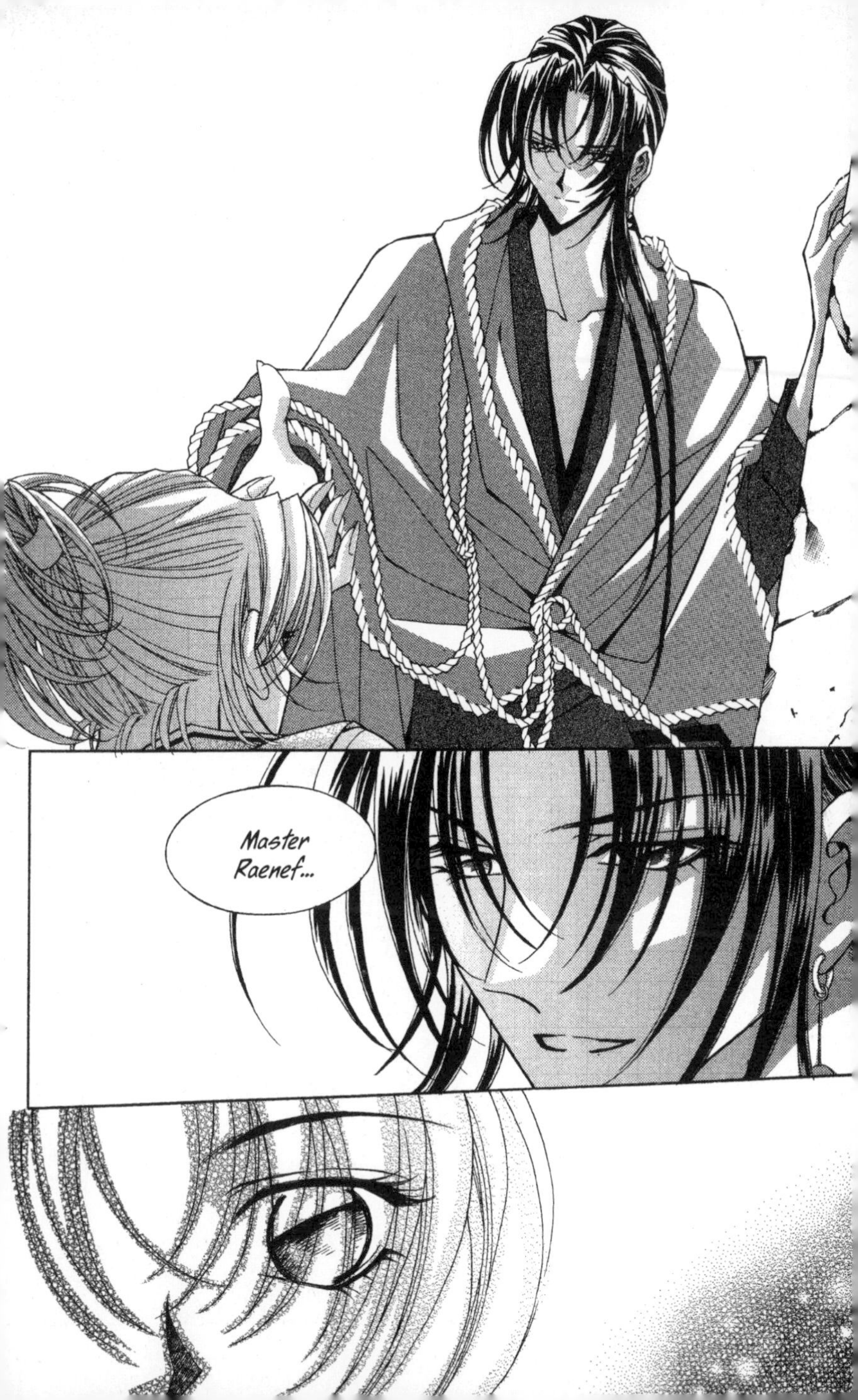
Master Raenef...

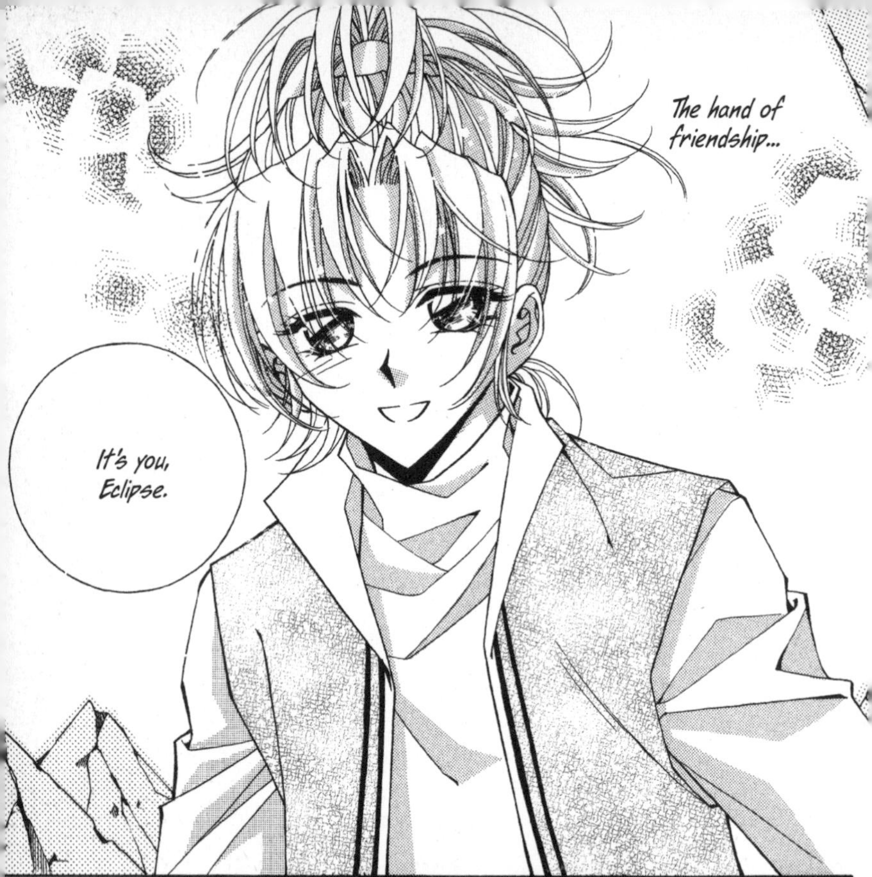
The hand of friendship...
It's you, Eclipse.
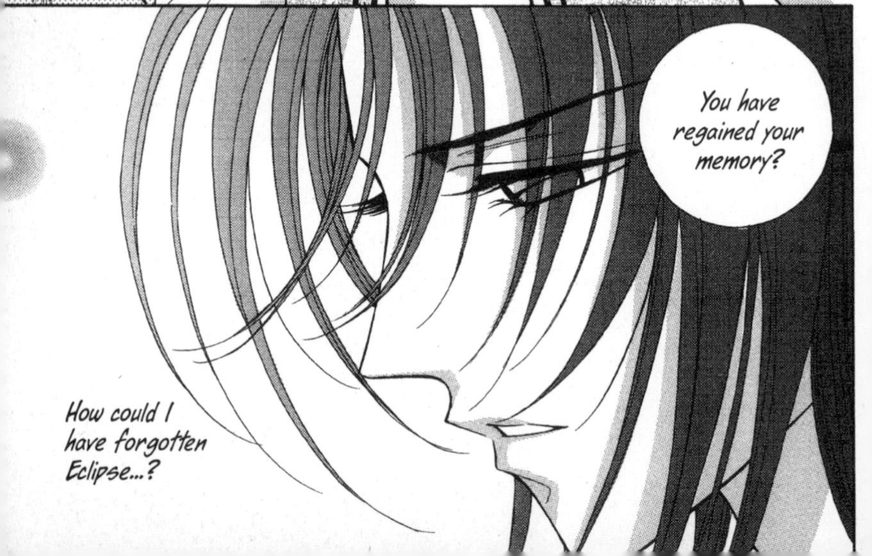
You have regained your memory?
How could I have forgotten Eclipse...?

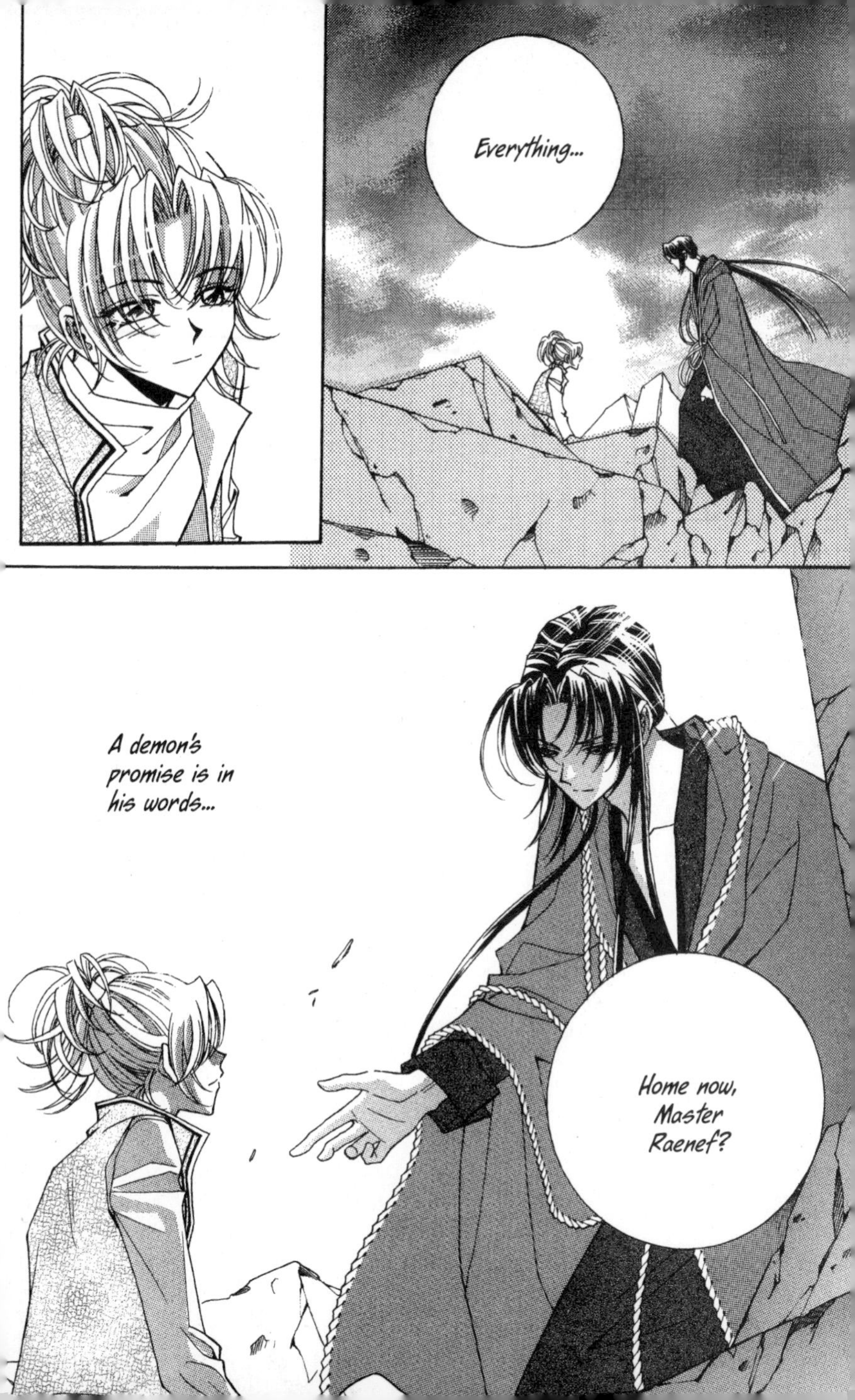
Everything...
A demon's promise is in his words...
Home now, Master Raenef?

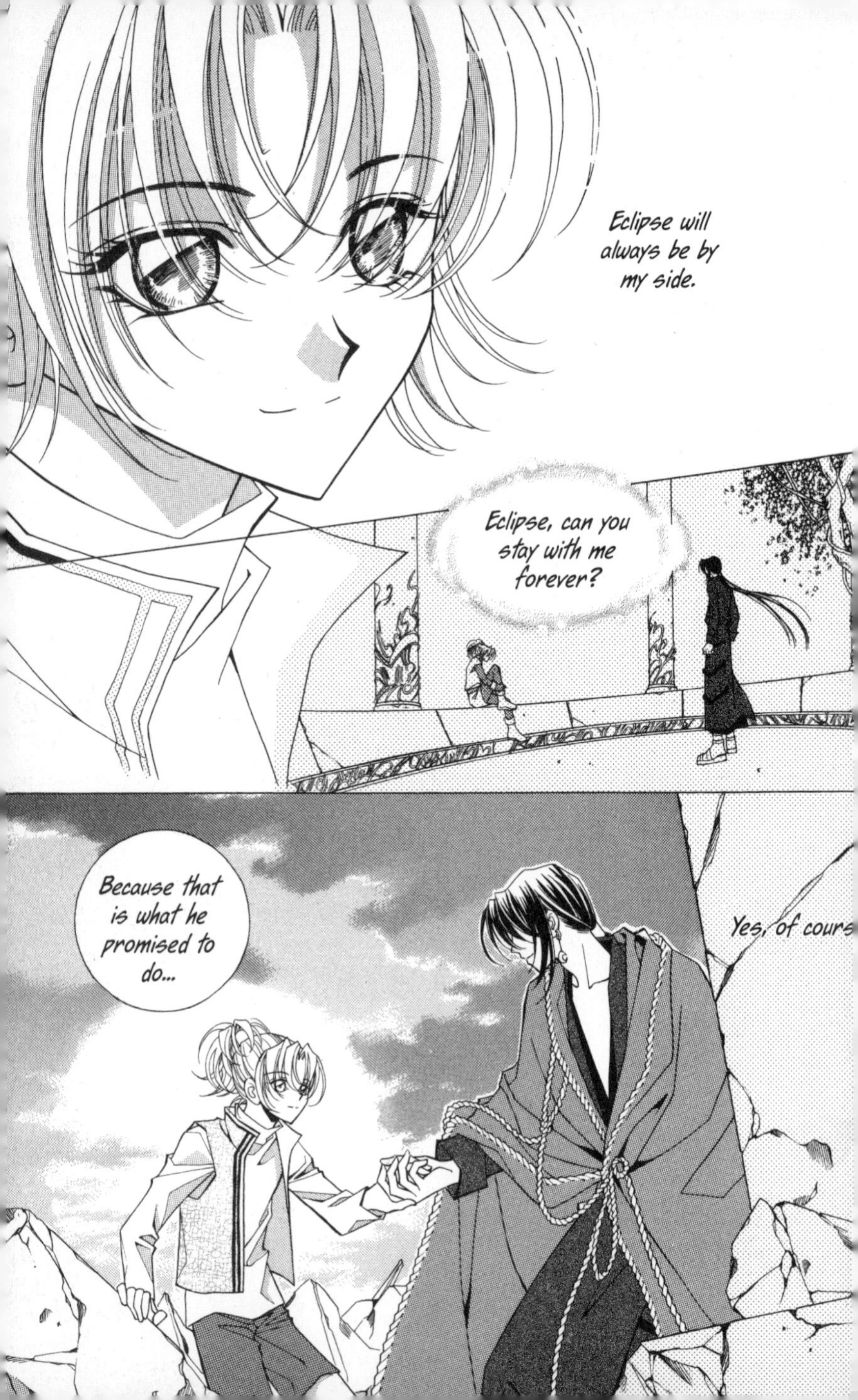
Eclipse will always be by my side.
Eclipse, can you stay with me forever?
Yes, of cours
Because that is what he promised to do...

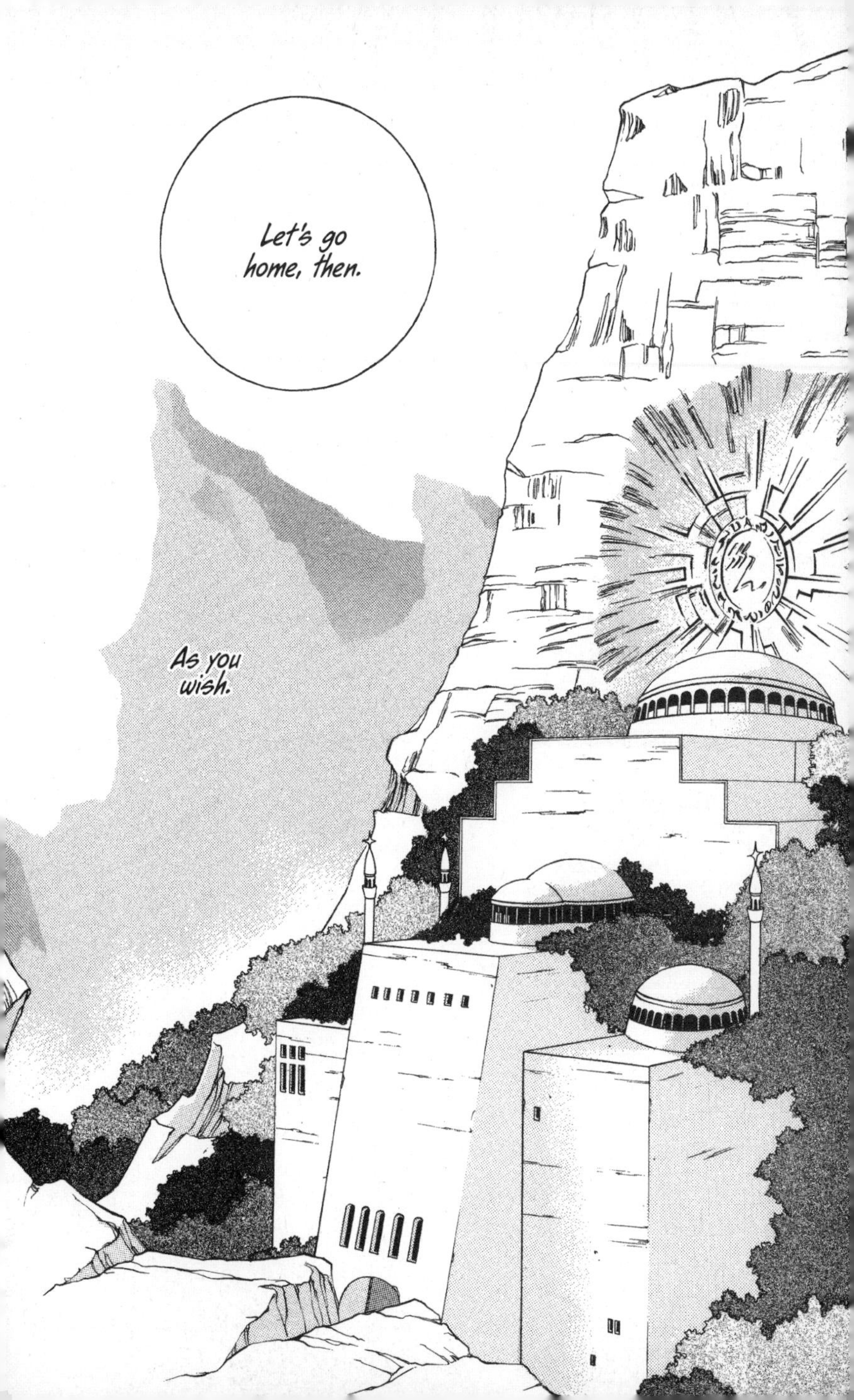
Let's go home, then.
As you wish.

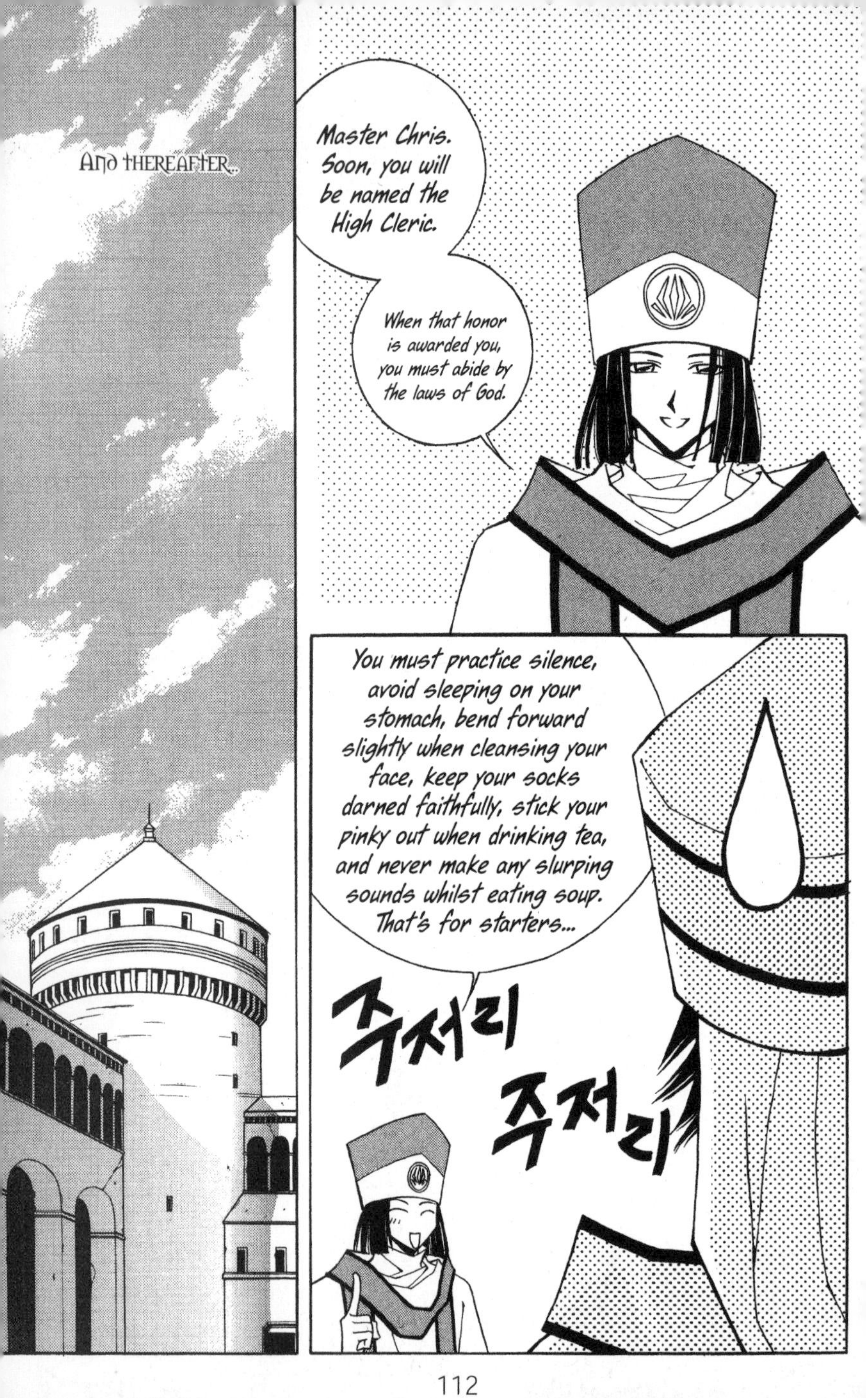
And thereafter...
Master Chris. Soon, you will be named the High Cleric.
When that honor is awarded you, you must abide by the laws of God.
You must practice silence, avoid sleeping on your stomach, bend forward slightly when cleansing your face, keep your socks darned faithfully, stick your pinky out when drinking tea, and never make any slurping sounds whilst eating soup. That's for starters...
주저리 주저리

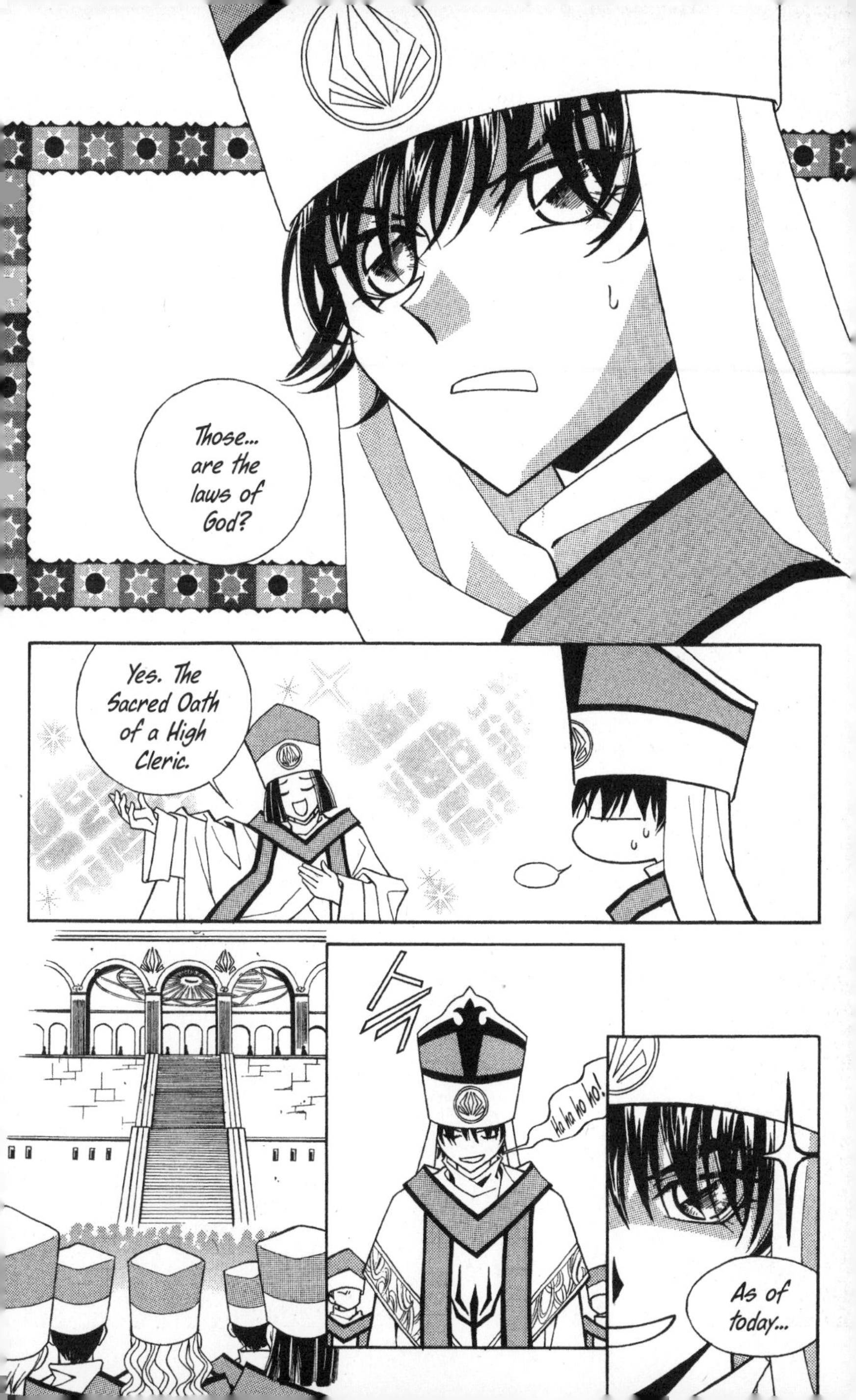
Those... are the laws of God?
Yes. The Sacred Oath of a High Cleric.
Ha ha ho ho!
As of today...

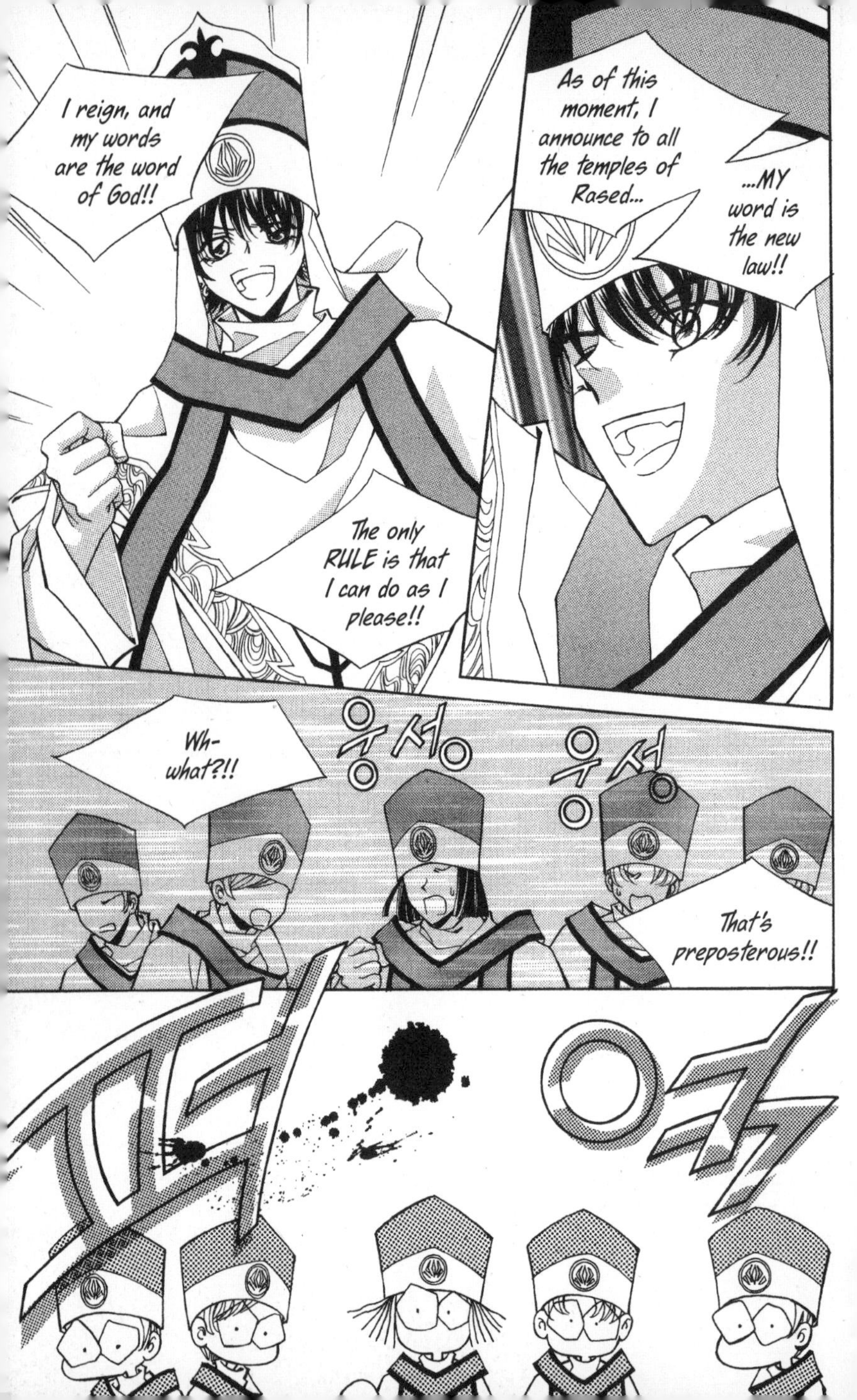
I reign, and my words are the word of God!!
The only RULE is that I can do as I please!!
As of this moment, I announce to all the temples of Rased...
...MY word is the new law!!
Wh- what?!!
웅성
웅성
That's preposterous!!

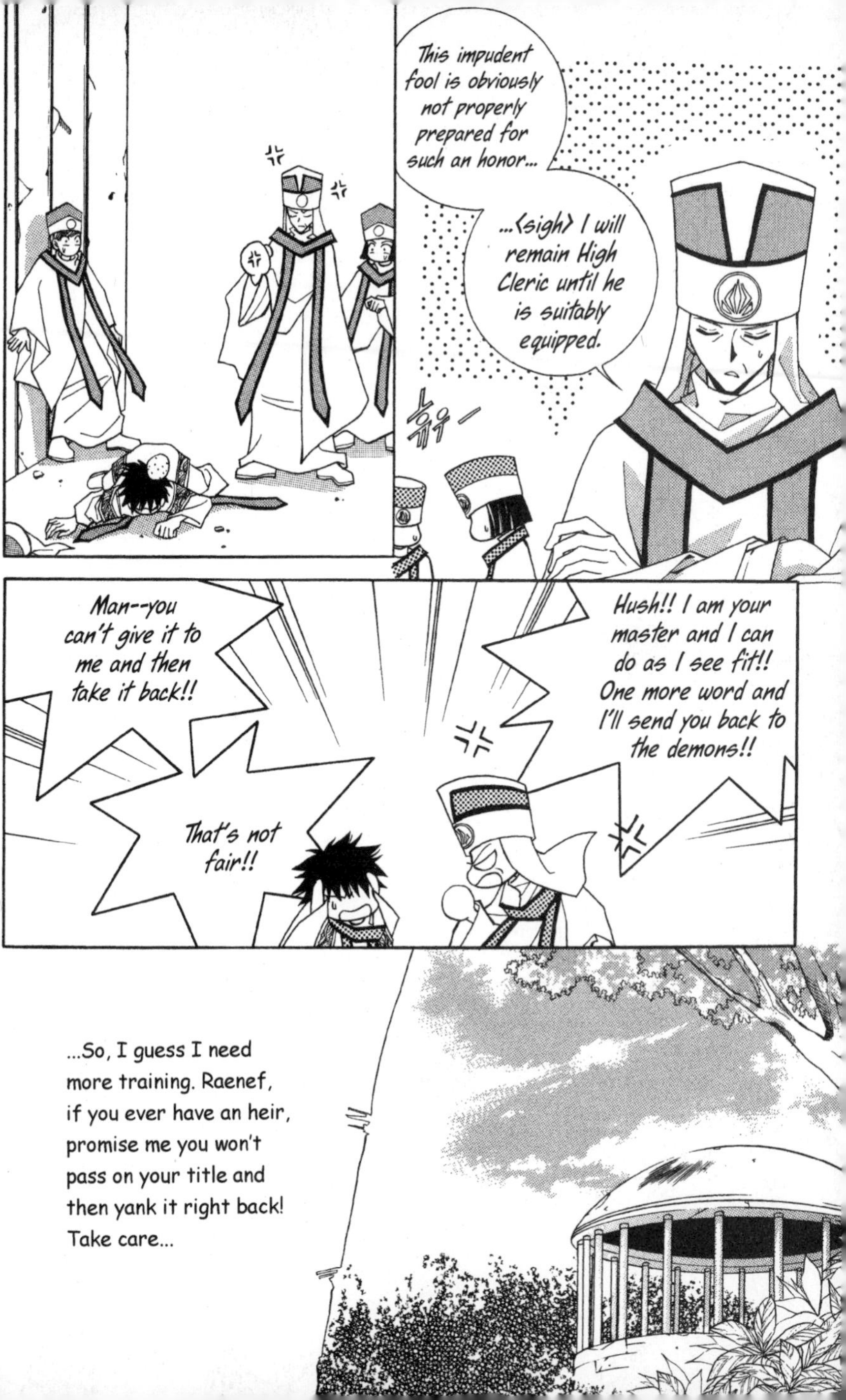
This impudent fool is obviously not properly prepared for such an honor...
...<sigh> I will remain High Cleric until he is suitably equipped.
Man--you can't give it to me and then take it back!!
That's not fair!!
Hush!! I am your master and I can do as I see fit!! One more word and I'll send you back to the demons!!
...So, I guess I need more training. Raenef, if you ever have an heir, promise me you won't pass on your title and then yank it right back! Take care...

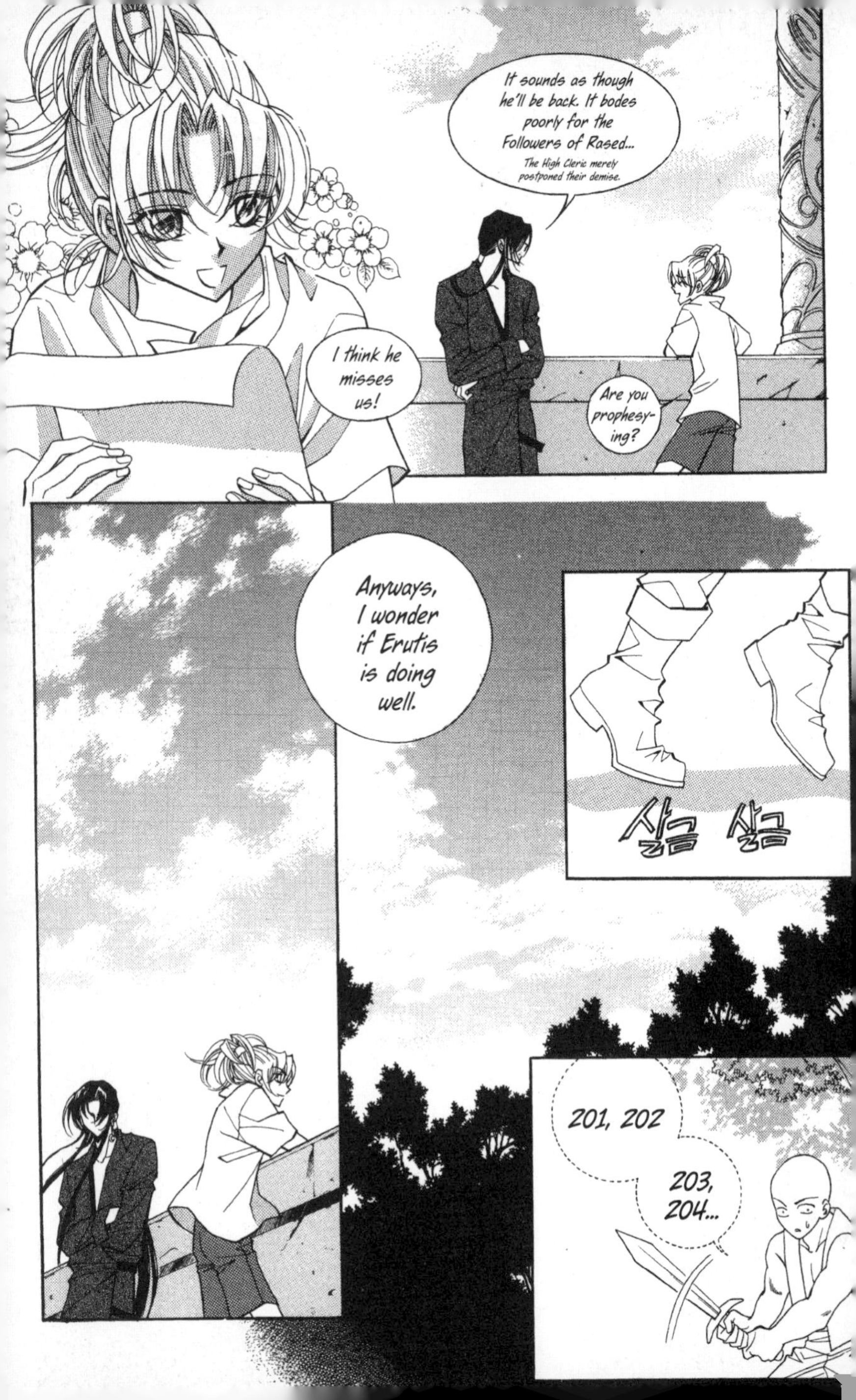
It sounds as though he'll be back. It bodes poorly for the Followers of Rased...
The High Cleric merely postponed their demise.
I think he misses us!
Are you prophesy-ing?
Anyways, I wonder if Erutis is doing well.
살금 살금
201, 202
203, 204...

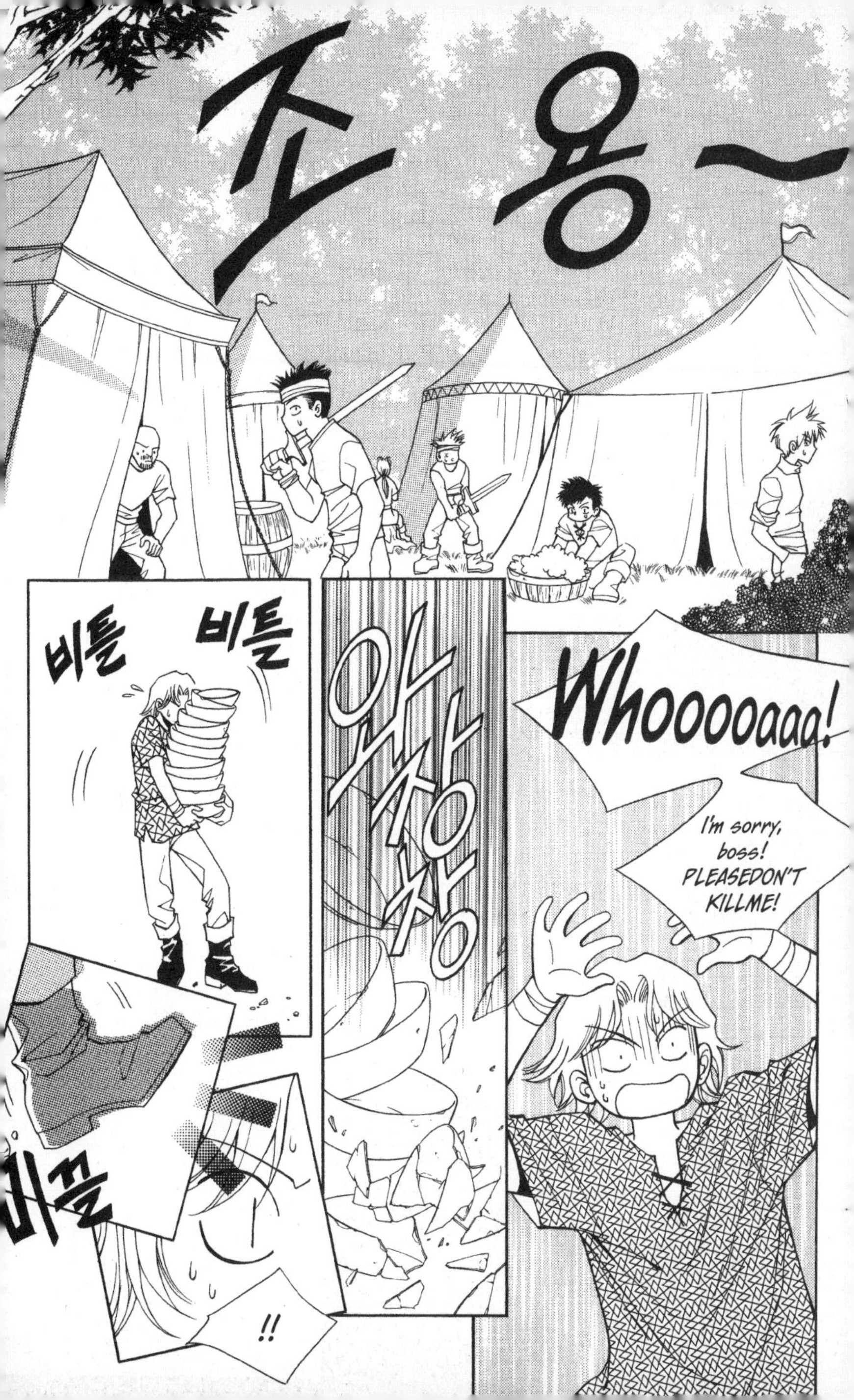
조용~
비틀 비틀
미끌
!!
와장창
Whoooaaa!
I'm sorry, boss! PLEASEDON'T KILLME!

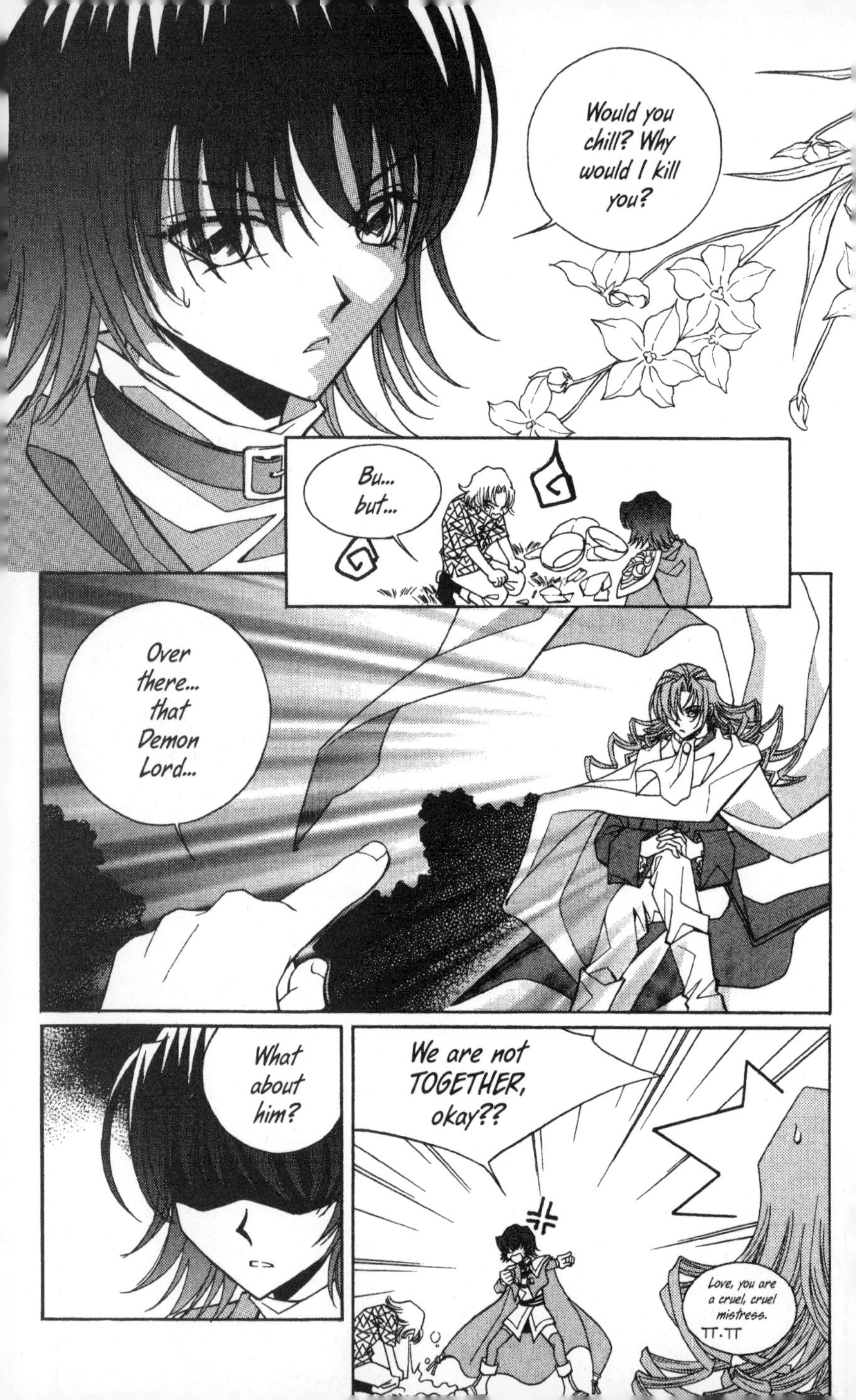
Would you chill? Why would I kill you?
Bu... but...
Over there... that Demon Lord...
What about him?
We are not TOGETHER, okay??
Love, you are a cruel, cruel mistress.
TT.TT

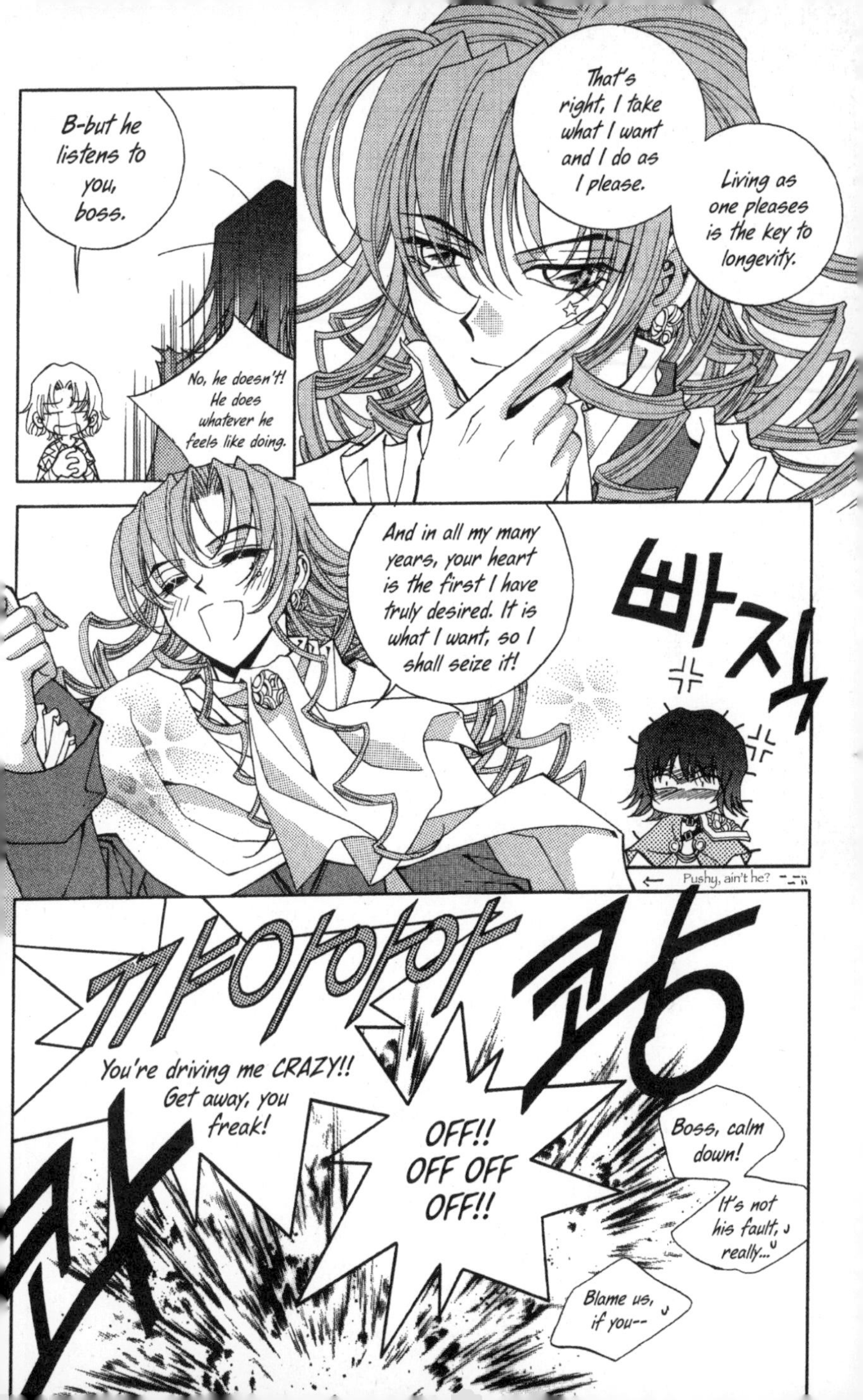
B-but he listens to you, boss.
No, he doesn't! He does whatever he feels like doing.
That's right, I take what I want and I do as I please.
Living as one pleases is the key to longevity.
And in all my many years, your heart is the first I have truly desired. It is what I want, so I shall seize it!
빠직
← Pushy, ain't he? -_-;;
You're driving me CRAZY!! Get away, you freak!
OFF!! OFF OFF OFF!!
Boss, calm down!
It's not his fault, really...
Blame us, if you--

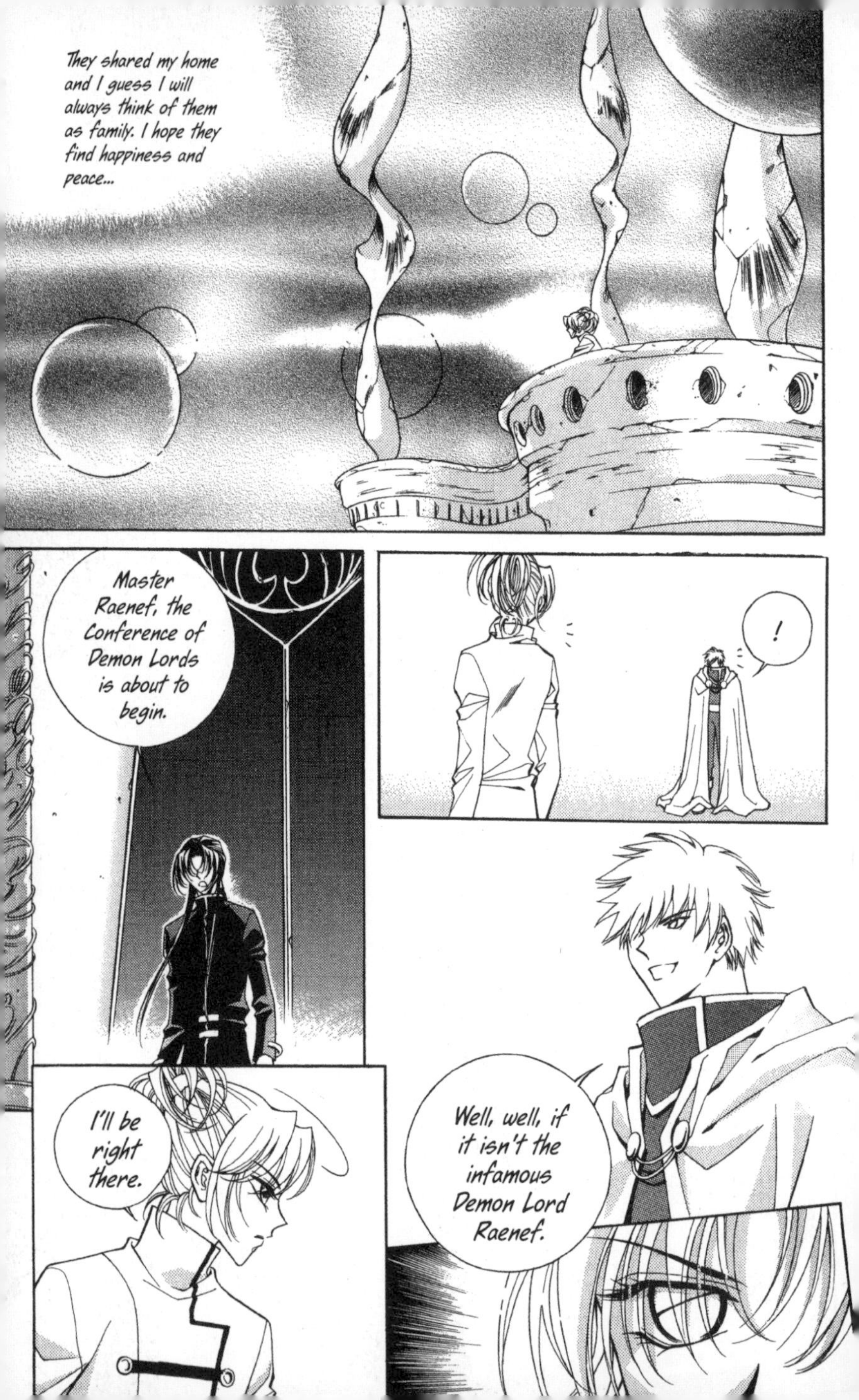
They shared my home and I guess I will always think of them as family. I hope they find happiness and peace...
Master Raenef, the Conference of Demon Lords is about to begin.
!
I'll be right there.
Well, well, if it isn't the infamous Demon Lord Raenef.

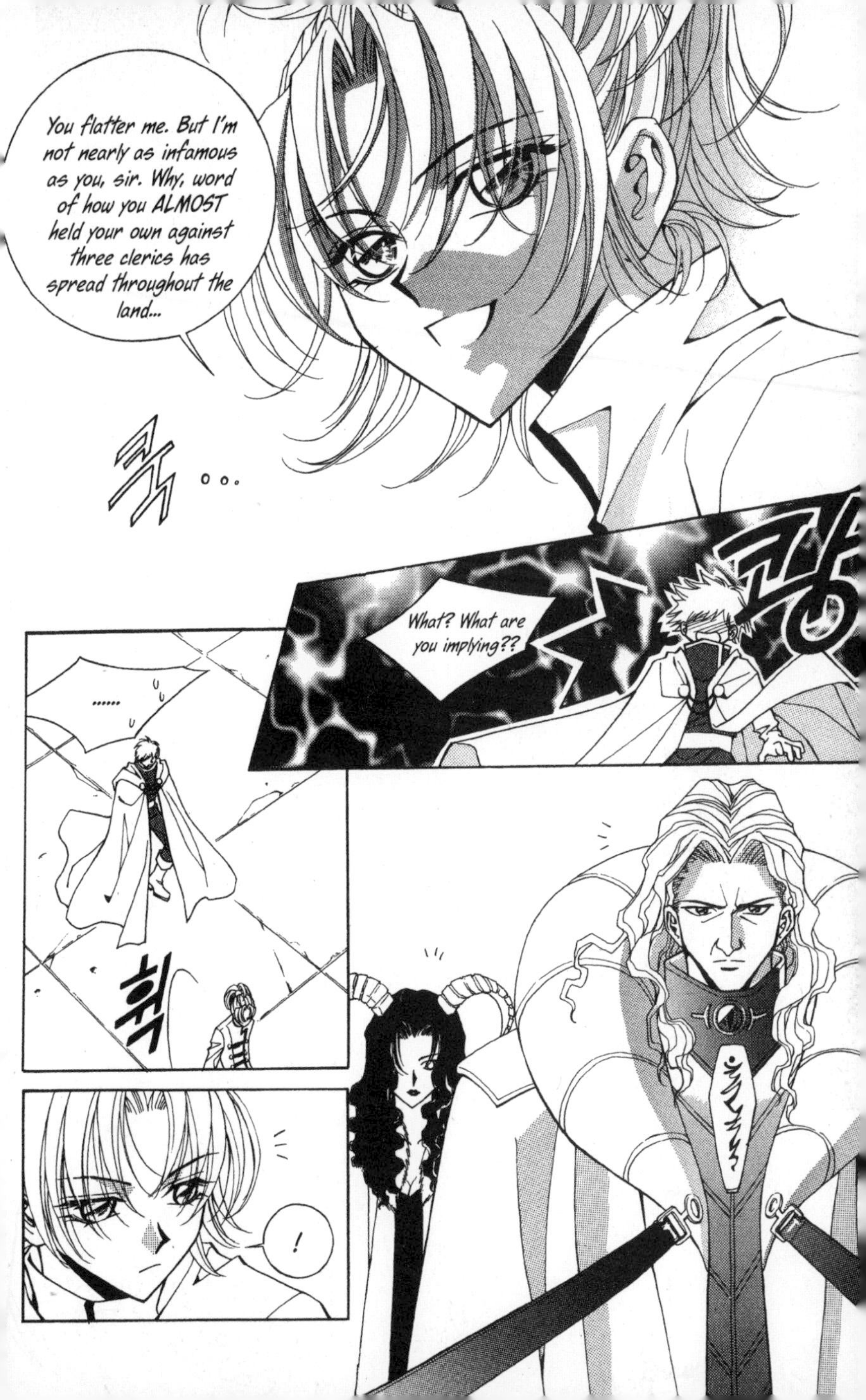

You flatter me. But I'm not nearly as infamous as you, sir. Why, word of how you ALMOST held your own against three clerics has spread throughout the land...
What? What are you implying??
......
!

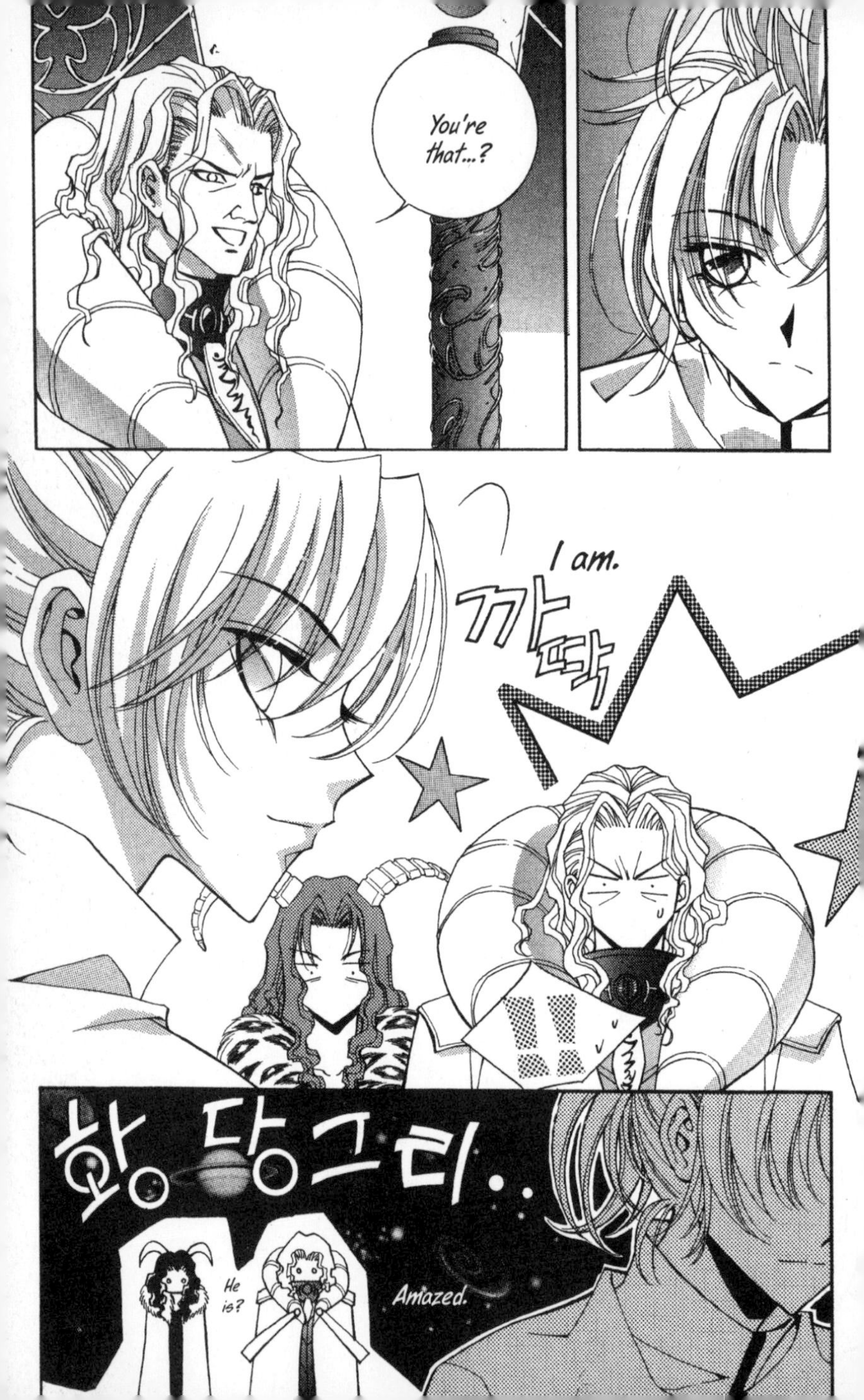
You're that...?
I am.
까딱
황당그리..
He is?
Amazed.

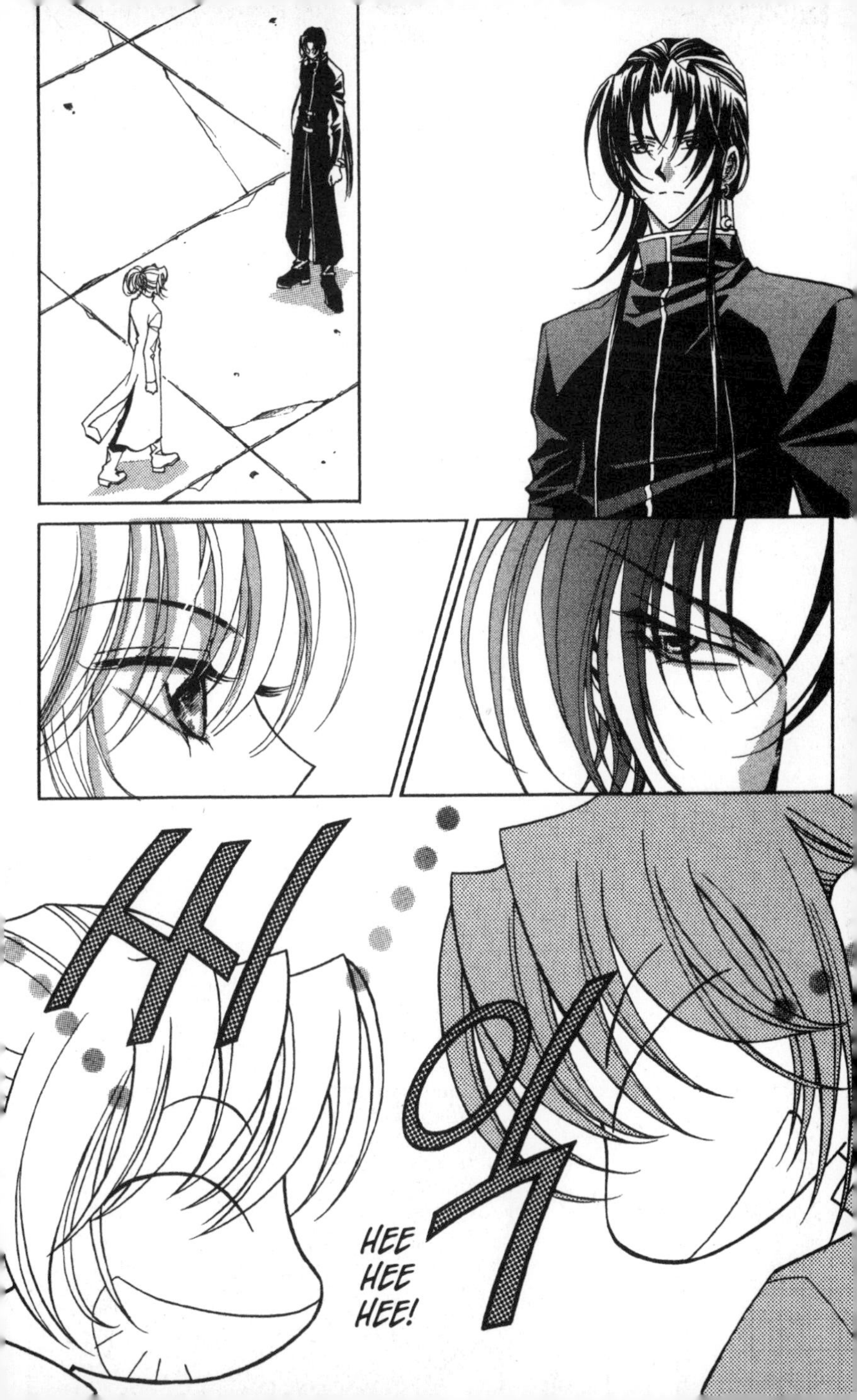
HH
OH
HEE
HEE
HEE!

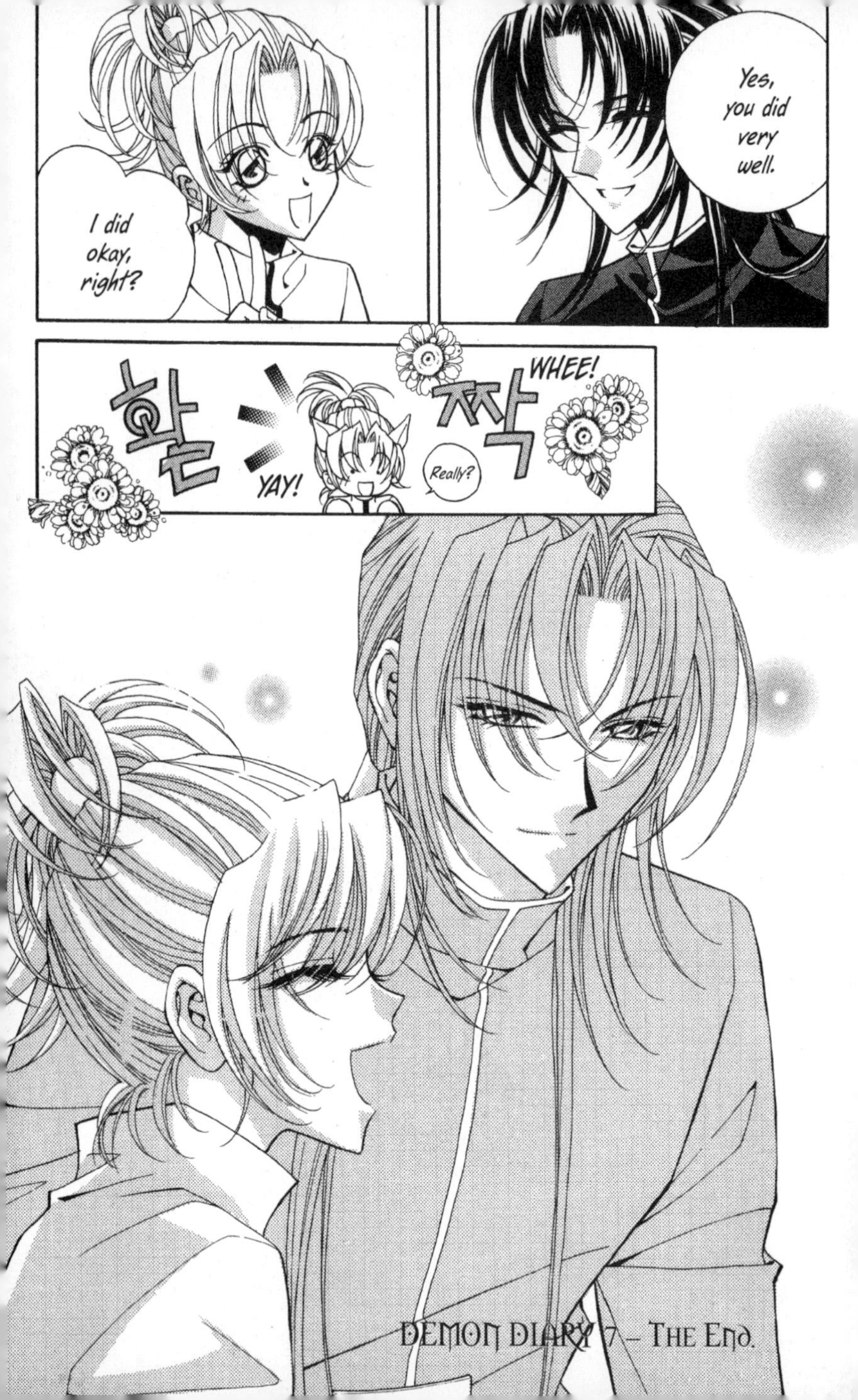
I did okay, right?
Yes, you did very well.
활
YAY!
Really?
짝
WHEE!
DEMON DIARY 7 – THE END.

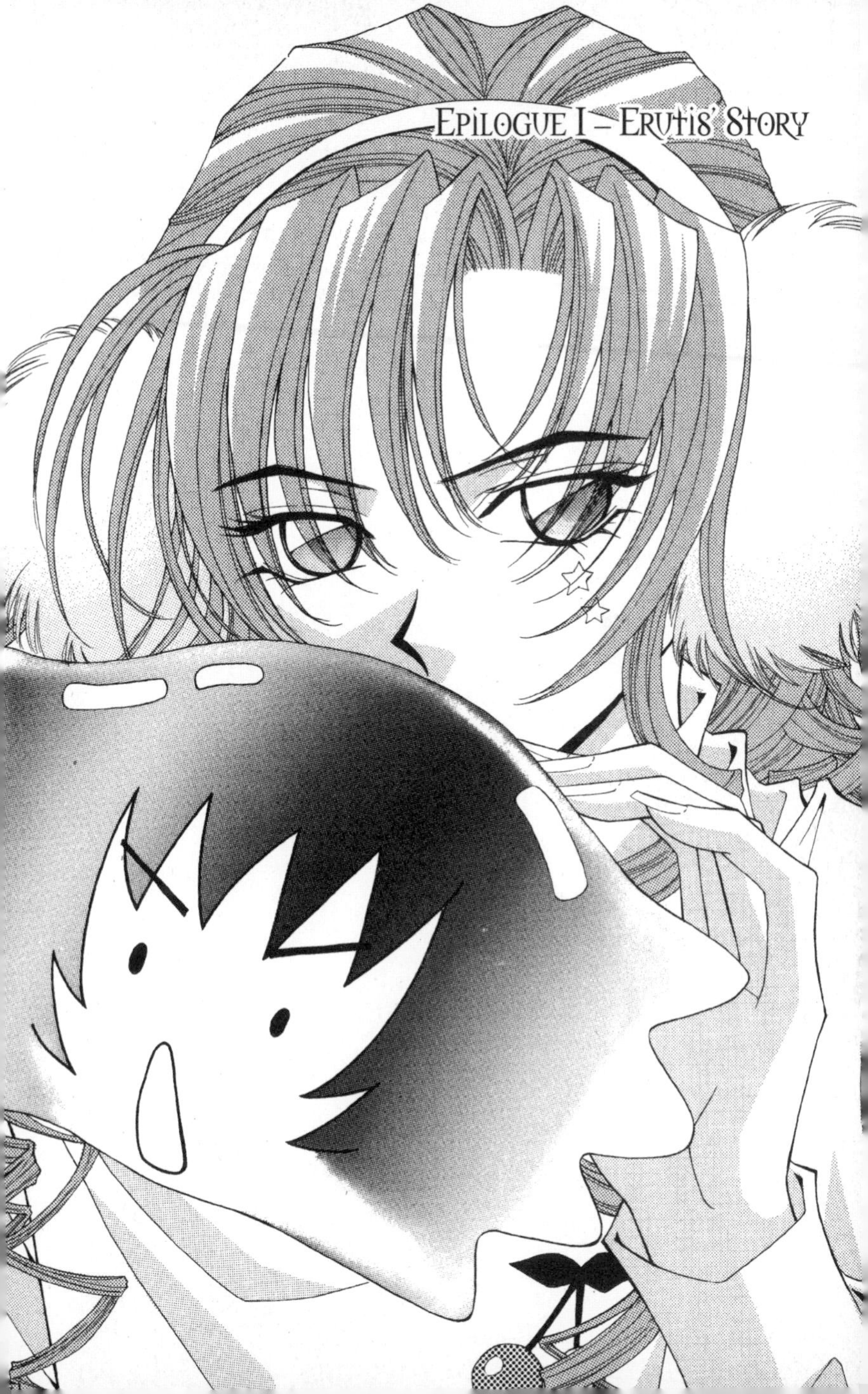
Epilogue I - Erutis' Story

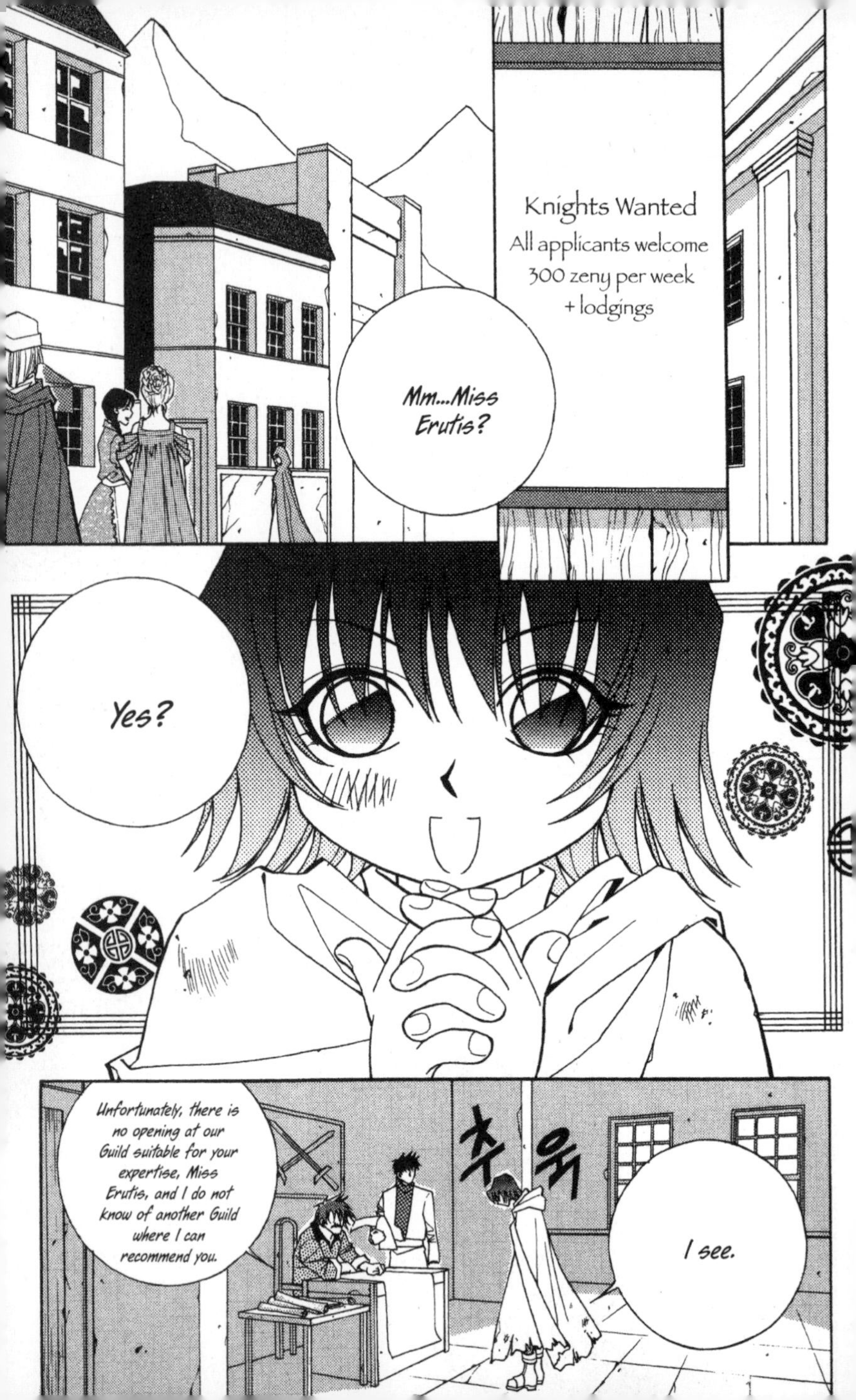
Mm...Miss Erutis?
Knights Wanted
All applicants welcome
300 zeny per week
+ lodgings
Yes?
Unfortunately, there is no opening at our Guild suitable for your expertise, Miss Erutis, and I do not know of another Guild where I can recommend you.
추욱
I see.

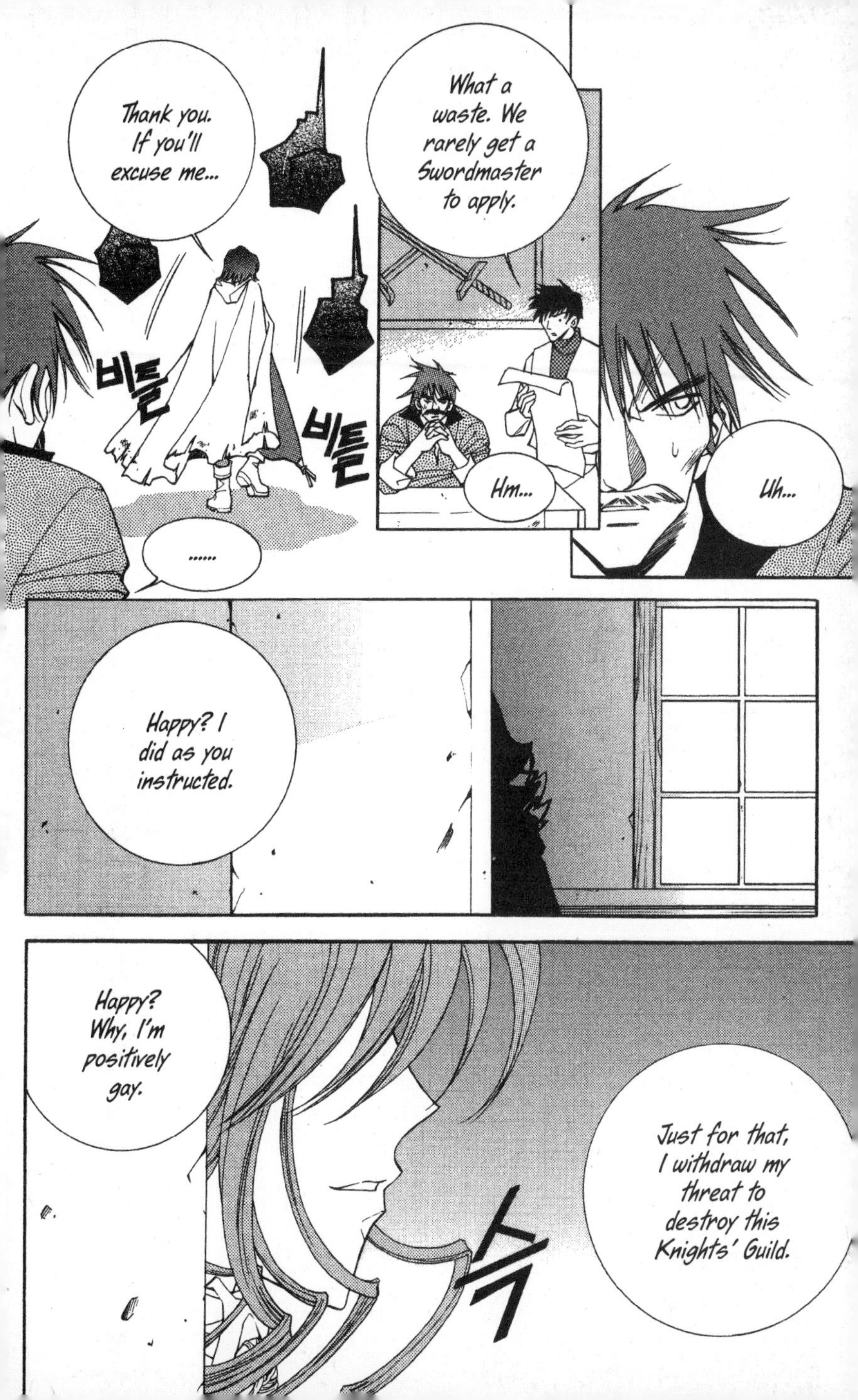
Thank you. If you'll excuse me...
비틀
비틀
......
What a waste. We rarely get a Swordmaster to apply.
Hm...
Uh...
Happy? I did as you instructed.
Happy? Why, I'm positively gay.
Just for that, I withdraw my threat to destroy this Knights' Guild.

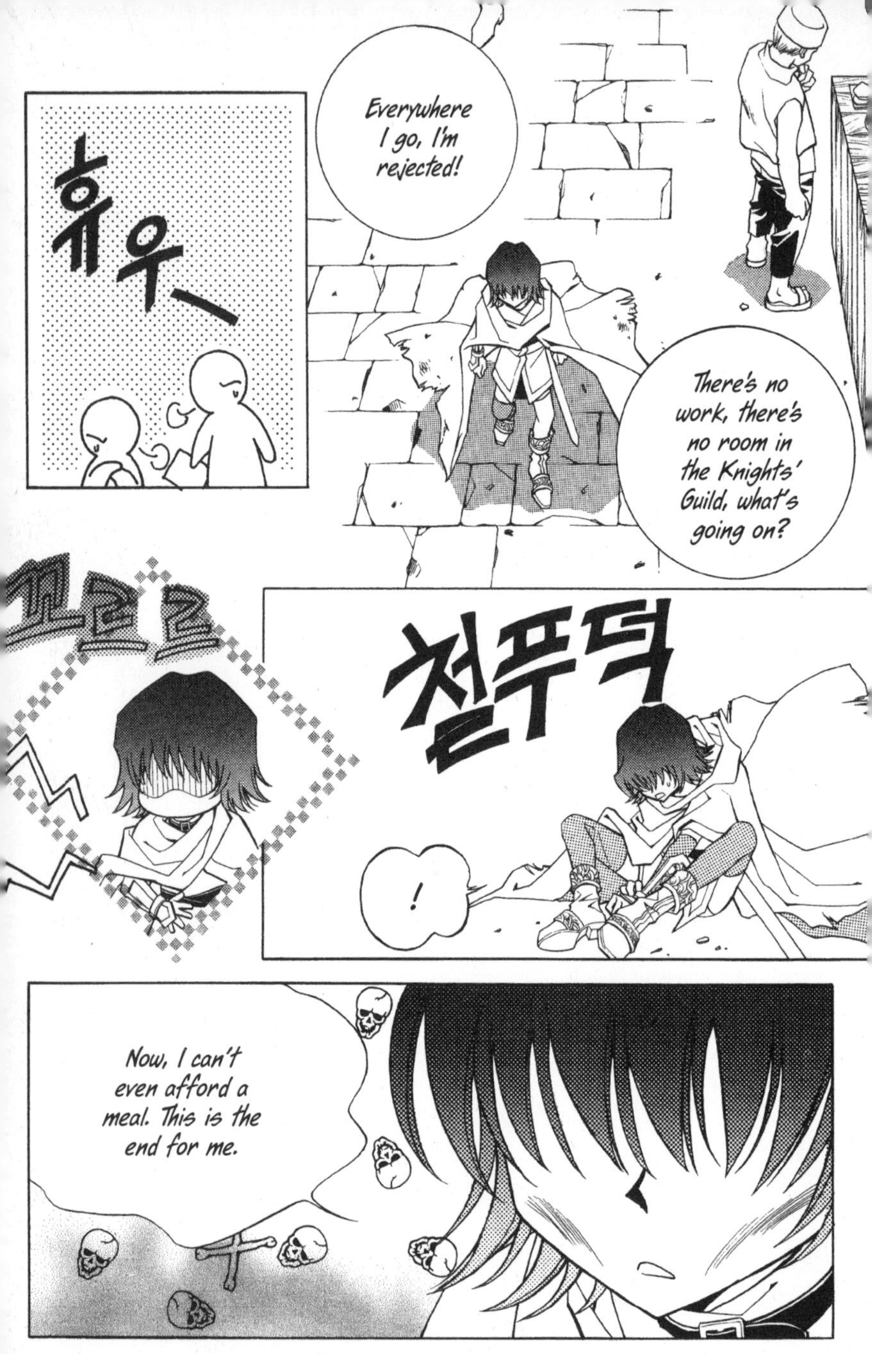
휴우~
Everywhere I go, I'm rejected!
There's no work, there's no room in the Knights' Guild, what's going on?
철푸덕
!
Now, I can't even afford a meal. This is the end for me.

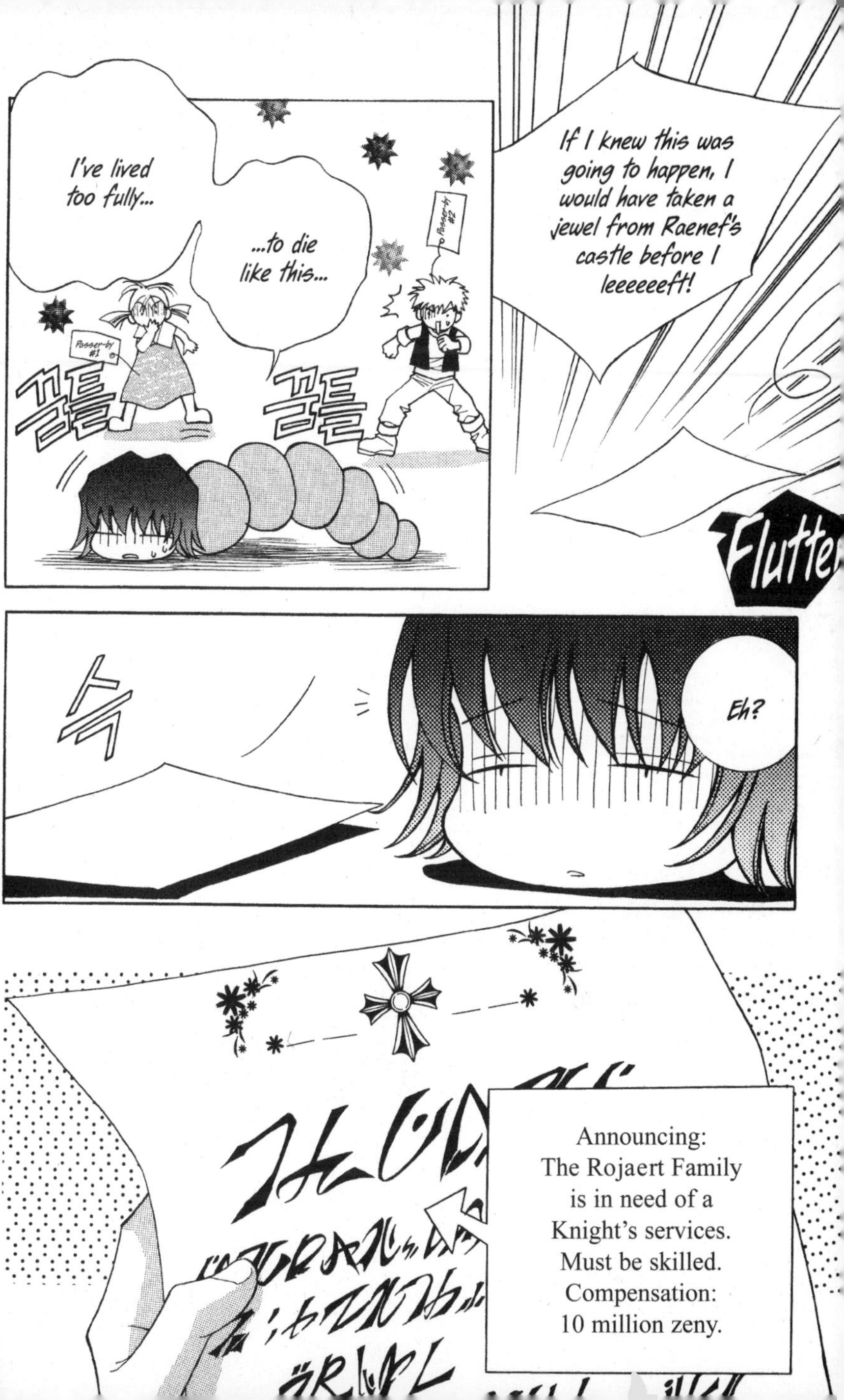

I've lived too fully...
...to die like this...
Passer-by #1
Passer-by #2
If I knew this was going to happen, I would have taken a jewel from Raenef's castle before I leeeeeeft!
Flutter
Eh?
Announcing:
The Rojaert Family is in need of a Knight's services.
Must be skilled.
Compensation:
10 million zeny.

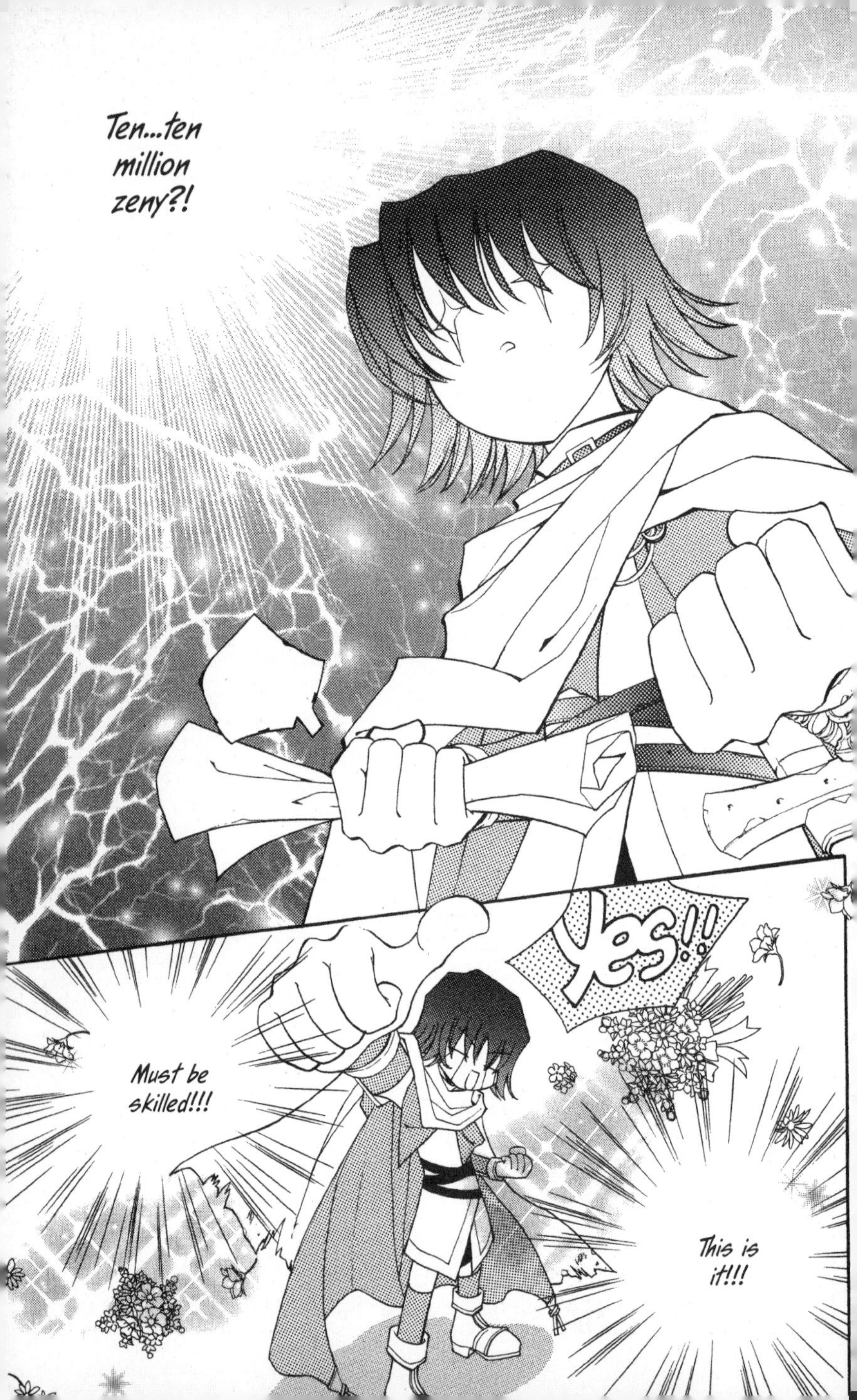
Ten...ten million zeny?!
Yes!!
Must be skilled!!!
This is it!!!

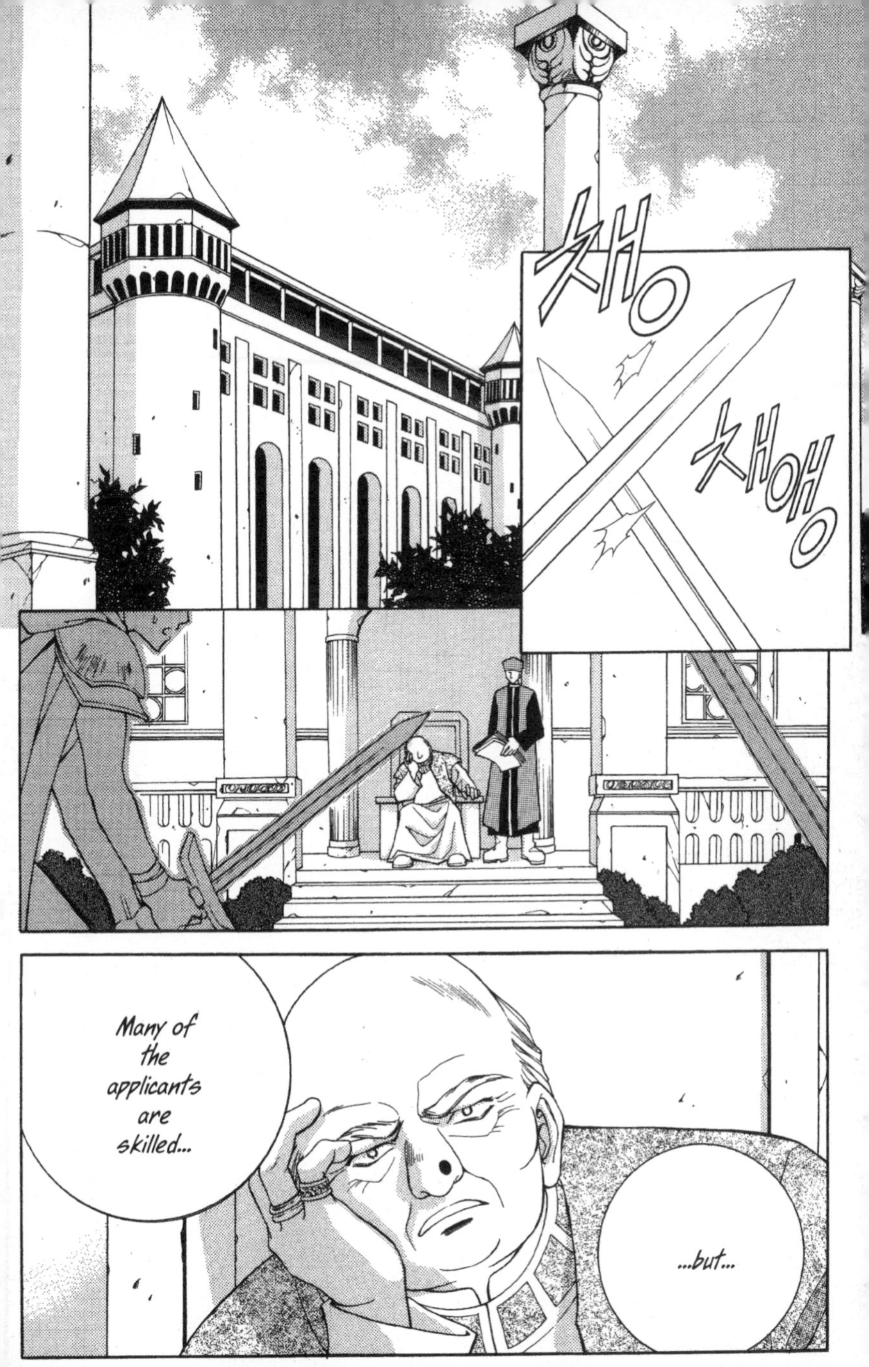

챙
챙챙
Many of the applicants are skilled...
...but...

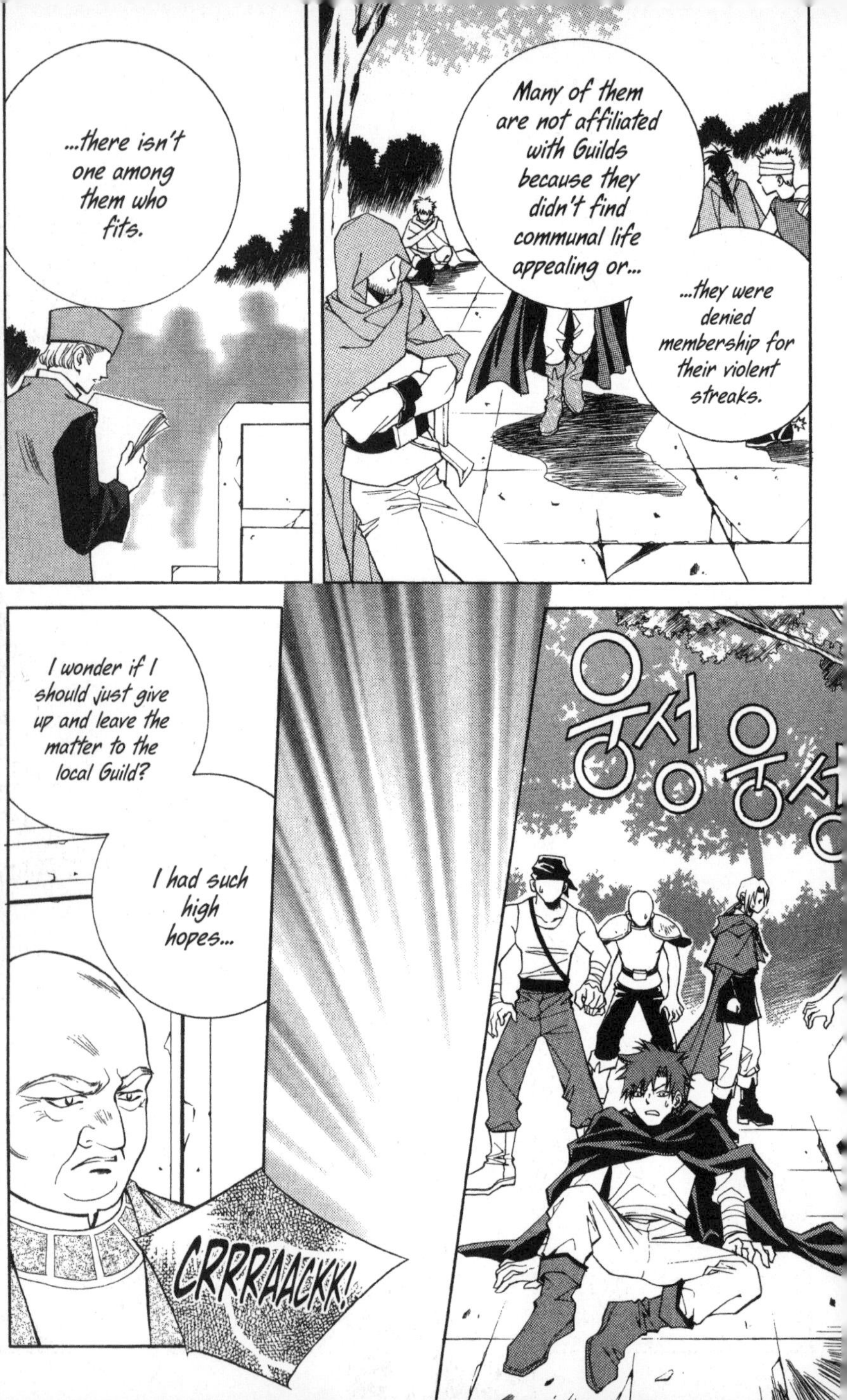
...there isn't one among them who fits.
Many of them are not affiliated with Guilds because they didn't find communal life appealing or...
...they were denied membership for their violent streaks.
I wonder if I should just give up and leave the matter to the local Guild?
I had such high hopes...
CRRRAACKK!
웅성 웅성

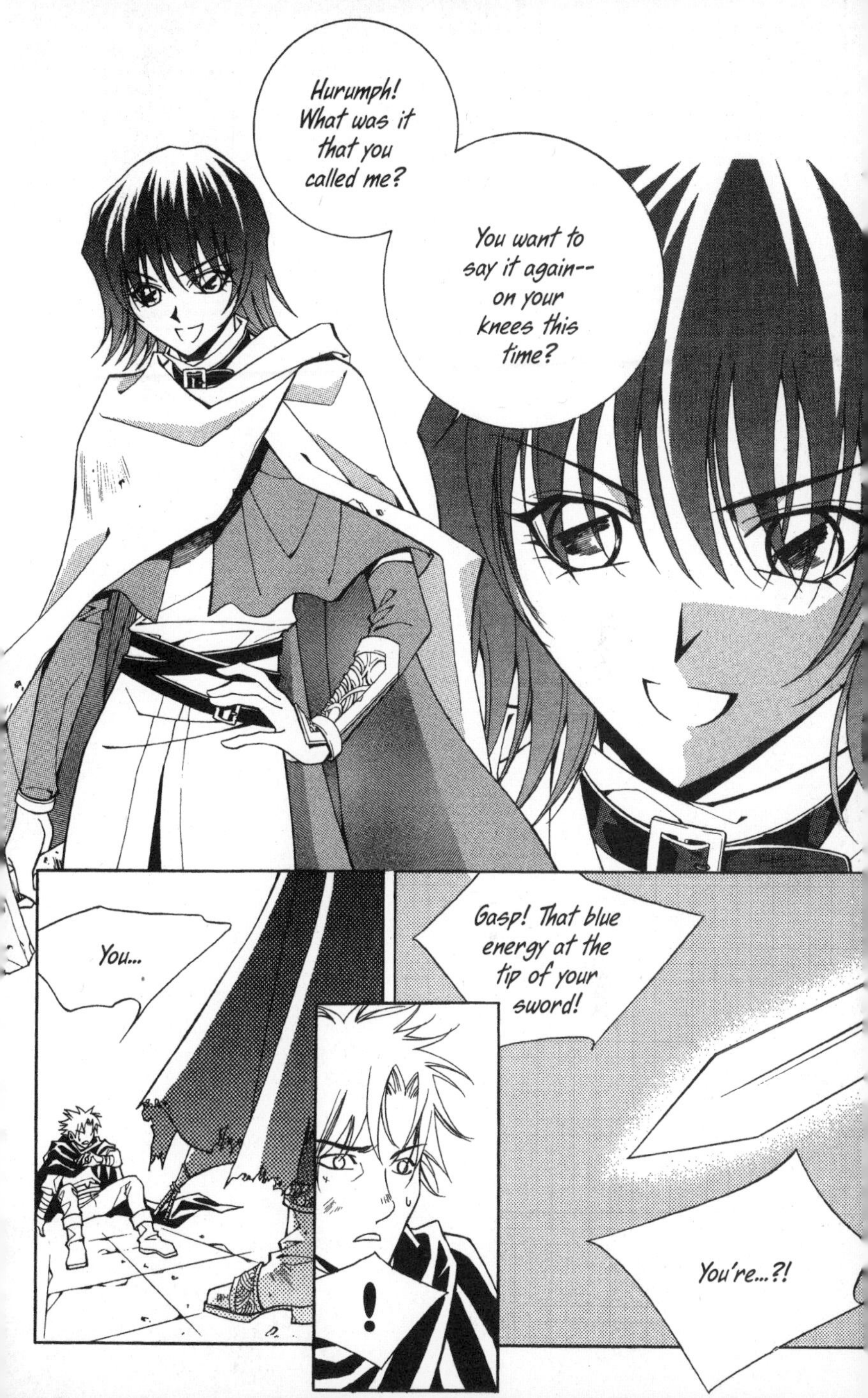

Hurumph! What was it that you called me?
You want to say it again--on your knees this time?
You...
Gasp! That blue energy at the tip of your sword!
!
You're...?!

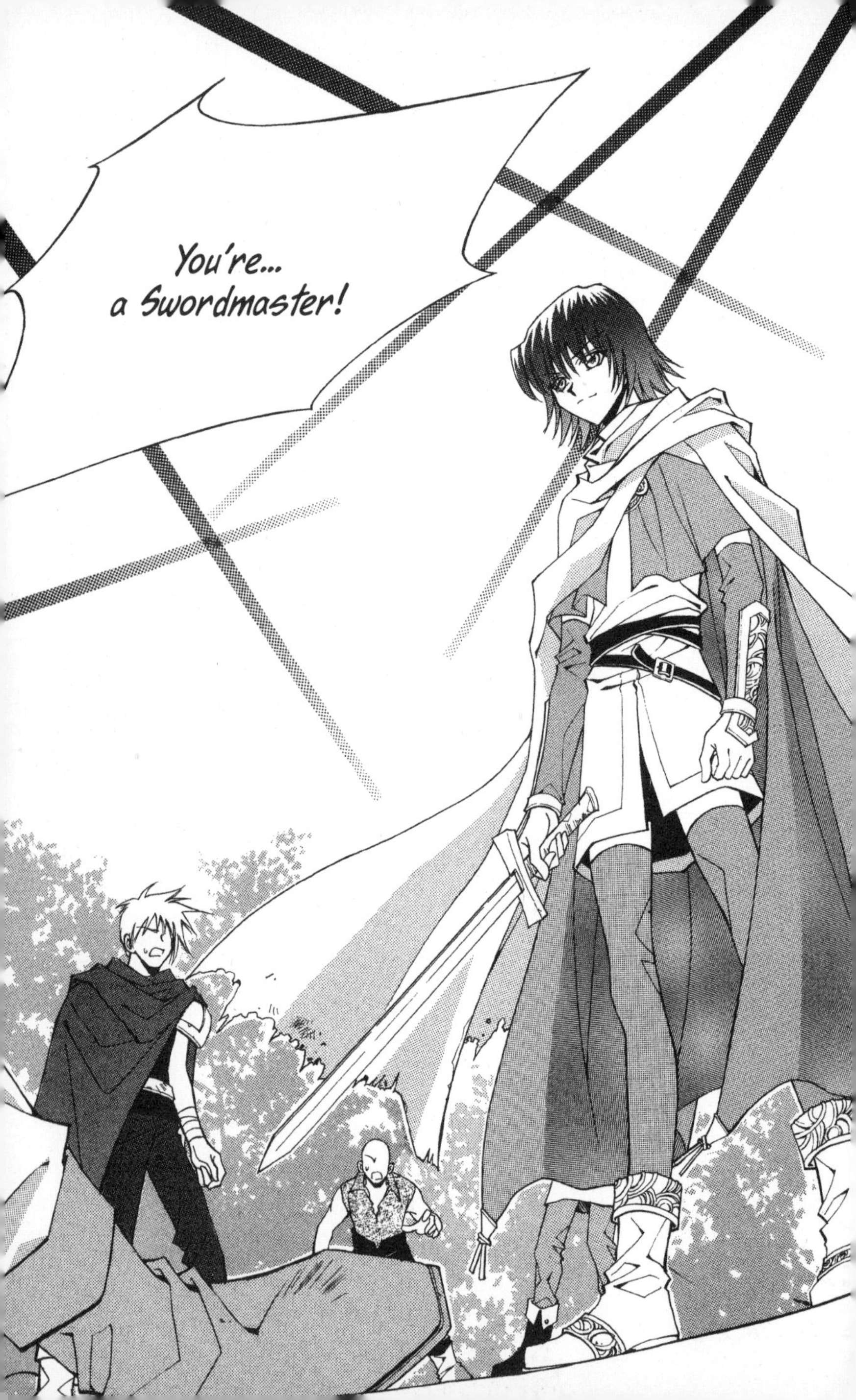
You're... a Swordmaster!

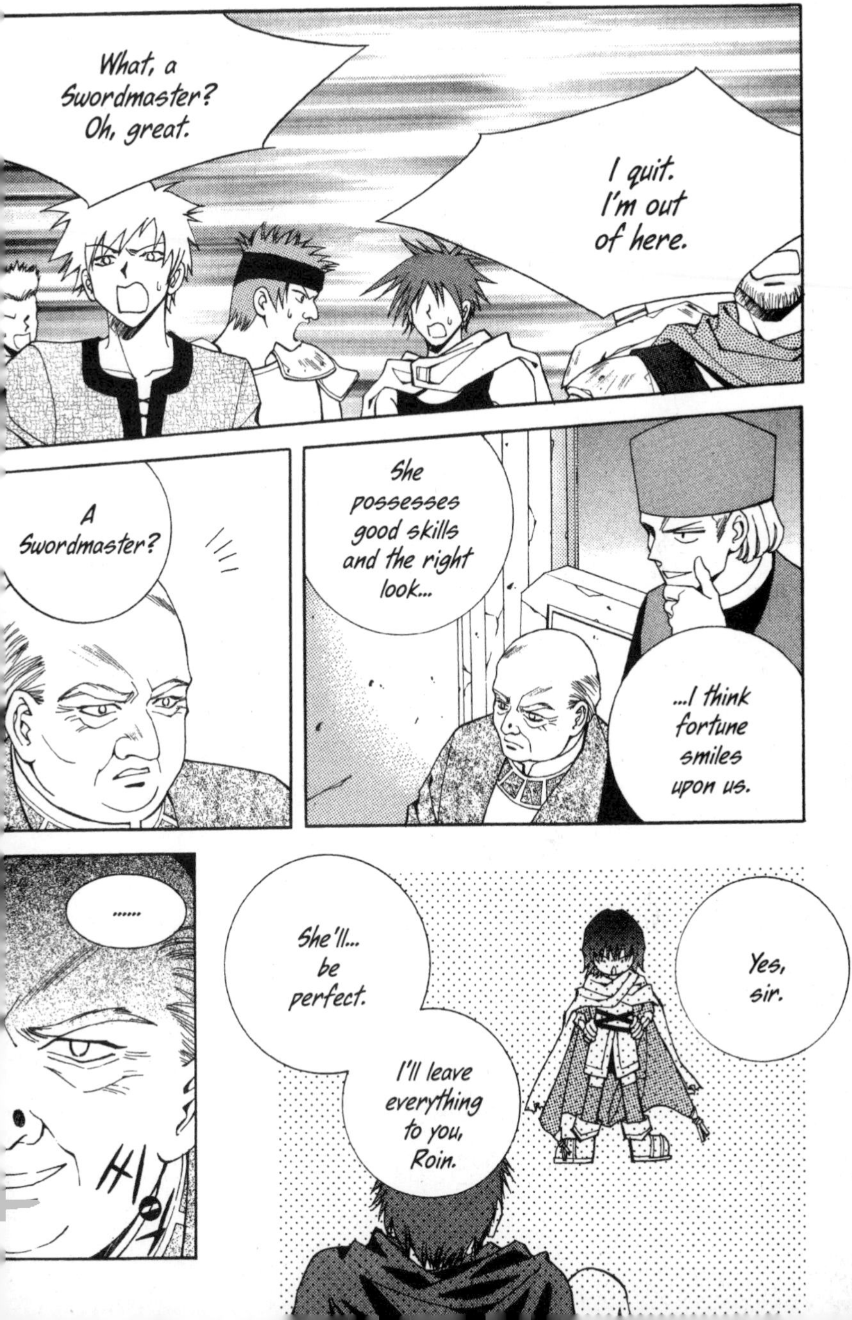
What, a Swordmaster? Oh, great.
I quit. I'm out of here.
A Swordmaster?
She possesses good skills and the right look...
...I think fortune smiles upon us.
......
She'll... be perfect.
I'll leave everything to you, Roin.
Yes, sir.

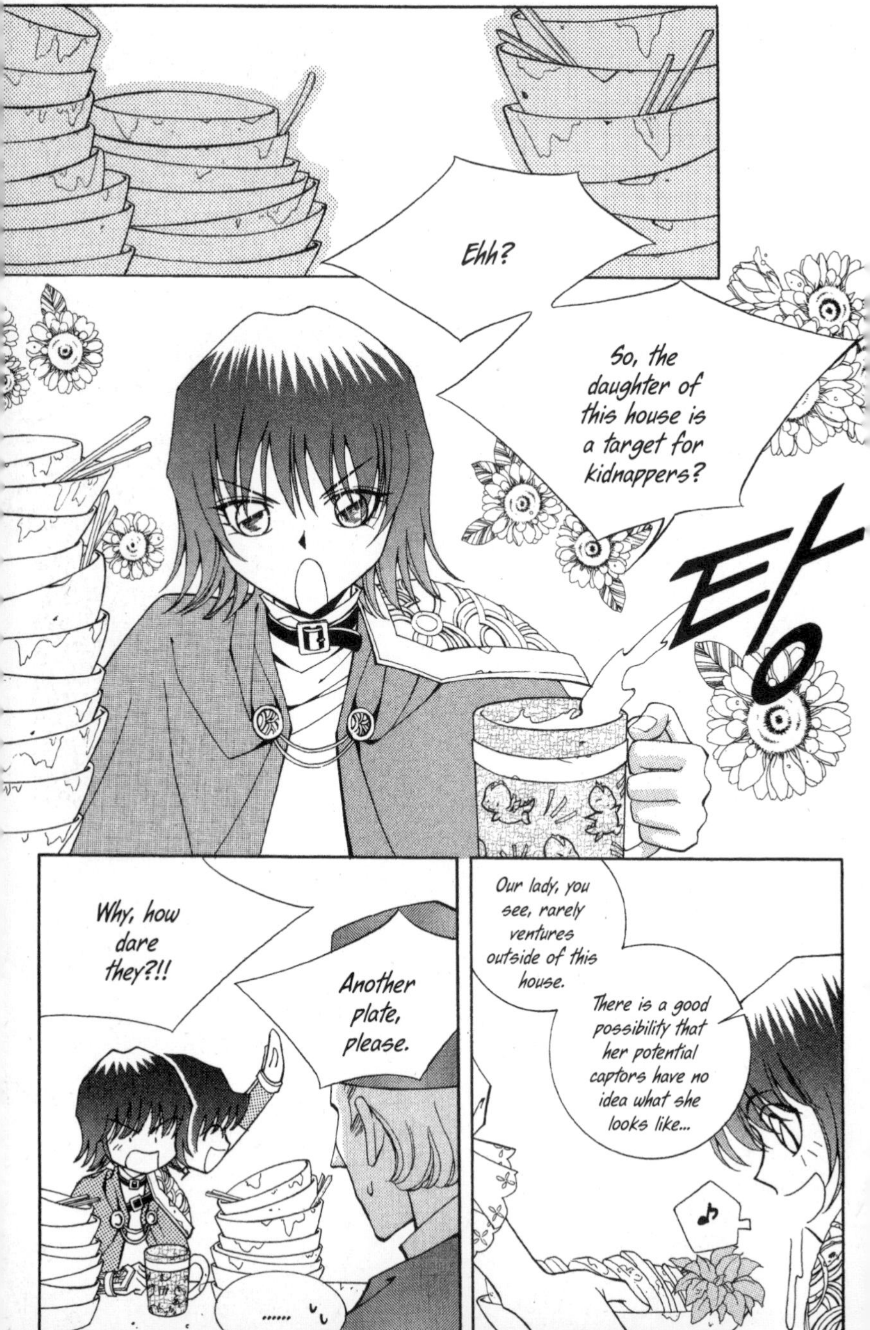
Ehh?
So, the daughter of this house is a target for kidnappers?
Why, how dare they?!!
Another plate, please.
......
Our lady, you see, rarely ventures outside of this house.
There is a good possibility that her potential captors have no idea what she looks like...

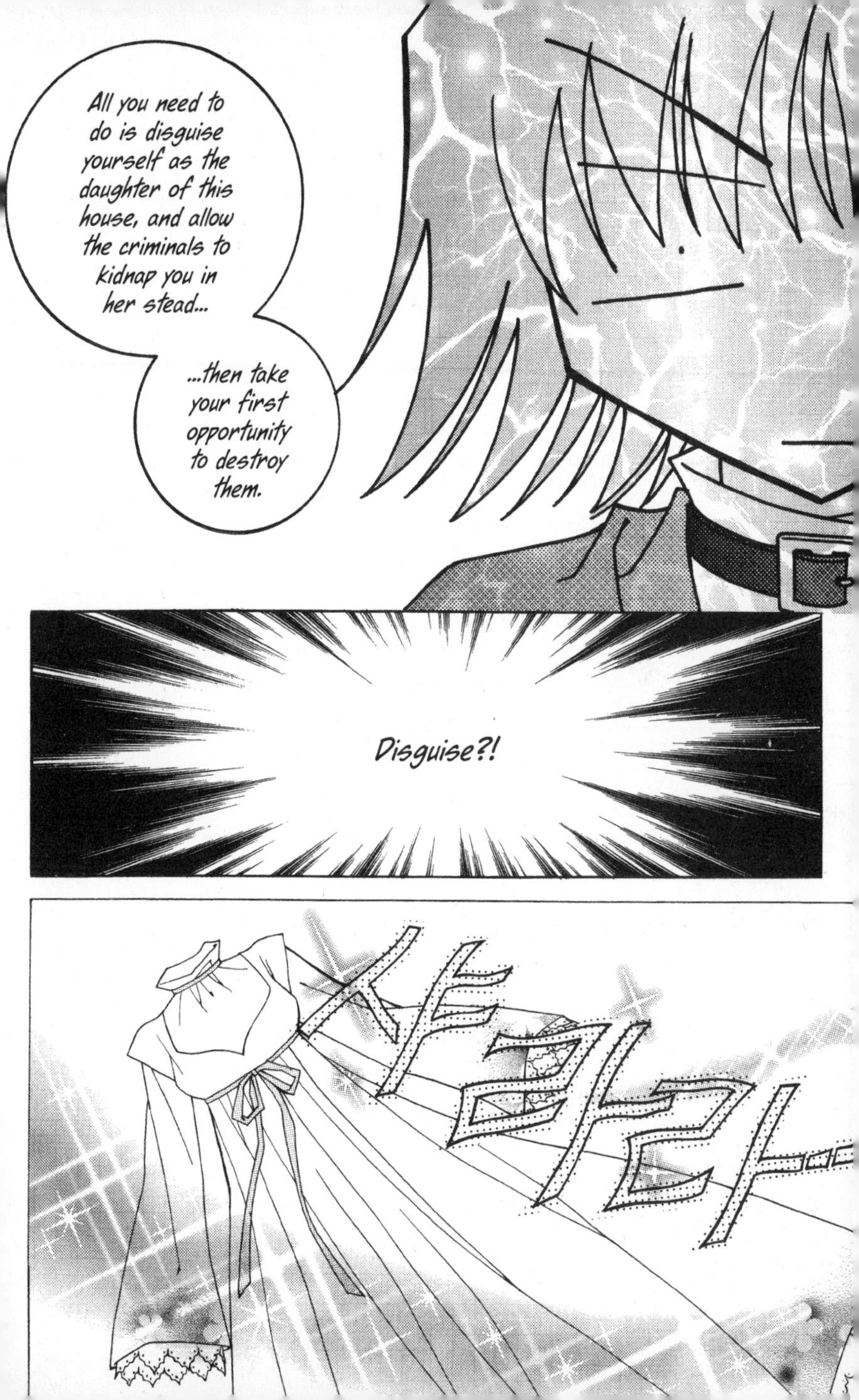
All you need to do is disguise yourself as the daughter of this house, and allow the criminals to kidnap you in her stead...
...then take your first opportunity to destroy them.
Disguise?!

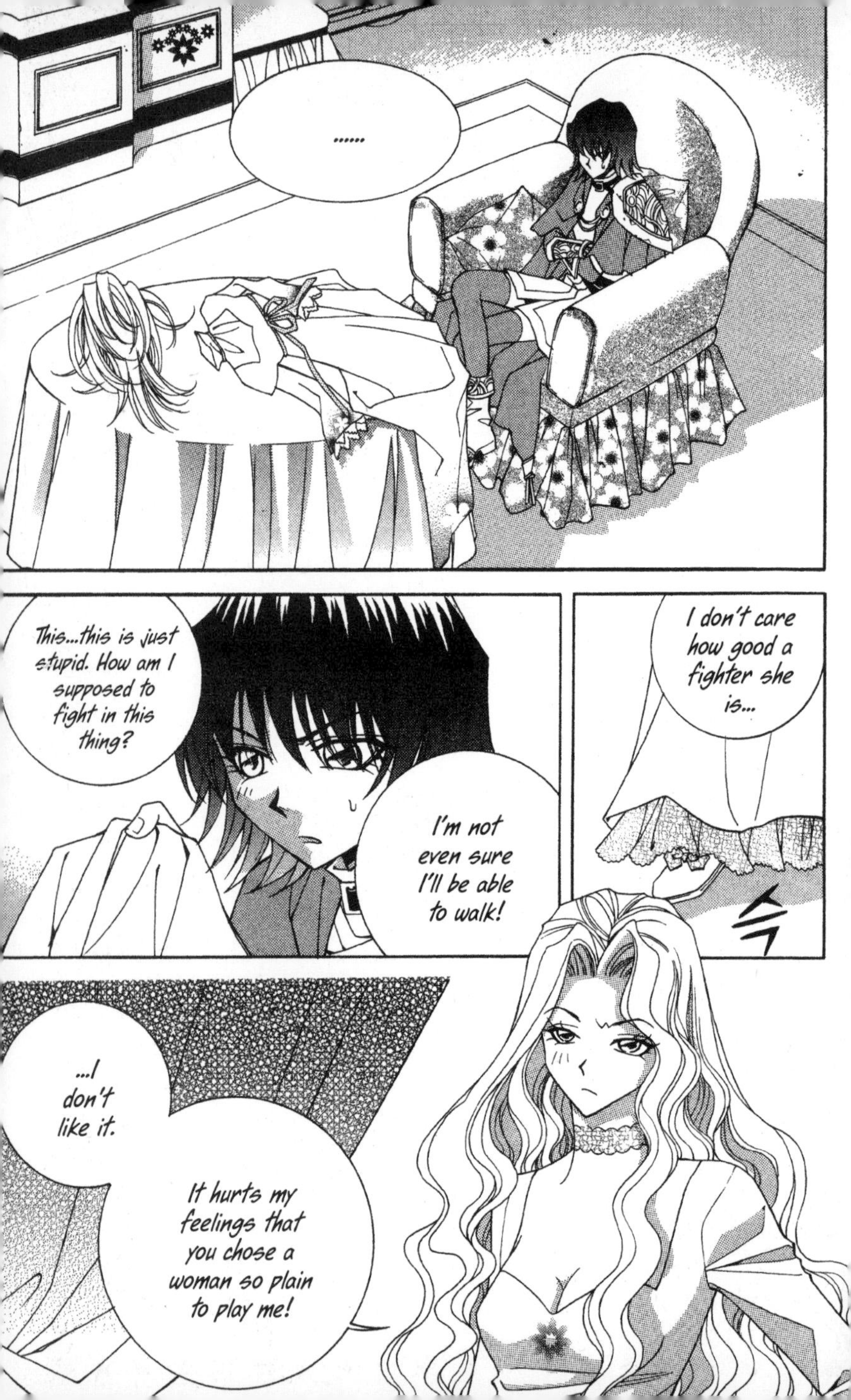
......
This...this is just stupid. How am I supposed to fight in this thing?
I'm not even sure I'll be able to walk!
I don't care how good a fighter she is...
...I don't like it.
It hurts my feelings that you chose a woman so plain to play me!

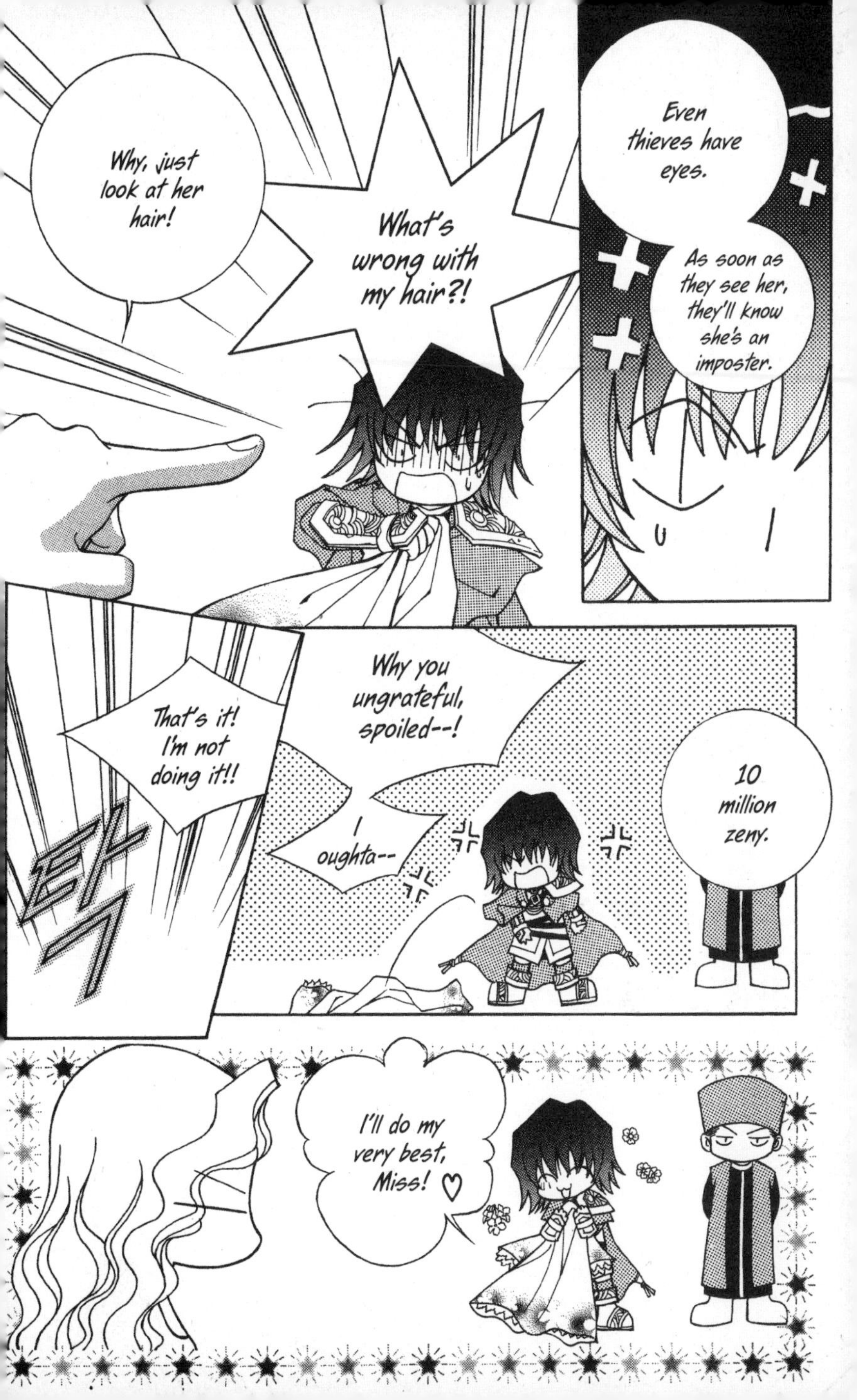
Why, just look at her hair!
What's wrong with my hair?!
Even thieves have eyes.
As soon as they see her, they'll know she's an imposter.
That's it! I'm not doing it!!
Why you ungrateful, spoiled--!
I oughta--
10 million zeny.
I'll do my very best, Miss! ♡

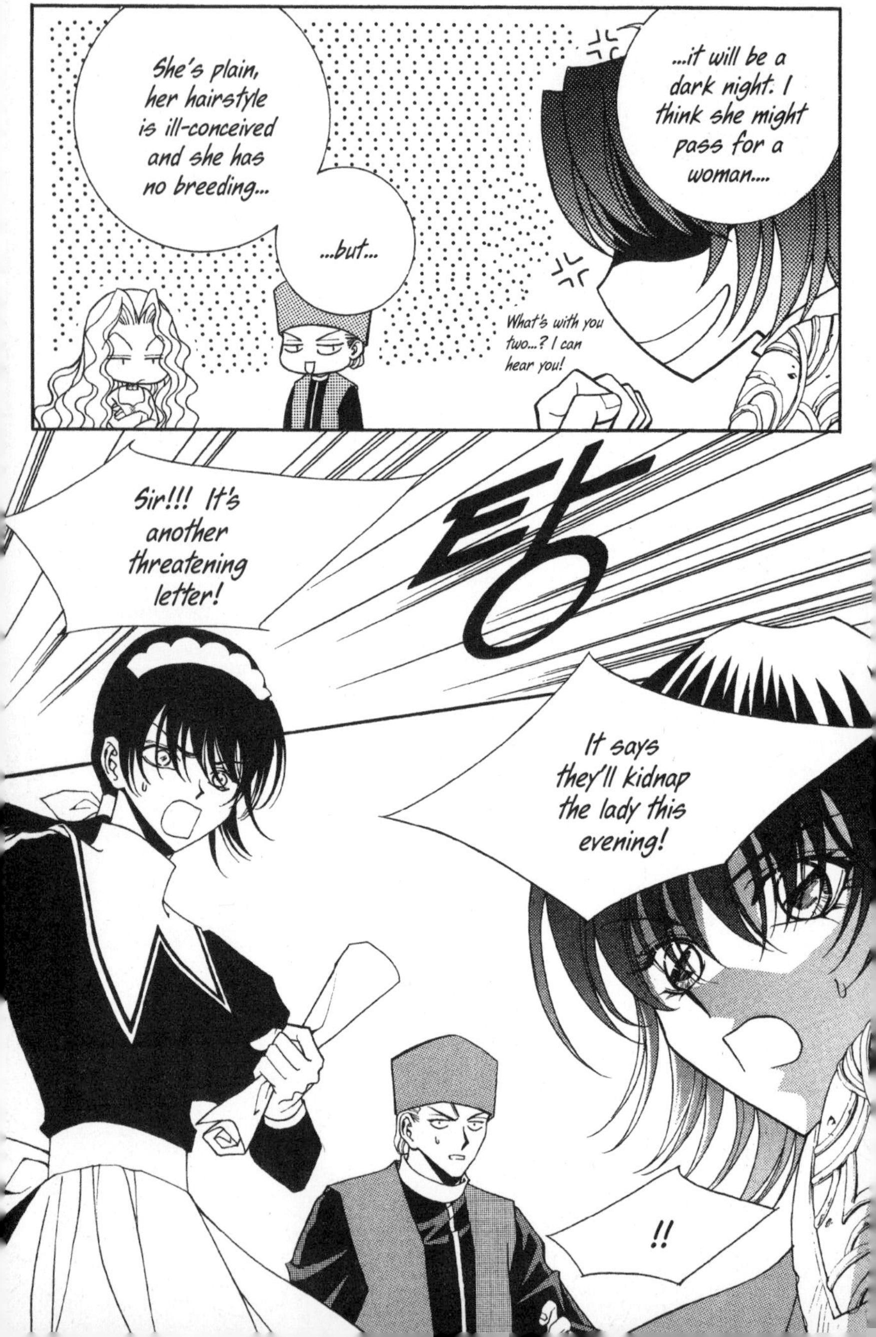
She's plain, her hairstyle is ill-conceived and she has no breeding...
...but...
...it will be a dark night. I think she might pass for a woman....
What's with you two...? I can hear you!
Sir!!! It's another threatening letter!
It says they'll kidnap the lady this evening!
!!

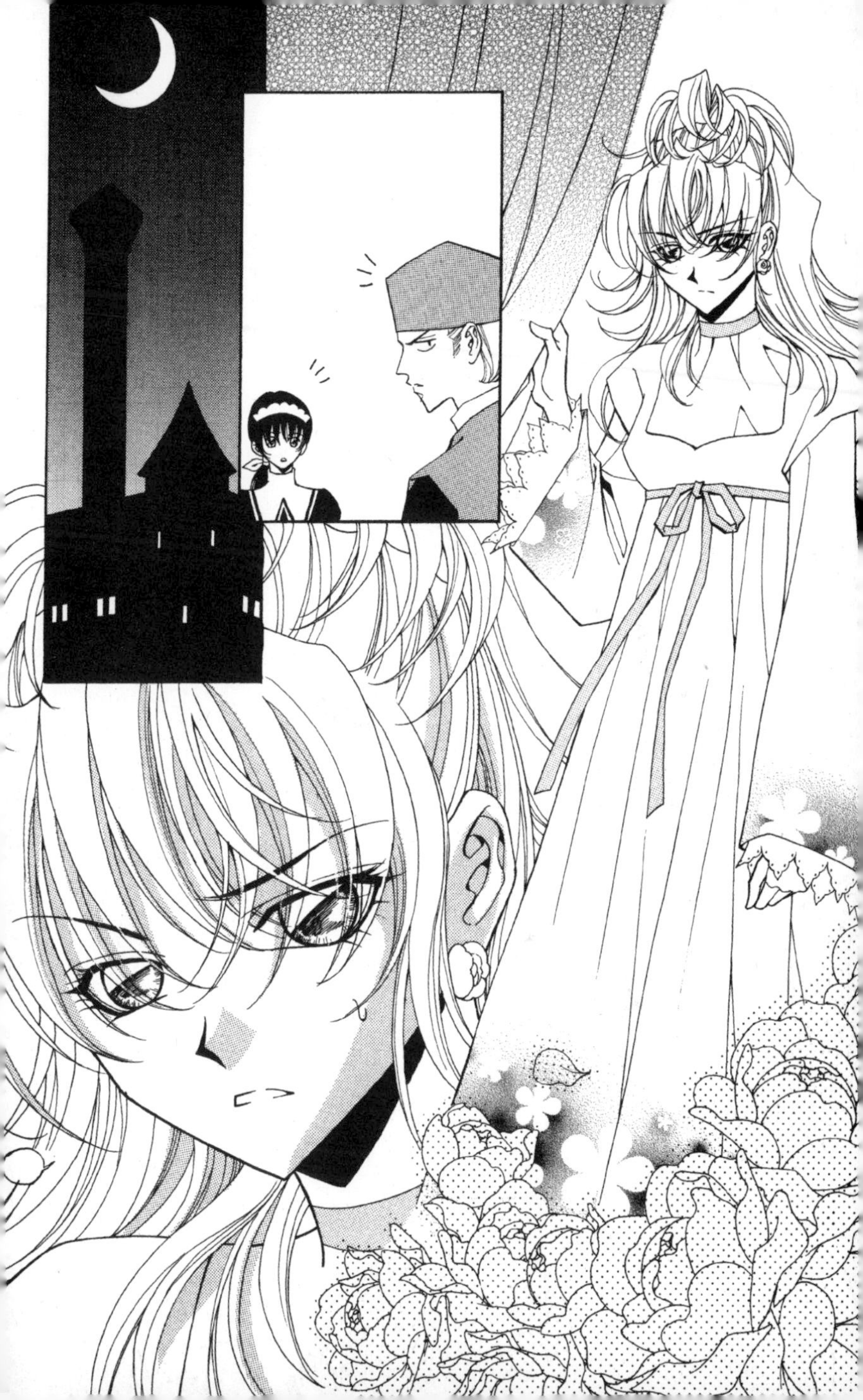

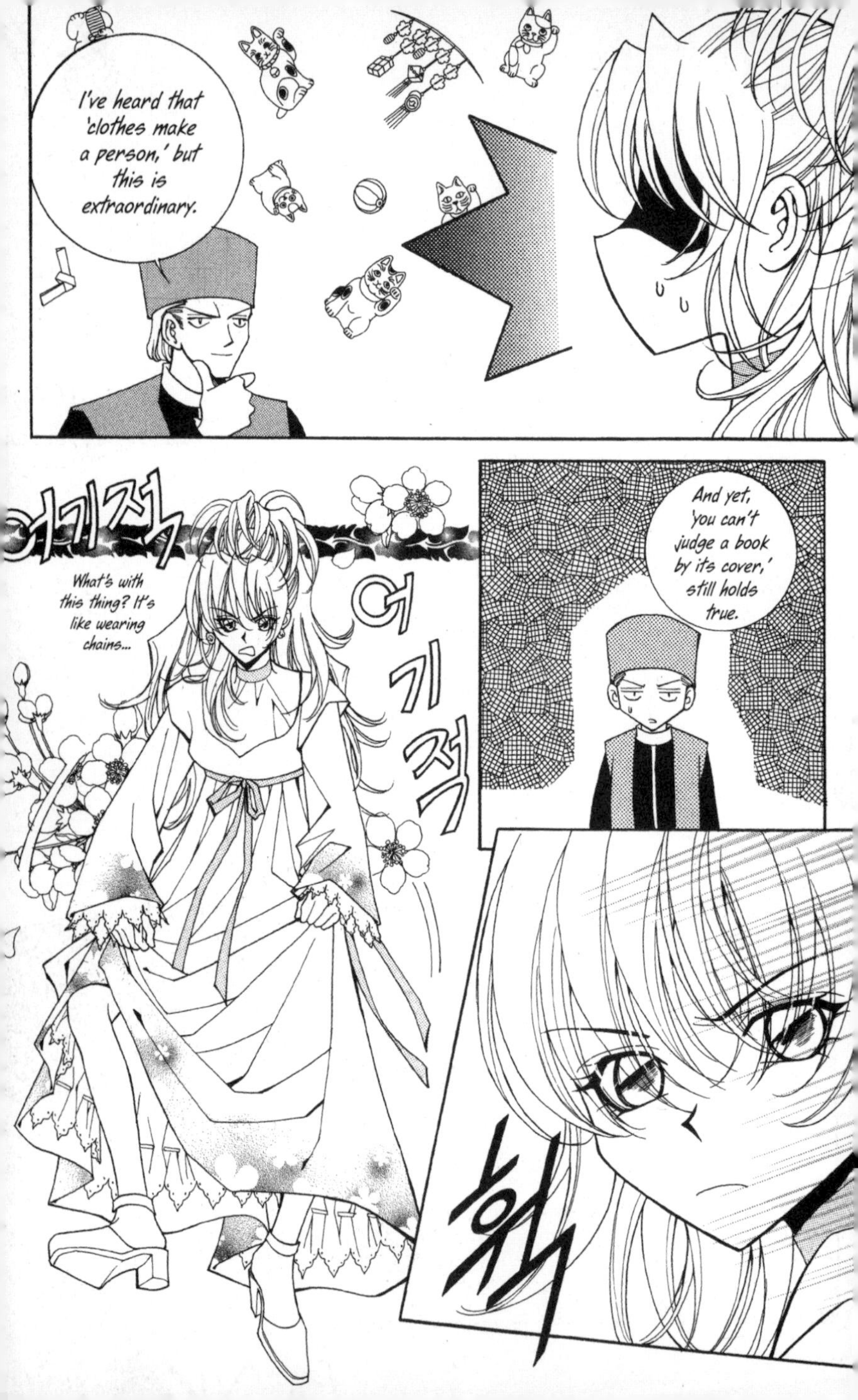
I've heard that 'clothes make a person,' but this is extraordinary.
어기적
What's with this thing? It's like wearing chains...
어기적
And yet, 'you can't judge a book by its cover,' still holds true.
휙

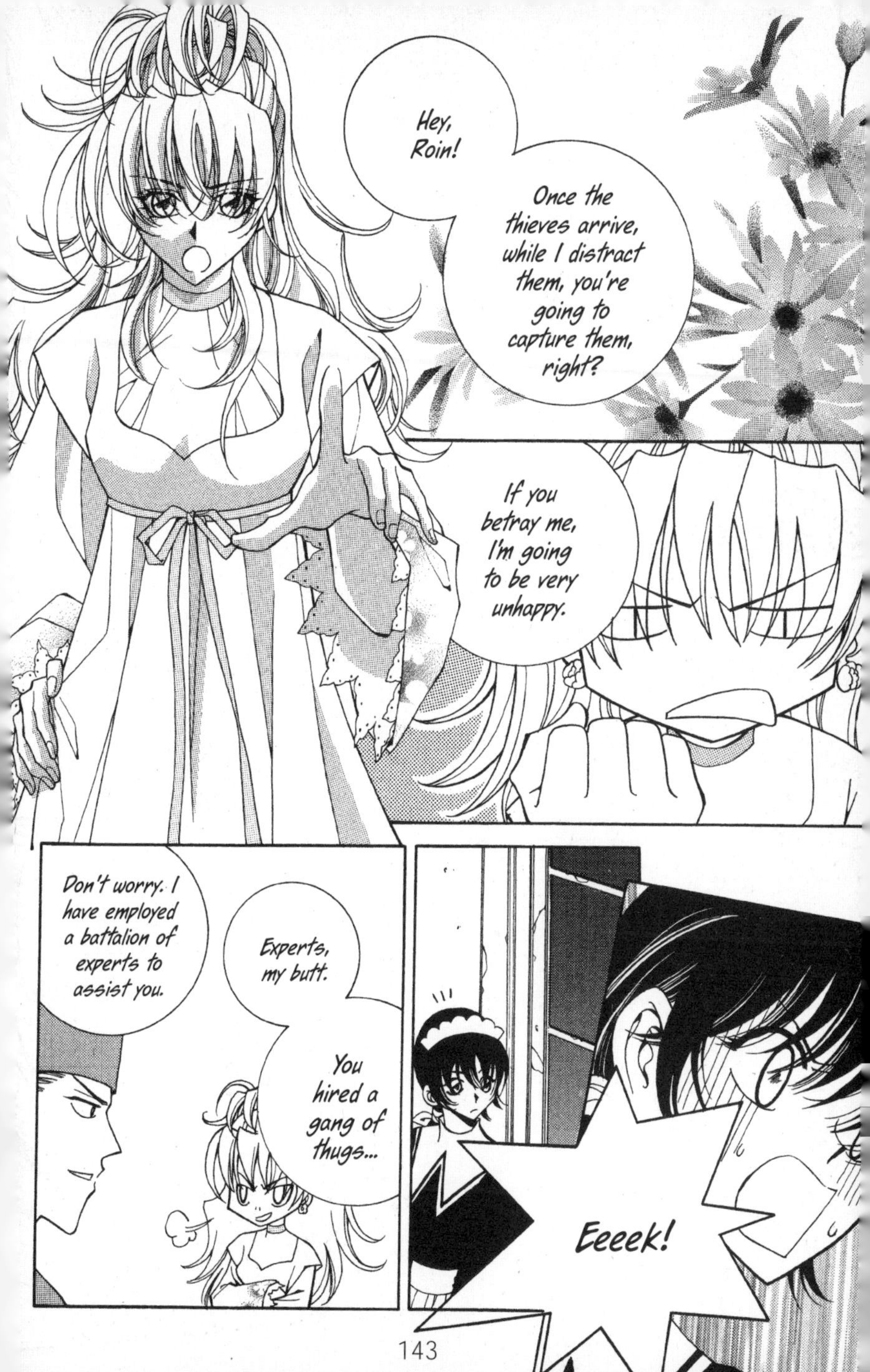
Hey, Roin!
Once the thieves arrive, while I distract them, you're going to capture them, right?
If you betray me, I'm going to be very unhappy.
Don't worry. I have employed a battalion of experts to assist you.
Experts, my butt.
You hired a gang of thugs...
Eeeek!

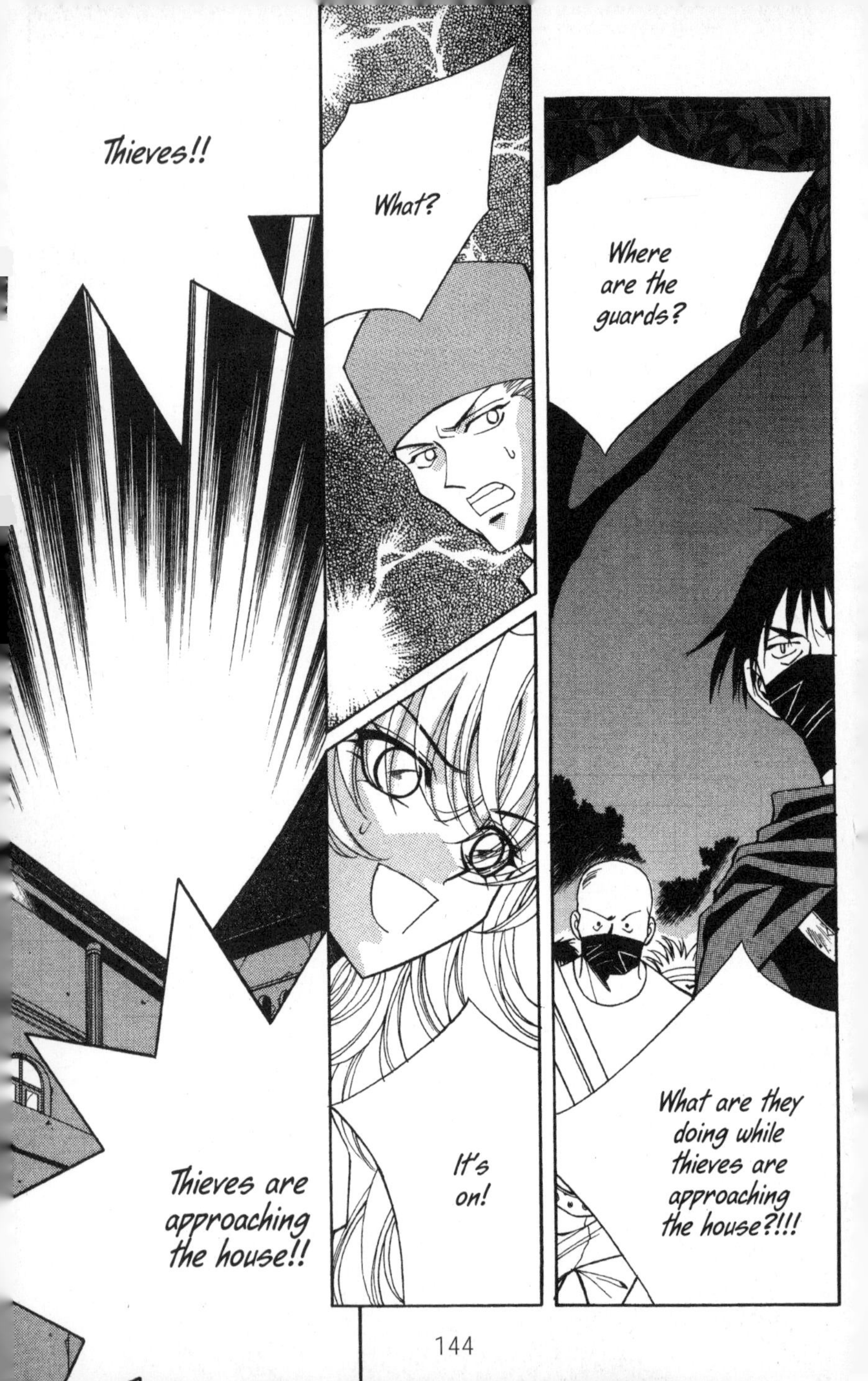
Thieves!!
Thieves are approaching the house!!
What?
It's on!
Where are the guards?
What are they doing while thieves are approaching the house?!!!

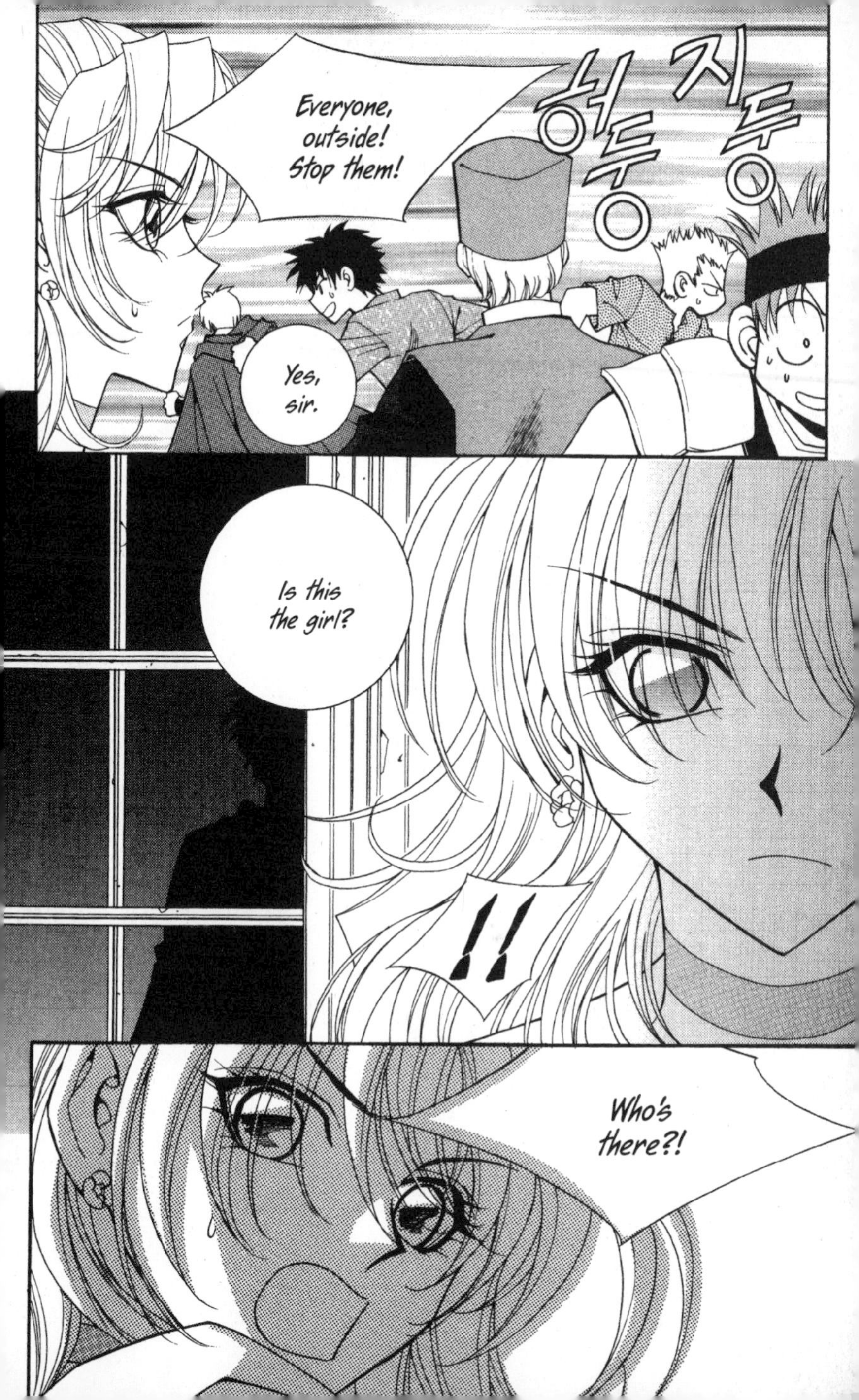
Everyone, outside! Stop them!
허둥지둥
Yes, sir.
Is this the girl?
!!
Who's there?!

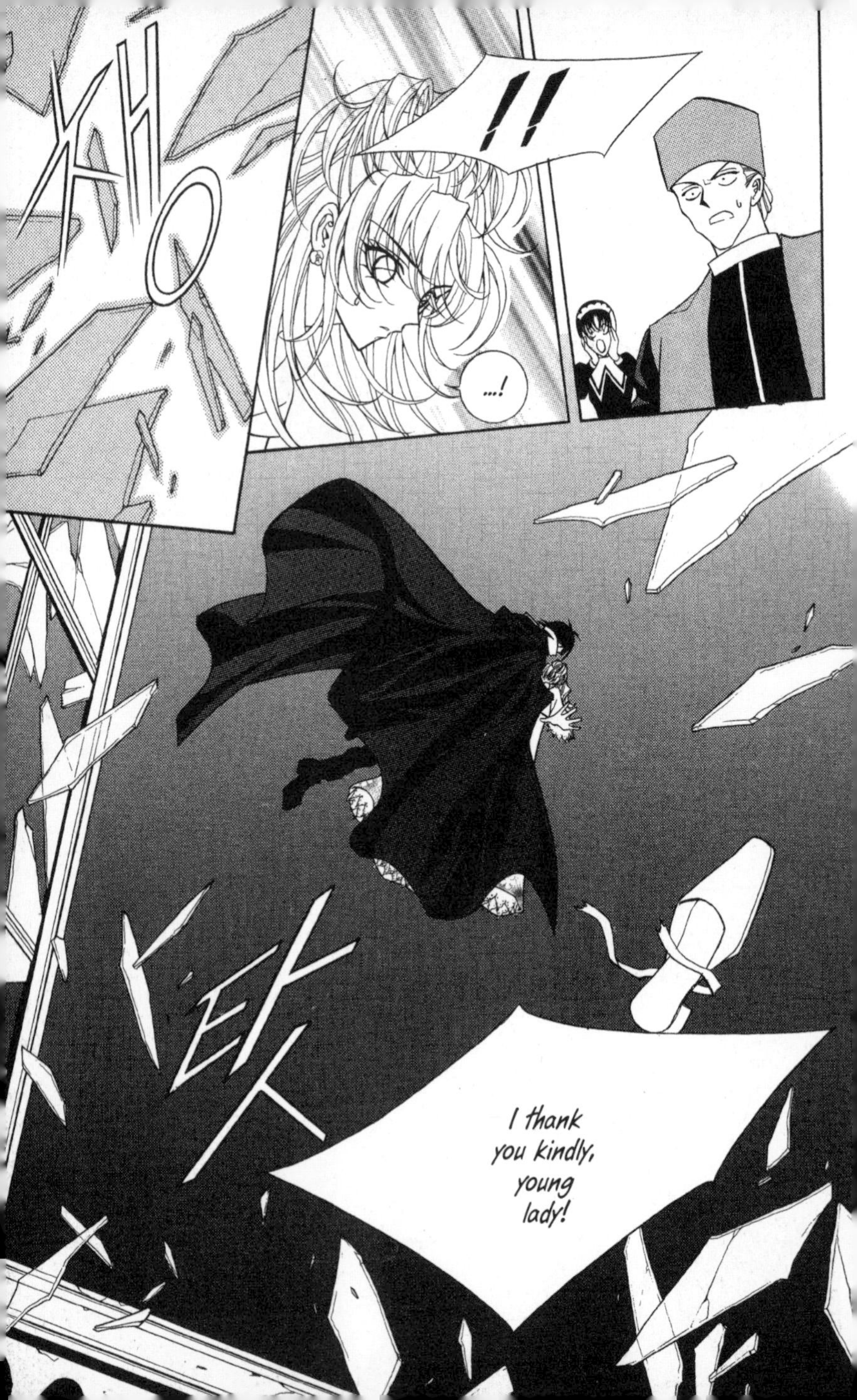

KSHH
!!
...!
KEEK
I thank you kindly, young lady!

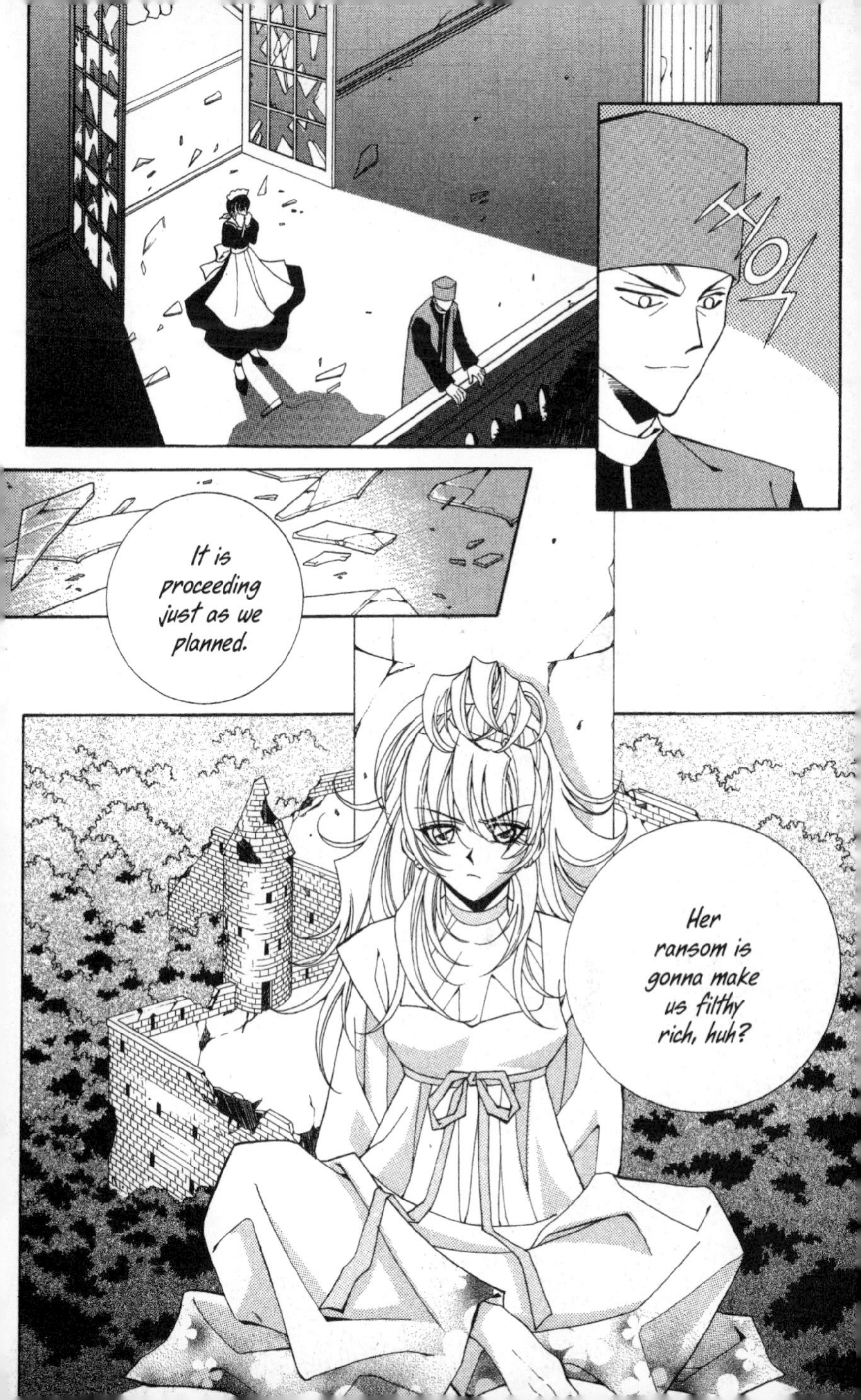
It is proceeding just as we planned.
Her ransom is gonna make us filthy rich, huh?

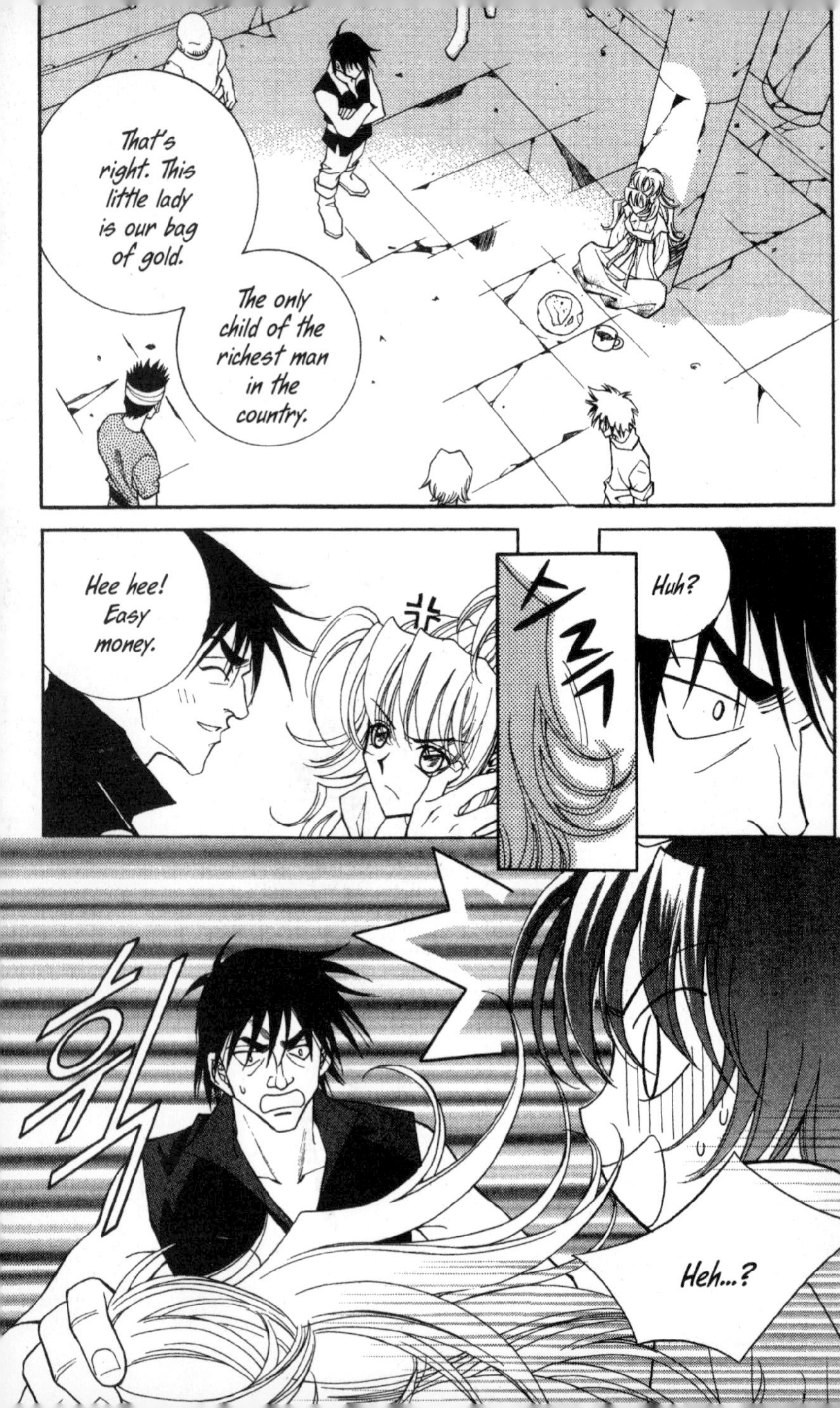

That's right. This little lady is our bag of gold.
The only child of the richest man in the country.
Hee hee! Easy money.
Huh?
Heh...?

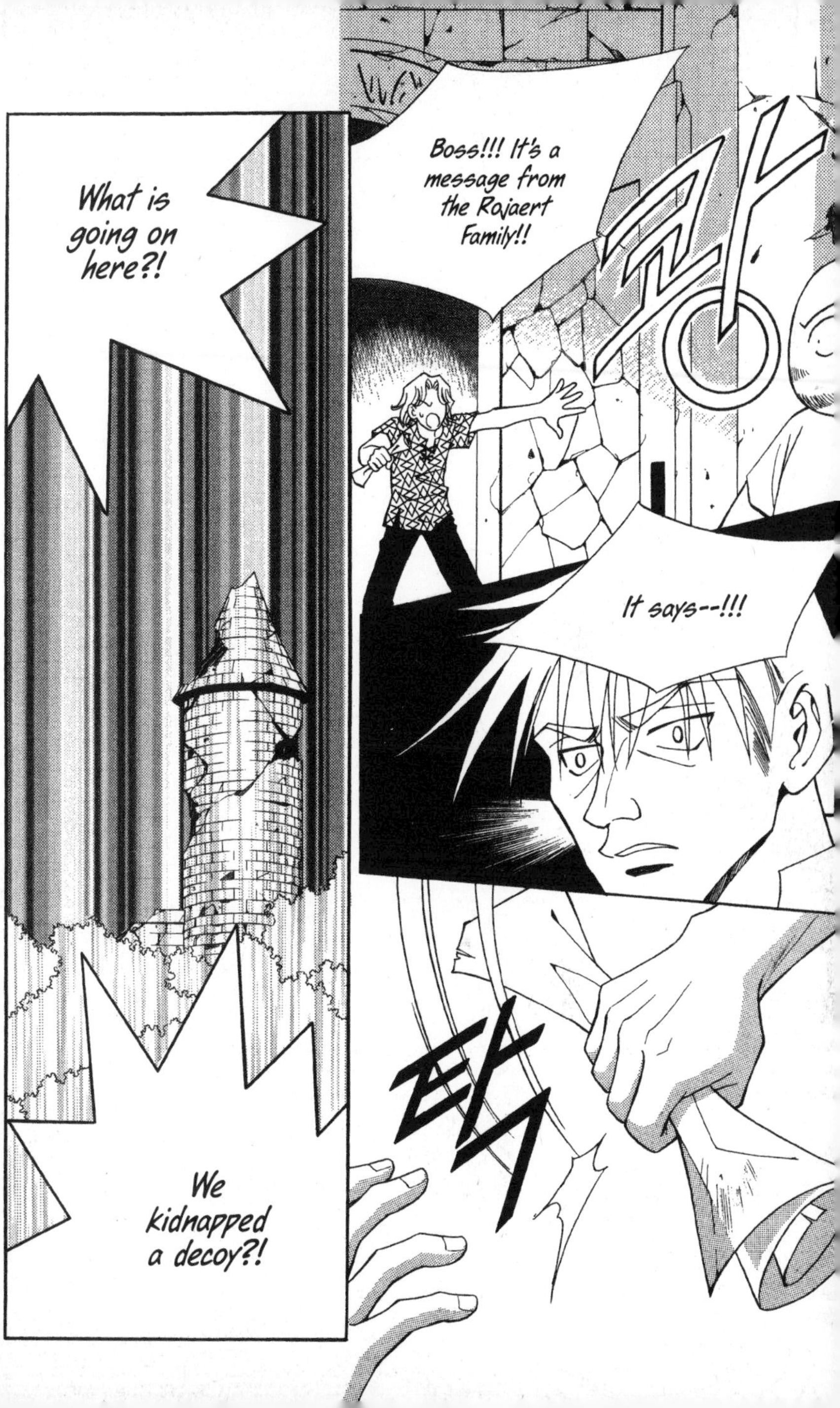
What is going on here?!
We kidnapped a decoy?!
Boss!!! It's a message from the Rojaert Family!!
It says--!!!

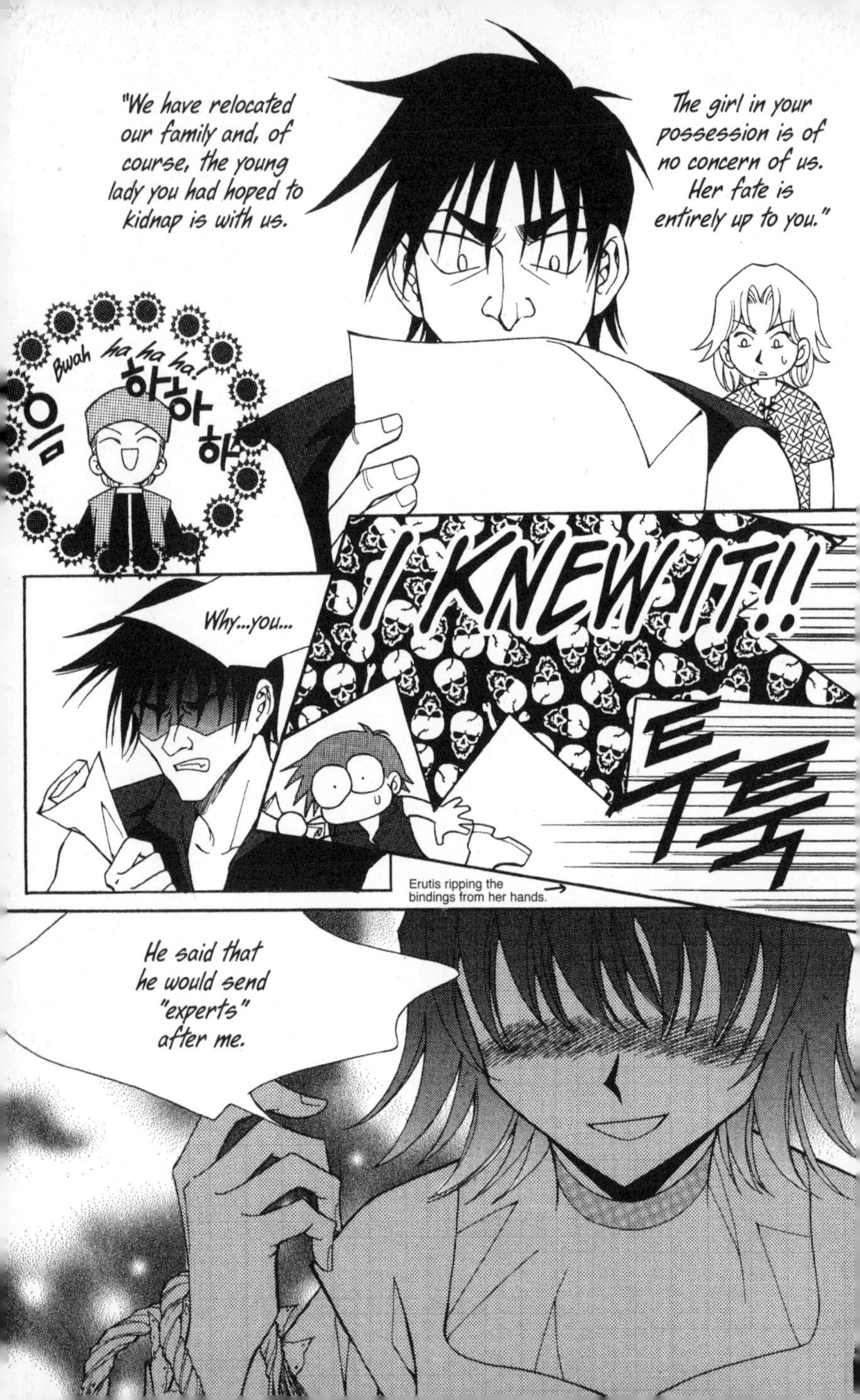
"We have relocated our family and, of course, the young lady you had hoped to kidnap is with us.
The girl in your possession is of no concern of us. Her fate is entirely up to you."
Bwah ha ha ha!
음하하하
I KNEW IT!!
Why...you...
Erutis ripping the bindings from her hands.
He said that he would send "experts" after me.

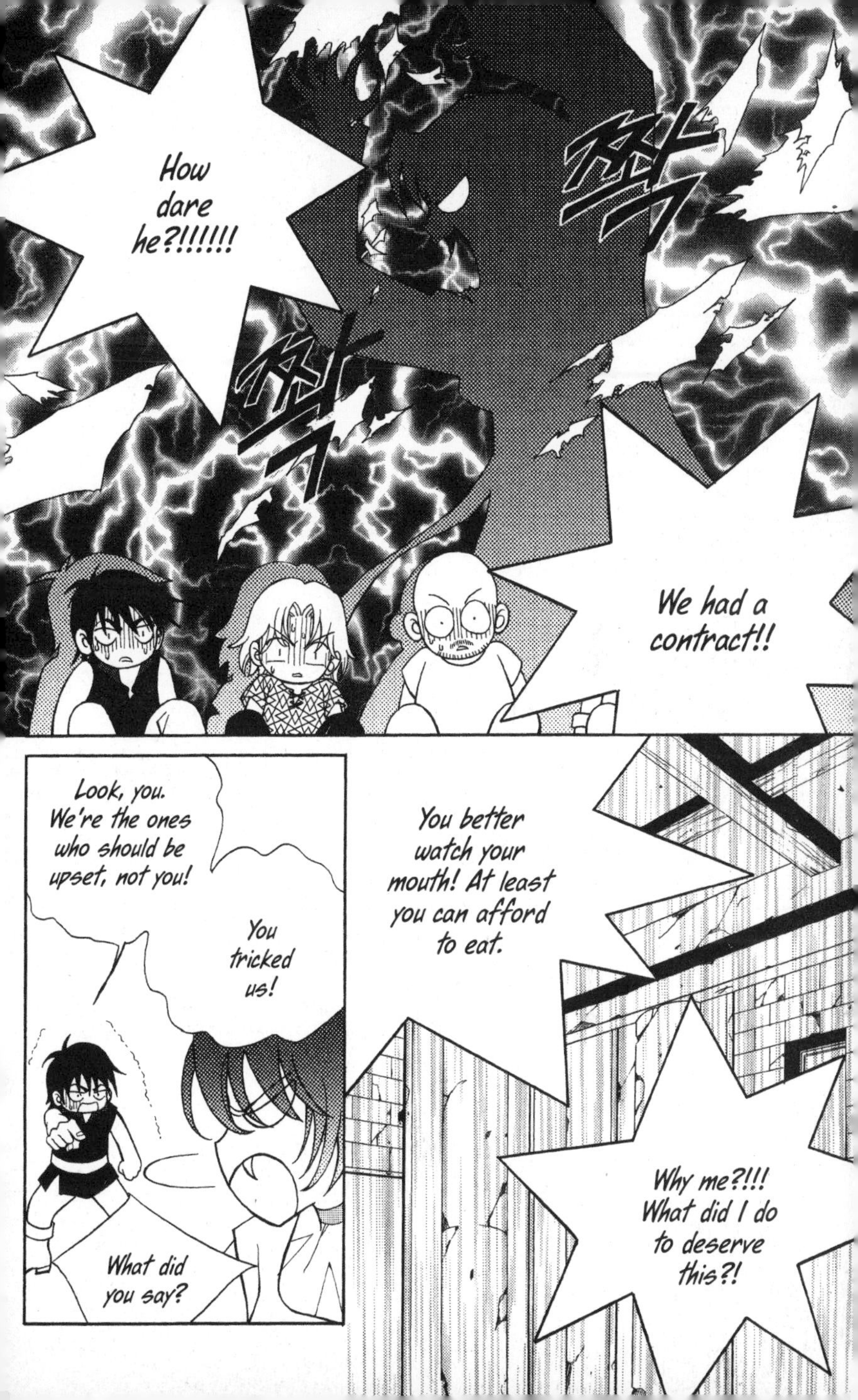
How dare he?!!!!!!
We had a contract!!
Look, you. We're the ones who should be upset, not you!
You tricked us!
What did you say?
You better watch your mouth! At least you can afford to eat.
Why me?!!! What did I do to deserve this?!

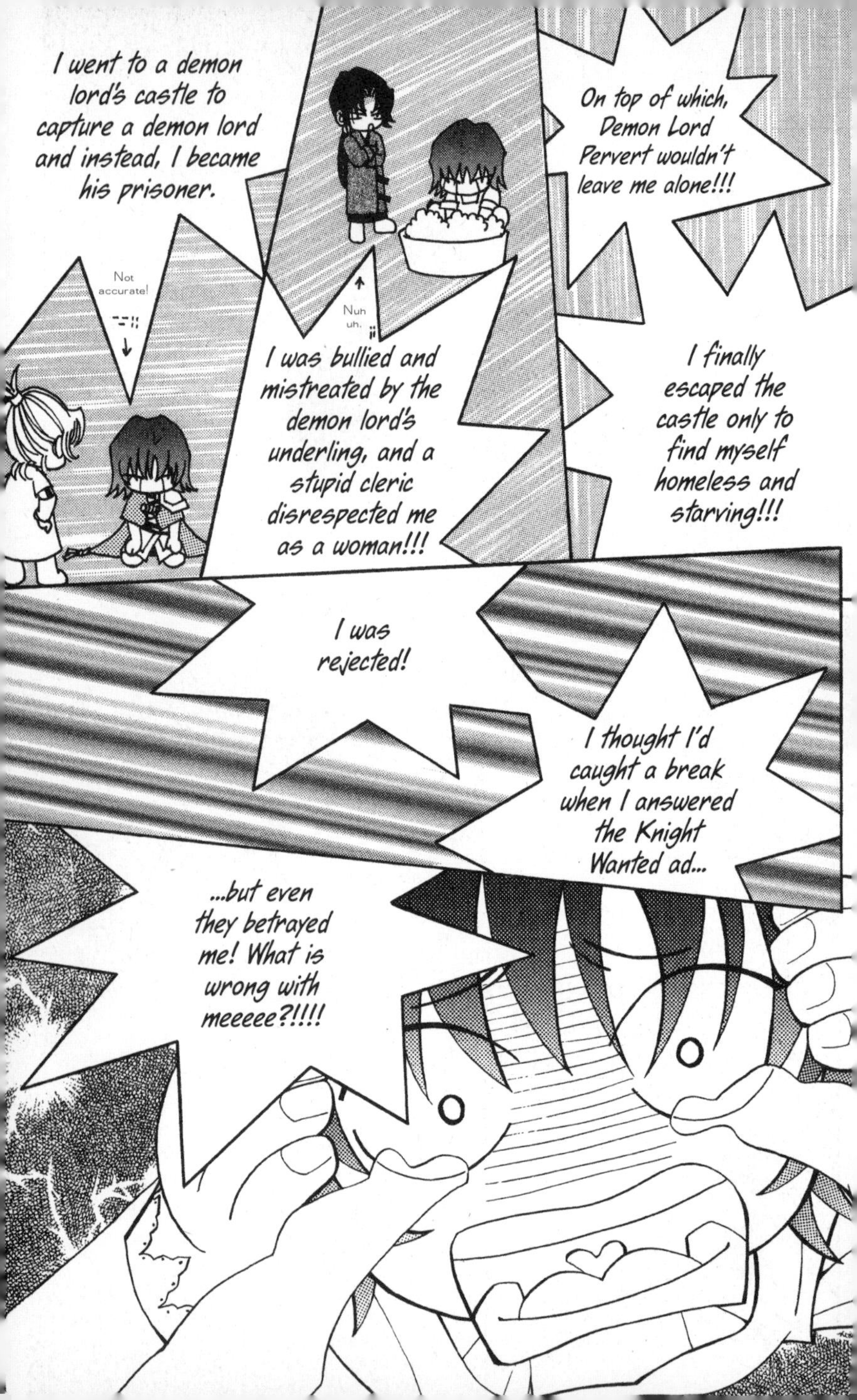
I went to a demon lord's castle to capture a demon lord and instead, I became his prisoner.
Not accurate!
Nuh uh.
I was bullied and mistreated by the demon lord's underling, and a stupid cleric disrespected me as a woman!!!
On top of which, Demon Lord Pervert wouldn't leave me alone!!!
I finally escaped the castle only to find myself homeless and starving!!!
I was rejected!
I thought I'd caught a break when I answered the Knight Wanted ad...
...but even they betrayed me! What is wrong with meeeee?!!!!

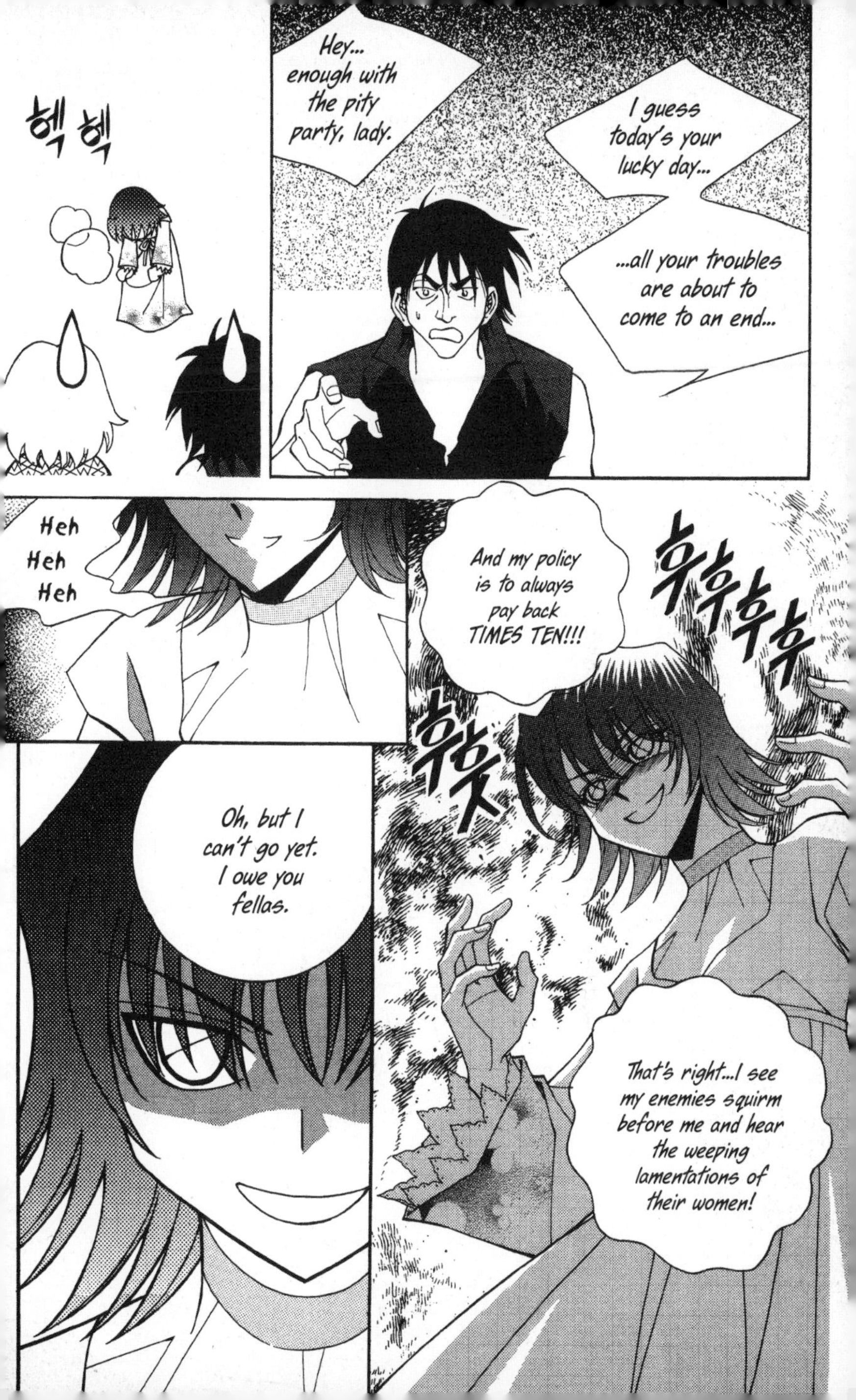

헥 헥
Hey... enough with the pity party, lady.
I guess today's your lucky day...
...all your troubles are about to come to an end...
Heh Heh Heh
Oh, but I can't go yet. I owe you fellas.
And my policy is to always pay back TIMES TEN!!!
후후후후
후훗
That's right...I see my enemies squirm before me and hear the weeping lamentations of their women!

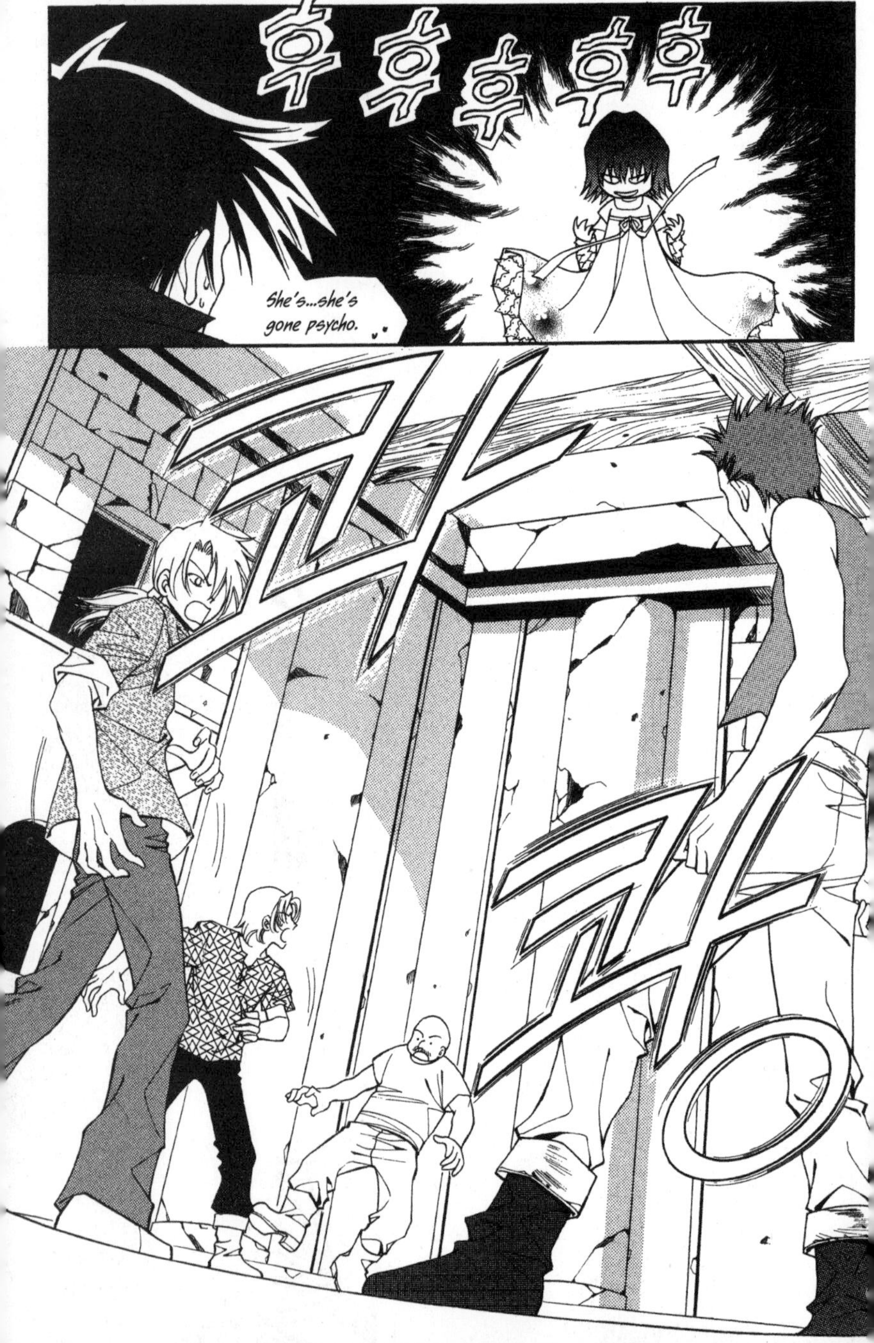
후후후후후
She's...she's gone psycho.

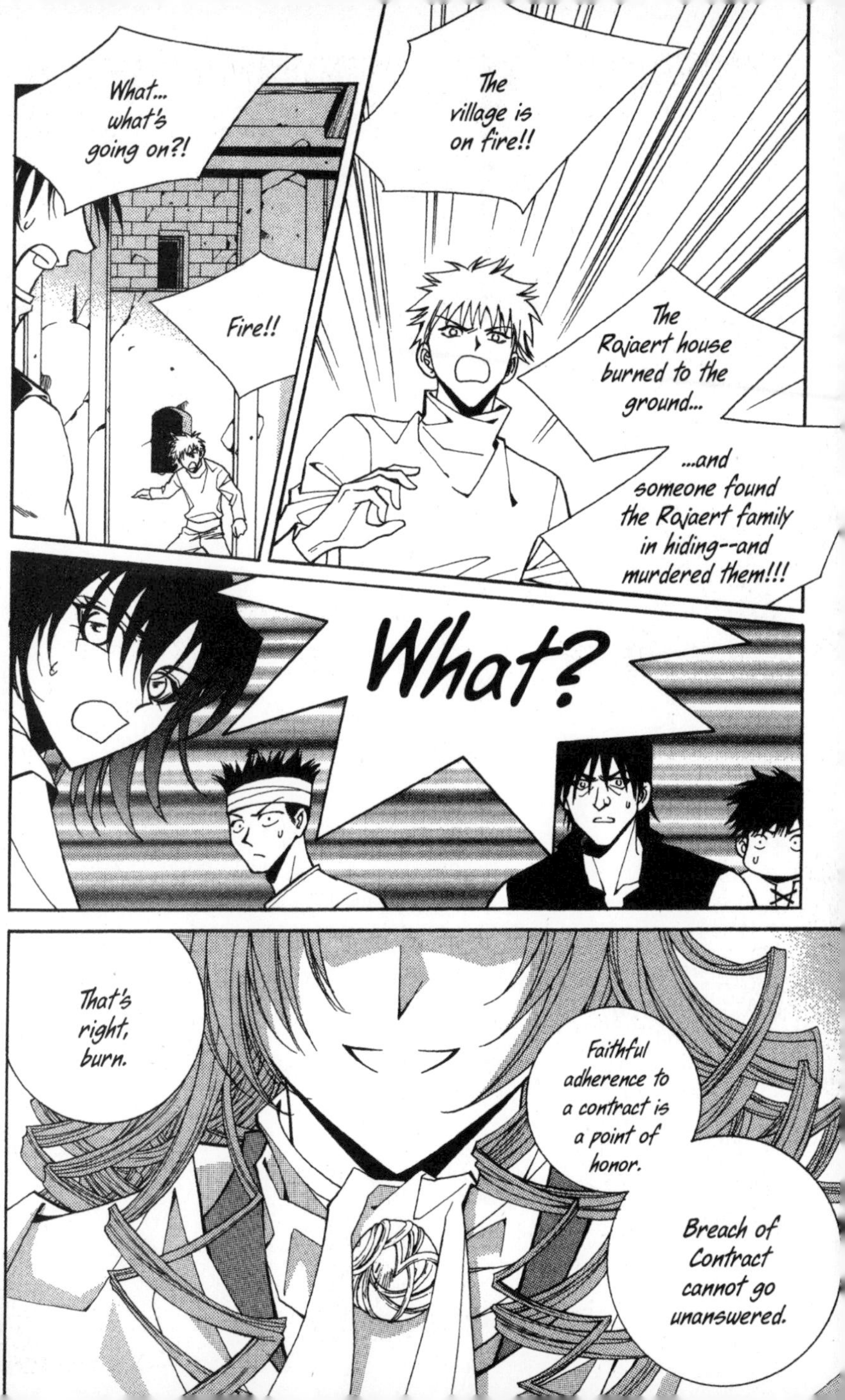
What... what's going on?!
Fire!!
The village is on fire!!
The Rojaert house burned to the ground...
...and someone found the Rojaert family in hiding--and murdered them!!!
What?
That's right, burn.
Faithful adherence to a contract is a point of honor.
Breach of Contract cannot go unanswered.

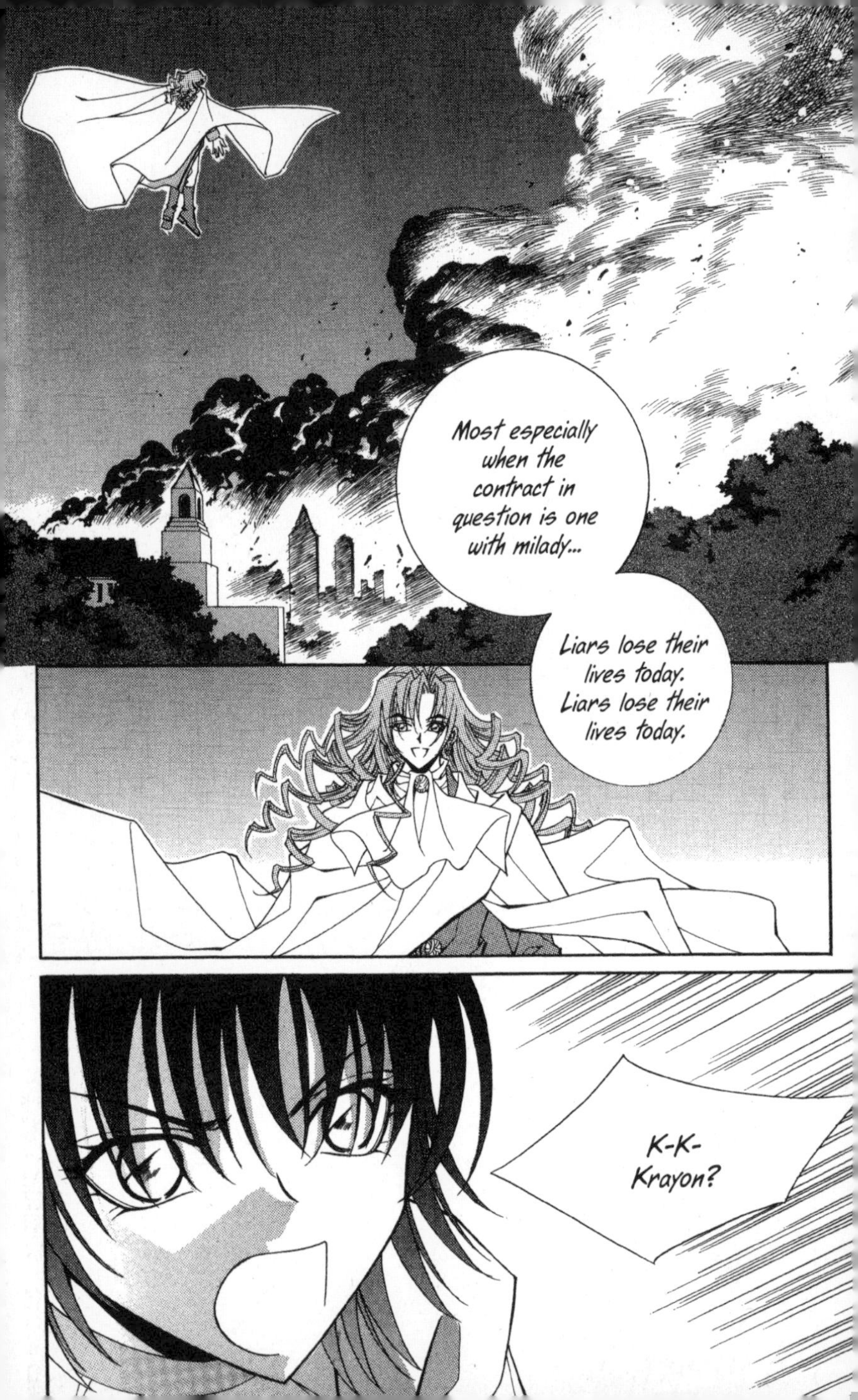
Most especially when the contract in question is one with milady...
Liars lose their lives today. Liars lose their lives today.
K-K-Krayon?

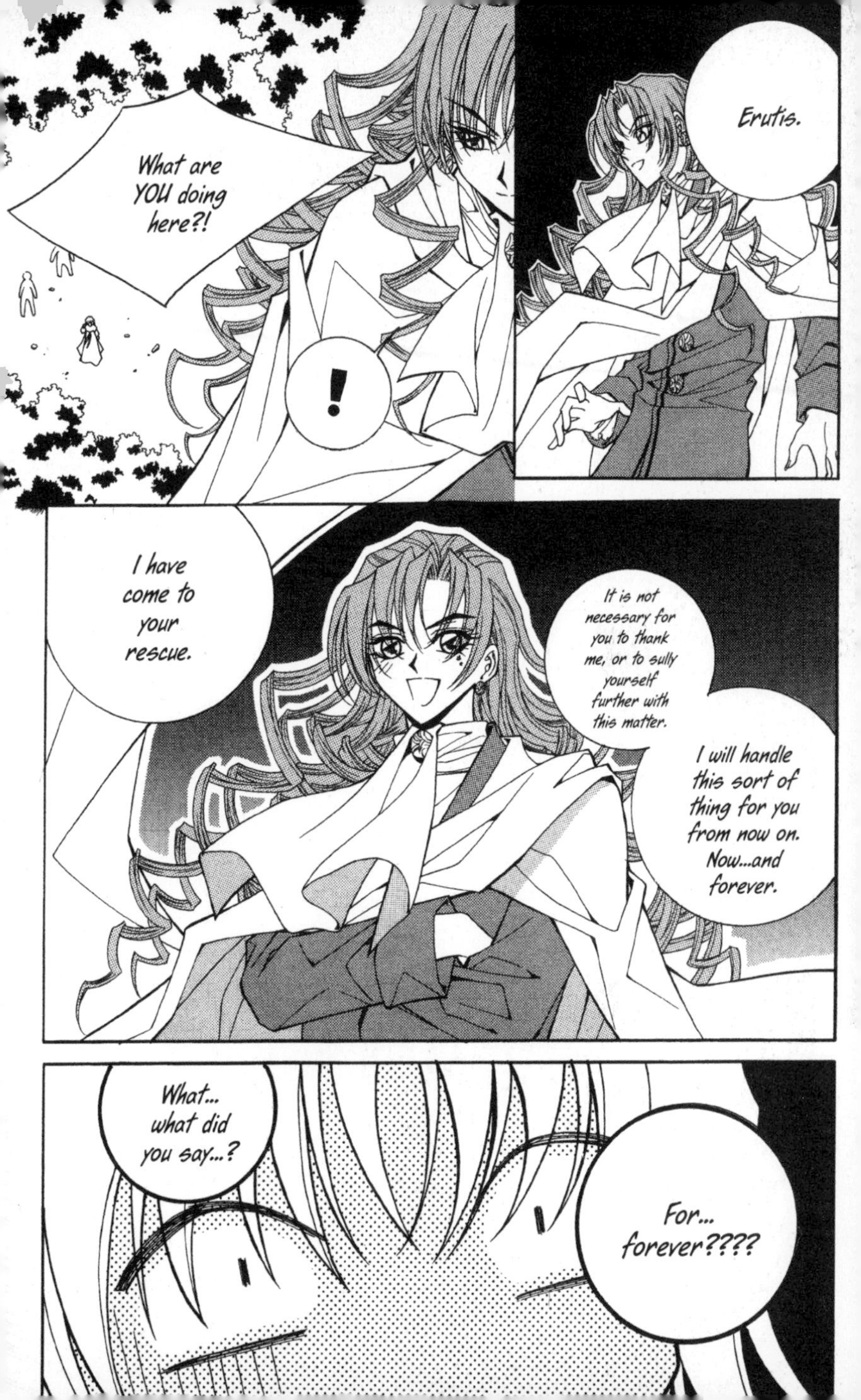
What are YOU doing here?!
!
Erutis.
I have come to your rescue.
It is not necessary for you to thank me, or to sully yourself further with this matter.
I will handle this sort of thing for you from now on. Now...and forever.
What... what did you say...?
For... forever????

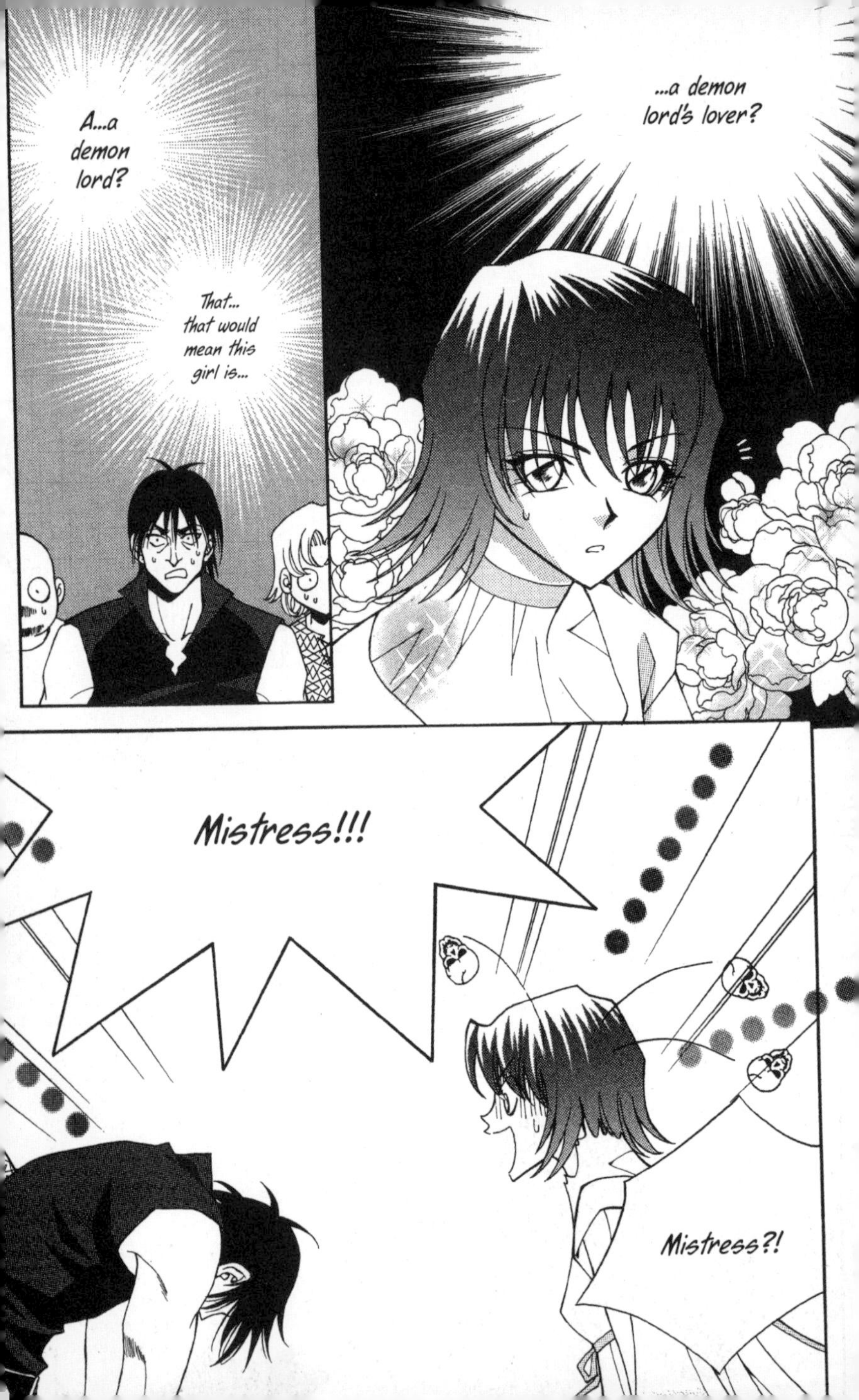
A...a demon lord?
That... that would mean this girl is...
...a demon lord's lover?
Mistress!!!
Mistress?!

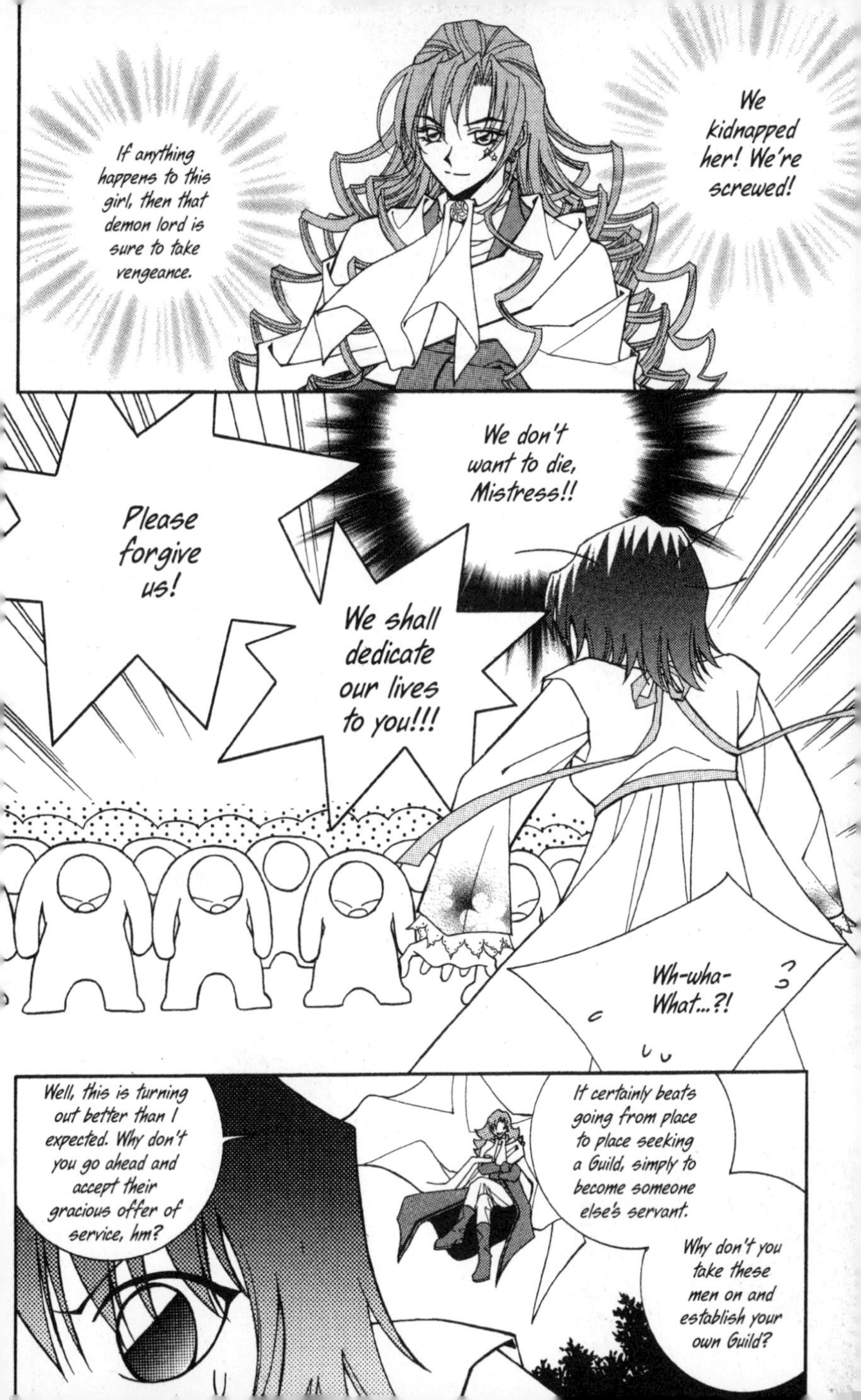
If anything happens to this girl, then that demon lord is sure to take vengeance.
We kidnapped her! We're screwed!
Please forgive us!
We don't want to die, Mistress!!
We shall dedicate our lives to you!!!
Wh-wha- What...?!
Well, this is turning out better than I expected. Why don't you go ahead and accept their gracious offer of service, hm?
It certainly beats going from place to place seeking a Guild, simply to become someone else's servant.
Why don't you take these men on and establish your own Guild?

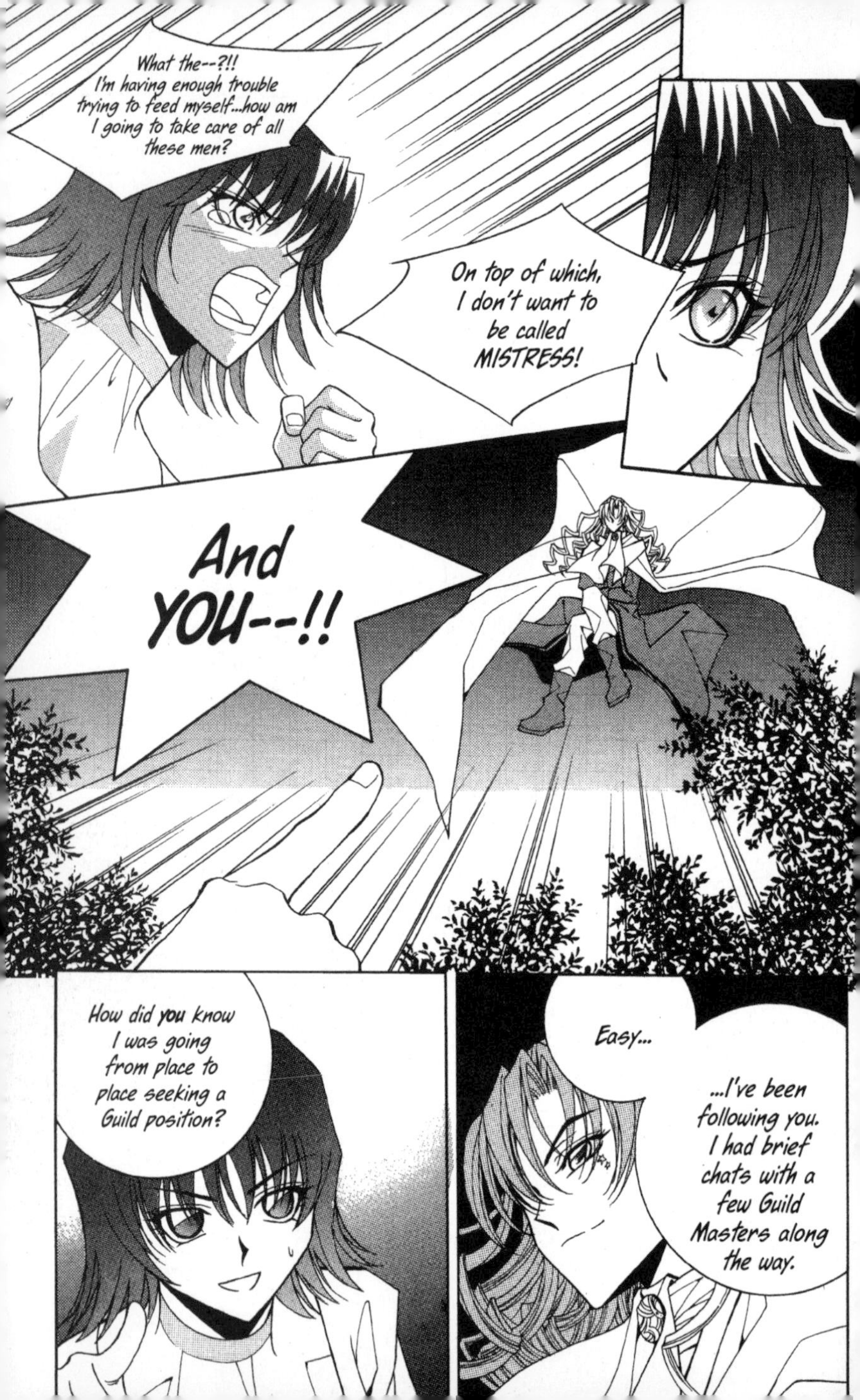
What the--?!!
I'm having enough trouble trying to feed myself...how am I going to take care of all these men?
On top of which, I don't want to be called MISTRESS!
And YOU--!!
How did you know I was going from place to place seeking a Guild position?
Easy...
...I've been following you. I had brief chats with a few Guild Masters along the way.

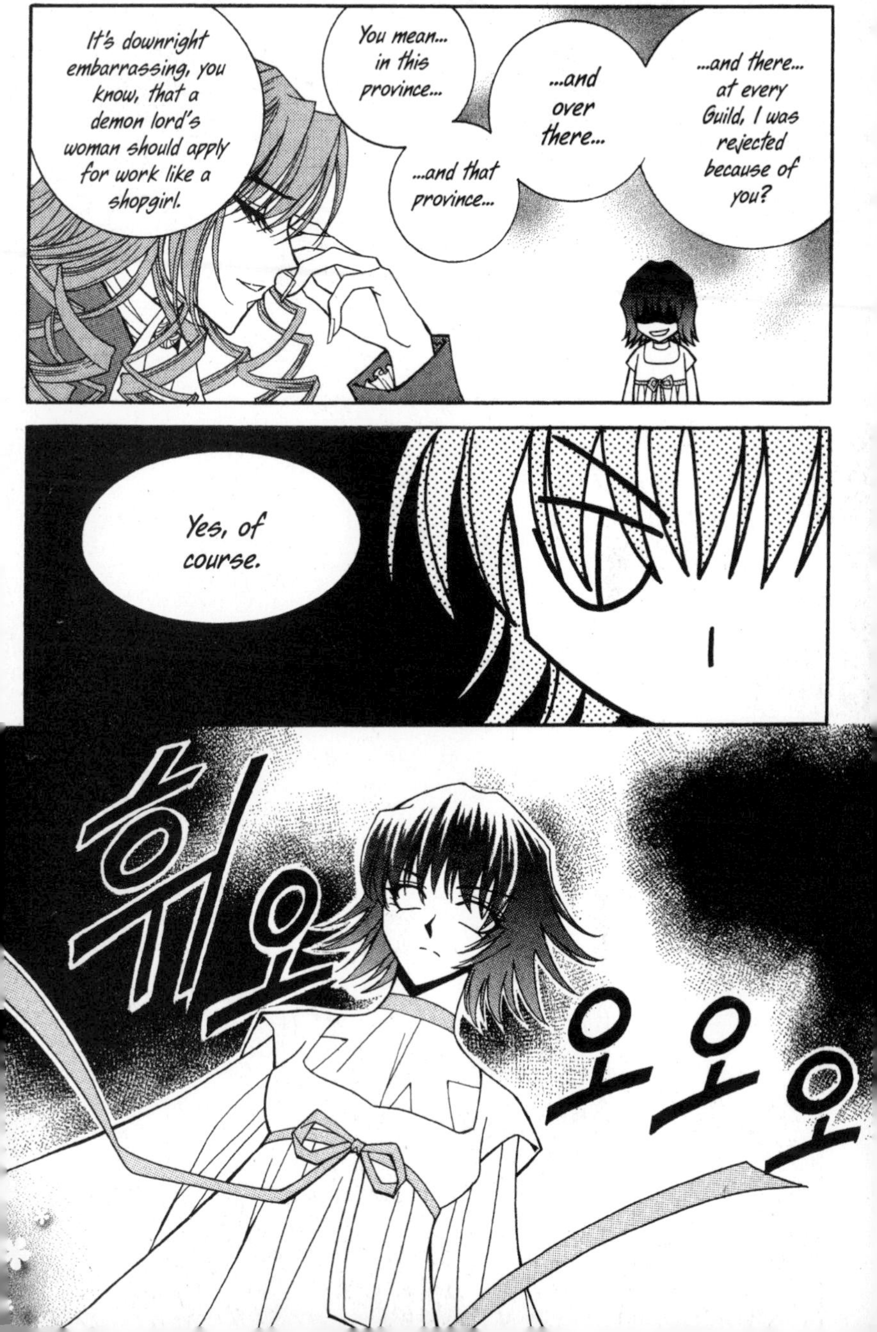
It's downright embarrassing, you know, that a demon lord's woman should apply for work like a shopgirl.
You mean... in this province...
...and that province...
...and over there...
...and there... at every Guild, I was rejected because of you?
Yes, of course.
휘오오오오

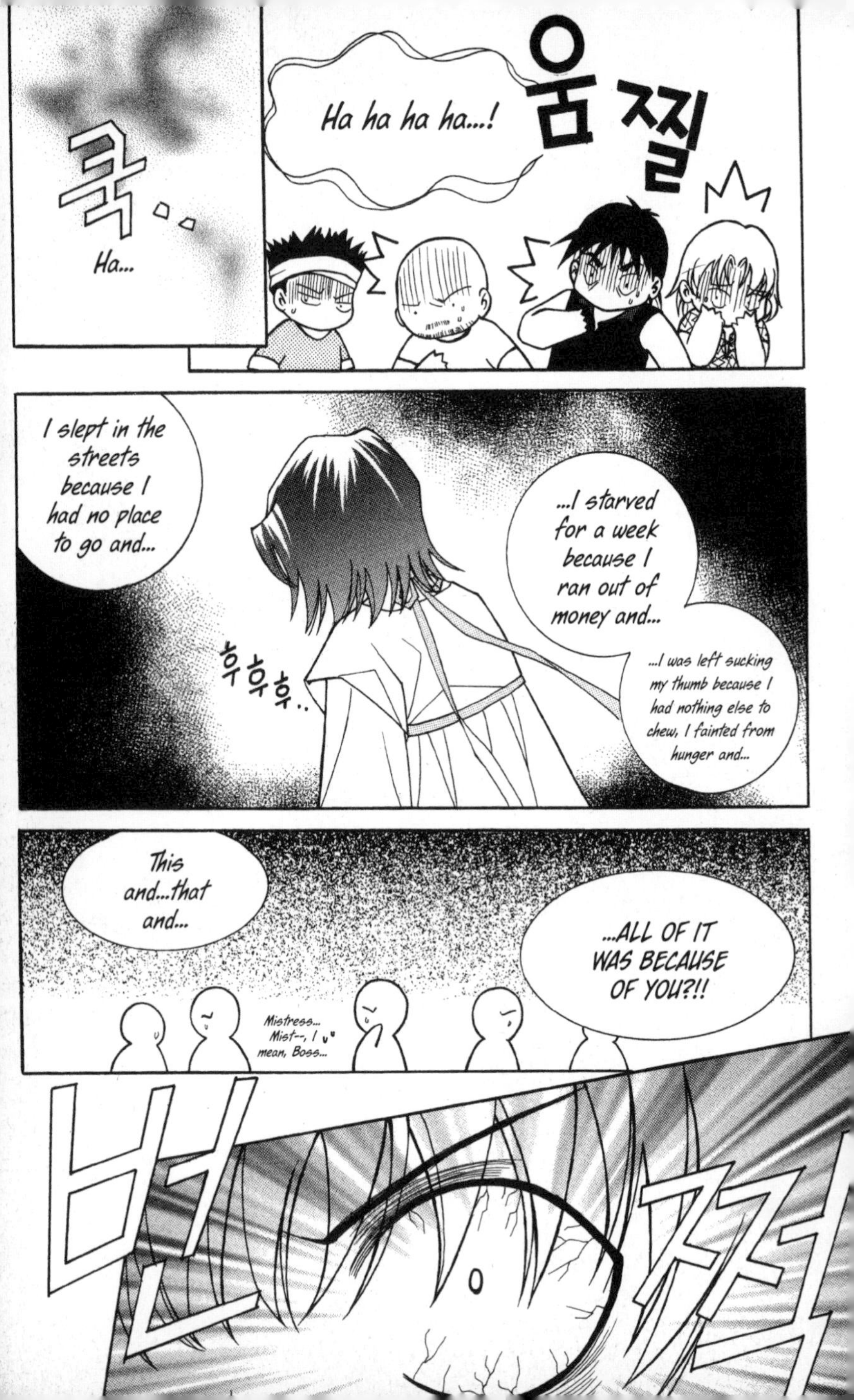
쿡..
Ha...
Ha ha ha ha...!
움찔
I slept in the streets because I had no place to go and...
후후후..
...I starved for a week because I ran out of money and...
...I was left sucking my thumb because I had nothing else to chew, I fainted from hunger and...
This and...that and...
Mistress... Mist--, I mean, Boss...
...ALL OF IT WAS BECAUSE OF YOU?!!
번쩍

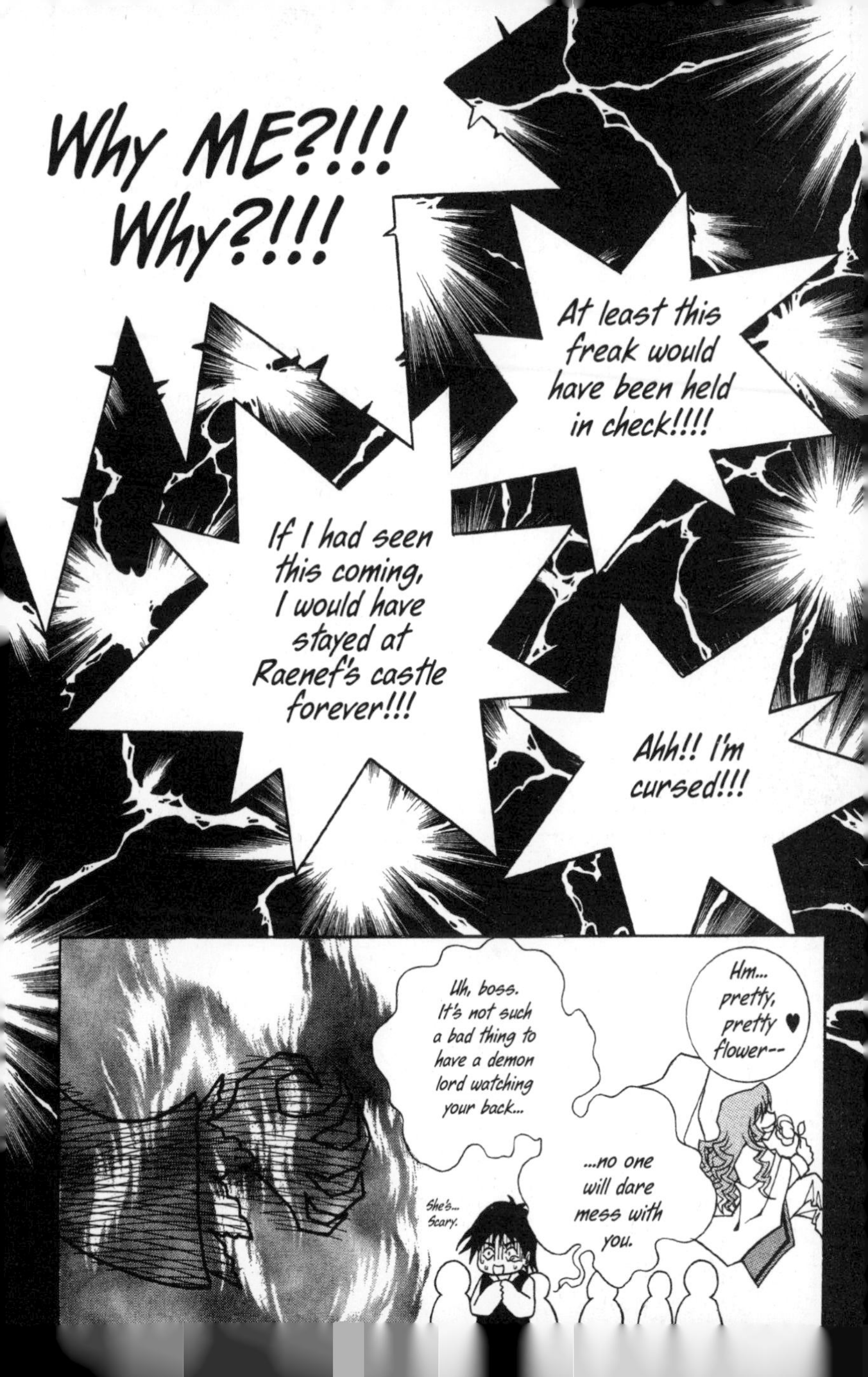

Why ME?!!! Why?!!!
At least this freak would have been held in check!!!!
If I had seen this coming, I would have stayed at Raenef's castle forever!!!
Ahh!! I'm cursed!!!
Uh, boss. It's not such a bad thing to have a demon lord watching your back...
Hm... pretty, pretty flower--
...no one will dare mess with you.
She's... Scary.

Epilogue II – Chris' Story

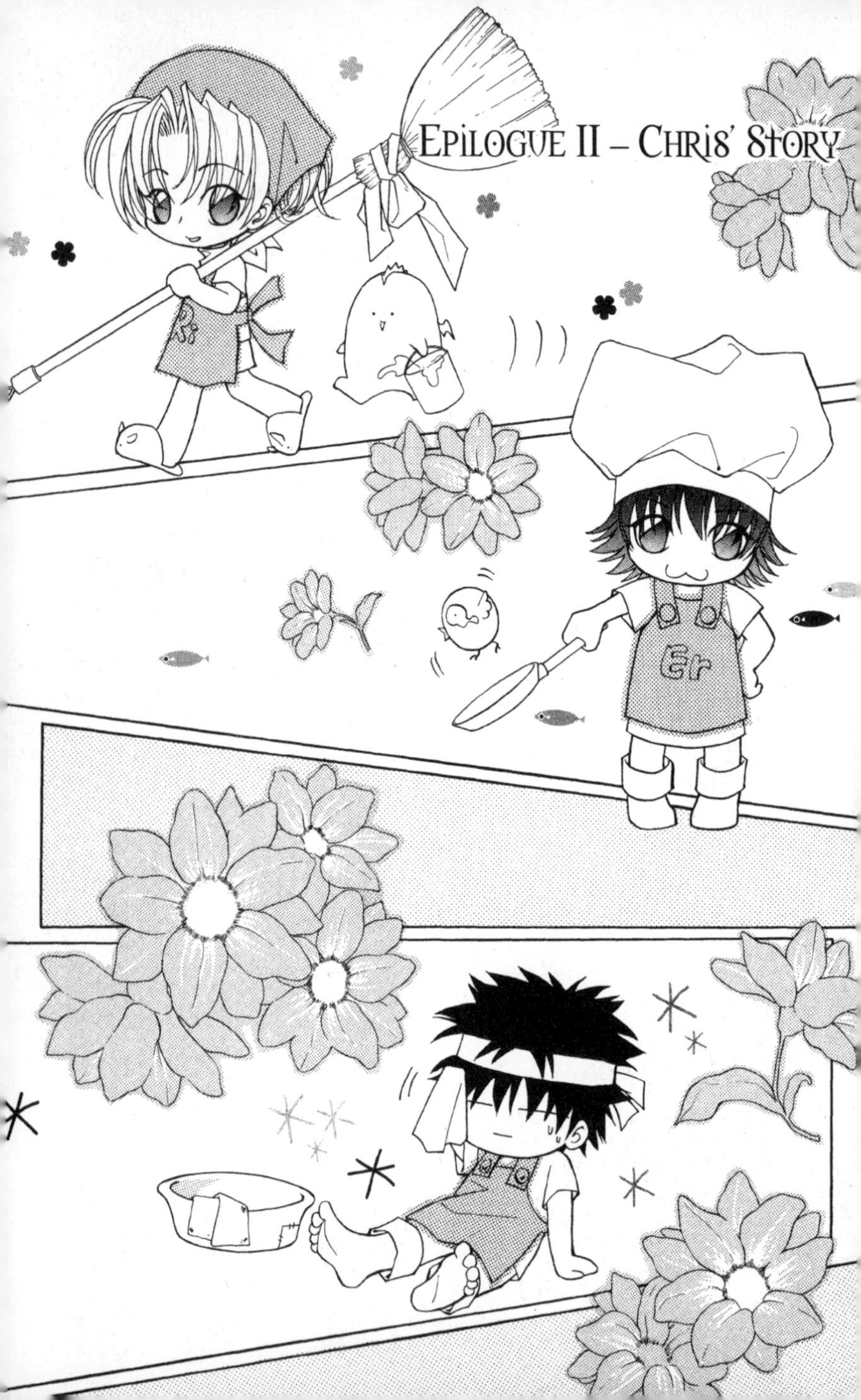

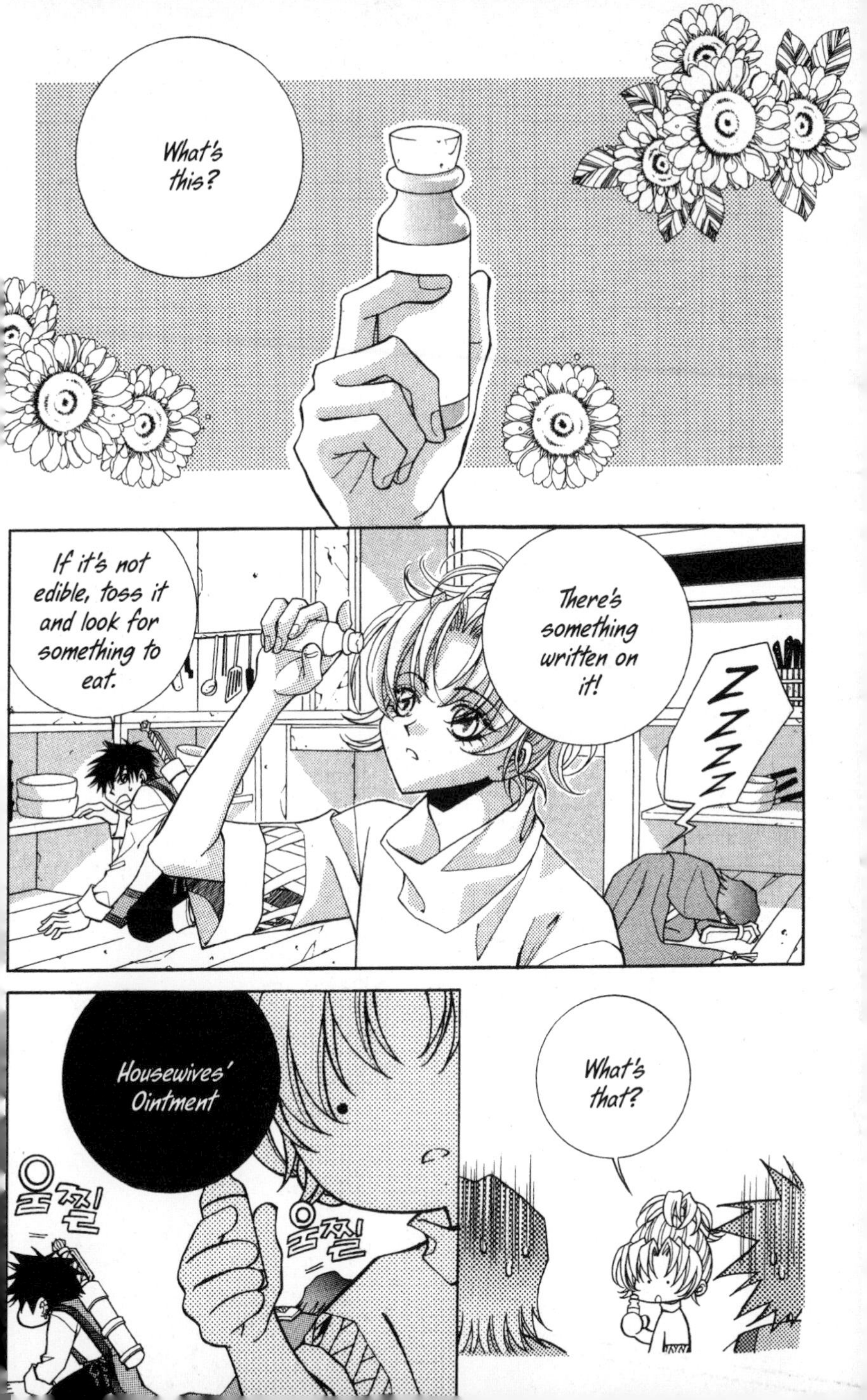
What's this?
If it's not edible, toss it and look for something to eat.
There's something written on it!
ZZZZ
Housewives' Ointment
What's that?

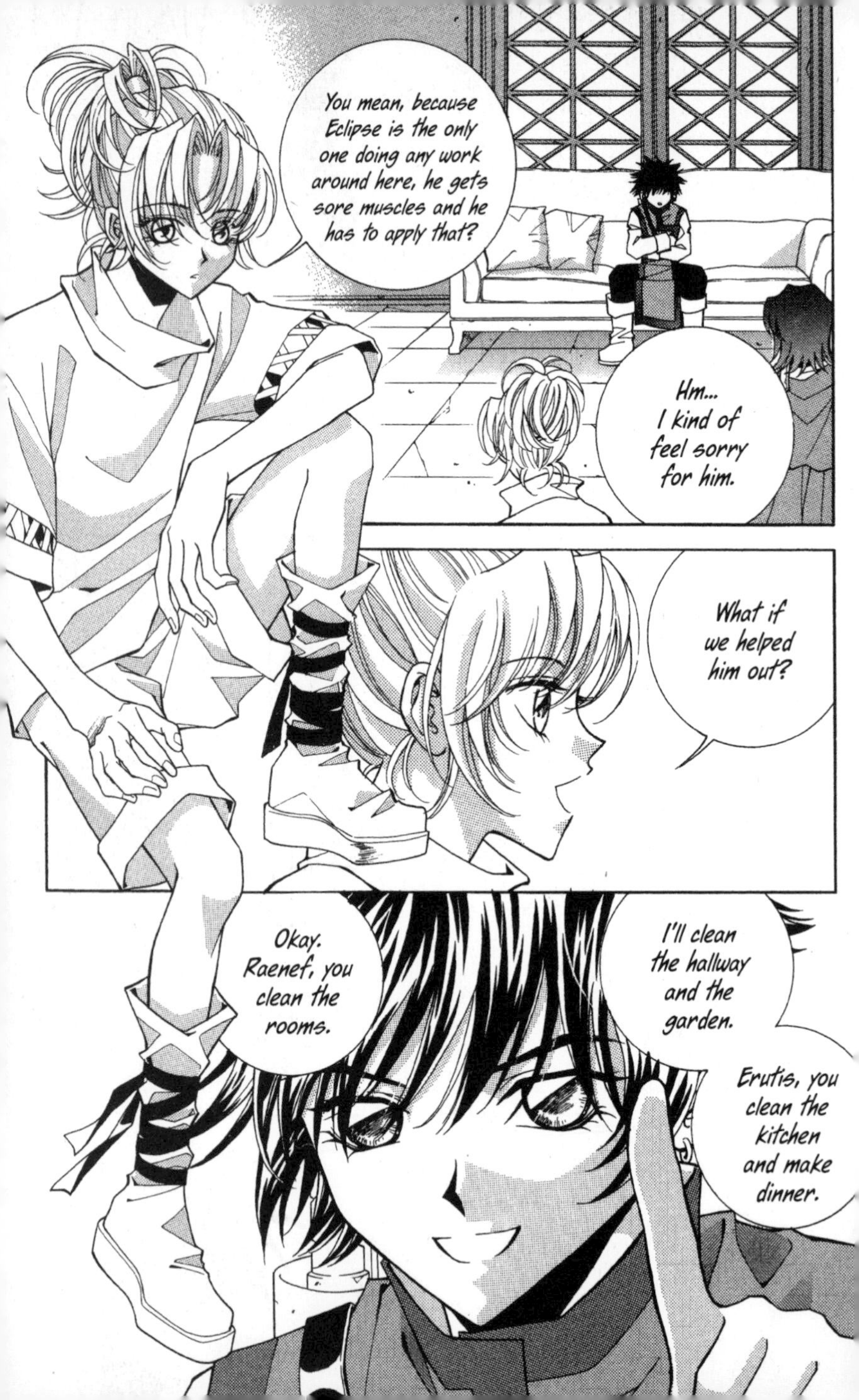
You mean, because Eclipse is the only one doing any work around here, he gets sore muscles and he has to apply that?
Hm... I kind of feel sorry for him.
What if we helped him out?
Okay. Raenef, you clean the rooms.
I'll clean the hallway and the garden.
Erutis, you clean the kitchen and make dinner.

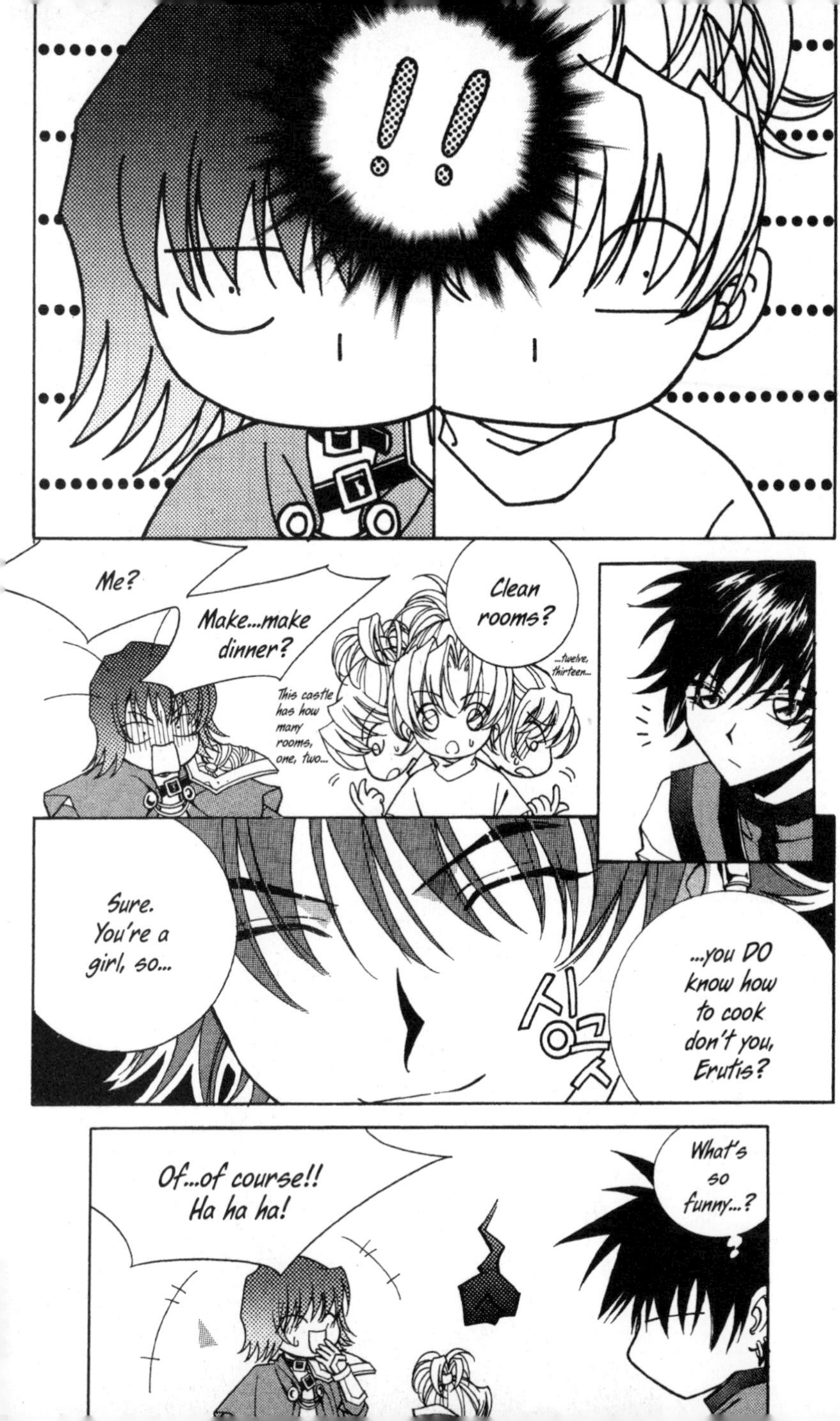
!!
Me?
Make...make dinner?
This castle has how many rooms, one, two...
Clean rooms?
...twelve, thirteen...
Sure. You're a girl, so...
...you DO know how to cook don't you, Erutis?
Of...of course!! Ha ha ha!
What's so funny...?

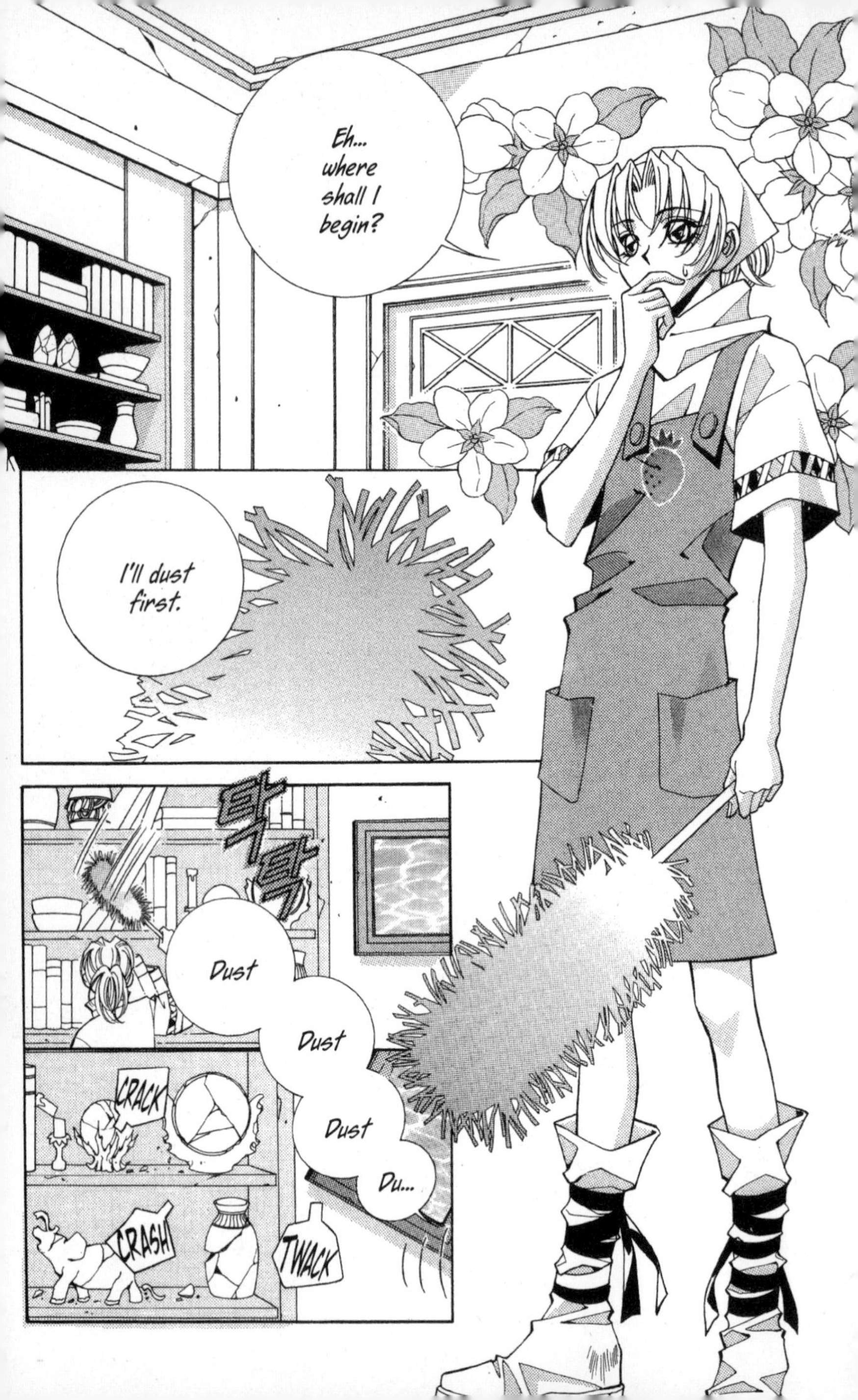

Eh... where shall I begin?
I'll dust first.
Dust
Dust
Dust
Du...
CRACK
CRASH
TWACK

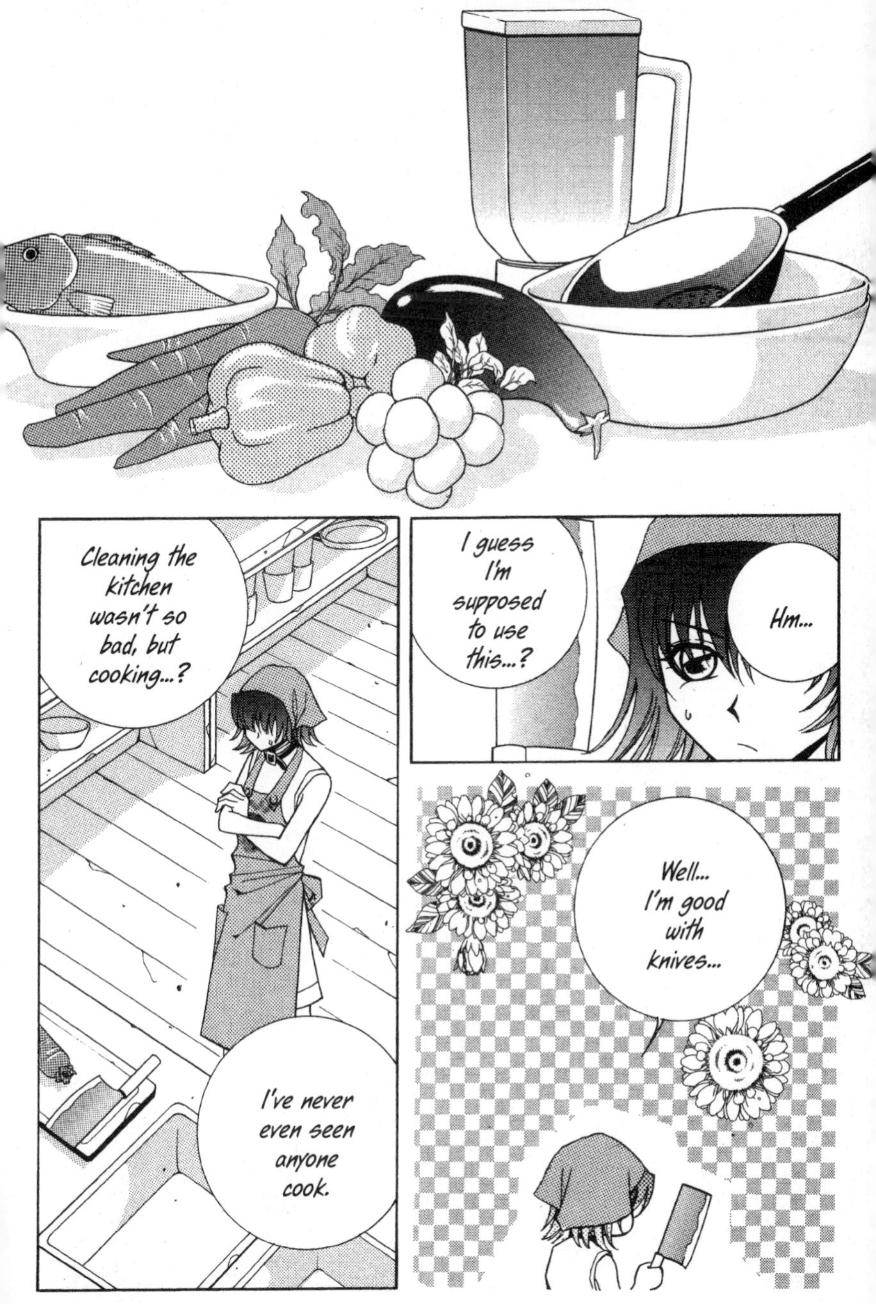
Cleaning the kitchen wasn't so bad, but cooking...?
I've never even seen anyone cook.
I guess I'm supposed to use this...?
Hm...
Well... I'm good with knives...

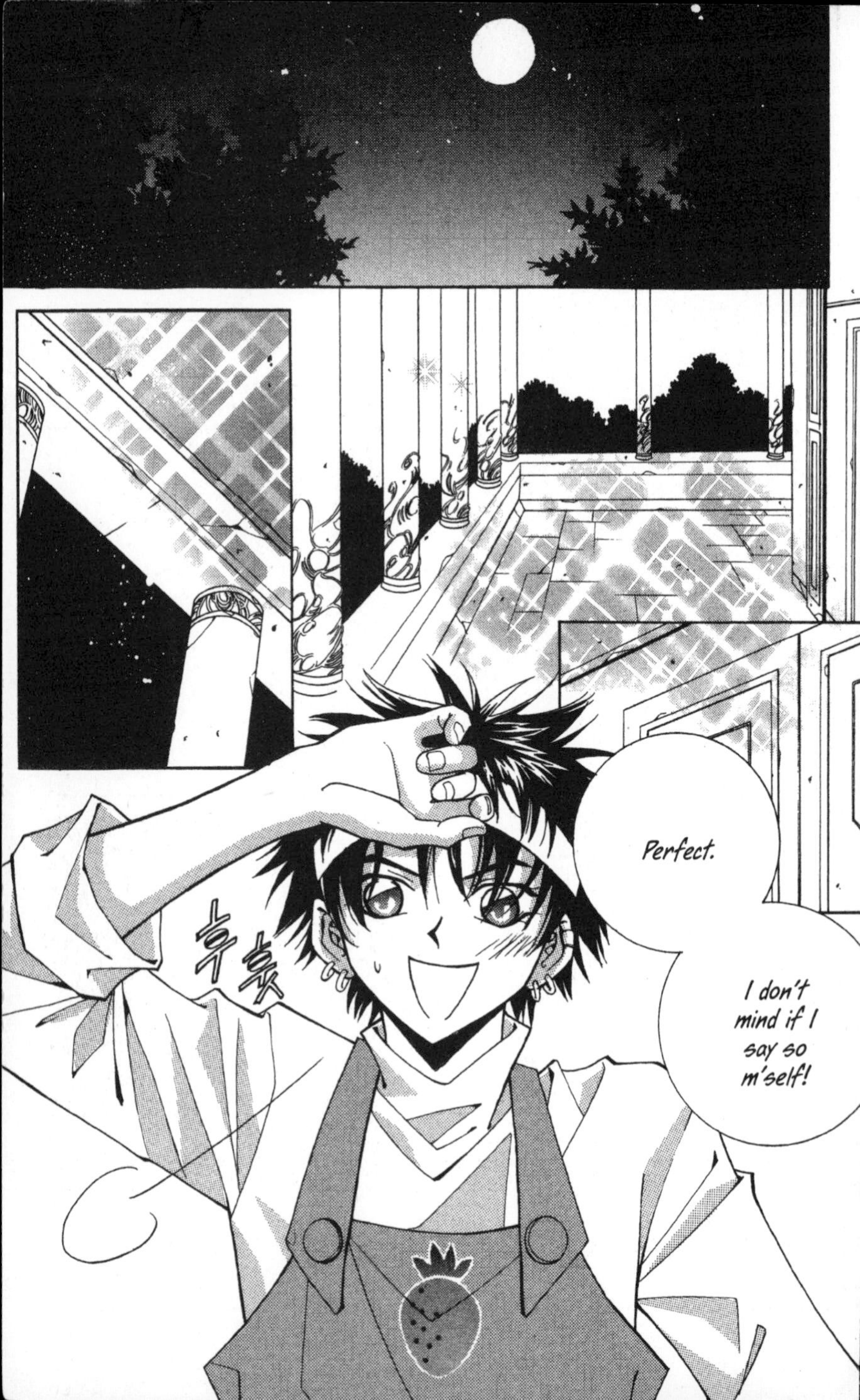
Perfect.
I don't mind if I say so m'self!
후훗

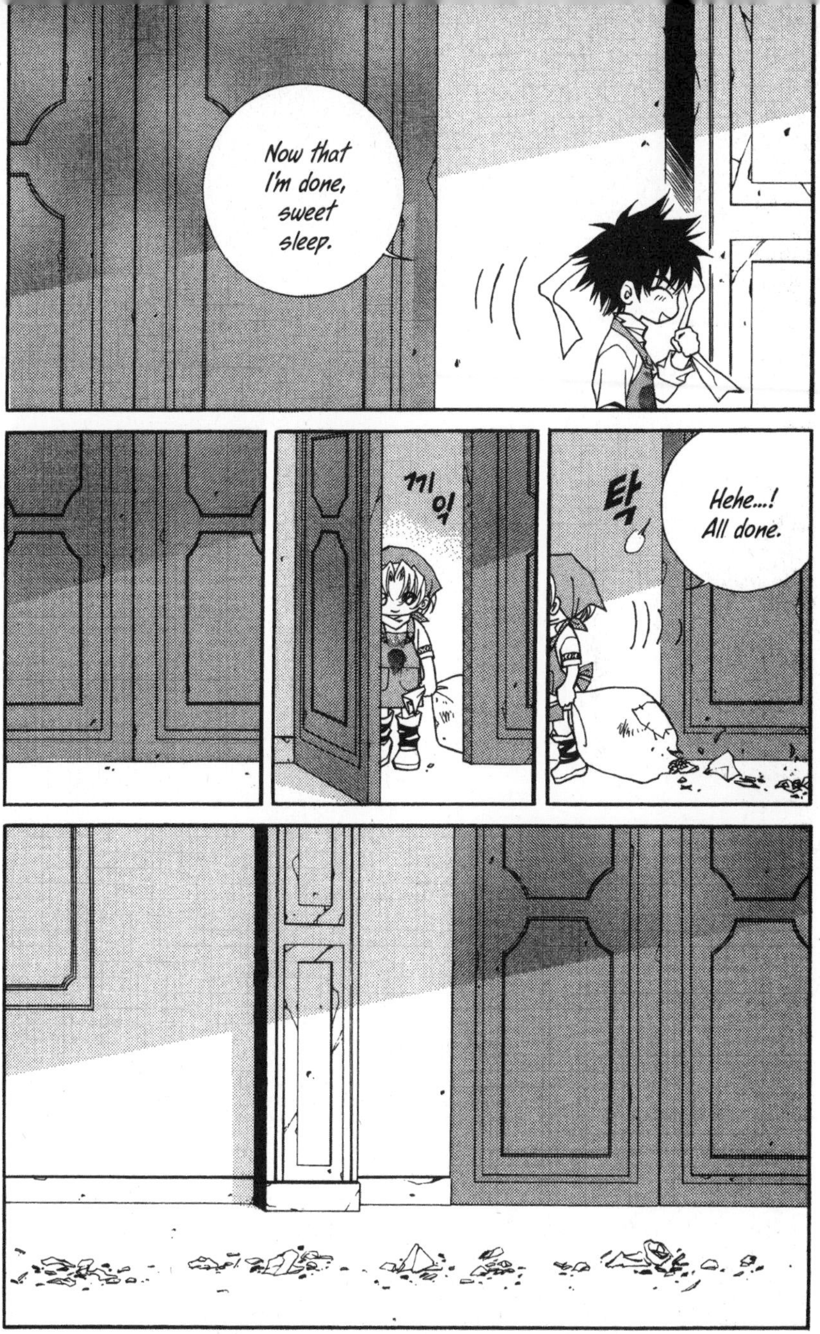
Now that I'm done, sweet sleep.
끼익
탁
Hehe...! All done.

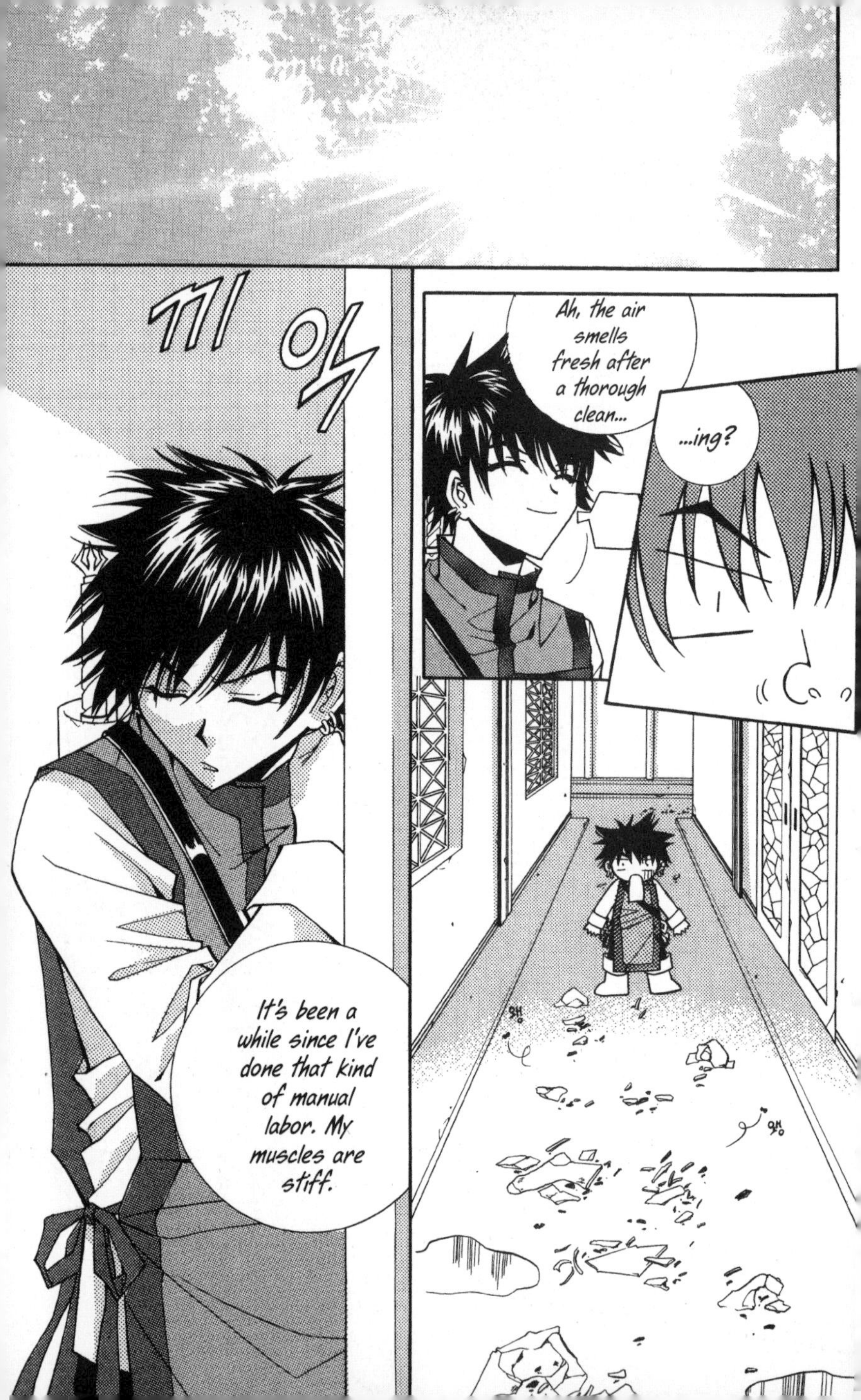
It's been a while since I've done that kind of manual labor. My muscles are stiff.
Ah, the air smells fresh after a thorough clean...
...ing?

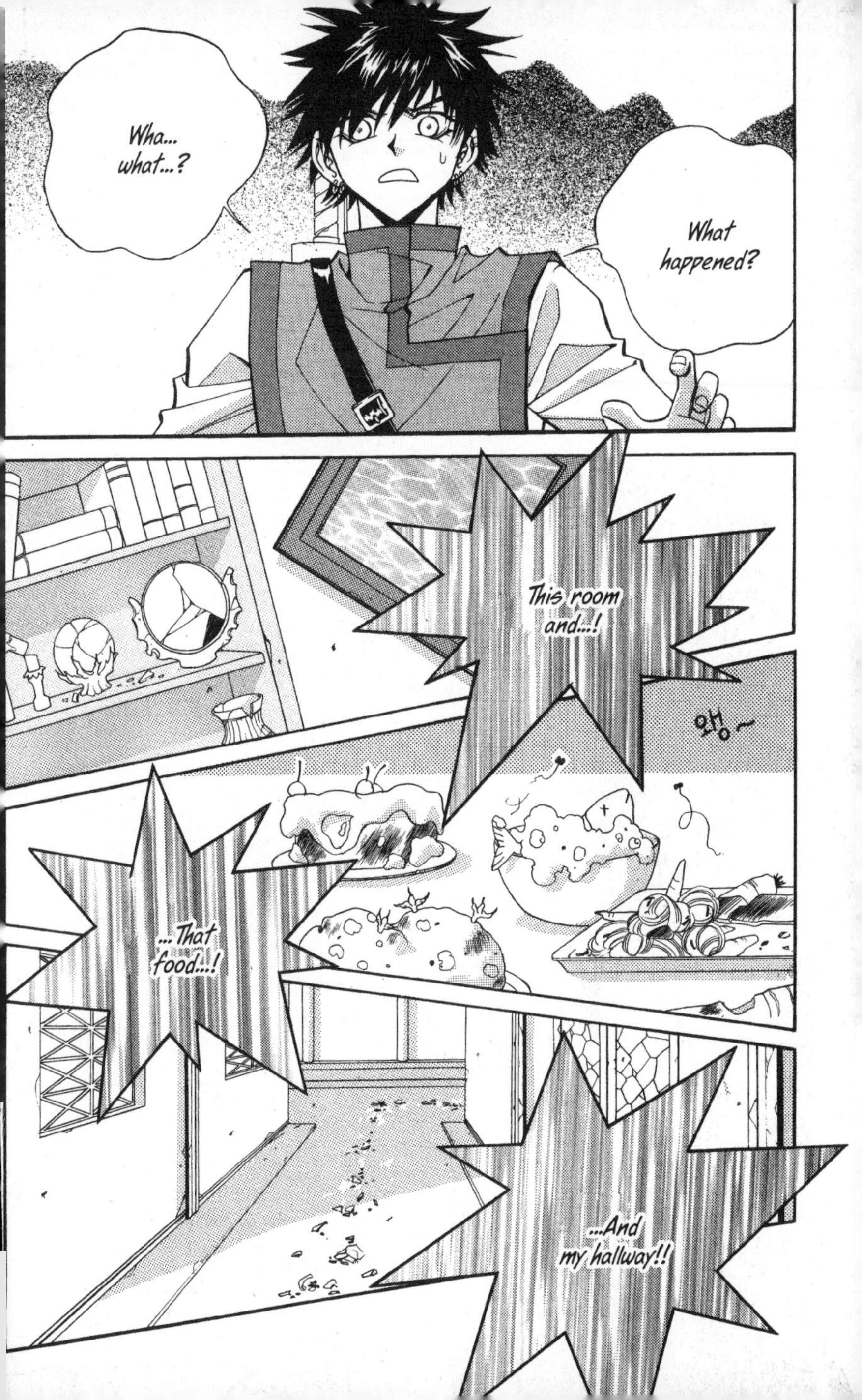
Wha... what...?
What happened?
This room and...!
OH HO ~
...That food...!
...And my hallway!!

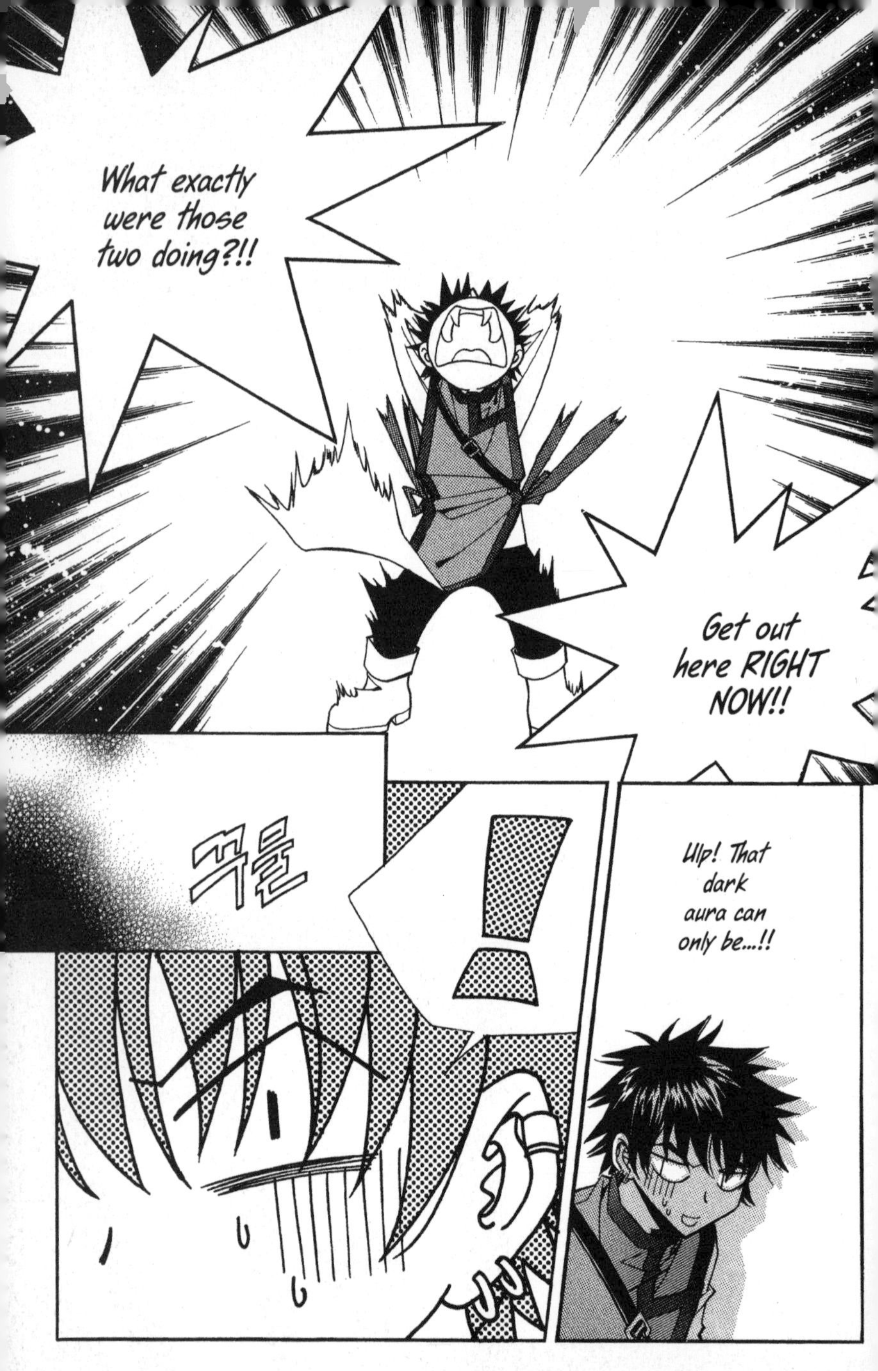
What exactly were those two doing?!!
Get out here RIGHT NOW!!
!
Ulp! That dark aura can only be...!!

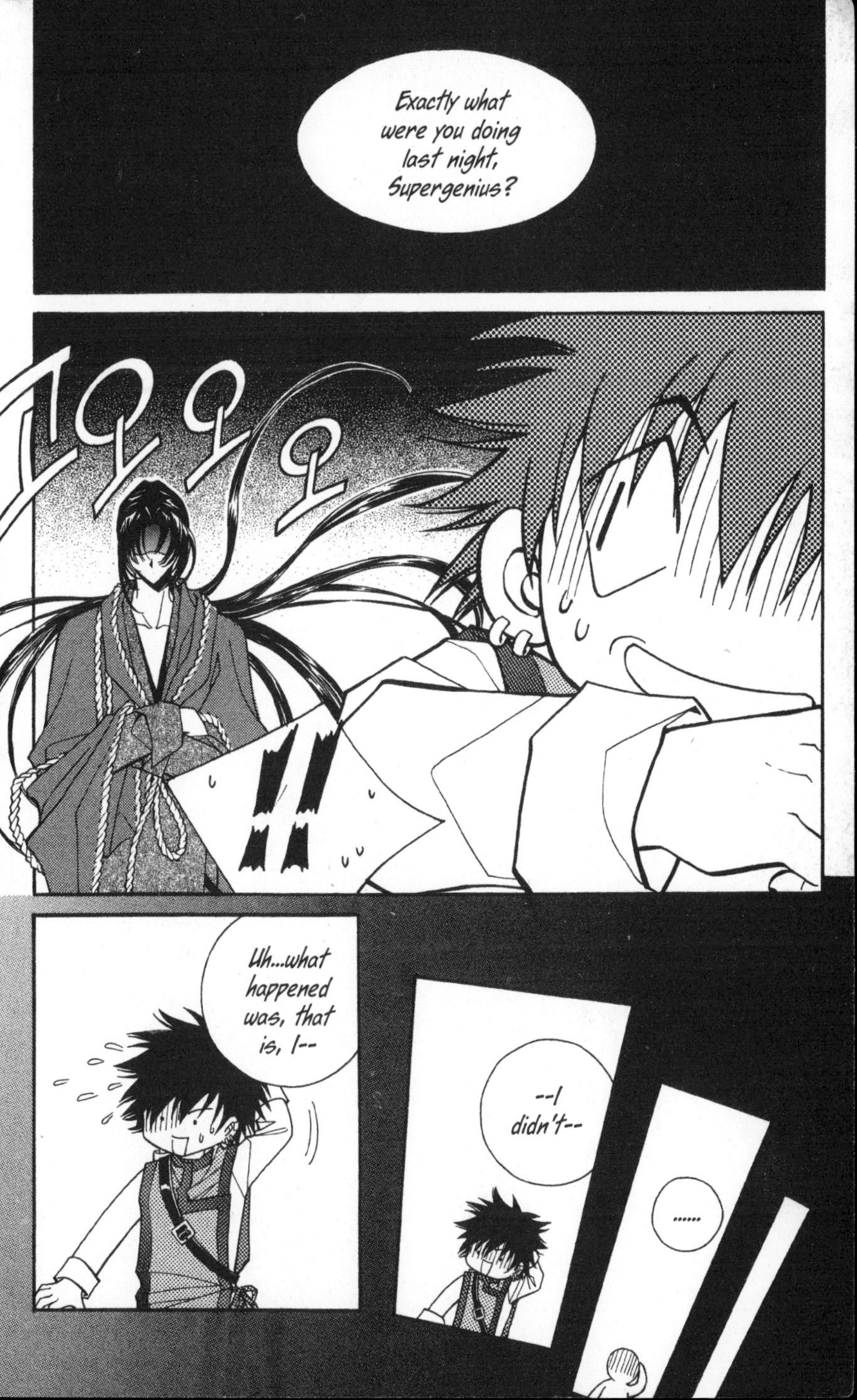
Exactly what were you doing last night, Supergenius?
!!
Uh...what happened was, that is, I--
--I didn't--
......

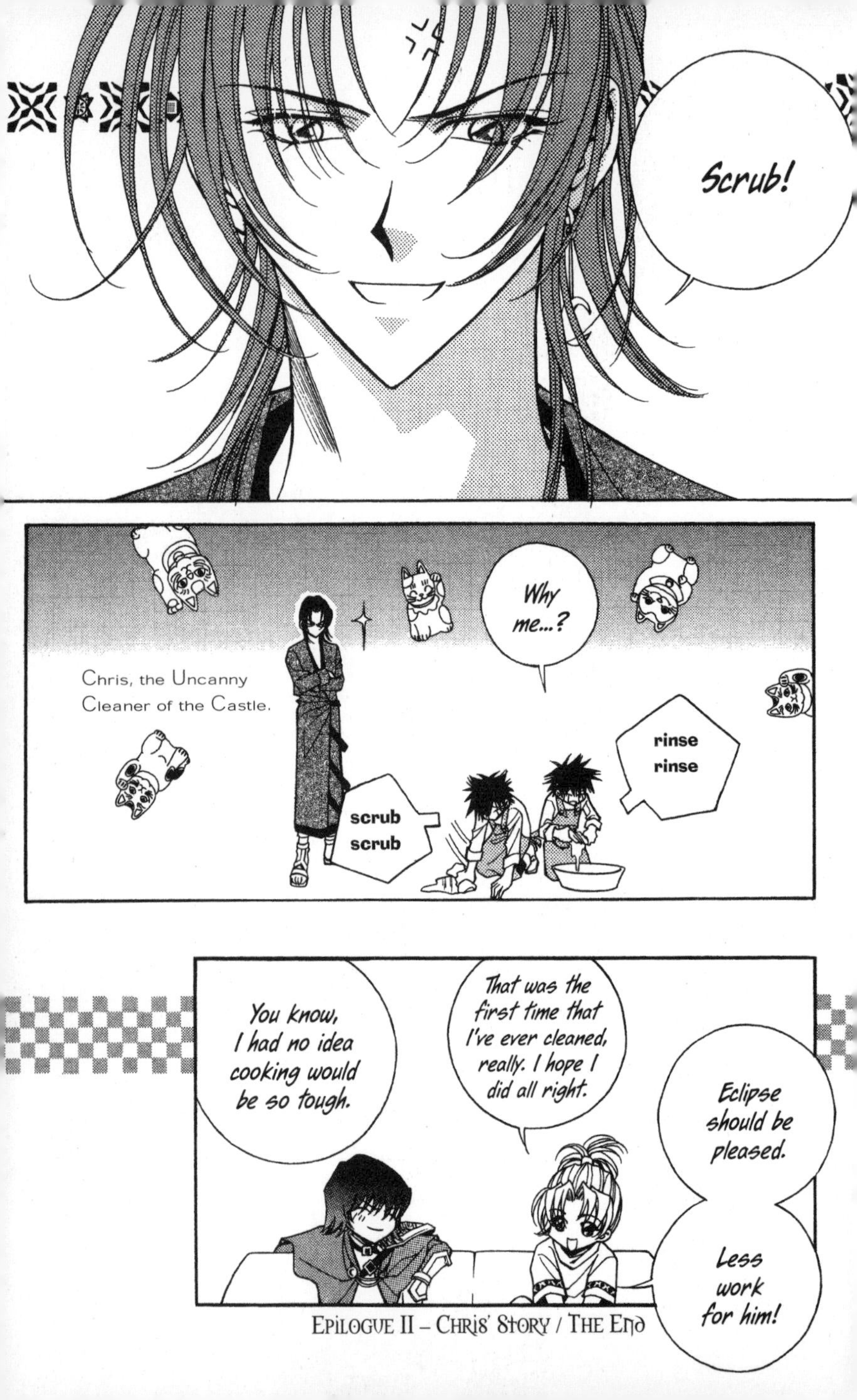
Scrub!
Chris, the Uncanny Cleaner of the Castle.
Why me...?
scrub scrub
rinse rinse
You know, I had no idea cooking would be so tough.
That was the first time that I've ever cleaned, really. I hope I did all right.
Eclipse should be pleased.
Less work for him!
Epilogue II – Chris' Story / The End

Illustrator's Parade

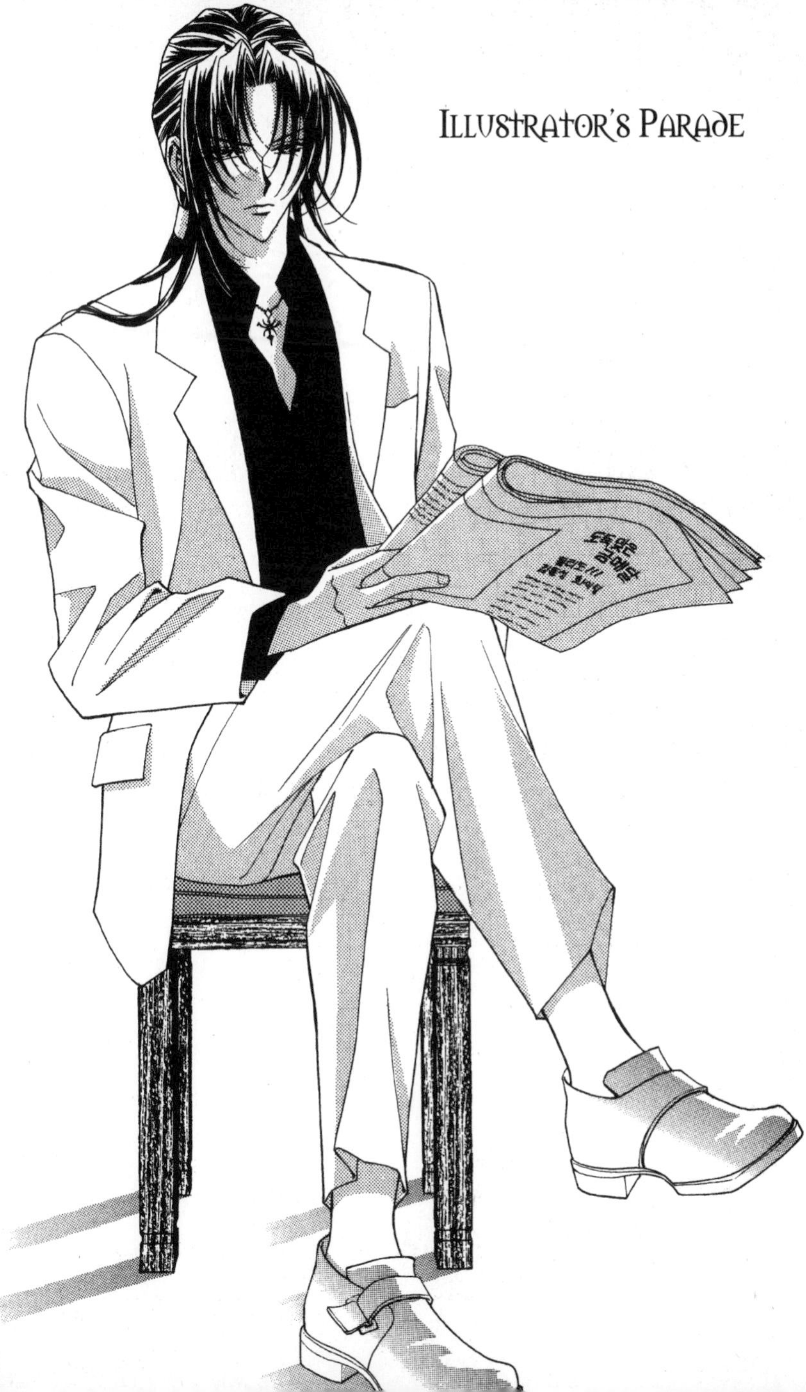

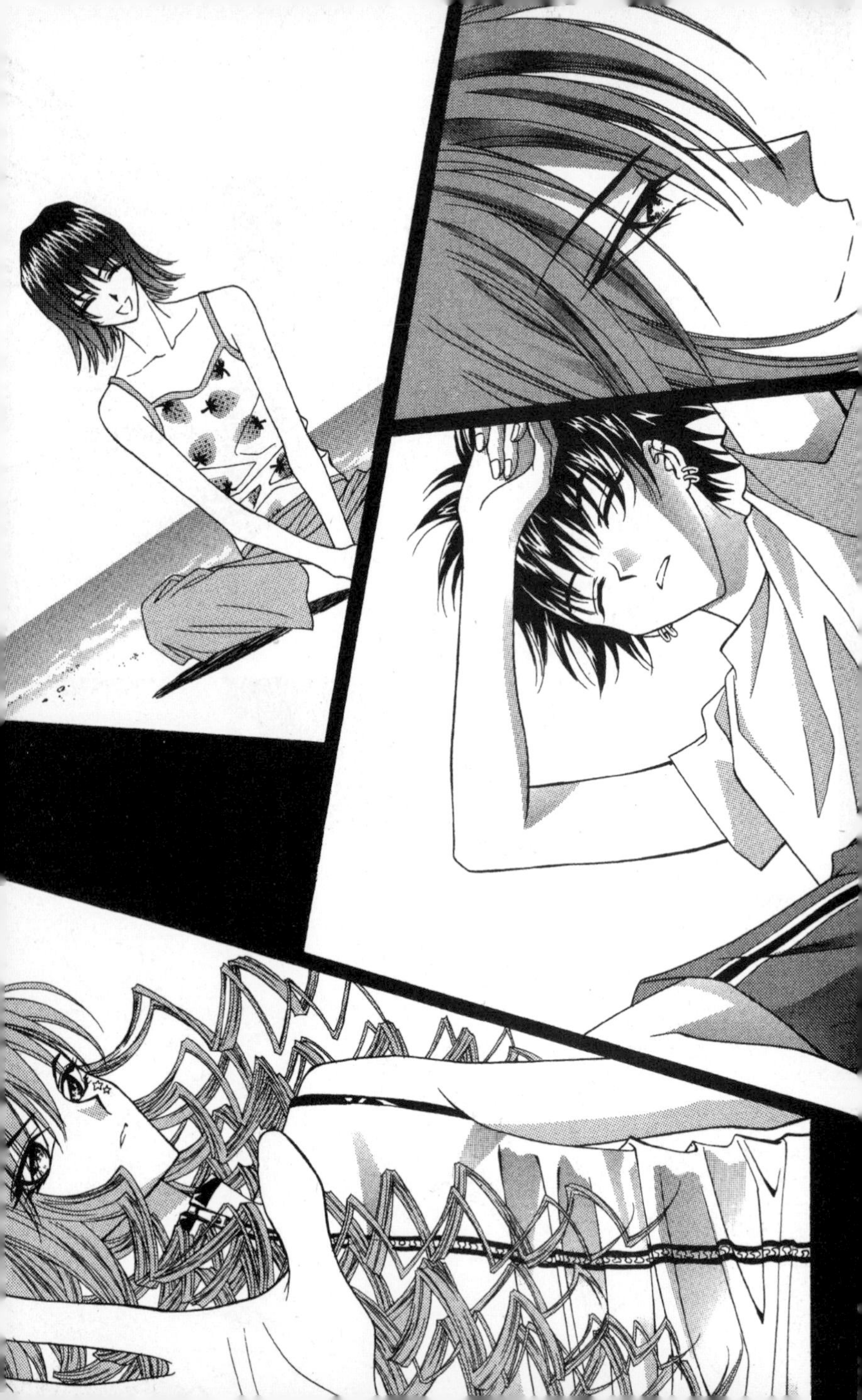

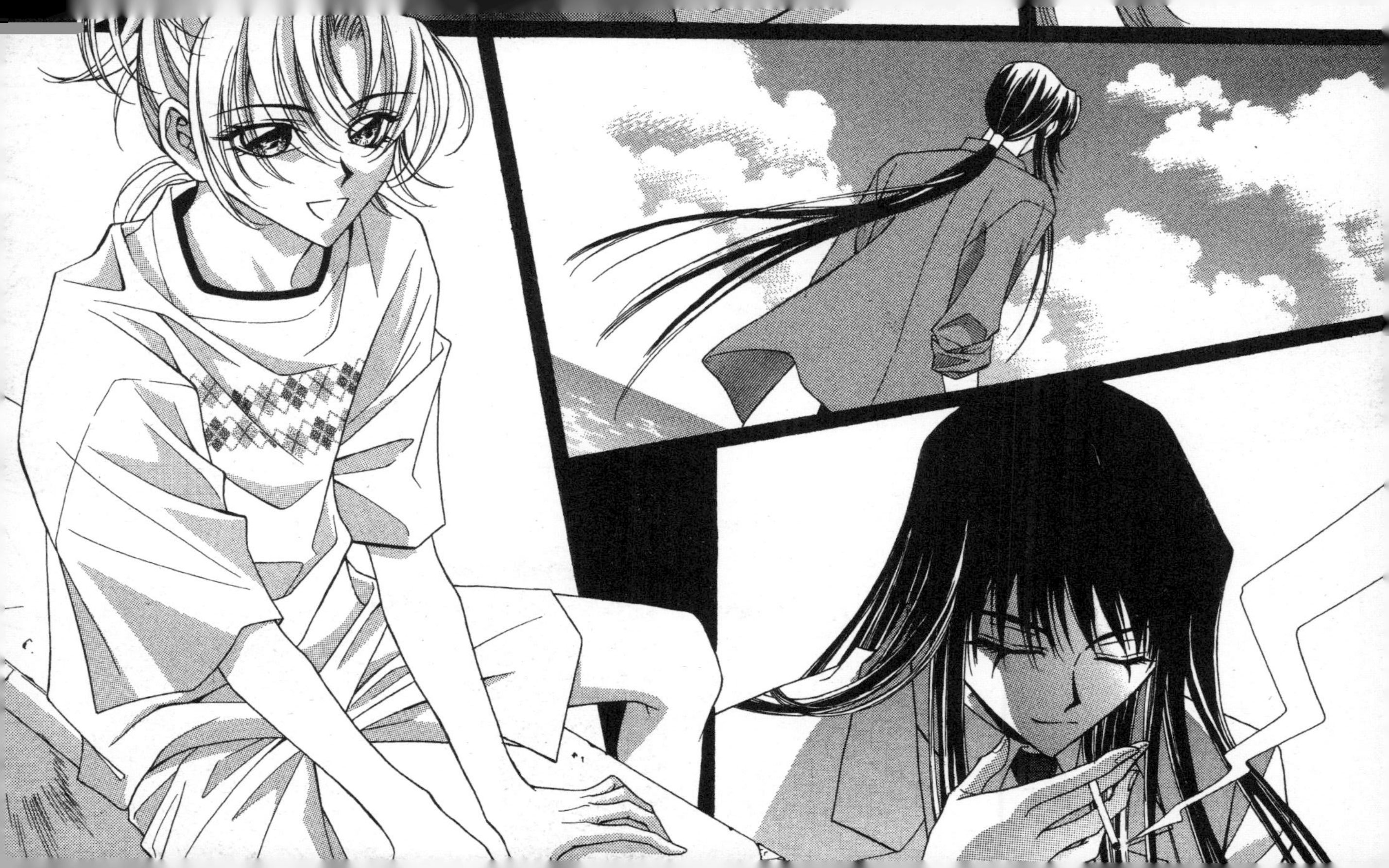

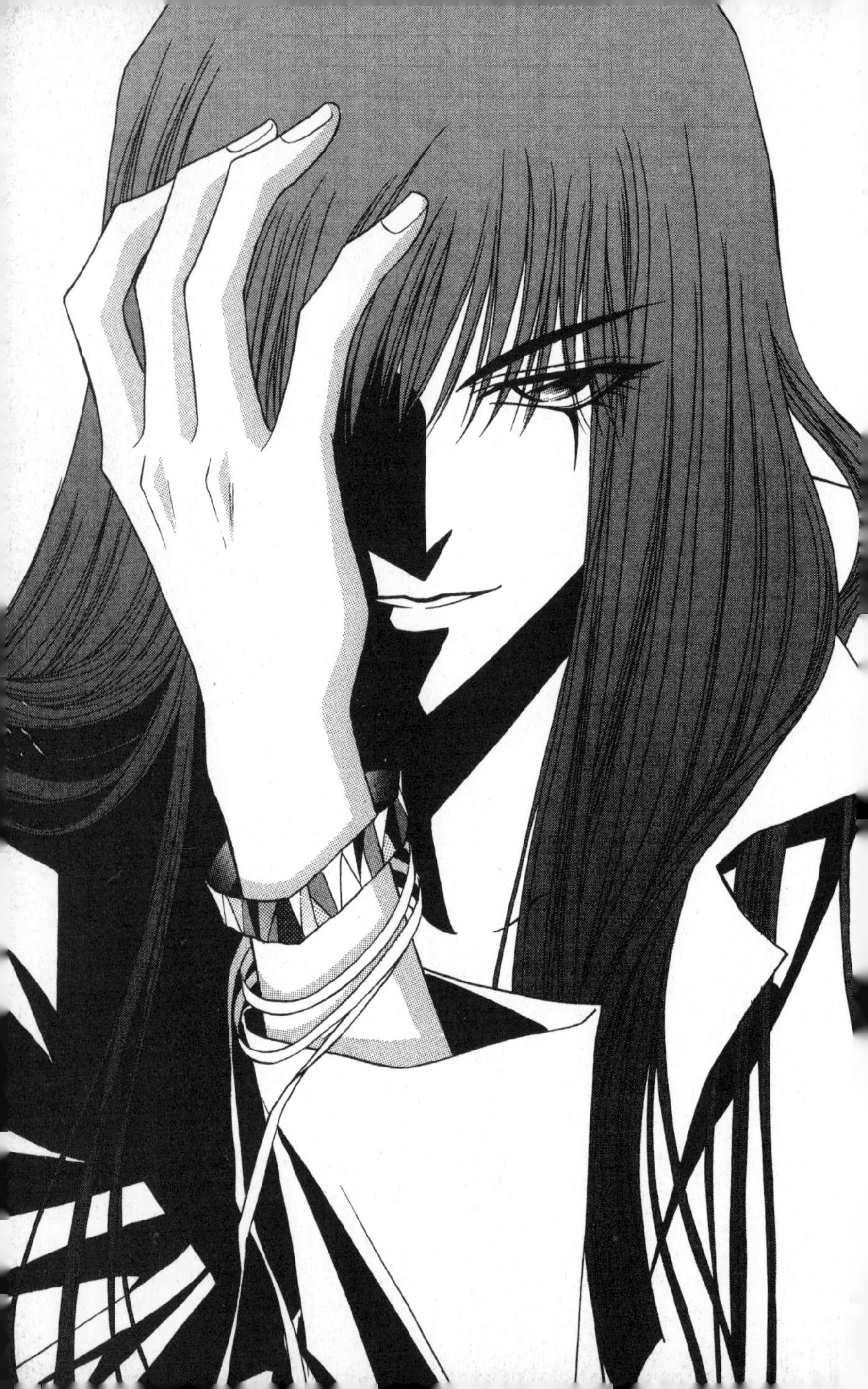

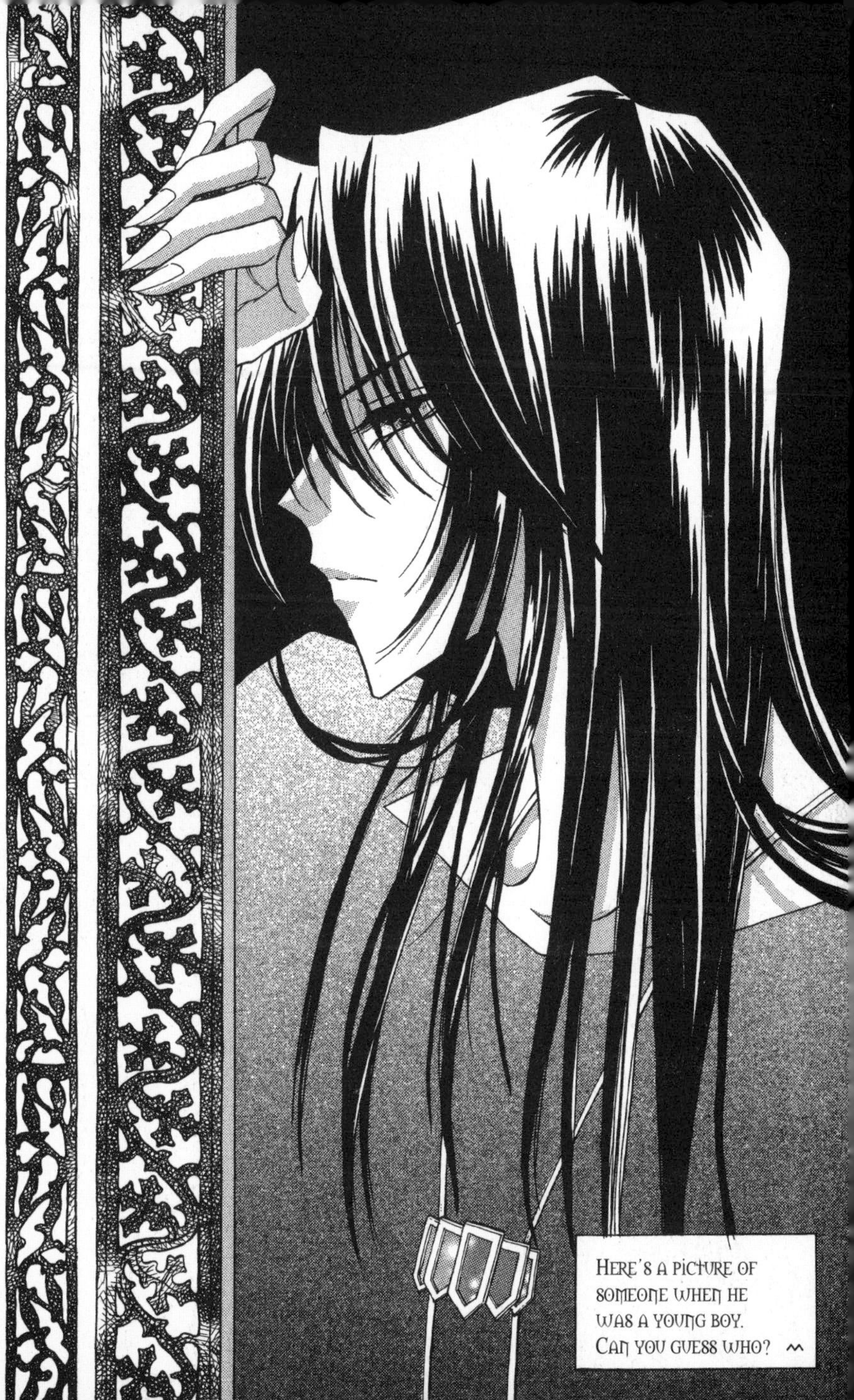
HERE'S A PICTURE OF
SOMEONE WHEN HE
WAS A YOUNG BOY.
CAN YOU GUESS WHO? ^^

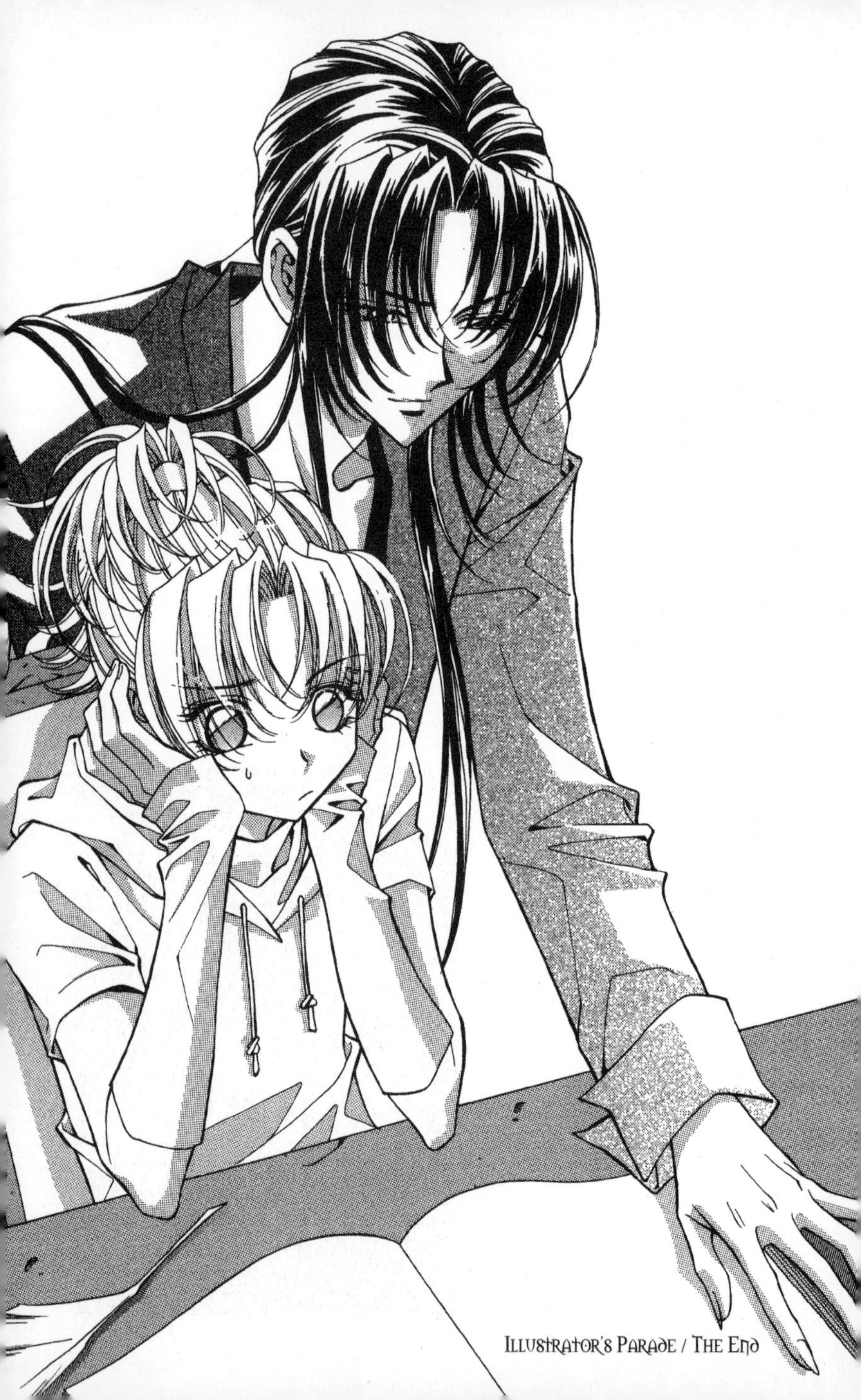

Illustrator's Parade / The End

Here's a brief look at the preceding volumes. Be sure to collect them all!

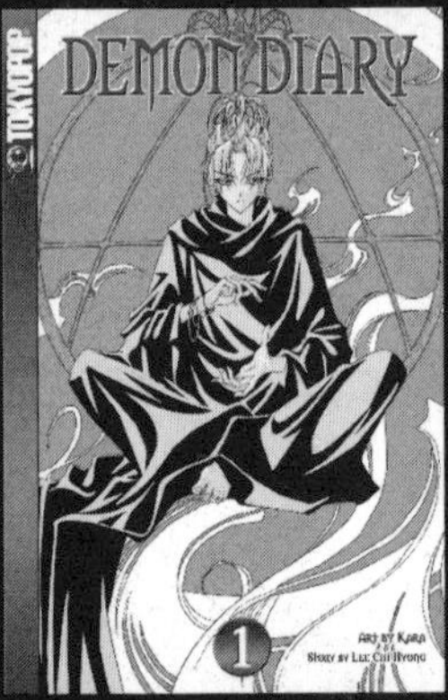

DEMON DIARY
TOKYOPOP
1

Volume 1:
Fools Rush In...

Meet Raenef. Meet Eclipse. Raenef meets Erutis...and Erutis very nearly meets her maker! See how it all started, including Raenef's very first meeting with the demon court. Includes two bonus stories: "Crystal Heart" and "Terra."

Volume 2:
When Rookies Rumble!

After failing Eclipse by sparing Erutis' life (very un-demonlike!), young Raenef decides to strike out on his own to become a true demon lord. But life in the outside world isn't easy for an unskilled demon...especially one with no money and a big appetite! Most people would kill a demon lord on sight...and Raenef finds himself in the temple of Rased facing someone who would love to do just that. Fortunately for Raenef, he isn't the only one still in training…

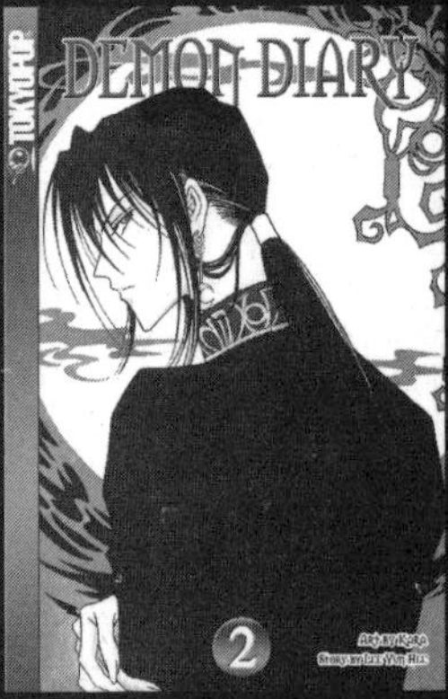

DEMON DIARY
TOKYOPOP
2

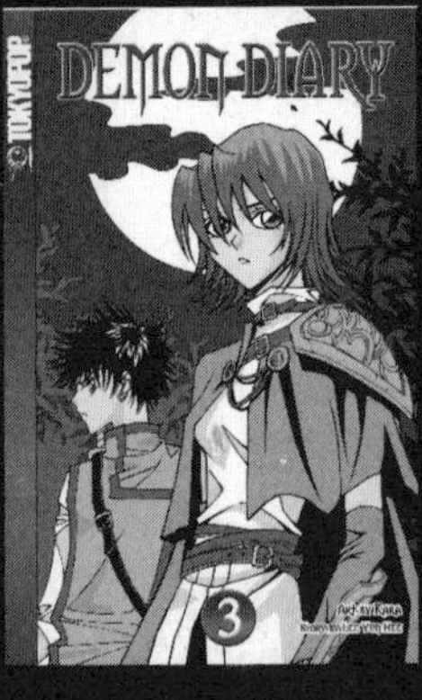

DEMON DIARY
TOKYOPOP
3

Volume 3:
Life in the Past Lane

The initial meeting of Raenef and Eclipse is revealed in a special glimpse of the days before *Demon Diary volume 1.* If you think their relationship is sometimes a bit...strained...now, you should see them before they got to know each other! Continuing the flashback frenzy, Chris' history is also revealed...along with the reason for his deep-seated grudge against all things demonic!

If you don't have every volume of *Demon Diary*, you don't have the whole story!

Volume 4:
Demonic Help Is Hard To Find

In a bid to steal Eclipse from Raenef, the Demon Lord Krayon--one of the five oldest demons in existence--puts Raenef to the test.

If Raenef passes, he can keep Eclipse. If Raenef fails, he could lose his life!

Volume 5:
Be Careful What You Wish For...

Fed up with his failures, Raenef does what he once considered unthinkable...and actually tries to study. However, when one hits the books in a demonic library, the books sometimes hit back. After Raenef suddenly becomes frightening and develops a terrible personality, will Eclipse consider his mission complete or will he start wishing for the "good" old days?

Volume 6:
You Only Hurt The Demons You Love

Considering that Chris lost his home, his family and everyone he ever knew to a demonic horde, you'd think it wouldn't be too hard to get him to attack a Demon Lord...and you'd be right! The evil Raenef V and Chris, successor to the High Cleric of the Temple of Rased, duke it out in a no-spells-barred magical melee!

ALSO AVAILABLE FROM TOKYOPOP

MANGA

.HACK//LEGEND OF THE TWILIGHT
@LARGE
ABENOBASHI: MAGICAL SHOPPING ARCADE
A.I. LOVE YOU
AI YORI AOSHI
ANGELIC LAYER
ARM OF KANNON
BABY BIRTH
BATTLE ROYALE
BATTLE VIXENS
BRAIN POWERED
BRIGADOON
B'TX
CANDIDATE FOR GODDESS, THE
CARDCAPTOR SAKURA
CARDCAPTOR SAKURA - MASTER OF THE CLOW
CHOBITS
CHRONICLES OF THE CURSED SWORD
CLAMP SCHOOL DETECTIVES
CLOVER
COMIC PARTY
CONFIDENTIAL CONFESSIONS
CORRECTOR YUI
COWBOY BEBOP
COWBOY BEBOP: SHOOTING STAR
CRAZY LOVE STORY
CRESCENT MOON
CULDCEPT
CYBORG 009
D•N•ANGEL
DEMON DIARY
DEMON ORORON, THE
DEUS VITAE
DIGIMON
DIGIMON TAMERS
DIGIMON ZERO TWO
DOLL
DRAGON HUNTER
DRAGON KNIGHTS
DRAGON VOICE
DREAM SAGA
DUKLYON: CLAMP SCHOOL DEFENDERS
EERIE QUEERIE!
END, THE
ERICA SAKURAZAWA: COLLECTED WORKS
ET CETERA
ETERNITY
EVIL'S RETURN
FAERIES' LANDING
FAKE
FLCL
FORBIDDEN DANCE
FRUITS BASKET
G GUNDAM
GATEKEEPERS

GETBACKERS
GIRL GOT GAME
GRAVITATION
GTO
GUNDAM BLUE DESTINY
GUNDAM SEED ASTRAY
GUNDAM WING
GUNDAM WING: BATTLEFIELD OF PACIFISTS
GUNDAM WING: ENDLESS WALTZ
GUNDAM WING: THE LAST OUTPOST (G-UNIT)
GUYS' GUIDE TO GIRLS
HANDS OFF!
HAPPY MANIA
HARLEM BEAT
I.N.V.U.
IMMORTAL RAIN
INITIAL D
INSTANT TEEN: JUST ADD NUTS
ISLAND
JING: KING OF BANDITS
JING: KING OF BANDITS - TWILIGHT TALES
JULINE
KARE KANO
KILL ME, KISS ME
KINDAICHI CASE FILES, THE
KING OF HELL
KODOCHA: SANA'S STAGE
LAMENT OF THE LAMB
LEGAL DRUG
LEGEND OF CHUN HYANG, THE
LES BIJOUX
LOVE HINA
LUPIN III
LUPIN III: WORLD'S MOST WANTED
MAGIC KNIGHT RAYEARTH I
MAGIC KNIGHT RAYEARTH II
MAHOROMATIC: AUTOMATIC MAIDEN
MAN OF MANY FACES
MARMALADE BOY
MARS
MARS: HORSE WITH NO NAME
METROID
MINK
MIRACLE GIRLS
MIYUKI-CHAN IN WONDERLAND
MODEL
ONE
ONE I LOVE, THE
PARADISE KISS
PARASYTE
PASSION FRUIT
PEACH GIRL
PEACH GIRL: CHANGE OF HEART
PET SHOP OF HORRORS
PITA-TEN
PLANET LADDER

03.03.04T

ALSO AVAILABLE FROM TOKYOPOP®

**For more
information visit
www.TOKYOPOP.com**

03.03.04T

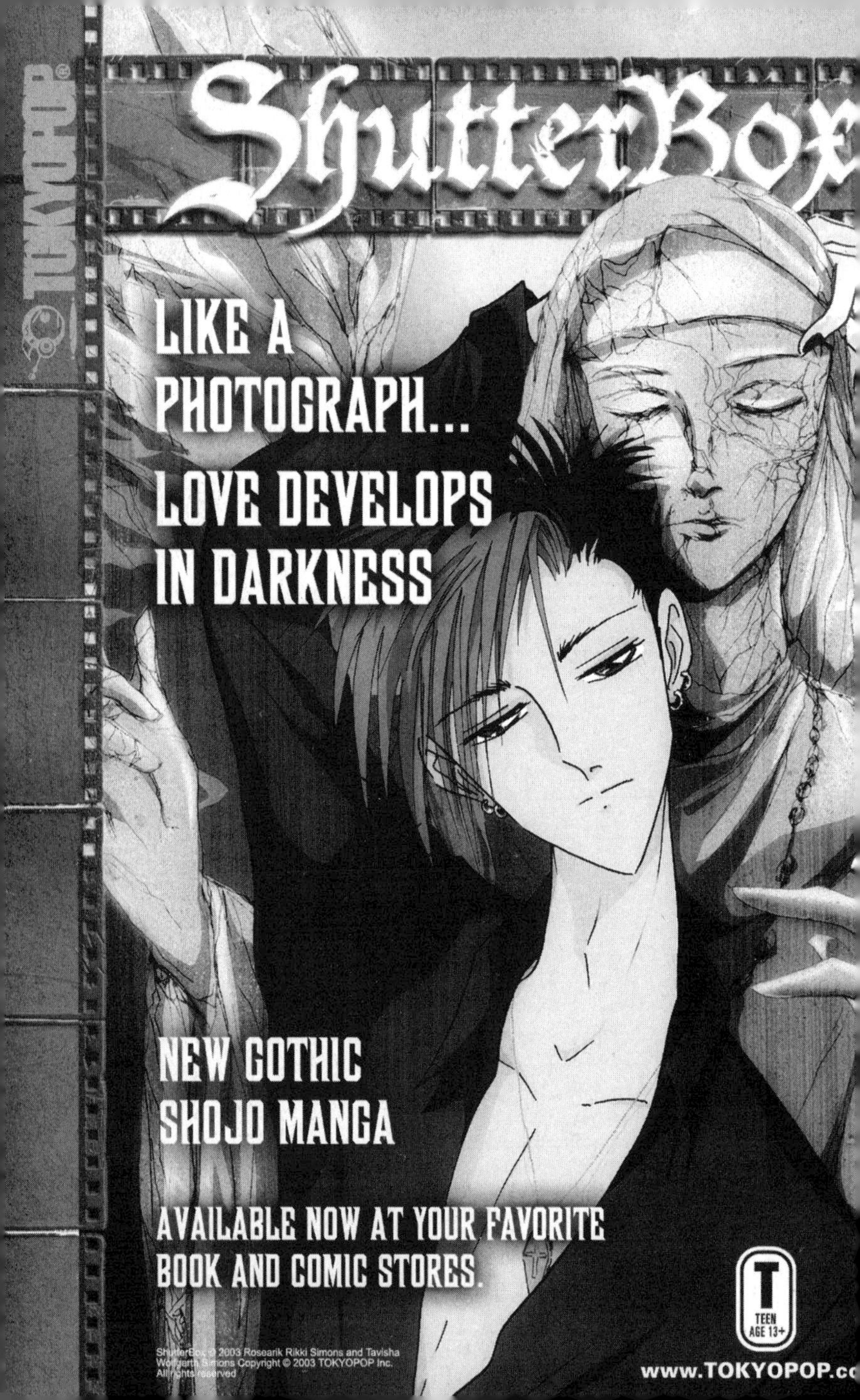
TOKYOPOP
ShutterBox
LIKE A PHOTOGRAPH...
LOVE DEVELOPS IN DARKNESS
NEW GOTHIC SHOJO MANGA
AVAILABLE NOW AT YOUR FAVORITE BOOK AND COMIC STORES.
T TEEN AGE 13+
ShutterBox © 2003 Rosearik Rikki Simons and Tavisha Wolfgarth Simons Copyright © 2003 TOKYOPOP Inc. All rights reserved
www.TOKYOPOP.co

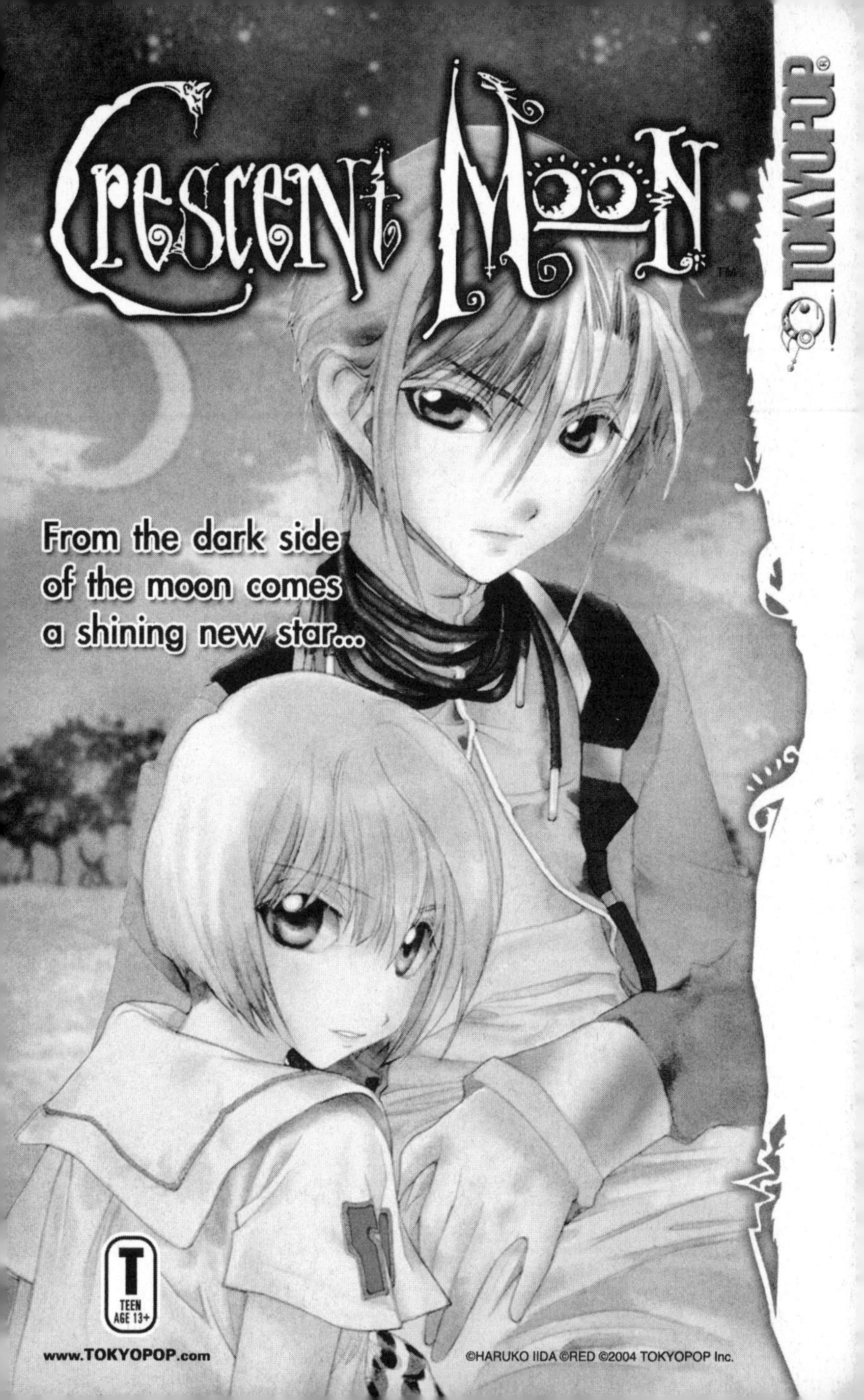
Crescent Moon™
TOKYOPOP®
From the dark side of the moon comes a shining new star...
T
TEEN
AGE 13+
www.TOKYOPOP.com
©HARUKO IIDA ©RED ©2004 TOKYOPOP Inc.

TOKYOPOP®

VAMPIRE GAME
by JUDAL

Reincarnation... Resurrection... Revenge...
All In the Hands of One Snotty Teenage Princess

T TEEN AGE 13+

www.TOKYOPOP.com

Available Now At Your Favorite Book and Comic Stores

©1996 JUDAL